8486

D0297306

AUSTERITY AND RECOVERY IN IRELAND

Austerity and Recovery in Ireland

*Europe's Poster Child and
the Great Recession*

Edited by
WILLIAM K. ROCHE, PHILIP J. O'CONNELL,
AND ANDREA PROTHERO

OXFORD
UNIVERSITY PRESS

OXFORD
UNIVERSITY PRESS

Great Clarendon Street, Oxford, OX2 6DP,
United Kingdom

Oxford University Press is a department of the University of Oxford.
It furthers the University's objective of excellence in research, scholarship,
and education by publishing worldwide. Oxford is a registered trade mark of
Oxford University Press in the UK and in certain other countries

Published in the United States of America by Oxford University Press
198 Madison Avenue, New York, NY 10016, United States of America

British Library Cataloguing in Publication Data
Data available

Library of Congress Control Number: 2016943125

ISBN 978–0–19–879237–6

Printed in Great Britain by
Clays Ltd, St Ives plc

Preface

The Great Recession was a cataclysmic event in modern Irish history and the genesis and effects of the crisis remain matters of enquiry and debate within Ireland. The dramatic recent rebound of the Irish economy shows no signs of dulling the edge of analysis and debate concerning the domestic and international lineage of the crisis, or the manner in which international institutions dealt with Ireland as the country sought to handle a calamitous fall in output, the near collapse of its banks, ballooning fiscal deficits, escalating unemployment, and the reoccurrence of mass emigration.

This book arose from the shared conviction of both editors and contributors that it was important that Ireland's experience of austerity, and subsequently of recovery, should be the subject of rigorous social scientific analysis, drawing on the highest quality data available. This view was further underlined by Ireland so often being cited internationally as an exemplar of how austerity can prime economic recovery and renewal.

The editors were gratified that a group of Ireland's leading social scientists were willing to contribute enthusiastically to the book. All are internationally acknowledged scholars in the areas which they contribute. Given the serious effects of the Great Recession and the austerity programme on many areas of Irish life, the book is necessarily interdisciplinary: drawing on the insights of economists, finance specialists, legal scholars, sociologists, political scientists, Europeanists, business, management, marketing, and industrial relations scholars, public management analysts, migration researchers, housing specialists, and cultural analysts. This, we believe, is one of the book's major strengths and contributions. Another contribution is that the book presents the first analysis of the Irish case that examines the crisis, the austerity programme agreed between Ireland and the Troika of the European Commission (EC), the European Central Bank (ECB), and the International Monetary Fund (IMF), *and* Ireland's dramatic economic rebound from 2014. This allows contributors to the book to consider whether, or in what way, the austerity programme can be viewed as having contributed to Ireland's recovery. In this context, a third major theme concerns the scepticism of the book's contributors that Ireland should in fact be viewed as a 'poster child' or exemplar of austerity-primed recovery and renewal in Europe that vindicates the response of the European Union (EU) and international institutions to countries beset by economic and fiscal crisis after 2008. A fourth theme explores the extent to which the crisis and austerity programme led to major and likely enduring changes in economic, financial, business, political, work, and labour market institutions, and in patterns of consumption.

A book dealing with such major themes and involving multiple contributors from many disciplines is a challenging undertaking. We would like to acknowledge with gratitude the support we received during our work on the project. Financial support towards a conference of contributors, held in June 2015 at the Michael Smurfit Graduate Business School, University College Dublin (UCD), was received from the UCD College of Business and the UCD Geary Institute for Public Policy. The conference allowed the editors and contributors to discuss the book's main themes and to highlight the main lessons of the Irish case. All contributions to the book were substantially revised in light of discussion at the conference. We would like to thank Adam Swallow, Commissioning Editor for Economics and Finance at Oxford University Press (OUP), for his encouragement for the project from its inception and for his very helpful comments and advice on how the book could best be given shape. We are grateful to the four anonymous reviewers for OUP, who contributed many helpful comments and suggestions on a detailed outline and on a range of draft chapters. Our thanks also to the delegates of OUP for accepting the book for publication and for further comments on the proposal and reviews. At OUP, Aimee Wright and Lowri Ribbons also provided much helpful advice and support. At UCD, Bernie Cramp provided excellent administrative support to the project throughout and we would like to record our thanks to her for her work on the book.

Bill Roche, Philip O'Connell,
and Andy Prothero
Dublin, April 2016

Contents

Contents

List of Figures

List of Tables

List of Abbreviations

AIB	Allied Irish Banks
ALMPs	active labour market policies
BOI	Bank of Ireland
BoP	Balance of Payments
BRRD	Bank Recovery and Resolution Directive
BTL	buy-to-let (mortgages)
CBIFSA	Central Bank of Ireland and Financial Services Authority
CEBS	Committee of European Bank Supervisors
COCOPS	Coordinating for Cohesion in the Public Sector of the Future
CSO	Central Statistics Office
CWS	Community Welfare Service
DECLG	Department of Environment, Community and Local Government
DPER	Department of Public Expenditure and Reform
DRHE	Dublin Region Homeless Executive
DSP	Department of Social Protection
EBS	Educational Building Society
EC	European Commission
ECB	European Central Bank
ECF	employment control frameworks
ECOFIN	Economic and Financial Affairs Council
ECRI	European Commission against Racism and Intolerance
ELA	Emergency Liquidity Assistance
ELG	Eligible Liabilities Guarantee (scheme)
ELS	Emergency Liquidity Support
EMC	Economic Management Council
EMU	Economic and Monetary Union
EPCU	External Programme Compliance Unit
EPL	employment protection legislation
EPP	European People's Party
ERC	European Research Council
ESRI	Economic and Social Research Institute
ETBs	Education and Training Boards

EU	European Union
Eurofound	European Foundation for the Improvement of Living and Working Conditions
FÁS	Foras Áiseanna Saothair (former National Training Authority)
FDI	foreign direct investment
FEMPI	Financial Emergency Measures in the Public Interest
FMP	Financial Measures Programme
FOI	freedom of information
GDP	gross domestic product
GIIPS	Greece, Ireland, Italy, Portugal, and Spain
GIPS	Greece, Ireland, Portugal, and Spain
GNI	gross national income
GNP	gross national product
HAP	Housing Assistance Payment
HoGs	Heads of Governments
HR	human resources
HSE	Health Service Executive
IBEC	Irish Business and Employers' Confederation
IBRC	Irish Bank Resolution Corporation
ICC	International Chamber of Commerce
ICT	information and communications technology
IDA (Ireland)	Industrial Development Authority (Ireland)
IFB	Irish Film Board
IFSC	International Financial Services Centre
IFSRA	Irish Financial Services Regulatory Authority
IFTA	Irish Film and Television Academy
IL&P	Irish Life and Permanent
ILO	International Labour Organization
IMF	International Monetary Fund
INBS	Irish Nationwide Building Society
Intreo	Integrated National Employment and Entitlement Service
IT	information technology
JA	Jobseeker's Allowance
JB	Jobseeker's Benefit
LPT	local property tax
LRC	Labour Relations Commission
LTU	long-term unemployment

MABS	Money Advice and Budgeting Service
NACE	Nomenclature générale des Activités économiques dans les Communautés Européennes/European industrial activity classification
NAMA	National Asset Management Agency
NCFA	National Campaign for the Arts
NEAP	National Employment Action Plan
NESC	National Economic and Social Council
NMS	new member states
NPG	new public governance
NPM	new public management
NRP	National Recovery Plan
NYCI	National Youth Council of Ireland
OECD	Organisation for Economic Co-operation and Development
PCAR	Prudential Capital Assessment Review
PDs	Progressive Democrats Party
PES	Public Employment Service
PEX	probability of exit
PLAR	Prudential Liquidity Assessment Review
PLC	post-Leaving Certificate
PMDS	Performance Management and Development System
PNR	Programme of National Recovery
PPPs	public–private partnerships
PRD	pension-related deduction
PRISM	Probability Risk and Impact System
PRSI	pay-related social insurance
PTW	Pathways to Work
R&D	research and development
RAS	Rental Accommodation Scheme
REIT	Real Estate Investment Trusts
RTÉ	Raidió Teilifís Éireann (State broadcasting authority)
S&P	Standard & Poor's
SFLCA	Special Firm-Level Collective Agreement
SIPO	Standards in Public Office Commission
SMEs	small and medium sized enterprises
SMI	Strategic Management Initiative
SOLAS	An tSeirbhís Oideachais Leanúnaigh agus Scileanna (Further Education and Training Authority)

SRPs	Site Resolution Plans
SSM	single supervisory mechanism
TDs	Teachtai Dála (members of the lower house of the Irish parliament)
TGI	Target Group Index
UCD	University College Dublin
VAT	value added taxes
WTO	World Trade Organization

List of Contributors

Frank Barry is Professor of International Business and Economic Development at Trinity College Dublin. His research areas include foreign direct investment (FDI) and Irish economic and business history.

Adele Bergin is a Senior Research Officer at the Economic and Social Research Institute (ESRI). Her research interests are in labour economics and macroeconomics.

Donald Taylor Black is an award-winning documentary filmmaker, writer, and educator. He was Head of the Department of Film & Media at the Institute of Art, Design and Technology, Dún Laoghaire (IADT) during 2001–7 and 2010–16, the first Creative Director of the National Film School at IADT from 2006–16, and Vice-Chair of Groupement Européen des Ecoles de Cinéma et de Télévision (GEECT) (2014–16), the European association of film schools.

Richard Boyle is Head of Research, Publishing, and Corporate Relations at the Institute of Public Administration in Ireland. His major areas of specialization, in which he has published extensively, include public sector performance management, monitoring and evaluation systems, and public service change and reform programmes.

Sara Cantillon is Professor of Economics at Glasgow Caledonian University and Director of Women in Scotland (WiSE) Economy Research Centre. Previously, she was Head of the UCD School of Social Justice. Her main areas of research are equality, poverty, gender, and intra-household distribution. Professor Cantillon was appointed to the Expert Group on Future Funding for Higher Education 2014–17.

Blanaid Clarke is the McCann FitzGerald Chair in Corporate Law at Trinity College Dublin. Her research interests include corporate governance, financial services law, and takeover regulation and she has published extensively in these areas. She is a member of the Irish Central Bank Commission, the European Securities and Markets Authority Takeover Bids Network, the Organisation for Economic Co-operation and Development (OECD) Corporate Governance Committee, and the EC's Informal Company Law Expert Group.

Marius C. Claudy is a Lecturer in Marketing at UCD. He has published widely on issues around sustainable consumption and the adoption of sustainable behaviours, practices, and technologies. Marius is involved in a UCD-funded multidisciplinary research project, which investigates how consumption has changed during the financial crisis and subsequent recession.

Gregory Connor is Professor of Finance at Maynooth University; his research interests are in financial risk modelling.

Margaret Crean is a graduate in both Science and Social Sciences from UCD, where she also completed her MSc and PhD in Equality Studies in the School of Social Justice. She has published a wide range of academic papers on equality issues, including papers on inequality in education, social class, and palliative care.

David M. Farrell, MRIA, holds the Chair of Politics at UCD, where he is incoming Head of the School of Politics and International Relations. From 2012–14 he was the Research Director of the Irish Constitutional Convention. A specialist in the study of parties, elections, and electoral systems, his current work is focused on deliberation and politics.

Thomas Flavin is Senior Lecturer in Financial Economics at Maynooth University, with research interests in international finance, particularly financial contagion and market integration.

Irial Glynn is Lecturer at the Institute of History in Leiden University. His research focuses on post-war Irish and Italian migration experiences, global trends in asylum policymaking from a historical perspective, and the links between memory studies and migration studies.

Rory Hearne is Senior Policy Analyst at Think-tank for Action on Social Change (TASC), a Dublin-based independent think tank whose focus is economic equality and democratic accountability. His work concerns housing, politics, political economy, privatization, human rights, social movements, and community development.

Andrew Keating is a Lecturer in Marketing at UCD. His research interests lie in the areas of consumer research and marketing and new venture development. His work has been published in journals such as *Entrepreneurship, Theory and Practice, Industrial Marketing Management*, and *Consumption, Markets and Culture*.

Stephen Kinsella is Senior Lecturer in Economics at the University of Limerick. His interests are stock flow consistent macroeconomics and the study of the impact of austerity.

Rob Kitchin is a Professor and European Research Council (ERC) Advanced Investigator at the National Institute for Regional and Spatial Analysis at Maynooth University. He specializes in social and urban geography broadly conceived, and has published widely across the social sciences.

Brigid Laffan is Director and Professor at the Robert Schuman Centre for Advanced Studies, European University Institute, Florence. She was

Vice-President of UCD and Principal of the College of Human Sciences from 2004 to 2011. She was the Founding Director of the Dublin European Institute UCD from 1999, and in March 2004 she was elected as a member of the Royal Irish Academy (MRIA). In September 2014 she was awarded the University Association for Contemporary European Studies (UACES) Lifetime Achievement Award.

Kathleen Lynch is a Professor of Equality Studies at UCD and an Irish Research Council Advanced Research Scholar 2014–17. She is guided by the belief that the purpose of scholarship and research is not just to understand the world, but to change it for the good of humanity.

Cian O'Callaghan is a Lecturer in Urban Geography at Trinity College Dublin. He specializes in urban political economy and geographies of the crisis, with a particular focus on housing, vacancy, and spatial justice.

Philip J. O'Connell is Professor of Applied Social Science and Director of the Geary Institute for Public Policy at UCD. His main areas of work are in labour markets and migration.

Brian O'Kelly is Adjunct Professor of Finance at Dublin City University, with research interests are in banking and bank regulation.

Seán Ó Riain is Professor of Sociology at the National University of Ireland Maynooth. He is the author of *The Politics of High Tech Growth* (2004) and *The Rise and Fall of Ireland's Celtic Tiger* (2014), and co-editor of *The Changing Worlds and Workplaces of Capitalism* (2015). He is currently directing the project 'New Deals in the New Economy', funded by an ERC Consolidator Grant.

Andrea Prothero is Professor of Business and Society at the College of Business, UCD. Andy's research interests focus on sustainability and business, and the relationships between marketing and society. She has published widely in these areas.

William K. Roche is Professor of Industrial Relations and Human Resources at the College of Business UCD, and Honorary Professor at the Management School, Queen's University, Belfast. He has published extensively on employment relations. He is co-author of *Recession at Work: HRM in the Irish Crisis* (2013).

Paul Teague is Professor of Management at Queen's University, Belfast. He has written widely on the theme of the employment relations consequences of deeper European integration and human resources in the recession. He is co-author of *Recession at Work: HRM in the Irish Crisis* (2013).

1

Introduction 'Poster Child' or 'Beautiful Freak'?

Austerity and Recovery in Ireland

William K. Roche, Philip J. O'Connell, and Andrea Prothero

Christine Lagarde took her place at the podium and smiled warmly at the large audience. Gathered to listen to her in the ceremonial splendour of St Patrick's Hall at Dublin Castle was a large appreciative audience of politicians, business leaders, senior civil servants, and diplomats. The managing director of the International Monetary Fund (IMF) offered congratulations for the manner in which the Irish Government and people had handled the crisis. Ireland, she told them, was setting standards. It was March 2013 and the country was within months of exiting the bailout arranged with the 'Troika' of the IMF, the European Central Bank (ECB), and the European Commission (EC). Looking on from the front row during an equally upbeat press conference later in Government Buildings was Ajai Chopra, head of the Troika team dispatched to Ireland in November 2010 to negotiate the terms of Ireland's rescue package. Chopra was the subject of an iconic press photograph taken at that time. Striding with his team towards the Irish Department of Finance, he encountered a beggar rattling a cup in the hope of soliciting some support—an apt visual commentary on the plight of the country he was there to rescue.

An ocean appeared to separate the Ireland of 2013 and 2010. Recovery had begun and would gather pace as the country eased its way out of the rescue programme without the need for a precautionary credit line from the departing international institutions. When Ireland ceded its economic sovereignty it became convenient to blame the Troika for unpopular taxes, spending cuts, and reform measures. Some political leaders thought to challenge 'Frankfurt's way', especially by attempting to institute burden-sharing with unsecured senior bondholders in the calamitous Anglo Irish Bank. But as Ireland progressed towards (again) becoming Europe's strongest performing economy, figures in the government were now pleased to accept plaudits from the Troika. They freely lectured their beleaguered Greek colleagues during the 2015 Greek crisis on the benefits that had flowed from austerity. Europe's basket case was now Europe's poster child.

This book provides an account of Ireland's experience of austerity and recovery. The Irish authorities are shown to have been the main authors of austerity. The major policies agreed with the Troika had been initiated by the Irish Government before the country was forced into accepting a bailout. To a greater degree than is commonly acknowledged Ireland's austerity was auto austerity. The book shows that the restructuring of the banks and fiscal consolidation were important in turning around Ireland's fortunes. But austerity and bailout reforms are shown to have occurred to varying degrees across different areas. The book examines the role of Troika institutions in improvising fixes for Ireland's troubled banks—indeed, one could argue, the Troika sailed close to the wind with respect to their legal mandates. The sophistication of Ireland's negotiators in their dealings with the IMF, the ECB, and the European Union (EU) is a significant feature of the story. The multiple costs of austerity are given their due weight in assessing Ireland's experience. Recovery is attributed, above all, to the trading position Ireland had built up over many decades and to the country's ability to benefit from global economic recovery, supported by an international financial system characterized by low interest rates and quantitative easing. The book also highlights the political and social context that sustained austerity. The government's decision to opt for austerity reflected a long-established pro-cyclical bias in fiscal policy and in politics. The sustainability of austerity was reinforced by support from the main political parties for the decision to implement austerity and for most of the measures involved. During the Great Recession, political and social dissent was limited, finding expression in left-wing protest against measures such as water charges, and in growing electoral support for the anti-austerity Sinn Fein Party and for independent members of parliament. Dissent and civil or industrial disorder on the scale evident in other bailout countries were absent in Ireland. Trade union resistance was muted in the private sector because employers refrained from an offensive on basic pay levels and collective bargaining. In the public sector unions were involved in, rather than excluded from, measures for cutting the public service pay bill.

To examine these themes, multidisciplinary chapters in the book draw on extensive empirical data covering a wide spectrum of Irish economic, political, social, and cultural affairs. They provide the fullest possible portrayal of the impact of this cataclysmic event on Irish life and allow for an assessment of whether Ireland can validly be regarded as a 'poster child' or exemplar for austerity-enabled recovery.

Two considerations explain the range of areas covered in the book. First, in order to understand fully the impact of the dramatic economic and social experiment wrought by the recession and resulting austerity, it is necessary to move well beyond the banking and fiscal crisis or related reforms that have dominated coverage of Ireland's collapse and that remain more or less centre stage in discussions of Ireland's recovery. Austerity affected many more areas of Irish life. As shown in the chapters of the book, it profoundly affected the labour market, workplaces, migration, public management, consumption, housing, inequality and disadvantage, and culture. The mood of reform to which austerity contributed also led to ambitious plans for radical change in political institutions. To understand how austerity in Ireland was shaped and sustained, it is necessary to examine how the Irish authorities dealt with the international institutions involved in the bailout programme: the ECB, EU, and IMF. To understand how Ireland found itself so exposed to cataclysmic collapse in 2008 it is also necessary to examine Ireland's longer-run development over the decades preceding the crisis.

A second consideration behind the broad scope of the book concerns Ireland's status as a poster child or exemplar for how austerity can be turned into economic recovery and renewed growth. A proper assessment of Ireland as an exemplar turns in part on understanding the full impact of austerity on Irish life. It depends as well on the extent to which austerity resulted in significant institutional reforms that directly contributed to recovery. But it turns also, crucially, on addressing a classical problem in comparative social science: whether the effects attributed to any particular set of reforms may have been predicated on their concurrence with other and perhaps less visible institutional arrangements, or with long-established patterns of development that could not easily, or not at all, be replicated by other countries.

One of the book's major themes is that Ireland's recovery—like its descent to near calamity—can only be understood in terms of the confluence of a series of features of the economy, polity, and society without direct parallels in other Troika programme countries. In the words of Kinsella in Chapter 3, Ireland's import is less that of a 'poster child' than that of a 'beautiful freak': a case marked by highly unusual and historically specific features and influences that acted in concert and shaped a pathway to recovery unlikely to have been, or to become, available to other countries affected by economic calamity.

In sustaining this understanding of Ireland's experience of the Great Recession and recovery, the following themes are examined by contributors to the book:

1. The features and effects of recession, austerity, and associated reforms across Irish economic, political, social, and cultural life.

2. Whether a viable alternative was available to the austerity programme agreed with the ECB, EC, and the IMF.

3. The degree to which austerity reforms and other associated reforms achieved their stated objectives.

4. The costs associated with recession and austerity, and where, or upon whom, the burden of these costs fell.

5. The degree to which austerity was a contributor to Ireland's recovery and whether Ireland should be considered a poster child or exemplar for other countries facing economic and fiscal calamity.

These themes provide a framework for Chapter 1 and are considered, in turn, in the rest of the chapter.

THE NATURE AND EXTENT OF AUSTERITY

There is no commonly agreed definition of austerity. Blythe (2013: 2) employs a broad definition of austerity as:

> [A] form of voluntary deflation where the economy adjusts through the reduction of wages, prices and public spending to restore competitiveness, which is (supposedly) best achieved by cutting the state's budget, debts, and deficits.

This approach incorporates fiscal contraction as well as wage and price cuts in order to meet investor demands and restore competiveness. Thompson (2013: 733), however, argues that the rationales for austerity may vary, that the fiscal crisis itself may require austerity to balance the books, and, moreover, that fiscal consolidation may be quite involuntary:

> At a certain point, the future cost of servicing debt is prohibitive and a full-scale debt crisis ensues, as Greece, Ireland and Portugal found. There is no necessity for an idea of austerity here; governments face a choice between default and the state not being able to meet basic financial commitments.

This seems closer to the Irish experience: the central thrust of austerity in Ireland consisted of severe cuts to expenditure and increases in taxation.

There were two distinct factors underlying the fiscal crisis of the Irish state: financing day-to-day activities and the cost of the bank crisis. First, when the property bubble burst in 2007–8 the contraction in economic activity and employment, combined with over-reliance on property-related taxes during the boom—which were used to fund rapid increases in expenditure—led to a dramatic shortfall of government revenue over expenditure. The General Government Balance, relating just to financing of day-to-day current and capital expenditures (i.e. excluding the cost of bailing out the banks), fell to −7.3 per cent of gross domestic product (GDP) in 2008, and by this measure the deficit grew to just under 12 per cent in both 2009 and 2010. Second, this deterioration in the fiscal position was aggravated by the massive transfers of funds to the banking system and direct injections of capital into the banks,

Table 1.1. The 32 billion euro austerity package, Ireland, 2008–15

	2008–10	2011	2012	2013	2014	2015	2008–15
				€ Billion			
Revenue	5.6	1.4	1.6	1.3	0.9	0.7	11.5
Expenditure	9.2	3.9	2.2	2.3	1.6	1.3	20.5
Total	14.7	5.3	3.8	3.5	2.5	2.0	31.8
Percentage of 2010 GDP	9.2%	3.3%	2.3%	2.1%	1.5%	1.1%	19.5%

Source: FitzGerald 2014.
Shaded area represents the period of the IMF–ECB–EC 'bailout' programme.

with the result that that gross government debt soared to almost over 120 per cent of GDP by 2013 (FitzGerald 2014). Almost one-third of this increased debt (or 40 per cent of GDP) was directly attributable to the money transferred to the banking system under the bank bailout. However, another 50 percentage points (of GDP) of the debt at the end of 2012 was attributable to the borrowing undertaken after 2008 to finance the fiscal imbalance between taxation and expenditure that had accumulated since the beginning of the crisis. So while Ireland had a relatively modest and apparently sustainable debt to GDP ratio of about 25 per cent in 2007, immediately before the recession, the combined effects of repeated fiscal deficits—due to the recession—as well as the banking bailout, were to result in Ireland becoming one of the most indebted countries in the world by 2012.

In the face of this fiscal crisis, the Irish Government embarked on a severe austerity programme to restore balance to the public finances with the aim of reducing the headline fiscal balance from over 12 per cent of GDP in 2008 to less than 3 per cent in 2015. Table 1.1 sets out a summary outline of the austerity package, entailing a total adjustment of 32 billion euros, consisting of 20.5 billion euros in expenditure cuts and 11.5 billion euros in tax increases (FitzGerald 2014).

The cumulative effects of this austerity package represent almost 20 per cent of GDP: it is this massive effort that various commentators have described as the 'sacrifice of the Irish people'. In the initial phase of the austerity package, 2008–10, more or less before the arrival of the IMF–ECB–EC Troika, adjustments amounting to almost 15 billion euros or 10 per cent of GDP were achieved. The second half of the austerity programme, of the same order of magnitude, was implemented over 2011–15, the first three of those years under the supervision of the Troika.

There were three key elements to the Memorandum of Understanding between the EC and Ireland governing the Programme of Financial Support:

1. Fiscal consolidation, including:
   - Increased taxes and introduction of new taxes on property, water, and carbon;

- Reduced government expenditure, including spending on social protection and cuts to public-sector numbers, pay, and pensions.
2. Financial-sector reforms, entailing:
   - Recapitalization and deleveraging of Irish banks;
   - Reorganization of the banking sector;
   - Burden-sharing by holders of subordinated debt.
3. Structural reforms:
   - Facilitate labour market adjustment by reducing the minimum wage and reforming wage setting arrangements;
   - Reform the social protection system, enhance activation measures, increase incentives to work and strengthen sanctions for non-compliance with job-search requirements of unemployment benefits;
   - Introduce legislation to remove restrictions to trade and competition in sheltered sectors such as the legal and medical professions.

In addition to fiscal consolidation and financial-sector reforms, the Troika programme introduced a number of additional elements to the financial support programme that had the potential to cut prices and wages, and presumably to restore competitiveness, including a short-lived cut in the minimum wage, labour market reforms, and removal of restrictive practices in sheltered sectors, such as the legal and health professions. However, as several chapters in this book demonstrate, these reforms were pursued with less vigour, or success, than fiscal consolidation.

It should be noted that the adoption of fiscal retrenchment from very early in the crisis entailed a return to the previous approach to crisis in the 1980s which entailed sweeping spending cuts in combination with negotiated wage restraint. The senior officials in the Department of Finance who oversaw fiscal consolidation from 2009 onwards would have been more junior civil servants when Ireland's earlier experiment with expansionary fiscal contraction was implemented after 1987, and would have witnessed that strategy seemingly bear fruit in sustained economic growth and prosperity in the 1990s. Ó Riain, in Chapter 2, sees this in institutional terms, arguing that Ireland was hampered by external and domestic political and institutional conditions that favoured austerity.

ALTERNATIVES TO AUSTERITY AND THE GENESIS OF THE BAILOUT PROGRAMME

As outlined, the Irish Government resolved early on in the crisis to pursue a pathway of fiscal austerity. Other responses had been proposed within Ireland as within the wider EU and beyond. Following the credit crunch and the occurrence of banking crises in the USA, the UK, and other European countries, British Prime Minister Gordon Brown initially won support for a Keynesian response based on an expansion of public investment. Soon, however, the focus within the UK and Europe shifted towards monetary policy and a continuation by Central Banks of cheap-money measures based on low interest rates and quantitative easing (Elliott 2016). A European Keynesian programme to address the crisis also existed on paper. This would have involved the mutualization of the debt of EU member states in serious difficulty, such as Greece, Portugal, Ireland, and Spain, through the creation of Eurobonds and a fiscal transfer mechanism to channel money from the richer to the poorer parts of the Eurozone (De Grauwe and Moesen 2009; Notre Europe 2012). Key member states in Northern Europe, most notably Germany, were implacable in their opposition to such options on the grounds that bailing out debtor countries in this way removed any incentives for fiscal prudence (Sinn 2013).

Several leading academic economists also opposed austerity as self-defeating, in particular Nobel Laureates Joseph Stiglitz and Paul Krugman (Krugman 2012a). Stiglitz was particularly trenchant in his criticism of Ireland's austerity programme and remained so following Ireland's subsequent economic rebound (Cragg and Stiglitz 2011; Keena 2009). In a 2016 World Economic Forum session, Stiglitz acknowledged that Ireland had shown signs of recovery and had done austerity 'better' than Greece, Portugal, and Spain, but he also maintained that Ireland would experience a 'lost decade' between 2008 and 2018, and that the country would have fared much better if it had introduced growth rather than austerity-based fiscal policies, and if the banks' debts had not been forced on the country by the EC and the ECB (RTE News 2016).

Within Ireland, alternative responses were proposed early on in the crisis by the tripartite state advisory agency, the National Economic and Social Council (NESC), and by the Irish Congress of Trade Unions (ICTU). The tripartite NESC had played a pivotal role in devising a response to deep and prolonged recession during the 1980s, and in March 2009 published a report outlining an 'integrated national response' to the crisis (NESC 2009). By then the main parameters of the government's austerity policy were already established and were taken as given by NESC. While proposing lower cuts in capital spending, the Council agreed with the government that there was a need for fiscal consolidation and the stabilization of the banking system, and also, in effect, accepted that there was a case for internal devaluation to restore competitiveness (NESC 2009: 55, 87–8). Furthermore, NESC sought to emphasize the importance of maintaining 'social solidarity', arguing that effective policy responses required consultation with the main economic and social interest groups and the protection of the most vulnerable from the highest burdens of adjustment. In the event, NESC was marginalized during the recession and only just escaped abolition as part of a programme of scrapping and merging state agencies to reduce public spending.

The concept of 'social solidarity' was pivotal to a Keynesian policy response pressed by ICTU in negotiations with the government and employers throughout 2009. The ICTU's idea of a 'social solidarity pact' explicitly opposed austerity in seeking to sustain pay levels and indeed to proceed with pay increases that were negotiated in September 2008; to reduce the deficit over a longer period than provided for in current fiscal policy and to involve all sections of society in sharing the burden of adjustment on a proportionate basis. Moreover, the ICTU proposal advocated measures to boost public capital and infrastructural spending, to be financed by government bonds and by redirecting investment by the National Pensions Reserve Fund (ICTU 2009). These proposals were strongly influenced by the handling of an earlier banking crisis in Sweden. The ICTU proposals received little traction from employers or government and lost ground completely with the collapse of social partnership in late 2009.

International critics of austerity, including Krugman and Stiglitz, continued to decry Europe's focus on monetary policy and fiscal retrenchment and extended their comments specifically to Ireland (Krugman 2010, 2012b; Newstalk 2014; Oxfam 2013; Paul 2015). Later, some of the architects of the Irish bailout programme, such as the IMF's Ajai Chopra and Ashoka Mody, were to criticize aspects of the Irish austerity programme (Beesley, Taylor, and Newenham 2015; RTE News 2013). However, alternatives to austerity had never received any serious consideration from the Irish Government. Austerity was the path chosen early on in the handling of the crisis. The preference of the government was to implement austerity outside of any formal international financial assistance programme by relying on borrowing in the bond markets and on liquidity supports to the banking system by the ECB to manage the financial crisis, recapitalize the banks, and finance public spending.

This strategy of 'auto austerity', as it might be termed, ran into problems during 2010 due to international reaction to the ongoing Greek crisis, fears within Europe of wider contagion, and the impact of sharply widening bond spreads on the cost of government borrowing. A subsequent report into the banking crisis by the Irish parliament outlined the sequence of events that resulted in Ireland being forced into a bailout programme in November 2010. The report makes clear that the ECB placed strong pressure on Ireland to accept a bailout (Joint Committee of Inquiry into the Banking Crisis 2016: 329–56). The extent of the pressure was evident in letters exchanged between the Minister for Finance, Brian Lenihan, and head of the ECB, Jean-Claude Trichet (*Irish Times* 2014).

In managing the banking and fiscal crisis, the Irish Government had favoured burden-sharing with unsecured senior bondholders in Irish banks.

The IMF had been prepared to consider 'haircuts' for senior bondholders. The ECB was emphatic, however, that Ireland could not institute burden-sharing and threatened to remove emergency liquidity assistance from Ireland's banks if such a strategy was implemented. Furthermore, the banking report states that Timothy Geithner, then Secretary to the US Treasury, played a role in ensuring losses were not imposed on senior bondholders, to prevent measures taken to handle Ireland's banking crisis from undermining the global financial system (Joint Committee of Inquiry into the Banking Crisis 2016: 361–2). While Ireland subsequently succeeded in refinancing aspects of the financial assistance provided by the Troika, further attempts to institute burden-sharing were equally resolutely resisted.

THE VARYING SUCCESS OF AUSTERITY REFORMS

Contributions to the book conclude that the Troika austerity programme and associated reforms set out in the National Recovery Plan (NRP) (2011–14) were of varying success, judged in terms of their objectives and their contribution to recovery. The highest levels of success were achieved in restructuring the financial institutions and in financial regulation. It is clear that a significant number of changes in these areas were initiated by the Irish authorities, or arose from what amounted to improvisation by the Irish Central Bank in conjunction with the international institutions.

The solvency of the sovereign was seriously imperilled by the bank guarantee introduced in September 2008 to prevent the collapse of the financial system. As Connor and his colleagues show in Chapter 5, the resulting €440 billion liability to the taxpayer was equivalent to more than double Irish GDP. Clarke's analysis in Chapter 6 of changes in financial regulation concludes that a 'paradigm shift in regulatory approach' had occurred in the years following the financial crisis, with a positive impact on the promotion of greater financial stability and consumer protection. Through a series of reforms, some originating internally, others emanating from the Troika programme, and yet others reflecting international regulatory developments, Ireland shook off its standing from the 2000s as the 'Wild West of European finance' (Lavery and O'Brien 2005). Some changes involved 'leadership and innovation' rather than simply relying on regulatory obligations or implementing European law. By acknowledging early on many of the mistakes associated with principles-based regulation and then-prevailing modes of corporate governance, a series of regulatory reforms were already underway when the Troika reform programme was agreed in November 2010. Particularly successful, according to Clarke (Chapter 6), have been more challenging and intrusive regulatory oversight introduced following the restructuring of the Irish Central Bank in July 2010, and subsequent higher levels of enforcement activity. The Central Bank's 'Prism Model' for assessing the stability of financial institutions and their capacity to withstand risks utilizes a series of quantitative impact metrics, allowing regulatory activity to focus most on areas of highest systemic risk for the financial system and its consumers. Corporate governance reforms, initiated by the Irish Central Bank via a 2010 statutory code (revised in 2015) and by the Companies Act 2014, involve higher standards than prevailing in other countries, in recognition of the particular experience of bank failure and mismanagement brought to light by the Irish financial crisis. Other reforms were integral to the Troika programme, in particular provisions for the immediate restructuring and stabilization of the banking system through the Credit Institutions (Stabilization) Act 2010—a key component of the NRP. Still others reflected evolving regulatory reforms in the EU and Eurozone, including the 'single supervisory mechanism' (SSM) that introduced provisions for the prudential supervision of all credit institutions and the 'single resolution mechanism' for managing banks that face serious difficulties. Overall, Clarke emphasizes that, just as the financial crisis was mainly 'home-made', many of the regulatory changes and innovations introduced were home-grown and contributed to a legal response to the crisis that has been 'strong and sustained'.

Connor and his colleagues' review in Chapter 5 of the restructuring of Ireland's financial institutions also strikes an optimistic note. A number of the key reforms resulted from improvisation and innovation by the Irish authorities and the Troika institutions, especially the ECB, that at times sailed close to the wind in terms of their strict legality or conformance with the mandates of sponsoring institutions. For example, the Byzantine 'promissory note' device used to manage the consequences of the disastrous implosion of Anglo Irish Bank and Irish Nationwide Building Society (INBS) was a compromise between the Irish Government, the ECB, and the Irish Central Bank that avoided the direct monetization of bank debt—this would have run contrary to European law—by, in effect, substituting a form of indirect debt monetization. The establishment of the National Asset Management Agency (NAMA) as a 'bad bank' for managing the property assets of Anglo Irish Bank and the recapitalized Irish banks was also an Irish Government initiative that Connor (Chapter 5) and his colleagues judge to have been successful in preventing the surviving banks from becoming 'zombie banks'. NAMA has ended up turning a modest profit on heavily discounted transferred assets. Other innovations introduced by the Irish authorities, in particular the so-called 'stress tests' for assessing the resilience of banking institutions, the Prudential Capital Assessment Review (PCAR) and the Prudential Liquidity Assessment Review (PLAR), became core features of banking reforms in the Troika programme. Less vigorously pursued were repossessions in the very many instances where defaults occurred on residential or investment mortgages. Here, a legal error or lacuna in the law that was allowed to stand until 2013 proved 'politically convenient' and resulted in an extremely low rate of repossessions—something that has changed little since the legal loophole involved was closed under pressure from the Troika.

The chapter's conclusion is that ECB-led pressure for Ireland to enter the Troika programme in 2010 resulted in the right course of action and that one of the programme's key goals, the 'restoration of confidence in the banking system', was achieved. However, Connor and his colleagues also identify a series of external developments that contributed to the success of the bank restructuring programme. These include unprecedentedly low interest rates set by Central Banks in the USA, the UK, and the Eurozone, and quantitative easing—measures that made the loan assets of the Irish banking system more attractive to foreign investors.

The consolidation of Ireland's public finances and recovery from the effective insolvency of the sovereign in 2010 counts as another significant achievement of the austerity programme. Kinsella in Chapter 3 emphasizes that the key reforms to resolve the fiscal crisis were underway from mid-2009—more than a year before the Troika programme had been agreed. While bailing out and restructuring the domestic banks cost €64 billion (equivalent to about 40 per cent of GDP) over the period from 2010 to 2012, about three-quarters of government debt was attributable to a general deterioration in the public finances. Cuts in spending, in public service pay, and in employment numbers were implemented from mid-2009. From 2010, a range of fiscal objectives and targets that were already guiding policy were included in the austerity programme agreed with the Troika.

Kinsella examines the large overall reduction that occurred in public spending. Revenue shortfalls caused by declining income streams as the economy contracted were made up from borrowing from Troika institutions as well as from bilateral loans by countries such as the UK and Denmark. The components of expenditure changed significantly as spending on social security and particularly unemployment (so-called 'automatic stabilizers') rose, while spending on health and education fell or remained flat. The share of income tax in public revenue rose significantly.

Chapter 12 by Boyle examines the scale of job reductions in the public service following on from the fiscal consolidations process. Thirty thousand jobs disappeared between 2008 and 2014: a 10 per cent reduction in employment. Chapter 11 by Roche examines the public service pay cuts that involved progressively tiered reductions in salaries of between 8 to 21 per cent over the period 2009–14. While public service jobs disappeared, demand for public services increased significantly—due to rising unemployment, growing numbers of social security claimants, and also to demographic pressures. A series of agreements with public service unions covering changes to patterns of staff allocation and working practices allowed the increased demand for public services to be absorbed as numbers employed dropped, resulting in a very significant increase in the productivity of the public service. However, Boyle shows that the quality of public service delivery declined across a range of dimensions.

If Troika measures for bank restructuring and regulatory reform and for fiscal consolidation can be judged as successful, the record in other areas of reform is more variegated. The vaguely formulated policy of internal devaluation or pay flexibility did not result in general reductions in nominal pay levels across the private sector, as shown in Chapter 3 by Kinsella and Chapter 11 by Roche. Nor did the significant cuts that occurred in public service pay spill over into the private sector, as some had anticipated. Structural reform measures promoting higher pay flexibility were either reversed, such as the 2010 cut in the minimum wage (reversed in 2011), or led to minor changes, such as modifications to pay fixing arrangements in low-paid, labour-intensive sectors and in construction. Roche shows that the suspension of these pay-fixing arrangements for a time during the recession arose from legal challenges by employers—whose opposition to these institutions had pre-dated the crisis. Overall, private-sector employers shied away from extensive cuts in basic pay and often opted instead for pragmatic and varied measures in retrenchment programmes agreed with trade unions. Soaring unemployment and continuing job insecurity dampened pay pressure and contributed to a decline in relative unit labour costs and a gain in Ireland's pay–cost competitiveness. The collapse of employment and economic activity in the bloated construction sector from 2008 was also behind the positive trend in nominal unit labour costs, and warrants caution in concluding that wage trends in Ireland contributed significantly to competitiveness or economic recovery.

Structural changes marked out in other areas of the austerity programme were also of limited success. Kinsella suggests that structural reforms to remove restrictions to trade and competition in sheltered sectors, including the legal and medical professions, barely scratched the surface (for the fate of proposal to reform the legal profession see Beesley 2016).

Chapter 13 by O'Connell examines labour activation measures introduced against the background of the steep rise in unemployment (peaking at 15 per cent) and long-term unemployment (LTU) (peaking at 9.5 per cent). A policy based around largely passive and ineffective labour market programmes shifted towards more active labour market measures from 2011, in line with commitments under the Troika programme. Income support and employment services were integrated, and job search and training supports became more sophisticated under the 'Pathways to Work' programme. However, staff capacity constraints hindered progress, and many placement and training measures were of limited success in getting participants back to work.

Over and above fiscal consolidation, the Troika programme sought to promote 'public service transformation'. As Boyle shows in Chapter 12, this had been a long-standing objective of government policy but had resulted in very limited progress, even from the mid-1990s when a wide-ranging reform programme was launched under the Strategic Management Initiative (SMI). Reforms introduced after the onset of the crisis were centrally driven and 'top down' in character—reversing the pre-crisis reform cycle, which had involved a gradual process of devolution of management authority and discretion to government departments and agencies. As shown by Boyle, and also in Chapter 11 by Roche, although changes in work and employment arrangements have impinged on the terms of the 'bargain' binding public service workers to the state, most reforms have involved going 'back to the future' by reintroducing or reinvigorating earlier cycles of reform. The character of public service careers was not fundamentally transformed.

Furthermore, in Chapter 11 Roche discusses how the NRP soft-pedalled reform objectives concerned with Ireland becoming a global innovation hub and location for high value-added employment. These objectives had clear implications for workplaces: envisioning a shift towards high-skill and high-involvement work and employment regimes. The research reported by Roche provides no evidence that such a shift has occurred in private-sector workplaces. Indeed, the evidence available suggests that improvements in productivity may have resulted more from higher work pressure or work intensification.

Having surrendered sovereignty in 2010 the Irish state remained in effect a protectorate of the Troika until the end of 2013. Prevailing political processes had been widely blamed for contributing to the economic and financial collapse through poor oversight and unsustainable economic and fiscal policies. The crisis and resort to the Troika resulted in a significant decline in trust and confidence in the political system. It also contributed to the unprecedented 'landslide election' of 2011 which swept an ostensibly reformist government to power, with the largest parliamentary majority in the history of the state. Starting from the premise that 'the failures of the political system over the past decade were a key contributor to the financial crisis', the new government pledged to introduce radical reforms of the political process (Fine Gael and Labour Party 2011: 19). Notwithstanding the high ambition of the incoming government, Chapter 9 by Farrell shows that political change remained nugatory over the period after 2008. The reforms that occurred are portrayed as 'distractive' rather than 'constructive'—designed to give the appearance of change without delivering substantive changes in the political system. In the two key areas that Farrell believes contributed to Ireland's economic collapse, a centralized system of government in which the Dáil (lower house of parliament) was weak relative to the executive, and a lack of openness and transparency, many reforms undertaken clustered around the 'distractive' end of the spectrum. The signal achievement of political reform was the inauguration of the Irish Constitutional Convention. This institution provides citizens with a voice in formulating constitutional and legislative reform proposals. But the issues addressed by the Constitutional Convention were an 'eclectic mix' and few, or none, addressed the political dysfunctions contributing to the economic and financial collapse.

Kitchin and his colleagues in Chapter 15 examine how housing policy during the boom contributed to the financial crisis. Austerity led to further problems, but economic recovery has brought yet more dysfunctions in the housing market. For Kitchin and his colleagues, Ireland's experience has been one of recurring crisis and policy failure. Policies protecting the interests of the banking and development sectors have prevented significant changes to housing and planning, which remain, in Kitchin and colleagues' words, 'fractured and fragmented'.

Exceptional economic growth and rising living standards during the Celtic Tiger years fuelled a consumption boom that was financed in part by rising personal debt. Chapter 7 by Claudy and his colleagues examines the effects of austerity on patterns of consumption. By deflating the domestic economy, the austerity programme resulted in sharp falls in personal consumption and in consumer confidence. The effects on consumer behaviour were complex. Data on micro-level consumption patterns that reveal people switched to lower cost goods and services and creatively delayed purchases. Trust in brands and advertising declined. There was a growth in sharing and the strong emphasis on personal consumption, equated with the boom years, declined in favour of other priorities and values such as 'reconnecting' with family and community.

Addressing the World Economic Forum in Davos in 2012, Ireland's Taoiseach, Enda Kenny, provoked controversy at home by commenting that the crisis was in part due to people having 'gone mad with borrowing'. As consumer confidence recovers in line with renewed growth, Claudy and his colleagues consider whether the effects of austerity on patterns of consumption may be long lasting or even transformative—leading people to reassess their values and their views towards possessions and relationships. The chapter concludes by showing that many spending habits and consumption practices that changed during the recession had now become normal for consumers. Particular changes in shopping habits and 'non-consumerist' values had continued beyond the recession and seemed likely to influence consumption into the future.

THE COSTS OF AUSTERITY

A number of chapters examine the costs associated with recession and austerity, and assess where, and on whom, the burden of those costs fell. In Chapter 13, O'Connell shows that the numbers unemployed rose from 100,000 in 2007 to 295,000 in 2012 before declining again as recovery took hold. LTU—particularly debilitating in respect of people's capacity to return to employment—rose from 1.4 per cent in 2007 to 9.5 per cent in 2010. Reflecting the collapse in construction employment and the decline of manufacturing, the burden of rising unemployment and of growing long-term joblessness fell mainly on men. Young people were particularly badly affected and have remained so, in what O'Connell describes as an 'extraordinary closing off of opportunities for labour market entry'. Many young people opted to remain in or return to education. Significant numbers of people taking up employment entered jobs requiring lower levels of education and skill than they possessed. Emigration was also concentrated among people with higher levels of education—many new migrants having been employed, rather than jobless, prior to leaving Ireland.

Chapter 16 by Glynn and O'Connell examines the dramatic rise in emigration during the recession, the numbers of people leaving Ireland peaking at 89,000 in 2012–13, before declining as recovery gained pace. In all, 610,000 people left Ireland between 2008 and 2015. Most were Irish nationals. Emigration clearly relieved the burden of unemployment to a significant degree. The per capita emigration rate in Ireland was very much higher than in other European countries in crisis. Unemployment, underemployment, and lack of job satisfaction were the major reasons people gave for leaving. For many, emigration was a positive experience and enabled them to find employment and to enjoy a better standard of living and quality of life. At the same time, some also paid an 'emotional price': families were missed and homesickness was sometimes a problem. Costs also arose for the families left behind by migrants: parents could suffer depressive symptoms and loneliness and communities were affected by falling numbers in clubs and social activities. The demographic structure also changed. There were fewer young people in the population, leading potentially to an unfavourable age dependency ratio in the future. Glynn and O'Connell are sceptical of the presumed 'brain drain' associated with emigration, notwithstanding the high levels of education of many of those who left. Whether they will return in large numbers as the economy improves remains, for now, an open question.

Inward migration to Ireland had grown dramatically in the years preceding the crisis as a result of high economic growth and the expansion of the EU from 2004. Outward migration by nationals of EU new member states (NMS) rose to 100,000 between 2008 and 2015; however, substantial inward migration also continued. Immigrants suffered more heavily from employment losses than Irish nationals, reflecting their concentration in sectors susceptible to the crisis: construction, retailing, accommodation, and food services. Glynn and O'Connell report that while migrants experienced multiple disadvantages and penalties in the labour market compared with Irish nationals, these had not intensified during the recession and may have declined in the areas of earnings and discrimination in access to jobs.

As shown in Chapter 11 by Roche, Irish nationals who remained in Ireland and retained their jobs often experienced declining earnings, as employers reduced working hours and cut back bonuses and other discretionary payments, or sometimes cut basic pay. Work pressure also increased as employers reduced headcounts and sometimes also tightened expected performance standards. Overall, qualitative features of work, such as the scope available to people to use their initiative on the job, or to influence decisions by their employer, remained unchanged.

Chapter 3 by Kinsella and Chapter 14 by Lynch and her colleagues examine various aspects of changes to fiscal policy and social expenditure. The austerity programme sought to address the deficit by loading two-thirds of the corrective on to spending cuts and one-third on to rises in taxes and charges. Taxation levels were increased and a new emergency tax, the Universal Social Charge was introduced. A new property tax was levied and a water charge was introduced. The combined effects of changes in salaries, taxes, and social transfers meant that median household disposable income fell by 16.4 per cent between 2008 and 2013. In Chapter 14, Lynch and her colleagues examine the effects of austerity on inequality. Ireland entered the crisis with one of the highest levels of income inequality in the Organisation for Economic Co-operation and Development (OECD). Overall income inequality, as measured by the Gini coefficient, was not exacerbated by austerity, although significant shifts occurred in the income shares of different groups. The average income of the bottom decile declined most sharply—marking a transfer of income from the poorest to the better off. Budgetary policies were neither consistently progressive nor regressive in their effects: the highest and lowest income groups experiencing broadly similar income losses arising from changes in tax, social security payments, and reductions in public service pay. Levels of basic deprivation and consistent poverty rose sharply. A rise in indirect taxes imposed a particularly heavy burden on people on the lowest incomes, and cutbacks in public services worsened the marginalization of people relying on disability supports, particularly children and young people, carers, travellers, and the physically and mentally ill. Furthermore, austerity was associated with a rise in the incidence of suicide by men and a rise in levels of non-fatal self-harm by men and women.

Chapter 15 by Kitchin and his colleagues shows how the collapse of the property market in 2008 and a precipitous fall in house prices (by well over 50 per cent) led to serious problems with negative equity and mortgage arrears. The number of households in negative equity grew to more than 50 per cent of mortgaged residential properties. By autumn 2013, 13 per cent of all mortgage holders were in arrears. Further problems arose from unfinished housing estates and from poorly constructed and unsafe housing and apartment developments. The provision of social housing was adversely affected by austerity, as state investment declined. Economic recovery has driven a new cycle of rapidly rising home purchase and rental prices and serious under-supply of social housing.

In Chapter 17, Taylor Black examines the deep cuts made to spending and investment in arts and culture. A cumulative reduction in Arts Council funding of over 35 per cent from 2009 had a direct impact on the living standards and work of artists and the viability of arts organizations. Public policy now promoted private philanthropy as a way of supporting the arts. The Irish Film Board (IFB) suffered even deeper cuts, losing 40 per cent of its public funds. Here, however, independent production activity grew significantly due to tax incentives and the early revival of the US economy. But this has favoured 'high-end' international productions more than Irish independent projects—the latter seriously affected by cutbacks in the state broadcasting authority, Raidió Teilifís Éireann (RTÉ). Audiences for arts activities fell significantly in the early years of the crisis, stabilizing thereafter. The recent exceptional international recognition achieved by Irish filmmakers and writers was seen to reflect the long-run investment in the arts that had been threatened by cuts in public investment introduced during the recession.

Taylor Black also reviews works by artists who have addressed the causes and consequences of austerity, especially those who contributed to his major documentary film, *Skin in the Game*. In this work and in further work in theatre, musical theatre, poetry, music, photography, and fiction, the actions and inactions of politicians, as much as those of bankers and developers, are the focus for explaining the genesis of austerity and its impact on the Irish people.

RECOVERY AND IRELAND AS EXEMPLAR

Chapters dealing with economic and fiscal policy and with business conclude that Ireland's strong revival is mainly attributable to the economy's position in international trade and the country's ability to benefit from the international economic revival. This reflects decades of industrial policy that positioned Ireland as a major hub for foreign direct investment (FDI), increasingly in high-technology manufacturing and traded services.

In Chapter 3, Kinsella is emphatic that Ireland's experience of austerity has been unique. The effects of severe cuts in current and capital spending and public-sector pay on domestic economic activity were offset by robust demand for exports in a way that could not be replicated in other Troika programme countries, or indeed more generally. Ireland's performance is comparable to economies like the USA and UK that pursued independent monetary policies, engaged in large programmes of quantitative easing, and adopted Keynesian-type fiscal expansions over the recession. In Chapter 4, Barry and Bergin's detailed examination of the structure and performance of the Irish business sector stresses Ireland's highly distinctive export orientation and high levels of FDI by multinationals. These features of the Irish business system partially reflect secular global trends in information and transportation technologies, the liberalization of international trade, and the deepening of European integration. They are also in part outcomes of Ireland's industrial policy and low corporation tax strategy.

During the Celtic Tiger era, the dramatic expansion of the construction sector, combined with a pro-cyclical fiscal policy, caused export growth to slow as the economy became more oriented to the domestic market. Ireland's international competitiveness also declined sharply. When the banking and fiscal crisis struck, for a time no offsetting external boom cushioned the shock, although pharmaceutical and information and communication technology (ICT) exports, where demand remained relatively buoyant, bolstered business performance through the worst years of the crisis. Small and medium enterprises (SMEs), wedded in the main to the domestic market, fared very badly, suffering the effects of an austerity-induced decline in domestic demand and a tight squeeze on the provision of credit by financial institutions. Recovery in the domestic economy has gained pace and domestic businesses are now making a significant contribution to growth. Barry and Bergin join other contributors to the book in underscoring the role of quantitative easing and historically low interest rates in stabilizing the restructured banking system, facilitating fiscal consolidation, and supporting economic recovery.

The contributions by Kinsella and Barry and Bergin conclude that, while fiscal contraction was necessary given the scale of the budget deficit and spiralling cost of borrowing, austerity was not responsible for the strength or timing of Ireland's economic recovery. The really significant factors, as they see it, were the strong export orientation of the economy, especially in high-demand sectors, and the buoyancy of the country's export destinations. These conclusions count against the case for Ireland as an exemplar, and Kinsella underscores this view by describing Ireland as a 'beautiful freak'.

Ireland's distinctiveness is again highlighted in Chapter 8, where Teague compares Ireland's experience of austerity with the experience of Greece, Italy, Portugal, and Spain (the so-called 'GIPS' countries). Teague argues that Troika-instigated 'structural adjustment' measures in the Irish case were less onerous than in the other GIPS countries, especially with respect to labour market and industrial relations reforms. This reflected the more flexible labour market and pay-fixing institutions that existed in Ireland, and their better alignment with the demands of Eurozone membership. Ireland's recovery and relative success under austerity is attributed to its extensive economic ties with economies outside the Eurozone, and also to the close alignment that existed between domestic industrial relations institutions and the highly open nature of the economy.

Moreover, other contributors point to the special and even unique character of the Irish case. The decision of the Irish Government in 2009 to opt for austerity reflected a long-running pro-cyclical bias in Irish public policy and Irish politics. Other than a brief and inglorious Keynesian interlude in the late 1970s, Irish fiscal policy and politics followed the maxim expressed by former Finance Minister Charlie McCreevy: 'when I have it I spend it. When I don't, I don't.' Around the onset of the crisis, when the UK's Prime Minister Gordon Brown canvassed European and international support for Keynesian measures, the Irish Government's focus was already squarely on austerity. As discussed in the alternatives to austerity section earlier in this chapter, the idea of a 'social solidarity pact', a core component of which was a public investment programme, gained little traction from the government before the massive resources required to stabilize the banking system and the billowing cost of Irish debt narrowed the options available. The Irish Government's preference had been to embark on a pathway of austerity without being tied into a formal international financial assistance programme.

The genesis of the auto austerity strategy and the sustainability of the subsequent austerity programme agreed with the Troika reflected particular features of the Irish case. As contributors to the book have observed, Ireland was subject to strong neoliberal influences on policy and politics well before the advent of the crisis. In Chapter 2, Ó Riain attributes the limited capacity of Irish policymakers to generate more diverse and creative solutions to the crisis to the role of financialization (Irish as well as European) in marginalizing the more creative corporatist developmental institutions at the core of Ireland's political economy during the early phase of the Celtic Tiger period. In Chapter 14, Lynch and her colleagues observe that political and administrative elites in Ireland had also committed to neoliberal views on the marketization of public services and public management well in advance of the crisis, and could readily accommodate the hardships and deprivations that went with austerity cutbacks and reforms. The strong tradition of responding to inequalities and their effects on a charitable basis rather than through citizen rights and institutional reforms further underscored the sustainability of austerity.

That Ireland opted for auto austerity and then reluctantly accommodated to Troika support leaves open the question of how support for the austerity programme was sustained as cuts began to bite and seriously affect large numbers of people. Things in Ireland had clearly taken a different course to the cycles of reluctant and grudging accommodation, followed by resistance, political volatility, and capital flight evident in other programme countries, especially Greece. The chapters by Ó Riain, by Roche, by Kinsella, and by Farrell discuss how the kinds of political and social dissent evident in other Troika programme countries were muted or contained in Ireland. All of the major political parties accepted the need for austerity early on and then sought to accommodate to the Troika austerity programme, challenging but, when threatened, pragmatically accepting the ECB's injunction against burden-sharing by unsecured bondholders. In Chapter 10, Laffan shows how Irish negotiators with Troika institutions studiously avoided the kind of volatility, overt public conflict, and tumult evident in the case of Greece and Portugal. Their resolve was to hit the agreed targets and to get out of the programme as soon as possible. For Laffan, this posture reflected the country's deeply pragmatic political and administrative culture.

Other than one public service-wide strike in late 2009 and rolling protests against the imposition of water charges, social dissent and protest never reached levels evident in other Troika programme countries. This was due in part to the pro-austerity postures of the main political parties. It was also due in a major degree to the absence of an offensive by employers in the private sectors against basic pay levels, and to the willingness of public service unions to agree pragmatic measures to moderate and shape cuts in the public service pay bill. Rather than acting as agents of protest and dissent, unions in Ireland opted for accommodation with the agents of austerity, seeing this as the lesser of evils. Kinsella argues that social dissent was further contained by Ireland's continuing high level of social expenditure. The role of emigration as a safety valve, so often evident in the country's history, also contributed to the weakness of dissent against austerity and associated cuts.

To what degree can Ireland's return to growth be viewed as sustainable, particularly given the limited extent of structural and institutional reforms beyond the restructuring of banking and related regulatory changes? Economic growth has burgeoned since about 2012 and the national debt has fallen from over 125 per cent of GDP in 2013 to less than 100 per cent in 2016 (*Irish Times* 2016). Ireland nevertheless remains the second most indebted industrial country in the world, with per capita debt of over €43,500. Servicing that debt will absorb resources that could otherwise be invested in Ireland's under-resourced public services. Unemployment has fallen from a high of 15 per cent in 2012 to about 8.5 per cent in 2016. However, the level of unemployment remains high, and further reductions in the numbers unemployed will require greater efforts, due to the composition of those remaining in unemployment.

Given the openness of the Irish economy and the importance of FDI, continued economic growth is dependent upon a stable and buoyant international economy. Here there are several causes for concern. In Britain, still Ireland's single largest trading partner, considerable support exists for an exit from the EU, the impact of which in Ireland is quite uncertain, but potentially severely negative. Sluggish growth in Europe and imbalances in the Chinese economy are also causes for concern.

A serious housing crisis has emerged, with rapidly escalating rents and house prices, and there has been a substantial increase in homelessness, mainly due to the inability of families to meet rent increases, as discussed in Chapter 15. The housing crisis causes social distress, but also threatens to undermine competitiveness and recovery. Poverty has also increased: the share of the population experiencing consistent poverty, which includes people who are both living under the poverty income threshold and experiencing enforced deprivation, increased from 4 per cent in 2008 to 8 per cent in 2013 and 2014, and has not decreased in the early stage of the recovery (CSO 2015). Following a sustained period of wage cuts in the public sector and wage restraint in the private sector, pressure has built up for pay rises and there are signs of growing industrial militancy in sectors such as transport. The orderly industrial relations arrangements that prevailed during the recession and into the early years of recovery could now unravel at significant economic cost. Thus, many commentators view Ireland's recovery as vulnerable to reverses in many of the forces that contributed to the country's dramatic rebound from austerity and the Great Recession.

REFERENCES

Beesley, A. 2016. 'Files Show Unrelenting Campaign by Legal Professions to Safeguard Privileged Position'. *Irish Times*, 12 February.

Beesley, A., Taylor, C., and Newenham, P. 2015. 'ECB Stewardship of Ireland's Bailout Attacked by Chopra'. *Irish Times*, 13 November.

Blyth, M. 2013. *Austerity: The History of a Dangerous Idea.* Oxford: Oxford University Press.

Cragg, M. and Stiglitz, J. 2011. 'ECB–IMF Deal is a Noose that Will Strangle Economic Recovery'. *Irish Times*, 9 April.

CSO (Central Statistics Office). 2015. *Survey on Income and Living Conditions (SILC) 2014.* Dublin: Stationery Office.

De Grauwe, P. and Moesen, W. 2009. 'Gains for All: A Proposal for a Common Eurobond'. *Intereconomics*, May/June.

Elliott, L. 2016. 'Keynes's Comeback Was Vital But Short-Lived', *The Guardian*, 8 February.

Fine Gael and Labour Party. 2011. *Programme for Government 2011–2016.* Available at: <http://www.taoiseach.gov.ie/eng/Work_Of_The_Department/Programme_for_Government/Programme_for_Government_2011-2016.pdf> (accessed 22 June 2016).

FitzGerald, J. 2014. 'Ireland's Recovery from Crisis'. *CESifo Forum*, 15(2): 8–13.

ICTU (Irish Congress of Trade Unions). 2009. *There is a Better Fairer Way: Congress Plan for National Recovery.* Dublin: Irish Congress of Trade Unions.

Irish Times. 2014. 'The Trichet–Lenihan Letters: The Full Text'. 7 November.

Joint Committee of Inquiry into the Banking Crisis. 2016. *Report of the Joint Committee of Inquiry into the Banking Crisis*, 3 vols. Dublin: Houses of the Oireachtas.

Keena, C. 2009. 'Fairness Needed When Dealing With Crisis, Says Stiglitz'. *Irish Times*, 9 October.

Krugman, P. 2010. 'Eating the Irish'. *New York Times*, 25 November. Available at: <http://www.nytimes.com/2010/11/26/opinion/26krugman.html?rref=collection%

2Fcolumn%2Fpaul-krugman&action=click&contentCollection=opinion&region=stream&module=stream_unit&version=search&contentPlacement=3&pgtype=collection> (accessed 20 March 2016).

Krugman, P. 2012a. *End This Depression Now!* New York: W.W. Norton & Company.

Krugman, P. 2012b. 'Those Revolting Europeans'. *New York Times*, 6 May. Available at: <http://www.nytimes.com/2012/05/07/opinion/krugman-those-revolting-europeans.html?rref=collection%2Fcolumn%2Fpaul-krugman&action=click&contentCollection=opinion&region=stream&module=stream_unit&version=search&contentPlacement=7&pgtype=collection> (accessed 20 March 2016).

Lavery, B. and O'Brien, L. 2005. 'For Insurance Regulators, Trails Lead to Dublin', *New York Times*. Available at: <http://www.nytimes.com/2005/04/01/business/worldbusiness/for-insurance-regulators-trails-lead-to-dublin.html?_r=1> (accessed 23 June 2016).

NESC (National Economic and Social Council). 2009. *Ireland's Five-Part Crisis: An Integrated National Response*. Dublin: National Economic and Social Council.

Newstalk. 2014. 'Economic Expert: Ireland Suffered Unnecessarily during Economic Crash (Audio Interview)', 30 May. Available at: <http://www.newstalk.com/Economic-expert:-Ireland-suffered-unnecessarily-during-economic-crash> (accessed 29 March 2016).

Notre Europe. 2012. *Completing the Euro: A Road Map toward Fiscal Union in Europe. Report of the Tommaso Padoa Schioppa Group*. Paris: Notre Europe, Institute Jacques Delors.

Oxfam. 2013. *The True Cost of Austerity and Inequality: Ireland Case Study*. Oxford: Oxfam Case Study. Available at: <https://www.oxfam.org/sites/www.oxfam.org/files/cs-true-cost-austerity-inequality-ireland-120913-en.pdf> (accessed 29 March 2016).

Paul, M. 2015. 'ECB to Blame for Irish Austerity, Says UK Labour Adviser'. *Irish Times*, 30 October.

RTÉ News. 2013. 'Reliance on Austerity is Counterproductive Says Former IMF Mission Chief', 11 April. Available at: <http://www.rte.ie/news/business/2013/0411/380836-too-much-austerity-in-bailout-imf-mission-chief/> (accessed 20 March 2016).

RTÉ News. 2016. 'Ireland's Economic Growth "No Victory Yet"—Says Stiglitz', 21 January. Available at: <http://www.rte.ie/news/2016/0121/761757-enda-kenny-davos-world-economic-forum/> (accessed 20 March 2016).

Sinn, H. W. 2013. 'Austerity, Growth and Inflation: Remarks on the Eurozone's Unresolved Competitiveness Problem', CESifo Working Paper No. 4086. Munich: Center for Economic Research & Information Institute.

Thompson, H. 2013. 'Austerity as Ideology: The Bait and Switch of the Banking Crisis'. *Comparative European Politics*, 11(6): 729–36.

2

The Road to Austerity

Seán Ó Riain

IRELAND'S AUSTERITY: SUDDEN, SEVERE, AND A LONG TIME COMING

Why was Ireland so helpless in the face of its crisis in 2008? Why was its austerity adjustment so severe, compared to other countries? Why did austerity appear to be such an inevitability, both economically and politically? As well as the challenges posed by facing a crisis of enormous scale, Ireland proved to be hampered by external and domestic political and institutional conditions that made a strong policy focus on austerity a highly likely outcome. Many of the very forces that brought Ireland to its position in the eye of the world's economic storm in 2008 made it more difficult for the Irish polity to respond in ways that might creatively work through what was inevitably an exceptionally difficult period.

There were three major causes for Ireland's particularly dramatic adjustment. First was the sheer scale of the financial crisis. This was not simply a matter of the massive debts in the banking system but also of the degree of entanglement of these bad debts with the real economy—primarily through the economic and employment impact of an immediate collapse in construction-related employment and the massive hole in the public finances left both by guaranteeing banking debt and by the disappearance of tax revenues related to property sales. Ireland was dealing not only with a massive debt overhang but also with a damaged and distorted economy.

Second, membership of the European Union (EU) and the Eurozone contributed to both the crisis in Ireland and the focus on austerity as a policy response. Despite the appearance of uncertainty, the EU in practice followed a remarkably consistent and narrow policy of pro-cyclical austerity at both the European and national levels, only moving to a more activist (and still limited) European policy well after the onset of the crisis.

Third, Ireland faced the crisis with a limited national capacity for adjustment. This may seem strange given the widespread international praise for

Ireland's adjustment and recovery. However, Ireland's capacities were strong in a narrow realm of action, primarily around reducing expenditure while limiting protest. The capacity of the policy system to generate more diverse and creative solutions was more limited, particularly at the level of national policy, as the financialization of the 2000s had marginalized some of the more creative institutional experiments of the 1990s. It is only in the uneven recovery since 2012 that echoes of these earlier policy successes were to be found.

Behind these proximate causes of Ireland's crisis and subsequent austerity lie a number of key questions, each of which are examined in this chapter. First, 'austerity' itself may serve as a label for quite different political and economic strategies. Therefore, the chapter starts with a discussion of the different meanings of 'austerity' (and its 'Keynesian' alternatives) and their place within the different varieties or worlds of capitalism. Second, it outlines the three major causes behind Ireland's road to austerity in more detail. Furthermore, it links each of these causes to a broader aspect of the social organization of 'liberalization'—looking in turn at financialization, regional projects of economic integration, and the weakening of the public and civic foundations of national political economic strategies. Third, the chapter turns to the complex question of the link between liberalism and austerity—in Ireland's boom, its crisis, and its current recovery.

AUSTERITY IN COMPARATIVE AND HISTORICAL PERSPECTIVE

Austerity is both a particularly striking aspect of the contemporary era and an idea with a long history (Blyth 2013). A variety of analysts link austerity directly to economic liberalism, primarily through the dominant emphasis within austerity policies on reducing public spending and therefore almost inevitably shrinking the size of the state. However, when we examine the responses to the economic crisis since 2008, the strongest focus on austerity—both in terms of the practical policies advocated and the rhetoric of the moral and economic need to 'live within the state's means'—has been in Northern Europe, apparently the least liberal and the most coordinated and 'social' of all the capitalisms (Ó Riain 2014).

Table 2.1 illustrates this puzzle, showing the significant differences that persisted across European countries in budget balances in the 2000s—both the actual balance and the 'potential' balance (calculated by the International Monetary Fund (IMF) to take into account the effects of the business cycle). These are contested concepts but the pattern is clear enough. The Nordic

Table 2.1. Actual and 'potential' budget balances in the 'varieties of capitalism' in Europe, 1999–2007

	1999–2007 (% actual GDP)	1999–2007 (% potential GDP)	1999–2002 (% potential GDP)	2003–7 (% potential GDP)
Nordics/Social Democratic	2.5	0.3	0.1	0.5
Continentals/ Christian Democratic	−1.5	−1.7	−1.7	−1.6
Mediterranean	−2.9	−4.0	−3.1	−4.7
Liberal	0.1	−2.5	−0.6	−3.8
Including: Ireland	1.6	−2.7	−0.7	−3.9

Source: Actual Balances—Eurostat; 'Potential' Balances—IMF.

economies do best in terms of 'fiscal discipline', running an actual surplus but also balancing their books, even on the basis of the underlying structural deficit (accounting for the effects of the Norwegian oil boom on Nordic surpluses). While running deficits a little larger than the social democracies, Europe's Christian democracies remained comfortably within the Eurozone criteria. The liberal economies of Ireland and the UK appear to do better, based on their actual balance, but this masked a significant bubble as their large underlying deficits indicate. The Mediterranean economies also had significant difficulties with budget deficits, which were already present in the early 2000s. It is clear, however, that it is the apparently expansionist 'social market' economies of Northern Europe who are the most fiscally conservative.

These patterns relate to the creation of the crisis—what of the response once the crisis hit? The alternative to austerity as a strategy for recovery was typically presented as some version of Keynesian stimulus policy that would drive recovery through expansion of the economy rather than direct consolidation of the debt, and that would repudiate the 'liberal' policy of austerity. Despite ongoing debates about the self-defeating nature of 'austerity' at the European level, EU elites have resisted what they see as the siren call of Keynesianism.

On the face of it, Europe should be the home of such Keynesian interventions as these should be politically and economically easier in countries with higher levels of social spending. Ironically, however, it is the countries of Continental Europe, with their larger public sectors and 'social economies', who have been cheerleaders for austerity policies, while the 'liberal', less free-spending states of the UK and USA have been more willing to engage in sustained quantitative easing.

Therefore, the political responses to the crisis in different worlds of capitalism have largely been consistent with their approaches prior to the crisis.

This points to a crucial distinction between austerity and fiscal conservatism—with the Northern European countries historically combining their higher levels of social spending (an antipathy to 'austerity') with an aversion to budget deficits (a deep commitment to 'fiscal prudence'). Fiscal discipline had less to do with German cultural memories of the 1930s inflation than with the general logics of these models of political economy (see Ó Riain 2014 for further discussion). In the 'social market' economies, fiscal prudence has historically been associated with the protection of the state and the public sector from the cycles of capitalism rather than with shrinking the state to respond to those fluctuations and pressures.

This also suggests that we need to revisit the place of 'Keynesianism' in contemporary debates. While Keynes is often read as an advocate of counter-cyclical spending and quantitative easing, this relies purely on a reading of Keynes as macroeconomic manager. Keynes also emphasized a more general role for government, particularly in securing social protection and investment, and generally managing the economy and ensuring appropriate levels of investment and other long-term economic requirements (Block 2012). While most commentators associate the social democratic worlds of capital-ism with Keynesianism, in practice it is this more general argument of Keynes for social investments and long-range planning and management that is most characteristic of the social democratic and Christian democratic countries. The Keynes who advocated counter-cyclical spending and macroeconomic reflation to escape from crisis is, in practice, more widely favoured in liberal political economies—as seen in the persistently higher deficits run in such economies.

Streeck (2014) links austerity to a structural shift in capitalism as a whole, as governments used looser private and public credit since the 1970s as a mechanism to meet increased expectations in an era of declining growth. Schafer and Streeck (2013) argue that escape from this failure is ever more difficult as declining growth made it more difficult to keep up with debt obligations (or to use inflation to erode debt). This made governments more responsive to the financial institutions that lent to them than to the citizens who elected them. However, instead of simply expressing an irresistible struc-tural shift in capitalism, the turn to austerity can be seen as a combination of established patterns of economic policymaking combined with significant shifts in European economies, in particular. The fiscal prudence and conservatism of Northern European economies had historically been counterbalanced by a number of central planks in their political economies. A banking system oriented towards long-term productive investments had helped to smooth out the cycles in the private economy. In the public sector, a strong emphasis on long-term social and economic investments, and on universalist collective systems of social protection, protected citizens while enabling them to adjust to challenges of external trading regime changes. These were key private and public aspects that both enabled and were reinforced by fiscal conservatism in the European model. However, many of these elements have been eroded, particularly since the 1980s, weakening the foundations of fiscal prudence even as the rhetoric of balanced budgets grew ever more intense and was formalized in EU rules.

We can see therefore that 'austerity' and 'Keynesianism' can, in practice, serve as labels for quite different approaches to fiscal prudence and macro-economic policy in different contexts; that these approaches are associated with different worlds of capitalism and different approaches to private invest-ment and social protection; and that the foundations of fiscal conservatism have, in practice, been eroding in recent decades as public sectors are increas-ingly weakened. It is in this context that we can now turn to examining the three key pressures that led Ireland on the road to austerity.

IRELAND'S ROAD TO AUSTERITY

Three of the grand themes of contemporary capitalism—financialization, a particular form of international economic integration and 'liberal' economic policies—intertwined to make Ireland's crisis particularly dramatic.

Financializing the Irish Economy

An attenuated version of the European model of development was at the heart of the genuine development of the Irish economy in the 1990s—productive investment, enabled by enterprise policy; European investment in social and regional cohesion within a trading zone; and a set of 'creative corporatist' institutions that mobilized capital and labour as well as managing relations between them. However, the 1990s project of productive investment in new industries, supported by lively developmental state agencies, was overwhelmed in the 2000s by the rise of property speculation, with cheap credit and speculative 'flipping' of residential and commercial buildings driving a prop-erty bubble. Ultimately this led to a banking crash, and massive bank debts were loaded onto the public purse.

On one reading, Ireland's financial crisis was a very local crisis. The sub-prime mortgages and securitized mortgage products that were central to the triggering of the US crisis were much less important in the Irish case, where lending to developers and inflated property prices were much more significant (Connor, Flavin, and Kelly 2012). While mortgage lending practices loosened in the 2000s, the crisis was not caused by mortgage defaults (although these became significant elements of the evolving crisis) but by developers failing to repay loans to banks when liquidity suddenly dried up in 2008.

However, other features of the Irish crisis were shared more broadly. As Connor, Flavin, and Kelly (2012) point out, Ireland shared with the USA features such as 'irrational exuberance' among market actors, a 'capital bonanza' (easy access to cheap capital for banks—in the Irish case through international borrowing), and failures of regulation and 'moral hazard'. To this list, we might add the absence of a significant public housing system. In addition, the various crises of the current period are linked through increasingly close financial integration, with the US crisis in 2008 the tipping point for Irish banks' collapse as interbank liquidity dried up very rapidly. This financial integration itself has been closely linked to a broader project of economic liberalization, most clearly since the 1990s.

Ireland proved a world leader in the financialization of the economy: 'the increasing role of financial motives, markets, actors and institutions in the operation of the domestic and international economies' (Epstein 2005: 3; Kus 2012). While there are many potential indicators of this process, Krippner (2011) takes the share of profits within the economy going to financial activities as her central measure of financialization, arguing that this measure reflects both the sectoral growth of finance and the accumulation of power within the economy. Figure 2.1 outlines trends in the profits of the 'financial intermediation' sector (banks and other financial institutions, but not including insurance, real estate, and other business services) for the years for which Organisation for Economic Co-operation and Development (OECD) statistics are available.

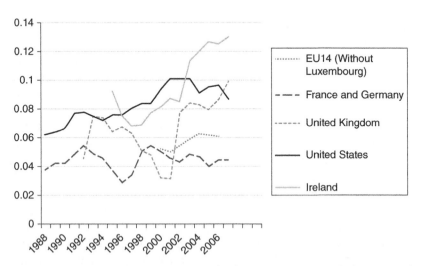

Figure 2.1. Proportion of all corporate profits (gross operating surplus) going to the 'financial intermediation' (banking) sector, 1988–2007

Note: EU14 and the France and Germany measures are an average of national rates, not a total of all profits across those countries.
Source: OECD STAN Database.

The statistics reveal some interesting variation in Irish banking profits. Despite their lack of contribution to economic development (Honohan 2006), Irish banks were comparatively profitable in the mid-1990s. Their share of corporate profits declined during the mid-1990s only to recover somewhat alongside the export boom of the late 1990s, and surge dramatically from 2003 to 2007. Ireland's financial expansion was only one leg of a 'triple financialization', also including Anglo-American financial systems and the financialization associated with European integration and the euro in the 2000s. While the USA was always more financialized than the European core, that gap widened significantly over the 1990s, and financialization is most closely associated with 'liberal market economies' (Hall and Soskice 2001) such as the USA, UK, and Ireland. Nonetheless, the EU economies closed the gap somewhat from 2001 onwards—with France and Germany showing a surge in the 2002–4 period. Since the proportion of Irish banks' liabilities derived from foreign sources grew dramatically in the 2000s (Lane 2011), these were very significant trends.

This financialization was both a driving force in economic liberalization and also enabled by 'liberal' policies. The key 'liberal' element in Ireland's policy regime during these years was the faith in the ability of private capital to allocate investment resources effectively in the economy. Crucially, the new government's budget of 1998 reduced capital gains tax from 40 per cent to 20 per cent, with a view to releasing pent-up capital into the economy. This goal was rapidly achieved—in the decade after the reduction of capital gains tax to 20 per cent in 1998, bank lending in the economy grew by 466 per cent. However, that capital flowed primarily and rapidly into property investment. Together, domestic banks and a small group of residential and commercial property developers misallocated capital in Ireland on a grand scale. A lending and investment coalition focused on domestic property was able to secure the lion's share of available capital, to the cost of competing sectors (most notably the medium- and high-tech sectors). Construction and real estate lending increased from 7 per cent to 28 per cent of total lending over the period. In contrast, the high-profile high-tech sectors attracted less than 2.5 per cent of credit (Ó Riain 2014).

With an institutionally and personally weak Financial Regulator, finance in Ireland was to be a liberal experiment based on governance by a set of market mechanisms. Unfortunately, these mechanisms failed to provide the necessary controls. Most basically, competition between the banks appears to have been a factor in 'crowding in' the two leading banks, Allied Irish Banks (AIB) and Bank of Ireland (BOI), into 'irrational' property lending. Anglo Irish Bank, the bank infamously most closely associated with property lending, saw a surge in profits to the point where it had significantly closed the gap with BOI by 2007. Executive compensation followed suit—including, as became apparent in 2008, secret loans to executives and directors of as much as €70 million.

AIB, Ireland's most profitable bank, responded to the Anglo surge with a shift into real estate and development lending, with a corresponding boost in profits—and subsequent disastrous collapse.

If market competition did not provide the discipline required, perhaps managerial authority could. In practice, however, the centralization of executive authority in the banks reinforced the convergence of optimistic assessments of asset quality, capital position, and economic growth (Ó Riain 2014). Bank executives faced few challenges to their perspectives. Authority within the banks was highly centralized, as an Anglo Irish Bank Annual Report noted:

> The Bank's centralized business model enables quick decision-making, ensuring consistent delivery of service to our customers and effective management of risk. It also allows us to operate in an efficient and streamlined manner, as reflected by our cost to income ratio of 27 per cent. (Anglo Irish Bank 2006: 4)

Senior bank executive salaries rose rapidly in all banks through the 2000s, with bonuses that were, in practice, increased by corporate strategies that inflated the bubble (TASC 2010).

Shareholders were the other candidates for providing sufficient external oversight from within the private sector as a 'market for governance' (Davis 2009). However, the stock market itself reinforced the tendencies towards financialization. Ó Riain (2014) examines trends in a variety of Irish Stock Market Indices from 1995 to 2005. The General Index showed strong growth in the late 1990s but dipped from 2001 to 2003 and only recovered by 2005. However, the financial stocks surged from 2000 onwards, after strong growth in the 1990s. The stock market was also a weak mechanism for distributing investment to the productive and innovative, rather than speculative, sectors. The technology-based Irish Technology Exchange Index never recovered subsequent to the dot.com bubble bursting in 2001, while the financial stocks increased rapidly in value. The stock market rewarded the lending patterns that were ultimately to crash the economy.

Nor did an increasing engagement with international financial institutions have the required effect. A crucial role here was played by the credit-rating agencies, private regulatory organizations that provide ratings of the quality of a wide variety of financial instruments, linked both to private and sovereign issuers. These agencies provided increasingly positive ratings of Ireland's banks, including for Anglo Irish Bank—which in turn was given a series of international accolades by consulting firms. The market institutions which were to provide a regulatory function to market actors and actions failed disastrously to limit the financialization of Ireland's economy, and actually facilitated and rewarded the dangerous expansion of the financial sector to a scale that would ultimately produce Ireland's dramatic austerity.

From Development to Financialization in the European Project

Ireland's financialization might have had domestic roots but was driven to dangerous heights by the changing dynamics of European integration. The entry of Ireland in 1973 was a major challenge for the EU as it was the first country admitted to the EU with significantly worse structural development and lower national income per capita than elsewhere in the EU (although there were regions within other countries, such as the Mezzogiorno in Italy and the 'Celtic peripheries' of the UK which were significantly poorer regions hidden within wealthier national nation states).

However, in the 1990s, European public funds were part of an effort to promote convergence across European regions and ultimately funded a high proportion of Ireland's investment during this decade of development. Much of this funding was related to agriculture but there were significant increases also in the total non-agricultural funds and in the European social funds that supported training and other measures for labour market inclusion. This increase persisted through the 1990s and only returned to the nominal levels of 1989 in 2007. Even in the booming late 1990s, EU funds accounted for over 15 per cent of Irish public capital expenditure—a very important contribution considering that the vast bulk of productive capital spending in the Irish economy during this period and later came from the public sector (White 2010).

However, Ireland's relationship with Europe changed significantly in the 2000s as the character of the European economic project itself shifted. A policy that incorporated strong elements of public developmentalism within a trading union was supplanted by private financialization in a monetary union. A growth model was available in the Eurozone and was behind Ireland's celebrated growth of the 1990s—and even more clearly contributed to the growth in Denmark and the Netherlands at the time (Behling and Ó Riain 2015; Hemerijck and Visser 1999). However, the project of financialization overwhelmed this growth model—both in the private sector, where financial activity drove an increasing share of profits, and in the political world, where the power of the idea of austerity, and the shrinking of the state, was deeply tied to the legitimation of the guiding role of financial markets (Blyth 2013).

The European form of financialization retained the historical emphasis on banks but the European banking system itself became increasingly marketized. European banks increasingly abandoned long-term relations with industrial clients, raised their funds through financial markets, and diversified their operations to place additional emphasis on speculative activities. They competed aggressively with US and UK banks in the 2000s to take advantage of 'innovation' in financial instruments and activities, creating a European banking bubble of their own. The bubble in German banking, for example, may have been shorter and less dramatic than in the liberal economies but nonetheless had some disastrous effects.

German commercial banks saw a rapid increase in their holdings of securitized assets and a disimprovement in their capital adequacy ratios between 2003 and 2007 (IMF 2009: Appendix Table 4). While significant elements of the banking system—including the savings and state banks—remained largely outside the bubble and continued to lend to small businesses before and through the crisis (Federation of Small Businesses 2012: 12), the large commercial banks expanded their international lending and became significant drivers of financialization in Europe. The triangle of Irish banks, international funders, and credit-ratings agencies connected the Irish financial world, based on personalized property development lending, to the international trade in securitized financial instruments through the standardizing effects of credit ratings. In the process, it further weakened the ties between financial and industrial capital in both the European periphery and the core.

This financialization was linked to the long-term twin project of monetary union and increased financial integration. Capital liberalization could support Germany's industrial competitiveness through laying the foundations for a single currency, ultimately the euro. The euro has been a significant subsidy for German exports, relative to the deutschmark which, had it continued, would have been a much stronger currency and have made German exports much more expensive. In addition, the banking sector itself became an important export sector in Germany, as in more liberal economies such as the UK and Ireland. While capital liberalization meant a significant shift away from the bank-centred hausbank system that had underpinned much of German industrial growth, it could still be seen as a strategy to boost the competitiveness of German exports.

In addition, at the macroeconomic level, the liberalization of finance was seen by key German policymakers as providing the external market discipline on public finances that was to be crucial to the European project (Ó Riain 2014). The financialization of European economies was linked to a broader project of apparently managed economic integration and, in particular, the monetary union of the 2000s. The financial integration that the euro facilitated was politically significant in shifting the balance of the different 'models of capitalism' within the EU, as the greatest threat to social democratic strategies came less from trade integration than from the danger posed by financialization to governments' ability to mobilize capital for productive investment (Scharpf 1991). In the process, the European economy became badly unbalanced, as, where this financialization took off most dramatically, (i.e. in the European periphery) it was funded through external financial systems. Where once Europe had invested heavily in the future, it now speculated on it.

Fiscal rules were to provide the protective shell around this financial system and the inevitable bubbles that would emerge. Much attention has focused on the failure to keep to these rules, particularly in France and Germany in the early 2000s, and the demonstration effect of the leniency towards these major countries. While legitimate, this focus obscures the more fundamental point noted earlier that the foundations of fiscal prudence were firmly in Europe's productive and welfare institutions which were themselves being undermined—notably by the very financialization that was supposed to discipline public finances. European policymakers may well have seen the Economic and Monetary Union (EMU) of the 2000s as the transplanting of the historically established European political economy and 'social model' from the national to the transnational stage. Indeed, Jacques Delors (the architect of the strategy of the 1990s and EMU) himself expected a crisis of sorts to materialize but believed it would force countries into the necessary adjustments (Begg 2016). In practice, however, the missing 'social Europe' materialized to a minimal degree, as 'negative' market integration dominated the European project (Scharpf 1999). Ultimately, this proved disastrous as it meant that some crucial elements of the European model were never transplanted to the transnational level.

Overall then, the EMU played a key role in making the crisis—even if the proximate causes are to be found in how various economic and political actors reacted to the new macroeconomic context. The euro's major flaw was one of its most touted successes—a particularly deep financial integration, which policymakers initially expected to provide an external discipline to businesses and states but which in fact it brought the exact opposite. This combined disastrously with the decline in flexibility available to governments to develop their own responses to such external pressures, and the tight coupling of their various national economies meant that weaknesses in one set of institutions (and especially financial systems) had strong transnational knock-on effects.

In addition, EMU was not as neutral as regards national models as was often portrayed. As we saw earlier in this chapter, the kinds of macroeconomic policy combinations that went with hard currency and low inflation were well suited to Nordics and Continentals and those countries were always better placed to manage the new context of the euro (including those Nordic economies, such as Denmark, that tracked the euro despite not joining it). More seriously still, the kinds of compensating investments and protections that were used in those countries to compensate for the disciplines of 'hard' monetary and currency regimes were absent at the European level (and were actually weakened after EMU was introduced), Most fundamentally, the euro covered a fault line within the EU itself. The major advantage of the euro for Germany was that it provided it with a far weaker currency than it would otherwise have had, strengthening its export competitiveness. However, this weakness of the euro depended upon the developmental weakness of peripheral economies. A significant upgrading of the peripheral economies would have challenged the German attraction to the euro project.

This hard edge to the euro project was institutionalized in the European Central Bank (ECB) and shown most clearly in the role played by Jean-Claude Trichet in a series of communications with the Irish Government. These are claimed to include an infamous phone message left before the bank guarantee of 2008 for the Minister for Finance to 'save your banks', before the Troika bailout, and when he warned the next unfortunate Minister of a 'bomb' that would go off if Ireland did not back away from a proposal to make lenders pay a portion of the costs of the crisis. Although full details have never emerged, Trichet's brand of 'destructive ambiguity' about the European reaction to Irish policy decisions clearly was designed to protect the European financial system above the EU's member states—whether out of desire to save the banks from the costs of their mistakes, or out of uncertainty as to the effects on the European banking system as a whole. The European project, as experienced by Ireland at least, had been transformed dramatically from Delors to Trichet.

A Flaw in the Social Contract

Given these twin pressures of financialization at home and a changing European region abroad, did Ireland have the domestic institutions and strategies that could navigate through these complex waters?

Ireland's apparent exit from the vicious circle of underdevelopment in the 1990s involved not only economic and social progress but also significant institutional innovations within the political economy. In particular, industrial development was driven forward both by multinational capital and by an emerging 'developmental network state' (Ó Riain 2004). Macroeconomic stability was provided through neo-corporatist social partnership agreements from 1987 onwards. Taken together, these provided a form of what Darius Ornston has called 'creative corporatism' (Ornston 2012). While many authors, including Ornston, have described Ireland as a case of competitive corporatism, in fact this label poorly described the Irish experience. In the 1990s, Ireland delivered support for active labour market policy (ALMP), risk capital, and (to a lesser extent) research and development (R&D) that approached the levels provided in the European social market economies (Ó Riain 2014). Irish corporatism in the 1990s, therefore, was more creative than the competitive corporatism description allows.

Ireland faced twin challenges at the end of the 1990s—to upgrade the economy to cope with rising costs and to tackle the significant inequalities that dogged Irish society, particularly the linked problems of income inequality and jobless households. The political challenge was substantial for Ireland in the early 2000s therefore, despite the significant successes of the late 1990s. Nonetheless, the degree to which the policy system and the society failed to manage these challenges was dramatic.

A number of the institutions that might have addressed these challenges were thus in place—although only weakly established in many cases. However, in the 2000s, the pendulum of governance swung away from these institutions and back towards a highly centralized government system that gave enormous power to a small group of key ministers, highly responsive to electoral cycles and partisan politics. The 2000s saw the erosion of developmental capacities and coalitions that had been developed in the 1990s but were now sidelined by property- and credit-growth machines—effectively sidestepping the challenge of economic upgrading.

This period saw the rise of strategies of growth in the UK and USA based on the expansion of private debt to inflate demand and drive consumption-based growth—a strategy that came to be called 'privatized Keynesianism' (Crouch 2009). This private-sector bubble proved to be central to 'the failure of Anglo-liberal capitalism' (Hay 2013). Given the developmental successes and massive employment expansion of the 1990s, the expansion of demand in Ireland was partly based on genuine and sustainable improvements in living standards. Furthermore, the critical effects of loose credit in the domestic economy were seen first and foremost in the business lending sector. However, as the 2000s went on, household debt expanded rapidly, including both housing and consumer debt—moving Ireland closer to the 'privatized Keynesian' model.

Disastrously, this financialization of business and households also found its way into the public finances through the structure of taxation and levels of public spending. As the bargains struck through social partnership and through partisan politics expanded in their scale through the 2000s, they relied most heavily on the return of after-tax income to citizens across the income distribution. With social security taxes and corporate taxes already low entering the Celtic Tiger years, the period from 1998 to 2002 saw major cuts in income tax, with the top rate dropping from 48 per cent to 41 per cent.

This focus on income tax reductions was reinforced by the structure of the Irish welfare regime, which placed a particularly strong emphasis on providing households with more after-tax income rather than significantly expanding the social services available to citizens. The structure of the Irish welfare state itself, in common with other liberal and Mediterranean welfare states, relied more heavily on transfer payments than on services. Indeed, the major policy report on the welfare state in the 2000s—the National Economic and Social Council (NESC) Report on the 'developmental welfare state'—argued for both a rebalancing of income transfers, social services, and active measures, as well as for a more flexible system of supports across the life course (NESC 2005). This notion found little support in the government, and welfare improvements in the 2000s emphasized increases in payments and eligibility. A welfare state that focused on cash payments rather than universal public services did little to build public support for protecting social services.

The combination of low tax and spending always rendered Ireland's fiscal model vulnerable (Ó Riain 2004, 2009). While many economists worried aloud about increased public spending through the 2000s and, in particular, increases in public sector wages, the factor that turned these structural weaknesses into an acute crisis was the increased dependency of the state on the 'bubble taxes' from capital gains and real estate sales. The financial and fiscal crises were tightly linked together through the property bubble, the core of the banks' business model and the source of the state's surging but vulnerable tax revenue. The flaw at the heart of Ireland's social contract was expressed in the reliance on bubble taxes—the increased spending of the 2000s was financed to an unsustainable degree by the bubble. When the financial crisis hit, those tax revenues disappeared and the weakness of the social contract was disastrously exposed. Overall, even as creative corporatism was eroded in the 2000s, so too was the prudent fiscal management of the late 1990s. Fiscal policies that drove the speculative bubble ever higher while weakening the national tax base followed the path of privatized Keynesianism and laid the foundations for later austerity.

RECOVERY WITHOUT TRANSFORMATION

Ireland's story offers some important lessons about actually existing economic liberalism. Ireland is often classified with the Anglo-American 'liberal' family of capitalisms, and some features of its experience are similar. Cutting capital gains tax and providing tax breaks to boost investment, relying on the stock market to provide oversight, insisting on 'light-touch' banking regulation, and limiting state capacity to even gather information about bank activities—all these crucial and familiar 'market mechanisms' contributed directly to Ireland's disastrous crash. These combined with other features common to liberal political economies—centralized governmental power and weak civic institutions, welfare states focused on transfers rather than services, structural budget deficits, and a macroeconomic strategy based on domestic consumption rather than export production—to produce economic crisis.

More than six years after its crash, Ireland's economy is now showing signs of a significant recovery. In particular, employment is growing and tax revenues are increasing, while budget deficits are narrowing. This employment growth is, however, only loosely related to 'internal devaluation' and the improvement of wage competitiveness. Even foreign firms have only been a part of this recovery. Improved investment and innovation underpin the growing importance of Irish-owned manufacturing, information technology (IT), and business services firms to employment, and the state has played a key role in creating new markets and investors in commercial property development, also a key driver of employment growth (Byrne forthcoming; Ó Riain forthcoming). In both these sectors, wages have not declined but in fact have grown modestly.

However, Ireland's ability to move forward is threatened by the same three trends that contributed to its crash. While banks are not lending as recklessly as they once did, they have provided little credit to productive businesses, and the government has only just created a long-promised state investment bank (which now seems to be stimulating new levels of activity in private bank business lending). Both finance and property are once again being boosted as growth sectors, and rising rents and prices are putting pressure on households and small businesses.

Alongside this emerging refinancialization, the Eurozone's policy response has been famously inadequate. Perhaps it is not surprising that European leaders have pursued austerity as even Europe's social democracies have historically been reluctant to run budget deficits and expose themselves to international financial markets. But it does seem surprising that these same social democracies have consistently rejected serious attempts to balance current spending cuts with significant investment plans to boost growth or social well-being. A current investment plan, channelled through public agencies, is dwarfed by a new round of 'quantitative easing,' which shovels funds into private finance. While 'cheap money' is helping Ireland's business gain some credit, the overall effect has been to refloat the financial sector with relatively little impact on investment, given the volume of funds transferred into the European economy. Much of Ireland's export recovery has been driven by stimulus elsewhere, given the crucial importance of US foreign investment and tourism.

Finally, tax cuts have re-emerged on the political agenda as growth has resumed, not surprisingly a popular move with a beleaguered population. This brings into focus a challenge for the forces opposing current European and Irish austerity policies. Contrary to common perceptions, balancing budgets has not been a tactic of Europe's economic liberals, but of the EU's social democrats. They have sought social solidarity in a social contract based on high employment, strong social services, and egalitarian wages—all wrapped in a protective shell of prudent finances. The Irish and European approaches today emphasize only the shell, including precious little of the social protection. The rediscovery of an older social democratic project involving prudence, protection, and economically and socially productive activity—an approach too long marginalized within EU policy debates—is long overdue.

REFERENCES

Anglo Irish Bank. 2006. *Annual Report and Accounts 2006.* Dublin: Anglo Irish Bank.

Begg, D. 2016. *Ireland, Small Open Economies and European Integration: Lost in Transition.* Basingstoke: Palgrave.

Behling, F. and Ó Riain, S. 2015. 'Varieties of centralized decentralization in Denmark and Ireland', Working Paper, New Deals in the New Economy, Maynooth University.

Block, F. 2012. 'End this Depression But How?' *Dissent,* summer. Available at: <https://www.dissentmagazine.org/online_articles/end-this-depression-but-how> (accessed 3 July 2016).

Blyth, M. 2013. *Austerity.* Oxford: Oxford University Press.

Byrne, M., forthcoming. 'Asset Price Urbanism and Financialization after the Crisis: Ireland's National Asset Management Agency'. *International Journal of Urban and Regional Research.*

Connor, G., Flavin, T., and Kelly, B. 2012. 'The U.S. and Irish Credit Crises: Their Distinctive Differences and Common Features'. *Journal of International Money and Finance,* 31: 60–79.

Crouch, C. 2009. 'Privatized Keynesianism: An Unacknowledged Policy Regime'. *British Journal of Politics & International Relations,* 11(3): 382–99.

Davis, G. 2009. *Managed by the Markets.* Oxford: Oxford University Press.

Epstein, G. A. (ed.) 2005. *Financialization and the World Economy.* London: Edward Elgar.

Federation of Small Businesses. 2012. *Alt+ Finance: Small Firms and Access to Finance.* London: Federation of Small Businesses.

Hall, P. A. and Soskice, D. W. (eds.) 2001. *Varieties of Capitalism: The Institutional Foundations of Comparative Advantage.* Oxford: Oxford University Press.

Hay, C. 2013. *The Failure of Anglo-Liberal Capitalism.* London: Palgrave.

Hemerijck, A. and Visser, J. 1999. *A Dutch Miracle.* Amsterdam: Amsterdam University Press.

Honohan, P. 2006. 'To What Extent Has Finance Been a Driver of Ireland's Economic Success?' *Economic and Social Research Institute Quarterly Economic Commentary,* winter, 59–72.

IMF (International Monetary Fund). 2009. *Germany.* Washington: IMF Country Report No. 09/15.

Krippner, G. 2011. *Capitalizing on Crisis.* Cambridge, MA: Harvard University Press.

Kus, B. 2012. 'Financialization and Income Inequality in OECD Nations: 1995–2007'. *Economic and Social Review,* 43(4): 477–95.

Lane, P. R. 2011. 'The Irish Crisis', IIIS Discussion Paper No. 356. Dublin: Trinity College Dublin.

NESC. 2005. *The Developmental Welfare State.* NESC Report No. 113. Dublin: NESC.

Ó Riain, S. 2004. *The Politics of High Tech Growth: Developmental Network States in the Global Economy.* Cambridge: Cambridge University Press.

Ó Riain, S. 2009. 'Addicted to Growth: Developmental Statism and NeoLiberalism in the Celtic Tiger'. In *The Nation-State in Transformation: The Governance, Growth and Cohesion of Small States under Globalization,* ed. M. Bøss. Aarhus: Aarhus University Press.

Ó Riain, S. 2014. *The Rise and Fall of Ireland's Celtic Tiger*. Cambridge: Cambridge University Press.

Ó Riain, S. Forthcoming. 'Ireland's Recovery: Explanation, Potential and Pitfalls'. In *Debating Austerity*, ed. E. Heffernan, J. McHale, and N. Moore-Cherry. Dublin: Royal Irish Academy.

Ornston, D. 2012. *When Small States Make Big Leaps: Institutional Innovation and High-Tech Competition in Western Europe*. Ithaca, NY: Cornell University Press.

Schafer, A. and Streeck, W. 2013. *Politics in the Age of Austerity*. London: Polity.

Scharpf, F. 1991. *Crisis and Choice in European Social Democracy*. Ithaca, NY: Cornell University Press.

Scharpf, F. 1999. *Governing in Europe*. Oxford: Oxford University Press.

Streeck, W. 2014. *Buying Time*. London: Verso.

TASC (Think-tank for Action on Social Change). 2010. *Mapping the Golden Circle*. Dublin: TASC.

White, R. 2010. *Years of High Income Largely Wasted*. Dublin: Davy Stockbrokers.

3

Economic and Fiscal Policy

Stephen Kinsella

INTRODUCTION

The purpose of this chapter is to examine Irish economic and fiscal policy from 1996 to 2016, looking particularly at the experience of austerity from 2009 to 2013 using macroeconomic data. The success of the Irish experience relative to other countries within adjustment programmes is frequently used by policymakers across the world to justify the imposition of austerity on other countries. Ireland is very often touted as the poster child for such policies. For example, the International Monetary Fund's (IMF) Christine Lagarde cites Ireland's experience as setting 'standards for the correct measures to follow towards a recovery' (IMF 2015: 12).

This chapter will try to answer why, exactly, a small open economy like Ireland was able to marry growth and large-scale fiscal consolidation. The answer lies in the institutional structure of the economy, its openness and particularly the sectoral structure of the economy.

Following Blyth (2013a: 866–7), let us define austerity, at least for the rest of this chapter as:

> [C]utting the state's budget to stabilise public finances, restore competitiveness through wage cuts, and create better investment expectations by lowering future tax burdens.

Thus, austerity is not simply fiscal consolidation, nor is it a static concept. Austerity is rooted in a dynamic conception of the economy as an evolving object with its own inter-temporal budget constraint. The objective of austerity is to inspire confidence amongst international investors that their investment will yield positive returns. The signal provided by the large drop in government expenditure or increase in taxes is traded for increased investment as a result of this increased confidence, generating a so-called 'expansionary fiscal contraction'. Using fiscal policy to influence investor expectations has been roundly criticized. Guajardo, Leigh, and Pescatori (2014) offer a good summary of these critical voices. Alesina and colleagues (2015) provides a rejoinder to these critics.

Ireland's evolution from the catch-up era from 1996 to 2002, characterized as the 'Celtic Tiger' years, will not be discussed. Readers should consult Ó Riain (Chapter 2, this volume, and 2014) for an overview of these years. Honohan and Walsh (2002) provide a compelling argument for the 'catch-up' thesis, essentially arguing that Ireland's Tiger years represented a regression to the European average living standard after decades of underperformance.

Instead, more recent fiscal and economic policies will be discussed, especially in terms of the decisions taken with respect to the fiscal stance—the relationship between government spending into the economy and the extraction of taxes from sectors of the economy to fund those services and effect a redistribution of income and wealth.

The Irish experience of fiscal policy has been studied previously by Lane (2011), Bergin and colleagues (2011), and Fitzgerald (2009), who found that Ireland's fiscal stance was worryingly pro-cyclical. Kinsella (2012) and Kinsella (2014) compare the Irish experience of fiscal retrenchment in the 1980s to the 2009–13 experience. Weymes and Bermingham (2012) examine the optimal structure of fiscal consolidations, finding a 50:50 mix of tax increases and spending cuts is broadly optimal, while Ball (2014) examines the long-run damage to Organisation for Economic Co-operation and Development (OECD) economies from the experience of austerity, finding austerity episodes may damage the long-run potential growth of the country. Considine and Duffy (2014) examine the role of expectations and the 'confidence faeries' in managing crises, using Ireland as a case study. Fiscal consolidations are supposed to inspire confidence in international investors. The argument is quite simple: cutting government spending calms markets, because it shows governments have a clear and credible strategy for reducing debt levels and thus avoiding default. With a rapid cut in government spending and deficit reduction, it should help bond yields remain low as the 'faeries' come on board. Considine and Duffy find, unsurprisingly, that the confidence faeries do not exist. Blyth (2013b) provides an overview of the intellectual architecture, and indeed the history of various austerity episodes, including Ireland. Perotti (2011) defends the theory of expansionary fiscal contraction critiqued in Kinsella (2012).

We examine three interrelated themes of fiscal policy. First, we discuss the components of both taxation revenue and expenditure, both current and capital, in some detail. Second, we examine the change in what we call 'the fiscal stance' over the period from 2002 to 2014. Third, we comment on the Irish experience of austerity relative to other European nations.

We make three, interlocking arguments related to these themes in this chapter.

First, Ireland's highly pro-cyclical fiscal policy has historically challenged its ability to weather sustained economic crises (Lee 1989). The majority of the decisions taken from 2002 to 2007 substantially decreased the ability of the economy to cope when the downturn of 2007 and 2008 took hold, particularly as a large amount of government revenue from standard income taxes was replaced with capital gains and capital acquisitions-type taxes over this five-year period.

Second, Ireland's experience of austerity from 2008 to 2013 was a unique one, given the level of openness of the economy and the lack of large-scale social unrest, neither of which are features of other countries who experienced austerity during the same period. The negative changes in current (non-pay), capital, and public sector wages were buttressed, to a certain extent, by robust demand for Irish exports, especially after 2009, while a large-scale emigration, particularly of the young, kept unemployment rates, with corresponding social protection spending, lower than otherwise.

Third, looking forward five or ten years, it is clear the Irish economy has a new 'target-driven' approach to fiscal policy based on regulating the Eurozone's macroeconomic imbalances, which will generate tensions of its own over time, especially when these targets are not met.

The rest of this chapter is laid out as follows. The section 'The Fiscal Evolution of the Irish Economy, 1996–2016' examines the fiscal evolution of the Irish economy. Then comes the section 'Austerity and the Arrival of the Troika', which discusses the issues surrounding austerity and looks at the crucial issue of Ireland's openness. This is followed by the 'Conclusion'.

THE FISCAL EVOLUTION OF THE IRISH ECONOMY, 1996–2016

Irish fiscal policy was, and to a certain extent, still is, highly pro-cyclical (Fitzgerald 2009; Weymes and Bermingham 2012). The composition of national revenue and expenditures have changed remarkably over the time period we study, which begins, roughly, when the 'Celtic Tiger' period of catch-up growth ended and a new phase of economic growth based largely on an asset price bubble took over.

Let us look in turn at the scale of the Irish government's revenues, its sources, and then at the uses of those revenues, and their changing compositions over time.

Pre-crisis taxation sources were largely made up of four groups: income taxes, taxes on consumption (valued added taxes (VAT) and customs/excise), corporation taxes, and taxes on capital transactions, particularly on property (stamp duties, capital gains, and acquisitions).

In 2002, roughly 31 per cent of all taxation revenue came from income taxes. In 2006 that had fallen to 26 per cent. By 2015, that proportion rose to 40 per cent. In comparison, revenues from VAT remained largely static, and averaged 29 per cent over the entire period, as did customs and excise taxes, averaging 15 per cent of all taxes. Capital gains and acquisitions taxes comprised only 7 per cent of all tax revenue in 2002. In 2006, this was 16 per cent, and by 2015 it had returned again to 15 per cent of all income, but this time included a local property tax (LPT). Corporation taxes fell from 16 per cent in 2002 to 12 per cent in 2008, reaching only 11 per cent by 2014 and jumping suddenly in 2015 to 15 per cent. Figure 3.1 shows the breakdown in percentage terms. It shows the composition and source of government revenue from 2002 to 2015, expressed as a percentage of the total tax take in each year. The large increase in the use of income taxes from 2009 onwards, and the large drop in stamp duties and corporation taxes, are apparent in the figure.

The crucial role income taxes have played in making up the difference between the government's expenditure and revenues allows us to infer that the

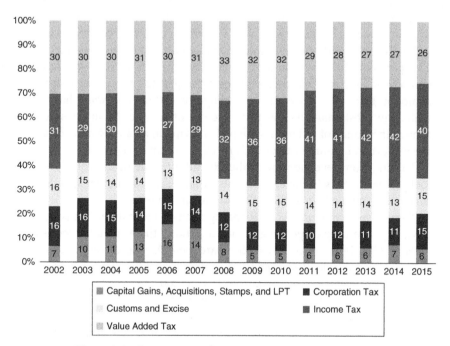

Figure 3.1. Components of government revenues, per cent

Note: 'LPT' is the local property tax, introduced in 2013.
Source: <databank.finance.gov.ie>.

largest burden of the adjustment fell on those with middle to high incomes, as this is the largest tax-paying segment of Irish society. Income tax was 28 per cent of the total tax take in 2003, and 40 per cent in 2015. In contrast, capital gains and stamp duties combined represented 10 per cent of the tax take in 2002, 15 per cent of the tax take in 2006, and 6 per cent of the tax take in 2015.

The distribution of tax and spend does matter in computing the overall welfare changes to the different cohorts represented in Ireland over this period. From 2002 to 2007, almost every sector of society benefited from lower tax rates, and higher levels of spending, particularly on social welfare elements like Jobseeker's Benefits (JB), pensions, and Child Benefit payments. Callan et al. (2014) looked carefully at the impact budgetary policies have had from 2009 to 2014, both on the top and bottom of the income deciles. They found budgetary policies reduced top incomes by 16 per cent, while incomes of those at the bottom fell by 12 per cent. The marginal effective tax rates on different household types also changed in the 2002 to 2007 period, as welfare rates increased, only to change again post-2007 as fiscal retrenchment, combined with a rapid deterioration in labour market conditions, forced income taxes on those remaining in work to balloon while payments on those without incomes either fell significantly, or stagnated.

The changing composition of the tax take was a policy judgement born out of sheer necessity. Faced with a 15 per cent drop in employment, a 22 per cent drop in domestic demand, an almost €40 billion euro bill required to bail out Ireland's banks, and a policy commitment to maintain corporation tax rates at 12.5 per cent, the state's options for revenue generation were relatively circumscribed. Income taxes have plugged the gap left by property and consumption taxes. The newer taxes on property, carbon, and water have yet to make any substantial changes to the composition of taxation revenue, and, though the profile of Ireland's tax base is moving in an anti-cyclical direction, the pro-cyclical nature of the state's revenue cannot be avoided.

Turning from revenue now to the expenditure side of the equation, if we look at the changes in the components of how the government spends those funds on an annual basis, the following picture emerges.

Three broad components of spending need to be analysed: current (non-pay), pay, and capital spending. Figure 3.2 shows these spending levels from 1994 to 2016, indexed to 2007 to compare their changes directly. The overall picture is one of relentless expansion in line or slightly above nominal gross domestic product (GDP) growth from 1994 to 2007, followed by a particularly deep retrenchment in capital expenditure from 2007 to 2013, and relatively modest increases thereafter.

Current (non-pay) expenditure was 60 per cent of its 2007 level in 2002, and only 26 per cent of its 2007 value in 1994. As mentioned, successive governments used large tax receipts to simultaneously increase the scale and scope of the welfare state, while decreasing the rate of tax many individuals and entities

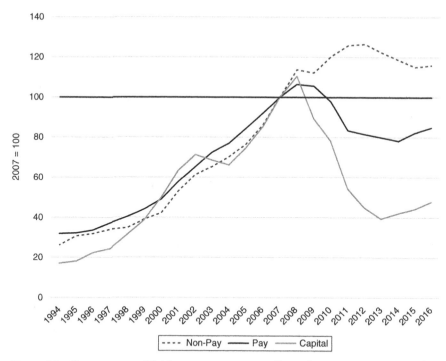

Figure 3.2. Components of Irish government expenditure from 1994 to 2016, with 2007 as the index year

Source: Department of Public Expenditure and Reform (DPER).

paid. These large nominal increases resulted in a 40 per cent increase relative to the government's 2007 level in current spending, which was cut back in certain areas after 2009, such as spending on Jobseeker's Allowance (JA) for younger workers, spending on expenses for public sector workers, decreases in funding to higher education, and many more cuts. However, large increases in payments for those not in work counterbalanced many of these decreases and so the relative size of the non-pay spend increased as automatic stabilization policies were employed.

By 2016, despite large cutbacks, current expenditure had increased to 116 per cent of its 2007 level. Capital spending was 72 per cent of its 2007 level in 2002, and only 47 per cent of its 2007 level in 2016. Public sector pay was 64 per cent of its 2007 level in 2002, only 34 per cent of its 2007 level in 1994, growing to 88 per cent of its 2007 level in 2016.

Current (non-)pay expenditure has many components, voted on by the Irish Parliament in annual finance bills. Figure 3.3 shows large elements of these 'votes', including a breakdown of the large social protection expenditure line in 2014. It shows, in billions of euros, the three largest components of voted current voted expenditure, on health, education, and social protection

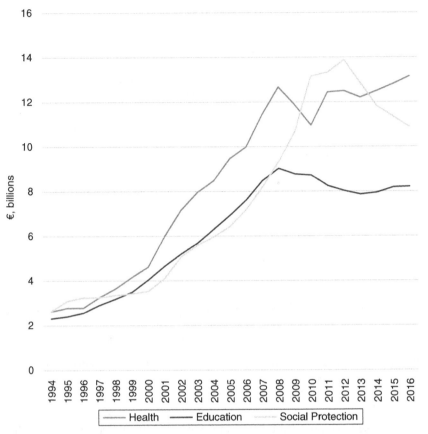

Figure 3.3. Three largest 'votes' of net government expenditure from 1994 to 2016, € billions

Source: DPER.

from 1994 to 2016. Together they represent almost 67 per cent of the total spend in 2016, and this proportion has increased from 52 per cent in 2002.

As with the revenue data reported in Figure 3.2 from 1994 to 2007 each heading increased in line with nominal GDP. Post-2007, however, education spending flatlined, while social protection spending continued to increase as unemployment increased, as a series of automatic stabilizers took effect. The sharp decrease in 2014 from €14 billion to €11 billion in 2016 came about as unemployment levels began to fall, reflecting the 'automatic' element of this element of voted expenditure. Despite decreases across the rest of the system, health spending has maintained its very high level of spending each year after 2007, requiring supplementary budgets each year since then, with spending almost returning to trend by 2016. In education, no increases have been seen after 2013, with 2016's voted expenditure roughly equivalent to its 2007 level.

In education especially, post-crisis, large infrastructural deficits and human capital shortages may well emerge as a result of the decreases in the growth rates of funding, especially as demographic pressures mount.

The breakdown of these services is significant, as reductions or increases to expenditure generally are not applied equally throughout a large 'vote'. Taking social protection—vote 37—as an example, we see the 12 billion euros spent in 2014 was spent in the following way. Housing took up 8 per cent of funds, survivors' benefits took up 7 per cent, payments to children and families another 12 per cent, state pensions took up 29 per cent, disability and sickness 21 per cent, and unemployment benefits in total absorbed 20 per cent of all payments. The complexity of the architecture of the state needs to be understood when discussing austerity, and the 'target-driven' approach to fiscal policy now employed.

Finally, putting both revenue and expenditure together and scaling by GDP gives us the basic funding position of the Irish state from 1996 to 2016, summarized in Figure 3.4. Without including spending on interest payments or other spending items, we can see the large difference between revenue and

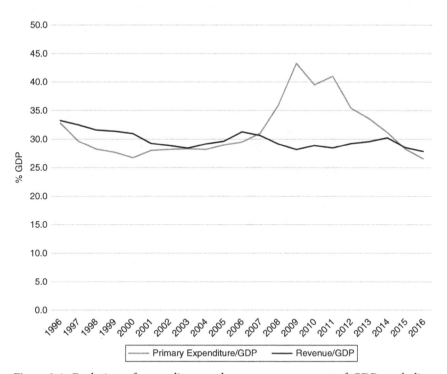

Figure 3.4. Evolution of expenditure and revenue as per cent of GDP, excluding interest payments

Source: CSO.

spending which took place after 2007. This gap was filled with state monies and borrowing from the private market until 2011, after which a loan package comprised of bilateral loans from countries like the UK and Denmark and the 'Troika' of the European Commission (EC), the IMF, and the European Central Bank (ECB), was used. Ireland regained access to the sovereign bond markets in 2013.

We can see the changing fiscal stance of the Irish state over this period. The ratio of tax to GDP changed slightly over this period. In 2002, the ratio was 28.3 per cent. In 2011, it was 28.7 per cent, and in 2016 it was 26.5 per cent. The real change, however, is in the division of the tax burden from labour, capital, and land. Labour's share has risen substantially over the crisis period in order to fund necessary services. Using the institutional sectoral accounts, and breaking down the 2015 figure of 31.3 per cent, again as a percentage of GDP we find 11 per cent comes from taxes on production and imports, 13.6 per cent comes from current taxes on income and wealth, 0.2 per cent comes from capital taxes, and 5.3 per cent comes from net social contributions. It is unlikely this fiscal stance will change in the short term, unless larger taxes on capital are introduced.

The fiscal position of the country deteriorated, requiring a large increase in debt. Figures 3.5 and 3.6 show the changes in debt per annum from 2007 to

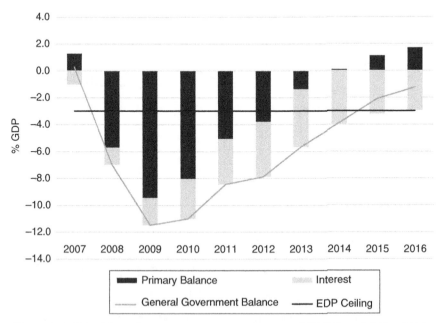

Figure 3.5. New debt and interest payments as per cent of GDP from 2007 to 2016
Source: CSO.ie.

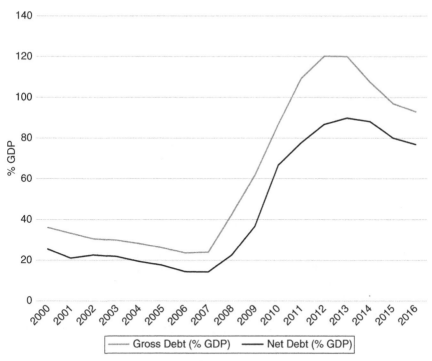

Figure 3.6. Gross and net debt for Ireland, expressed as per cent of GDP, 2000 to 2016
Source: CSO.

2016, and break these changes down into new debt issued to maintain a funding balance, and interest payments incurred. The clear increase in net debt, which takes account of all cash equivalents on the state's balance sheet, from 14 per cent of GDP in 2007 to 90 per cent by 2013, is obvious. What is not obvious is the path of debt reduction post-2016, and this path is highly dependent on external factors.

Moving from the government's finances to the interplay between financial corporations, non-financial corporations, and households, it is appropriate to focus on the role the expansion of credit played, given the financialized nature of the crisis. Credit was typically extended for asset purchases of residential and commercial properties. In 2002, the net amount of new personal loans produced by the Irish economy was roughly €370 million, and grew by about 25 per cent per annum from 2002 to 2007.

By 2006, almost €1.2 billion in new credit was being produced by a euphoric banking system to meet the ever-growing demands of the household sector. Household credit simply could not stay at these boom levels, absent a large and liquid international wholesale market for interbank lending, which was disrupted following the collapse of Lehman Brothers

on 15 September 2008. Net new lending fell precipitously from 2007 onwards, reaching an historic low of less than €100 million in 2012, before
rising again to around €300 million in 2014. The expansion of credit, the
societal euphoria this produced, and the subsequent collapse in both
asset prices and credit flows have followed the classical Minsky cycle
rather closely.

Minsky (1986: 42) wrote that:

> Whenever profits decreased hedge units [when anticipated cash flows from
> operations exceeds anticipated commitments at all future times] become
> speculative and speculative units [situation when anticipated cash commit-
> ments will exceed anticipated cash flows at some points in the future] become
> Ponzi firms [situation when anticipated cash inflows falling short of antici-
> pated commitments at most or all future times]. Such induced transformation
> of the financial structure lead to falls in the price of capital assets and therefore
> to decline in investment. A recursive process is readily triggered in which a
> financial market failure leads to a fall in investment in which leads to a fall in
> profits which leads to financial failures, further declines in investment, profits,
> additional failure, etc.

This is precisely what happened in Ireland. In 2008, the private debt generated
by transactions between the household and financial sectors of the economy
was transferred in large part to the government sector via a state guarantee
of the assets and liabilities of the banking sector worth roughly €440 billion
in 2008.

This guarantee, enacted in September 2008 by then Finance Minister Brian
Lenihan to calm market fears about illiquid banks quickly became a fiscal
straitjacket as questions about the illiquidity, and then the solvency, of the
banking system were replaced with questions about the solvency of the Irish
state. The Eligible Liabilities Guarantee (ELG) scheme made sure that deposits
in Irish banks were kept safe, and kept the taxpayer on the hook for some
losses in the banks if they occurred. (Because the state summed a contingent
exposure for the banks, there was a fee charged to each covered bank. The state
in fact earned €4.4 billion from 2008 to 2015 when the ELG scheme was
discontinued.)

It is worth viewing the change in the fortunes of the Irish economy from the
lens of the balance sheet, where assets and liabilities are valued at a particular
moment in time and their difference, or net worth, can be seen. Table 3.1, from
Barnes and Smyth (2013: 20), shows the deterioration of the balance sheet of
the Irish state from 2009 to 2012 in both nominal terms and relative to
GDP. In terms of the health of its balance sheet, from 2008 onwards, the
Irish sovereign moved from one of the stars of the Eurozone to a experiencing
a balance sheet crisis, as described by Koo (2009). The marked increase in
liabilities, from 114 billion euros in 2009 to 208 billion euros in 2012,

Table 3.1. The balance sheet of the Irish sovereign

	2009	2010	2011	2012
1. Non-Financial Assets	61	58	57	57
2. Financial Assets	72	65	62	73
3. Liabilities	114	138	167	208
4. Net Financial Assets (=2+3)	−41	−73	−105	−135
5. Net Worth (=1+4)	20	−15	−48	−77
		%		
Net Worth, Per Cent of GDP	12	−9	−29	−47

Source: Barnes and Smyth (2013: 20).

illustrates this deterioration. The negative net position more than triples from 2009 to 2012. The remarkable change in net worth as a percentage of GDP is testament to this, with Ireland's net worth valued at around 12 per cent of GDP in 2009, and a striking −47 per cent of GDP in 2012.

The individual sectors of the economy also experienced large changes in their fortunes. A very useful way to see these changes is by computing the sectoral balances of the private sector (savings minus investment), the public sector (government spending minus taxes), and the rest of the world (exports minus imports plus net factor income from the rest of the world). The sum of the private and public balances must equal the rest of the world's financial balance by simple arithmetic. Because these are identities, and not equations, these relationships hold true regardless. The sectoral balances represent an ex post accounting identity resulting from rearranging the components of aggregate demand, showing how the flow of funds affects the financial balances of the private sector, government sector, and foreign sector. Figure 3.7 shows these changes over time for Ireland.

The balance for the private sector shows investment falling rapidly after 2008, with precautionary saving and retrenchment taking place after this period, combined with a rapid movement away from highly indebted positions, which economists call deleveraging. The trade balance shows a marked upswing after 2008, with exports returning rapidly to their pre-crisis levels while imports do not. This strange effect is explained by the extremely open nature of the Irish economy, and the dominance of the export sector by multinationals. Faced with a world economy which partially had recovered by 2009, exports returned to trend. The domestic economy, meanwhile, had to cope with a large negative change in unemployment, a collapse in construction-related activities, and a fiscal crisis by the sovereign. Import demand, therefore, did not recover, pulling the 'rest of the world' sector upwards after 2009. The public sector, as we have discussed extensively, moved from a condition of rough balance from 2002 to 2007, to an excess

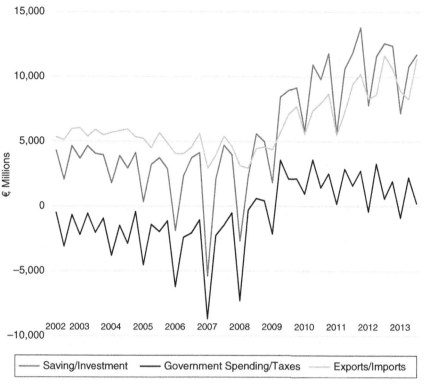

Figure 3.7. Sectoral balances—Ireland, quarterly, millions of euros
Source: CSO.

of government spending over taxes, which necessitated, first, large-scale borrowing, and then reduction via austerity.

Overall, using the sectoral balance approach, we can see a sharp movement
from foreign surplus composed of deposits and equity from 2002 to 2007, to
foreign surplus composed of loans and equity from 2007 to 2016. The turnaround is remarkable, both in its speed and its scale. Because we have these
balances as accounting identities and not causal relationships, it cannot be said
where these balances will tend in the future with any certainty.

However, we can say that austerity policies have achieved the rather dubious objective of making the difference between government expenditure and
taxation as small as possible. In this movement towards fiscal balance, the
domestic authorities imposing austerity were accommodated, first, by a
private-sector balance adjustment and, more crucially, by the rest of the
world via the 'rest of the world' balance. This meant that Irish austerity, rather
than being a domestic success, was in fact facilitated by Ireland's openness to
the rest of the world.

AUSTERITY AND THE ARRIVAL OF THE TROIKA

Once private capital markets became closed to the government in 2010, creating an effective ceiling on any expansionary fiscal policy, a loan facility was arranged with official funders (the IMF, EC, and the ECB) in exchange for the adoption of austerity policies, many of which were already underway by mid-2009, when a mid-year budget began the process of increasing income taxes, reducing planned expenditure, and effectively cancelling capital developments.

Three separate reports and a parliamentary banking enquiry into the Irish crisis have established that macro-prudential regulation of banking was lax, that fiscal policy, and in particular Ireland's fiscal stance, was inappropriate given its membership of the Eurozone during a period of low real interest rates, and, finally, that Ireland's political elite was inappropriately enmeshed with property developers, whose interests were served before those of the national interest. Each report has noted with dismay the failure of macroeconomic models used by Ireland's Department of Finance and the ECB to accurately predict the crisis (Honohan 2010; Regling and Watson 2010; Nyberg 2011).

The Troika rescue plan, negotiated in 2010 after Ireland had lost its access to private bond markets, had a specific strategy. The IMF's Memorandum of Understanding (IMF 2010) set out, in detail, the austerity measures the Irish undertook until 2014. Briefly, they fell under the following categories and subcategories.

1. Fiscal consolidation
   a. Taxes were to be raised. Carbon, property, and water taxes were to be introduced, personal income tax bands lowered, and credits to be pursued.
   b. Government expenditure, including social protection expenditure and numbers of public sector workers, was to be reduced.

2. Financial sector reforms
   a. A deleveraging of Irish banks by €72 billion over three years.
   b. A reorganization of the banking sector. Smaller banks merged with larger 'pillar' banks.
   c. Increases in Tier 1 capital ratios of 'pillar' banks.
   d. Burden-sharing by holders of subordinated (not senior) bond debt.

3. Structural reforms to the labour market and protected sectors
   a. The IMF proposed a reduction of the minimum wage.
   b. Increased workplace training and internship positions.
   c. Government was to introduce legislative changes to remove restrictions to trade and competition in sheltered sectors including the legal and medical professions.

It is clear from this list that the proposed and implemented solution to the problem of fiscal imbalances in particular was a range of austerity measures across the real and financial sectors of the economy. Of the three major elements of the Troika programme, only elements 1 and 2 were carried out effectively. No serious reforms of any professions were carried out, and the minimum wage reduction was cancelled. Reforms were introduced to increase the activation elements of labour market policies for the unemployed, although as O'Connell argues in Chapter 13, these reforms were implemented slowly, despite the scale of the unemployment crisis, and questions remain about the effectiveness of many training and employment schemes.

The key issues of restoring fiscal balance and recapitalizing and reorganizing the banking system stand as the key achievements of the Troika's time in Ireland. Much of the broad strokes of a fiscal consolidation were underway from mid-2009, and so it is unclear to what extent the Troika can be blamed, or take credit for, this return to fiscal balance. Certainly, their presence provided a convenient scapegoat for highly unpopular policies.

These policies had a specific mix: one-third of the measures to reduce the budget deficit would be increases in taxation, while two-thirds would be decreases in government expenditure. The result was, of course, a fall in domestic demand and an increase in unemployment. A minimum 18.3 per cent of GDP was extracted by government since 2008 in a near-zero inflation environment.

The collapse in domestic demand and in investment in gross fixed capital formation meant that unemployment peaked at 15.1 per cent in 2011. Unemployment has been falling, partly due to emigration, since 2012. The net result, however, has been the attainment of the objective of a narrowing of the gap between spending and revenue. Austerity policies have achieved the rather dubious objective of minimizing the difference between government expenditure and taxation as they were accommodated by private-sector balance adjustment and, crucially, by the rest of the world via the current account balance. As mentioned, the key to understanding the seeming contradiction between austerity and growth in the Irish case lies within the structure of the Irish economy.

One important feature of the Irish economy is its relatively high levels of redistribution of income taxes, with relatively generous social welfare schemes and a large social protection programme. The scale and extent of this has already been discussed. The redistributive arm of Ireland's fiscal policy affected income inequality and helped to reduce the impact of austerity. Figure 3.8 shows the percentage change in the Gini coefficient from 2009 to 2013 against social expenditure in 2009 (including social protection payments and health and education expenditures) for a range of OECD countries. Irish social expenditure is on a par with Denmark, Finland, and the Netherlands. Despite changes in inequality, social expenditure has helped to buttress the effects of the downturn.

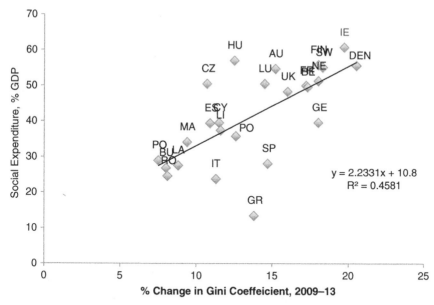

Figure 3.8. Changes in social expenditure and inequality as measured by the Gini coefficient

Source: Eurostat.

Note the key differences between Portugal and Greece and Ireland. Both of the former spend far lower proportions on social expenditure, and both have experienced large changes in inequality. This may be one reason why incidences of social unrest have been much higher in programme countries other than Ireland. Simply put, Ireland's social welfare system was not allowed to deteriorate to the extent other countries' systems were, and the redistributive systems of the state, broadly speaking, did their jobs.

The definition of austerity given by Blyth (2013a) includes a reference to regaining competitiveness. When a devaluation is not possible through the exchange rate, only a devaluation through the wage channel will suffice. So, did Ireland perform a large, across-the-board change in wages in response to its economic crisis? Several sectors, most notably the public sector, with around 330,000 workers, experienced a drop in real wages, but broadly across the economy wages did not adjust downward by more than 4 per cent. Wage bills were controlled through unemployment, for the most part. Computing changes in the Labour Cost Index over time for Germany, Ireland, Greece, Spain, Cyprus, and Portugal, we can see the year-on-year change from 2010 to 2014. It is clear that Ireland's change was barely above zero, relative to European Union (EU)/IMF programme countries like Greece, Portugal, Spain, and Cyprus, which all experienced negative wage changes over this period as measured by the Labour Cost Index. The Irish

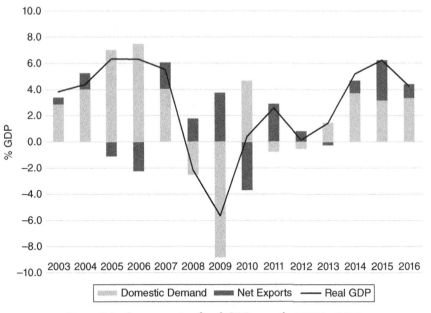

Figure 3.9. Components of real GDP growth, 2003 to 2016
Source: CSO.

experience of austerity is therefore not well described by a neoclassical theory where wages adjust downward to clear markets, but by an adjustment in the quantity of labour employed, which is precisely what is predicted by simple Keynesian economics, and which can only be restored by increasing effective demand, precisely what is being stripped from the economy during periods of austerity.

To see how the contribution of demand altered over the crisis, Figure 3.9 computes the contributions to real GDP growth from domestic demand, which is the sum of government expenditure, private consumption and investment, and net exports. In 2008 and 2009, domestic demand fell by 2.2 per cent and 8.8 per cent of GDP respectively. Thus austerity, at the very moment demand is required to buttress the change in private-sector spending, removes that demand.

Finally, we must understand how Ireland managed to grow through its austerity experience. In this it is an outlier. To see this, compare the average percentage change in the primary balance, which is the difference between government expenditure and taxes before interest payments, adjusting for the cycle, where a positive value indicates a large decrease in expenditure or increase in taxes, or both, to the average percentage change in real GDP over the 2009 to 2013 period for selected countries.

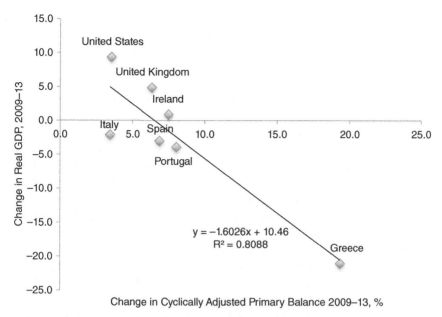

Figure 3.10. Changes in real gross domestic product and the cyclically adjusted primary balance from 2009 to 2013
Source: IMF.

Figure 3.10 shows us Ireland has managed to grow, along with the USA and the UK, while countries like Italy, Spain, Portugal, and Greece have experienced large changes with no corresponding growth. In the case of Greece, as we know, lack of growth and a failing welfare state have caused widespread societal problems. Indeed, these countries bear out the tautology that fiscal contractions are contractionary. Not so with Ireland, it seems. Ireland is also remarkable because it is clustered with two economies with their own monetary policies, both of whom enacted large-scale quantitative easing programmes as well as Keynesian-style fiscal expansions over this period. Comparing Ireland to Portugal, which experienced a drop in its real GDP of around 4 per cent combined with a large change in its primary balance of around 8 per cent, seems to suggest the Irish did something differently to the Portuguese.

In practice, the Portuguese bailout was very similar in scope, scale, and intent to the Irish bailout. Like Ireland, in 2010 the Portuguese bailout plan targeted an improvement in the structural primary budget balance of 10 percentage points of GDP. The improvement between 2010 and 2013 has been about three-quarters of that. Public debt is forecast to peak at almost 130 per cent of GDP rather than the 115 per cent previously expected. The Portuguese current account has moved from a deficit of over 10 per cent of

GDP in 2010 to a surplus of 0.5 per cent in 2013, but their banks are still heavily reliant on ECB funds, are still unprofitable, and still have high loan-to-deposit ratios, averaging around 115 per cent, albeit falling from a high of 167 per cent.

So what *is* different? How did Ireland manage to grow when Portugal, Spain, and Greece, did not? The answer is the degree of openness of the Irish economy. Ireland scores highly in any measure of openness. In one simple measure, the sum of exports and imports as a proportion of GDP, Irish openness (4.2) is 1.5 times Portugal's (2.5) and double Greece's (2.1). In another measure of openness, using foreign direct investment (FDI), Ireland scores 3.5 while Greece scores 2.6 and Portugal scores 3.4. Over the time period studied in this chapter, the degree of openness of the Irish economy has grown by eight times more than either Greece or Portugal. The macro-economic significance of this is clear: because of its extremely large 'tradable' sectoral composition, Ireland was able to absorb the impacts of austerity in ways that Greece, Portugal, and Spain could not. Rather than being touted as a poster child for austerity, Ireland is instead a beautiful freak, whose institutional make-up, and relatively high levels of expenditure on social programmes, cushioned the impact of austerity on large sections of the population, while its exporting sectors managed to rebound earlier, and keep growth much higher, than in other countries facing the same fiscal problems.

CONCLUSION

This chapter set out to explain the evolution of Ireland's fiscal and economic policies from 2002 to 2016. We found three striking features of Irish fiscal policy. First, it was highly pro-cyclical in the 2002 to 2007 period, becoming less so after 2009, with the introduction of carbon, water, and property taxes. Second, the large increase in the proportion of taxes coming from income over the 2009 to 2014 period was, by necessity, harmful to the middle classes, but was important to keep the redistributive apparatus of the state working while reducing spending on capital, public sector pay, and non-essential spending. Third, the complexity of the state's finances needs to be understood when computing both the distributional impacts of austerity and its long-run consequences. We gave the example of social protection expenditure in the section 'The Fiscal Evolution of the Irish Economy, 1996–2016', but all government services have a similarly complex and articulated structure.

Ireland's extremely open and export-focused economy, with its tradeable sectors dominated by multinationals, allowed it to increase its trade balance after 2007, partially compensating for the fiscal consolidation begun in 2009 and intensified under the Troika, while the private sector deleveraged and restructured itself. Ireland's experience of austerity from 2009 to 2013 is not a good example for other nations to attempt to emulate for these reasons. This unique structure, combined with a compression of borrowing costs from an ECB exercising a full backstop after July 2012, allowed GDP growth to coincide with large doses of austerity. The growth statistics, in fact, masked much of the decline in domestic demand and the large build-up of non-performing private debt in both the household and non-financial corporate sectors. So, for example, despite relatively robust growth and falling unemployment since 2012, the total impairment rate on private loans went from 12 per cent in Q4, 2010 to 25 per cent in Q1, 2016, and has been stable at this level for fourteen quarters at the time of writing.

The argument this chapter has advanced is that austerity was harmful but offset by Ireland's extraordinary openness. Thus, despite austerity being imposed, the economy grew, thanks to extraordinary changes in the international environment. An important question arises: would the structural features of the Irish economy have been sufficient to bring about recovery without the ECB's policies such as quantitative easing, the series of long-term refinancing operations which increased liquidity to Ireland's banks, and the express commitment to 'do whatever it takes' to save the euro, all of which have improved Ireland's competiveness through lower interest rates, lower sovereign borrowing costs, and by weakening the euro relative to Ireland's major trading partners, the USA and UK.

The same openness which helped Ireland survive the crisis may well prove its undoing. Four large downside risks are present at the time of writing. First, the possibility of a 'Brexit', where the UK votes to leave the EU. A Brexit will harm Ireland's labour market, change the nature of the border the Republic shares with Northern Ireland, alter Ireland's energy markets, and a 1 per cent reduction in UK GDP is estimated to lead to a 0.3 per cent fall in Irish GDP over the short term. A sharp depreciation of sterling could also hurt Irish exports (Barrett et al. 2015).

Second, the Chinese economy is undergoing large changes to its structure, with flagging industrial production, excessive household debt, and capital outflows necessitating changes to its fiscal and monetary policies. Should the Chinese economy continue to disappoint in terms of its growth rates, the outlook for Ireland, exposed as it is to the vagaries of the global economy, would diminish rapidly.

Third, Ireland is a net importer of energy, importing over 90 per cent of its energy from abroad. Low oil and gas prices are helping Irish households and firms' profit margins, but these may well reverse. These price rises may well coincide with the changes in the UK and Chinese economies.

Finally, moving forward, Ireland's fiscal policy choices will also be constrained by expenditure ceilings and debt-reduction targets mandated by the Eurozone but now part of the Irish legal and fiscal framework. These targets ensure the large spending increases which we saw from 2002 to 2007 above the growth rate of potential GDP will most likely not be possible, while large changes to the structure of Irish taxation will perforce be much more gradual. Bottlenecks will appear, as underinvestment in capital programmes clash with societal priorities and with the long-term transformation of the population, both demographically and spatially, and this may necessitate larger capital investment programmes over the medium term, keeping current expenditure levels roughly constant. Either way, fiscal policy choices are effectively constrained, making the tools of macro-prudential and micro-prudential policies much more important as policy levers.

REFERENCES

Alesina, A., Barbiero, O., Favero, C., Giavazzi, F., and Paradisi, M. 2015. *Austerity in 2009–2013*. Cambridge: National Bureau of Economic Research.

Ball, L. M. 2014. *Long-Term Damage from the Great Recession in OECD Countries*. National Bureau of Economic Research.

Barnes, S. and Smyth, D. 2013. *The Government's Balance Sheet after the Crisis: A Comprehensive Perspective*. Irish Fiscal Advisory Council.

Barrett, A., Bergin, A., FitzGerald, J., Lambert, D., McCoy, D., Morgenroth, E., and Studnicka, Z. 2015. 'Scoping the Possible Economic Implications of Brexit on Ireland'. *Economic and Social Research Institute (ESRI) Research Series*, 48, November.

Bergin, A., FitzGerald, J. Kearney, I., and O'Sullivan, C. 2011. 'The Irish Fiscal Crisis'. *National Institute Economic Review*, 217(1): R47–59.

Blyth, M. 2013a. 'Austerity as Ideology: A Reply to My Critics'. *Comparative European Politics* 11(6): 737–51.

Blyth, M. 2013b. *Austerity: The History of a Dangerous Idea*. Oxford: Oxford University Press.

Considine, J. and Duffy, D. 2014. 'Keynes and the Confidence Faeries'. *Cambridge Journal of Economics*, 40(1): 309–25.

Fitzgerald, J. 2009. 'Fiscal Policy for Recovery', Working Paper 326. Dublin: Economic Social Research Institute.

Guajardo, J., Leigh, L., and Pescatori, A. 2014. 'Expansionary Austerity? International Evidence'. *Journal of the European Economic Association*, 12 (4): 949–68.

Honohan, P. 2010. 'The Irish Banking Crisis: Regulatory and Financial Stability Policy 2003–2008. A Report to the Minister for Finance by the Governor of the Central Bank'. Available at: http://www.bankinginquiry.gov.ie/The%20Irish% 20Banking%20Crisis%20 (Regulatory%20and%20Financial%20Stability%20Policy %202003–2008.pdf (accessed 15 August 2016).

Honohan, P. and Walsh, B. M. 2002. 'Catching Up with the Leaders: The Irish Hare'. *Brookings Papers on Economic Activity*, 1: 1–57.

IMF (International Monetary Fund). 2015. 'Ireland: Lessons from Its Recovery from the Bank-Sovereign Loop'. Available at: <https://www.imf.org/external/pubs/ft/dp/2015/eur1501.pdf> (accessed 30 March 2016).

IMF (International Monetary Fund). 2010. 'Ireland: Letter of Intent, Memorandum of Economic and Financial Policies, and Technical Memorandum of Understanding'. Available at https://www.imf.org/external/np/loi/2010/irl/120310.pdf (accessed August 15 2016).

Kinsella, S. 2012. 'Is Ireland Really the Role Model for Austerity?' *Cambridge Journal of Economics*, 36(1): 223–35.

Kinsella, S. 2014. 'Post-Bailout Ireland as the Poster Child for Austerity'. *CESifo Forum* 15(2): 20–5.

Koo, R. C. 2011. *The Holy Grail of Macroeconomics: Lessons from Japan's Great Recession*. Singapore: John Wiley & Sons.

Lane, P. R. 2011. 'The Irish Crisis', in *The Euro Area and the Financial Crisis*, ed. Miroslav Beblavy, David Cobham, and L'udovit Odor. Cambridge: Cambridge University Press, 59–80.

Lee, J. J. 1989. *Ireland 1912–1985: Politics and Society*. Cambridge: Cambridge University Press.

Minsky, H. P. 1986. *Stabilising an Unstable Economy*. New York: McGraw-Hill.

Nyberg, P. 2011. 'Report of the Commission of Investigation into the Banking Sector, Misjudging Risk: Causes of the Systemic Banking Crisis in Ireland'. Available at: <http://www.bankinginquiry.gov.ie/> (accessed 15 April 2016).

Ó Riain, S. 2014. *The Rise and Fall of Ireland's Celtic Tiger: Liberalism, Boom and Bust*. Cambridge: Cambridge University Press.

Perotti, R. 2011. 'The "Austerity Myth": Gain Without Pain?' Paper presented at the BIS Conference on Fiscal Policy and its Implications for Monetary and Financial Stability, Palace Hotel, Lucerne, Switzerland, 23–24 June. Available at: <http://www.bis.org/events/conf110623/perotti.pdf> (accessed 15 April 2016).

Regling, K. and Watson, M. 2010. 'Preliminary Report on the Sources of Ireland's Banking Crisis'. Available at: <http://www.bankinginquiry.gov.ie/> (accessed 15 April 2016).

Savage, M., Callan, T., Nolan, B., and Colgan, B. 2015. 'The Great Recession, austerity and inequality: evidence from Ireland'. ESRI Working Paper No. WP499. Available at: https://www.esri.ie/pubs/WP499.pdf (accessed 15 August 2016).

Weymes, L. and Bermingham, C. 2012. 'Fiscal Compact-Implications for Ireland'. *Central Bank of Ireland, Economic Letter Series* 9: 1–7.

4

Business

Frank Barry and Adele Bergin

INTRODUCTION

From the late 1980s, Ireland began to converge rapidly on the UK in terms of income per head, and by the early years of the new millennium, as seen in Figure 4.1, parity had been breached.[1]

There were initial fears that this rapid convergence was characterized by 'jobless growth'. From the mid-1990s, however, employment growth far exceeded the rates prevailing in the UK and the USA, which were also strong performers over this period (Figure 4.2).

The year 2007 was the peak one in both of Figures 4.1 and 4.2. The economy contracted sharply in 2008 and recovery began only in late 2012. As of early 2016, the recovery is ongoing.

The capacity of the Irish economy to exhibit such pronounced cycles as is apparent in Figures 4.1 and 4.2 draws attention to its extreme openness to international flows of both capital and labour. This suggests, as Paul Krugman (1997) notes, that we might think of Ireland as a *regional economy*. In such an economy, employment is determined primarily by labour demand since supply is extremely elastic. The regional perspective focuses attention on the economy's export base, with employment in the rest of the economy—construction and both public and private services—arising largely to service that base. Expansion in these other sectors must be financed either by the performance of the export base or by external borrowing, which is likely to be unsustainable. This is a useful, if overly simplified, analytical framework to bear in mind as background.

---

[1] Gross national income (GNI) is preferable to gross domestic product (GDP) as a measure of Irish national income as it includes net factor income from abroad. For Ireland, the latter is a large negative number—coming to around 20 per cent of GDP—because of the profits accruing to foreign multinational corporations (MNCs) for which the country serves as a significant export platform. For most countries, the gap between GNI and GDP is insignificant.

Figure 4.1. Per capita gross national income (PPS): Ireland relative to the UK
Source: Eurostat.

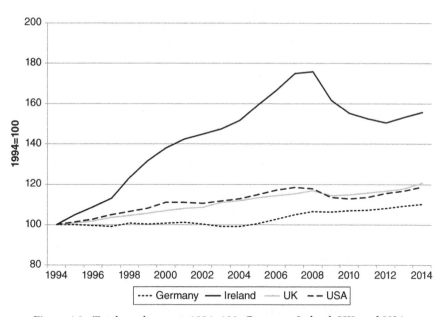

Figure 4.2. Total employment, 1994=100: Germany, Ireland, UK, and USA
Source: OECD Labour Force Statistics.

We begin with an overview of developments in the business sector over recent decades, along with a snapshot of its structure over this period. This is followed by a chronological account of the key changes and drivers of change over the export-led growth phase of the 1990s, the credit-fuelled boom of

2000–7, the collapse of 2008, and the recovery that began in late 2012. That fiscal contraction was necessary when the budget deficit and the cost of borrowing spiralled out of control in no way suggests that the strength and timing of the recovery can be attributed to austerity. The strong export orientation of the economy, the sectoral pattern of exports, the country's particular set of export destinations, and the asymmetric effects for Ireland of euro weakness have all been hugely significant contributory factors.

THE IRISH BUSINESS SECTOR: OVERVIEW OF DYNAMICS AND A SNAPSHOT OF STRUCTURE

The sectoral structure of an economy can be described in either output or employment terms. For Ireland, because of the very high productivity recorded for foreign-owned industry, these two approaches yield dramatically different images. This is particularly true of the foreign-dominated pharmaceuticals sector, which, according to Eurostat data for 2012, accounted for 9 per cent of manufacturing employment but 40 per cent of manufacturing value added. Within services, the foreign-dominated information and communications sector accounted for 7 per cent of market services employment and 26 per cent of value added. There were no equivalently large discrepancies for the EU15.[2]

Because foreign industry in Ireland is heavily export oriented, most export sectors feature much more prominently in value-added than in employment terms. Though we largely use employment as our measuring rod in this chapter, our analysis of the contribution of exports must necessarily be conducted through the lens of output.

Figure 4.3 charts employment over the period since 2000 in non-market or public services, and in the three sectors—manufacturing, construction, and market services—that we define as comprising the business economy.[3]

Table 4.1 compares the evolution of the shares of these three business sectors in Ireland to developments in the Western European EU15.

There are three points to be noted from Table 4.1 The first is the downward trend in manufacturing's share, which is common across the developed world.

---

[2] For the EU15, pharmaceuticals accounted for 2 per cent of manufacturing employment and 5 per cent of value added, while information and communications accounted for 6 per cent of market services employment and 13 per cent of value added.

[3] Non-market services comprise the categories of public administration, defence, and compulsory social security; education; health and social work. Though we exclude these and some other sectors (utilities and the primary sector, which is largely agriculture) from consideration, we recognize that they provide inputs into the business economy and can be significant elements in the cost of doing business.

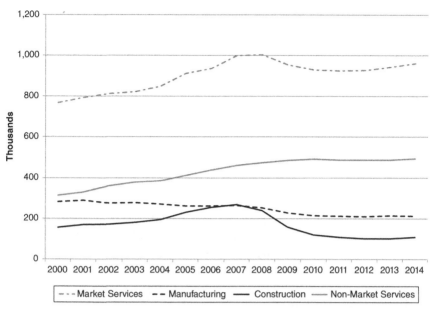

Figure 4.3. Sectoral employment, thousands, Ireland
Source: Eurostat.

Table 4.1. Percentage shares of business sector employment

		2000	2007	2014
Manufacturing	Ireland	23	17	17
	EU15	26	28	21
Construction	Ireland	13	18	9
	EU15	12	10	10
Market Services	Ireland	64	65	75
	EU15	61	62	69

Source: Eurostat.

The second is the volatility in the share of construction in Ireland, and the third the high share of market services in the Irish case. We deal with the first two points in our chronological narrative in the next section on the drivers of developments in the business sector. The third arises as a consequence of the two related characteristics already alluded to and that apply to services as well as to manufacturing, that is, the extent of foreign ownership and the associated high degree of export orientation of the sector.

Foreign affiliates account for almost one-half of Irish manufacturing employment compared to a little over a quarter for the other European Union (EU) member states for which data are reported (Table 4.2). In the case of

Table 4.2. Shares of foreign-owned affiliates in manufacturing and services

	Manufacturing, 2007		Services, 2006	
	Employment	Value added	Employment	Value added
Ireland	46	79	27	42
EU Average	28	36	13	20

Notes: EU average for manufacturing refers to sixteen EU member states other than Ireland for which data are available; EU average for services refers to twelve EU member states other than Ireland.
Source: OECD 2010: 157.

services, foreign affiliates account for a little over a quarter of Irish employment, which is again around twice the figure for the other EU member states in the data.[4] This is not simply a consequence of the small size of the Irish economy; Ireland is significantly more foreign direct investment (FDI) intensive than all of the other small countries in the sample. Also notable from Table 4.2 is the much larger share of foreign affiliates in value added than in employment, as adverted to at the beginning of this section.

The sectoral structure of Irish exports is also largely determined by the strong presence of foreign affiliates in the economy.[5] In 2012, foreign affiliates accounted for over 80 per cent of employment in highly export-oriented manufacturing sectors such as chemicals and pharmaceuticals, and computer, electronic, and optical products. Within market services they accounted for almost 50 per cent of employment in the information and communication segment and over a quarter in administrative and support service activities.

This foreign presence, combined with Ireland's high measured productivity and strong export orientation, affects the sectoral structure of Irish exports in a number of ways. First, exports of chemicals and related products (including pharmaceuticals) have come, since around 2005, to comprise over one-half of Irish merchandise exports. This can be seen in Table 4.3, which illustrates the differences in export structure between Ireland and the EU15. Chemical and pharmaceutical exports come almost exclusively from the foreign-owned sector. Second, and unusually by international standards, Irish services exports have grown to equal in size the value of merchandise exports. Third, as most services exports are produced by foreign-owned MNCs, they tend to be in modern rather than traditional categories. Computer and information services account for around 40 per cent of Irish services exports, 'other business services' almost 30 per cent, and finance and insurance almost 20 per cent (Table 4.4).

---

[4] Department of Finance (2014: Figure 7) reports a somewhat lower share for services employment in Ireland.
[5] Data from Forfás (2012) suggest that over 80 per cent of merchandise exports and around 90 per cent of services exports are produced by foreign firms.

Table 4.3. Sectoral percentage shares in Irish and EU15 goods exports

	SITC Code	Ireland				EU15			
		1995	2000	2008	2015	1995	2000	2008	2015
Food, Animals, Beverages, and Tobacco	0–1	19	8	9	10	9	7	8	9
Chemicals and Related Products, n.e.s.	5	19	33	52	58	13	13	16	18
…(of which) Medicinal and Pharmaceutical Products	54	5	6	20	27	2	3	5	7
Office and Data-Processing Equipment	75	21	23	11	4	4	5	3	2
Instruments and Appliances, n.e.s., for Medical, Surgical, Dental, or Veterinary Purposes	872	1	2	3	4	0	1	1	1

Note: n.e.s. = not elsewhere specified.
Source: Eurostat External Trade Statistics.

Table 4.4. Sectoral percentage shares in Irish and EU15 services exports

	Ireland					EU15		
	1998	2000	2005	2008	2013	2005	2008	2013
Insurance Services	15	13	14	12	9	2	3	2
Financial Services	7	10	10	10	8	9	10	9
Computer and Information Services	30	38	33	35	41	6	6	6
Other Business Services	15	10	27	30	29	26	27	30
Rest of Services	33	30	16	14	14	57	54	53

Note: These are the most recent consistent figures available as statistical agencies are shifting to a new BoP methodology.
Source: CSO Balance of Payments for Ireland; Eurostat Balance of Payments (BoP) for EU15.

The domestic value-added share in Irish gross exports is low by international standards, reflecting the high import content of much foreign-affiliate output (Byrne and O'Brien 2015). This means that €1 million of foreign MNC exports contributes much less to Irish national income than €1 million of indigenous-company exports. A different perspective on the relative importance of the foreign MNC sector emerges, however, when we evaluate the extent of backward linkages *per job* rather than per volume of sales, as done in Table 4.5. In the case of the rapidly growing foreign-affiliate services sector, for example, expenditure per employee on Irish-sourced services is very high, and this backward linkage may be particularly employment intensive. In addition to the direct linkages illustrated in the table, it should also be noted that foreign-owned industry is the source of most corporation tax revenues raised in Ireland.

While foreign-owned firms tend to be large and, on account of this, to receive a lot of media attention, it is noteworthy that small and medium

Table 4.5. Backward linkages per job in indigenous and foreign industry in Ireland, 2013

	Manufacturing		Services	
	Indigenous €k	Foreign €k	Indigenous €k	Foreign €k
Payroll Cost per Employee	40	63	52	66
Irish Materials Purchased per Employee	106	33	13	16
Services Sourced in Ireland per Employee	24	37	27	144

Source: Own calculations from Forfás 2013.

enterprises (SMEs) (i.e. enterprises employing fewer than 250 persons) accounted for 99.7 per cent of active enterprises and 68 per cent of business-sector employment in 2012. SMEs employed 96 per cent of those working in construction, around 73 per cent of those working in 'other services' and distribution, 55 per cent of those in industry, and 30 per cent of those in finance and insurance.[6]

Most SMEs are Irish-owned and almost 70 per cent of SME employees are in firms that are focused solely on the domestic economy, engaging in neither exporting nor importing. Micro-enterprises, which employ fewer than ten workers, are particularly significant in construction, where they account for almost 70 per cent of employment. They are far less significant in other sectors. SMEs stand out as having fared particularly badly over the financial crisis, largely because of their dependence on the domestic market.

DRIVERS OF DEVELOPMENTS IN THE BUSINESS SECTOR: A CHRONOLOGICAL ACCOUNT

The evolving structure of the business sector is driven by the relatively slow-moving processes of globalization and technological change, upon which higher-frequency macroeconomic shocks are superimposed.

The declining cost of air shipping has lessened the disadvantages of geographic peripherality and facilitated Ireland in developing into sectors such as pharmaceuticals and microchips that have low bulk-to-value ratios. Advances in information technology (IT) have made many formerly non-traded services internationally tradeable, which has allowed Ireland to develop as an export platform for computer and IT services, finance, insurance, and other business

[6] In this particular Central Statistics Office (CSO) publication, industry comprises manufacturing, mining, quarrying, and utilities, while 'other services' denotes services other than distribution, finance, and insurance (CSO 2012: Appendix 3).

services. Since transmission of these services is almost costless, it is not surprising that some 35 per cent of Irish service exports go to locations other than the EU and North America, compared to a figure of only 20 per cent for Irish merchandise exports. Deeper integration into emerging global value chains has been facilitated by the protection afforded to the free movement of goods and services by EU and World Trade Organization (WTO) rules. Eastwards enlargement of the EU and the integration of China into the global economy, however, have meant that export comparative advantages can now change much more rapidly than previously. The more flexible the economy is—and Ireland appears to have become increasingly flexible since the 1960s and 1970s—the less disruptive these shocks are.

EU integration processes—the Single Market programme of the early 1990s and the single currency project—have also been hugely consequential.[7]

The Celtic Tiger Era of the 1990s

After many decades of lacklustre growth, the Irish economy took off over the 1990s in what came to be known as the Celtic Tiger era. The economy slowed somewhat with the bursting of the dot.com bubble and the 9/11 shock of the new millennium, given Ireland's exposure to the US economy and to the IT sector in particular, but growth then resumed until the crash of 2007–8. We treat these two rapid-growth eras separately.

Towards the end of the 1980s, a series of beneficial shocks—policy-induced and otherwise—created a virtuous circle of economic progress. A change in fiscal strategy in 1987 contributed to the rapid resolution of that era's crisis in the public finances. The contractionary consequences were dampened by a concurrent boom in the UK, which remains an important market for the labour-intensive exports of Irish indigenous firms. The early years of social partnership brought wage moderation, while the doubling of the EU Structural Funds in 1989 made it possible to implement the badly needed infrastructural projects that had been put on hold as part of the change in fiscal stance.

Ireland's low corporation tax strategy, which had been in place since the mid-1950s, came into its own in the 1990s with the advent of the Single Market and the US high-tech boom. These triggered a strong increase in FDI flows into and around Europe. Restrictive public procurement policies had formerly forced transnational corporations in certain sectors to locate in

---

[7] A range of other EU policies—on competition, energy and the environment, food security, etc.—have also had effects on the business sector. These are beyond the scope of the chapter to address.

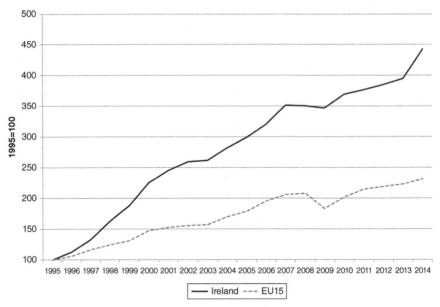

Figure 4.4. Growth in Irish and EU15 exports, 1995=100
Source: Eurostat, constant price data.

larger EU member states. With the outlawing of these practices under the Single Market initiative, Ireland captured a growing share of the available FDI.

Data from the Census of Industrial Production show that employment in Irish-owned manufacturing firms expanded by 23 per cent between 1988 and 1999, while employment in foreign-owned firms rose by 49 per cent. By the end of the period, manufacturing employment was about equally divided between the two segments.

The export orientation of the foreign-owned sector was the key driver of the massive (and continuing) rise in Irish exports seen in Figure 4.4. From the mid-1990s to 2000, growth in the volume of Irish exports exceeded that of the EU15 by a factor of around 2.5.

Internationally traded and international financial services employment was also growing, from a level of 8,500 in 1988—which was about equally divided between domestic and foreign firms—to some 50,000 in 1999, of which foreign firms accounted for two-thirds.[8]

The foreign-owned segment of services is also strongly export oriented and is the main driver of the rising share of service exports seen in Figure 4.5. In 1995, service exports accounted for around a quarter of both Irish and EU15 exports.

[8] Forfás (1995, 2007).

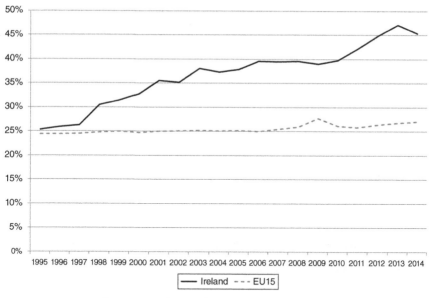

Figure 4.5. Shares of services in total exports
Source: Eurostat, constant price data.

By 2013 the Irish share had almost doubled while that for the EU15 had remained broadly stable.

The Bubble Economy, 2000–7

By the early years of the new millennium the nature of Irish growth had changed. While the earlier period had been export-led and underpinned by wage restraint, this later period was fuelled by the construction sector, whose expansion sustained economic growth up to 2007 despite the deterioration in wage competitiveness seen in Figure 4.6.

The sharp fall in interest rates following euro membership fuelled the expansion in credit-dependent construction and property development as well as housing demand. The threefold increase in real property prices over the decade to 2006 was dramatic not just by Irish but by international standards.

From 2003, all of the banks on the Irish market eased lending conditions, such as maximum loan-to-value ratios, in the face of competitive pressures from what ultimately proved to be maverick banks. Net foreign borrowing by Irish banks jumped from 10 per cent of GDP in 2003 to over 60 per cent by early 2008 to fund loan demands. Because currency risk had been completely removed, this borrowing did not push up interest rates as would have occurred

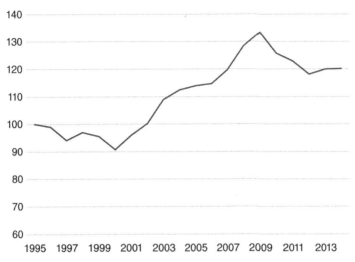

Figure 4.6. Relative hourly earnings in manufacturing in a common currency, 1995–2014 (1995=100)

Note: A rise in the index indicates a loss in competitiveness.
Source: Central Bank of Ireland (unpublished data).

in the past. Only when funding seized up at the onset of the global financial crisis in 2008 was such behaviour belatedly punished.

Government revenues over the period became more dependent on volatile sources, particularly the booming property sector, as centralized wage agreements continued to be shored up by income tax concessions. The tax base became increasingly vulnerable to a downturn while fiscal expenditure became strongly pro-cyclical.

The expansion of the construction sector and pro-cyclical fiscal policy both contributed to a crowding-out of export sectors and a deterioration in the balance of payments.[9] In contrast to the earlier period when employment growth was far stronger in exporting establishments (both indigenous and foreign), over this later 'crowding-out period' these establishments declined as a share of all establishments, and suffered far greater proportionate losses than did non-exporting establishments.[10]

The sectoral make-up of the manufacturing sector was also changing over this period, though arguably driven more by globalization and technological change than by the business cycle and declining competitiveness. Employment in the pharmaceutical sector grew 30 per cent, while employment in office machinery

---

[9] O'Brien (2007) provided a perceptive contemporaneous analysis of the bubble, focusing on developments in the current account deficit.

[10] This is based on the performance of manufacturing establishments alone, as this is the only enterprise sector for which such data are available for this period.

Table 4.6. Employment in a selection of manufacturing and service sectors, 2000 and 2007

	2000	2007
Pharmaceuticals (NACE 244)	8,573	11,136
Office and Data-Processing Equipment (NACE 30)	20,723	12,500
Internationally Traded Services other than Financial Services	55,084	64,568

Source: Census of Industrial Production and Forfás 2007.

and computer manufacturing fell by 40 per cent (Table 4.6). As Barry and Van Egeraat (2008) show, however, while information and communications technology (ICT) firms were shifting their computer assembly operations out of Ireland, the firms themselves remained in place, transitioning their Irish operations into higher-paid service activities including software, sales and support, and research and development (R&D).

Collapse and Recovery, 2008–the Present

The collapse of the property bubble decimated the bloated construction sector. Given the limited degree of monetary integration in the Eurozone and the shock waves emanating from events in the USA, it also triggered the near-collapse of the domestic financial sector. The government responded by pumping over 40 per cent of GDP into the banking system to cover its losses and recapitalize the surviving banks. Real estate in Ireland had grown to be a major source of revenue for the exchequer so the property market collapse also had a very severe impact on the public finances. From a position of surplus in 2007, the general government deficit exceeded 11 per cent of GDP in 2009, despite significant cuts in that year's budget.

With the private sector deleveraging, banks shrinking their balance sheets, construction at a standstill, export markets stalled, and competitiveness out of kilter, the massive budget deficit and sharp rise in borrowing costs necessitated fiscal contraction. There was no ameliorating external boom to cushion the fiscal shock as there had been in the late 1980s. The cumulative ex ante fiscal adjustment (i.e. when no account is taken of the feedback to government revenue and expenditure) came to just under 20 per cent of GDP, while the fall in GNP from peak to trough was over 15 per cent (FitzGerald 2014).

The burden of adjusting to imbalances in the Eurozone fell almost entirely on the deficit countries in the periphery (De Grauwe 2013: Figure 4.8). Almost all sectors suffered, both in terms of jobs and number of surviving enterprises, before signs of a turnaround began to emerge in late 2012. Though the export sector performed much more strongly than the domestic economy, it too was hit hard in the early stages of the recession. Exports fell slightly in 2008 and more dramatically in 2009 before recovering in 2010. A broadly similar pattern is evident for the EU15, though the export contraction in 2009 was much more severe than in Ireland.

Figure 4.6 shows that there was some improvement in Ireland's competitiveness relative to its trading partners over the crisis period. This improvement came about, however, not by downward hourly real wage reductions—which, as is widely recognized, are very difficult to achieve in a zero inflation environment—but by a general standstill in Irish wages while those in Ireland's trading partners increased (O'Farrell 2015).[11]

Currency movements are also of importance in the construction of this index. Of all the Eurozone economies, Ireland has the highest proportion of its trade with the USA and the UK. The sharp fall of the euro against both sterling and the dollar between 2009 and 2015 yielded a substantial competitiveness gain to Ireland. To the extent that this was driven by the increasingly aggressive monetary policies associated with Mario Draghi's tenure as European Central Bank (ECB) President, Ireland gained more than the other troubled economies of the Eurozone periphery from these actions, while benefiting along with them, of course, from the resulting low interest rates which reduced debt-service payments and moderated the extent of fiscal contraction required.

The sectoral structure of the export sector was a further important determinant of how the economy fared. Ireland was relatively highly specialized in sectors in which USA, UK, and Eurozone import demand proved resilient (Table 4.7). The broad chemicals sector (including pharmaceuticals), for example, was the most significant Irish merchandise export sector over the period 2000–13. During this time, chemical and pharmaceutical imports grew as a share of total Eurozone, UK, and USA imports. The same pattern is evident in the case of computer and information services. The fact that Ireland was relatively specialized in goods and services for which international demand remained buoyant significantly bolstered the country's economy during the worst years of the crisis, and has facilitated recovery.

Figure 4.7 illustrates the contributions of various subsectors to manufacturing export growth over time. Office machinery made a substantial contribution in the 1990s; since then its contribution has been reversed as the sector migrated out of Ireland. Pharmaceutical and medical device exports have generally made positive contributions, though pharmaceuticals dragged down export growth in 2012 and 2013 when a number of leading medicines produced in Ireland went off patent.[12] The decline in employment, however,

---

[11] Walsh (2012) and Bergin, Kelly, and McGuinness (2013) also show that there was relatively little adjustment in hourly earnings.

[12] The patent cliff can lead to a dramatic fall in revenue for the firms involved. If the firms are foreign-owned and continue to produce the drugs in Ireland in the same quantity as before, this

Table 4.7. The sectoral structure of Irish exports and world import demand

	Exports				Imports					
	2000		2013		2000			2013		
	World	Ireland	World	Ireland	Eurozone	UK	USA	Eurozone	UK	USA
Goods	79.3	78.0	78.8	49.9	77.7	76.7	85.0	75.7	76.7	83.1
... of which										
Agricultural and Food	9.0	9.21	9.9	12.3	10.4	9.8	5.7	11.4	11.4	6.5
Chemicals and Pharma	9.6	34.5	11.4	59.0	11.4	9.7	6.3	14.6	12.1	8.9
Office Machinery and Electrical	15.8	34.5	9.9	6.5	12.5	18.4	17.9	7.3	9.2	13.7
Other	65.5	21.9	68.8	22.2	65.6	62.1	70.1	66.6	67.3	70.8
Services	20.7	22.0	21.2	50.1	22.3	23.3	15.0	24.3	23.3	16.9
... of which										
Computer and Information	5.3	34.5	8.6	41.7	4.9	4.1	5.5	5.6	7.5	7.6
Insurance and other Financial	8.2	19.0	9.3	16.7	6.6	5.3	10.1	1.2	9.2	15.0
Business Services	21.4	17.9	26.4	28.6	7.0	16.8	11.1	7.3	25.3	20.4
Other	65.1	28.7	55.7	13.0	81.5	73.8	73.2	85.9	58.0	57.0

Source: Byrne and O'Brien 2015.

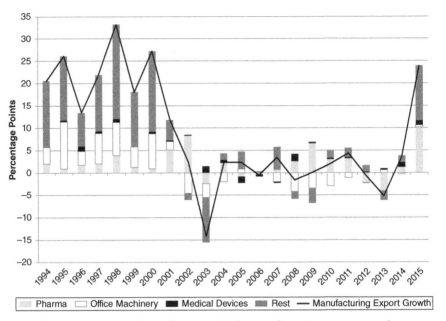

Figure 4.7. Sectoral contribution to Irish manufacturing export growth
Source: CSO External Trade Statistics.

proved to be much more moderate. While the value of pharma exports fell by almost 20 per cent between 2011 and 2013, the fall in employment was much less significant.

Figure 4.8 provides a similar breakdown for services exports. Computer and information services stands out as the only sector to make a positive contribution in 2008. It also made a small positive contribution to growth in 2009, and since then it has accounted for half or more of services exports growth. This contribution is particularly interesting in that it has been made by the indigenous as well as the multinational segment of this high-tech sector (Barry and Bergin 2012).

Ireland's trade links with the UK and the USA assisted recovery through a channel additional to the currency effects discussed in this section, in that both recovered more rapidly from the global crisis than did the EU as a whole. The US recovery was particularly rapid. While the USA is of some significance as a destination for Irish services exports (of which it accounts for around 10 per cent), it is much more significant for merchandise exports, and its importance has been increasing. In 2014, the US market served as

will show us largely as a loss in GDP rather than gross national product (GNP), since the reduction in value is offset by a reduction in profit outflows (FitzGerald 2013a).

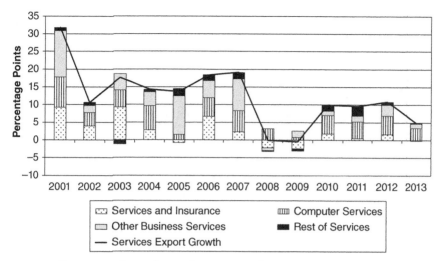

Figure 4.8. Sectoral contributions to Irish services export growth
Source: CSO Balance of Payments.

destination for almost one-quarter of Irish goods exports, up from a figure of 18 per cent in 2000.[13]

Further evidence of the role of the export sectors in stabilizing the economy emerges from the *Annual Business Survey of Economic Impact*, from which estimates of the employment directly generated by production of exports can be derived (Table 4.8).[14]

The cycle is readily apparent in these data. Overall employment in export production declines over the 'crowding-out' period 2000–7. It drops more dramatically at the onset of the global crisis, reaches its trough in 2009, and begins to recover rapidly thereafter (Figure 4.9). This recovery was driven by indigenous manufacturing exports and by the growth of both indigenous and foreign-affiliate services exports. Employment in the production of foreign-affiliate manufactured exports continued to decline.

The home-market-oriented sectors of the economy fared very poorly over the crisis. Public and private spending dipped sharply and the number of active enterprises fell across almost all sectors of the economy (Table 4.9).

---

[13] Brazys and Regan (2015) present evidence that Ireland, as an export platform for US companies, benefited disproportionately from the increased availability of funding to firms in high-tech sectors associated with quantitative easing in the USA.

[14] This entails multiplying employment levels in each of the four categories shown in Table 4.8 by exports as a share of sales for each category. The Forfás data we use for manufacturing also include a small trace of non-manufacturing primary industries.

Table 4.8. Employment directly generated by production of exports

	2000	2007	2013
Indigenous Manufacturing Exporters	46,219	38,085	42,342
Foreign-Owned Manufacturing Exporters	108,075	93,676	75,851
Indigenous Services Exporters	11,630	14,464	23,965
Foreign-Owned Services Exporters	43,059	47,725	59,921
Total Employment in Production for Export	208,983	193,950	202,079

Source: Calculations on data reported by Forfás 2013.

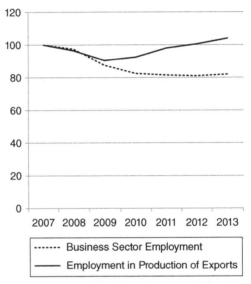

Figure 4.9. Employment recovery in production of exports, 2007=100
Source: Calculations based on data in Forfás 2013.

SMEs suffered far more than large firms over the downturn. By 2012, employment in SMEs stood at 76 per cent of the 2007 figure, while for large enterprises the equivalent figure was 90 per cent. Nor was this solely due to the massive decline in construction, the sector most affected by the downturn. In fact, it was only in construction that large firms suffered a greater proportional drop in employment than SMEs. Within industry, employment in SMEs in 2012 was 25 per cent down on its 2007 level, while for large firms the figure was closer to 20 per cent. Of the sectors into which these data are divided (industry, construction, services, distribution, finance and insurance), the only sector in which employment increased, in both SMEs and large firms, was finance and insurance (CSO 2012).

Table 4.9. Number of active enterprises by sector, 2007–12

	2007	2008	2009	2010	2011	2012
Manufacturing	13,583	13,697	13,363	12,790	12,290	11,999
Construction	61,082	57,042	46,655	40,459	36,747	33,879
Wholesale and Retail Trade	44,834	45,732	45,347	43,981	42,966	42,210
Transportation and Storage	11,990	11,926	11,306	10,572	10,171	9,937
Accommodation and Food Services	16,361	16,905	16,822	16,511	16,340	16,279
Information and Communication	9,696	10,137	10,076	10,057	10,297	10,764
Financial and Insurance Activities	4,747	4,901	5,271	5,282	5,454	5,658
Professional, Scientific, and Technical	29,709	31,078	31,718	30,801	30,440	30,325
Administrative and Support Services	12,150	12,537	12,382	11,789	11,395	11,289
BUSINESS ECONOMY	216,198	216,265	206,575	195,431	189,055	185,530

Notes: Wholesale and retail trade includes motor repairs; financial and insurance excludes activities of holding companies, as does business economy.
Source: CSO Business Demography.

As noted in the section entitled 'The Irish Business Sector', the poor performance of the SME sector over the crisis is largely ascribable to its dependence on the domestic market. From 2009 to 2012, most reported that their greatest challenge was in finding customers, even though Central Bank researchers found that Irish SMEs over the crisis faced the toughest credit conditions in Europe.[15] In the period up to September 2012, in the face of the aggregate demand deficiency prevailing, access to credit appeared to have been a binding constraint for only one in nine such firms (O'Toole, Gerlach-Kristin, and O'Connell 2013).[16]

While the SME sector continued to languish in 2012 there was some recovery in the numbers employed in large firms. Signs of a turnaround in late 2012 appeared in the data on aggregate employment, hours worked, GNP, and unemployment. Having increased by 10 percentage points between 2007 and 2012, the unemployment rate fell by more than 2 percentage points between end 2012 and end 2013 (Fitz Gerald 2014). The number of new business owners also rose in 2013.[17]

While all of the exporting jobs shown earlier are in agency-assisted firms, not all of the jobs in agency-assisted firms are involved in export production, since these firms also serve the domestic market.[18] The data on permanent full-time employment in agency-assisted firms are shown in Table 4.10, which provides clear evidence of the turnaround in the economy over recent years.[19]

Table 4.10. Permanent full-time employment in agency-assisted firms

	Foreign				Indigenous			
	2008	2010	2012	2014	2008	2010	2012	2014
Manufacturing and Other Industry	88,677	78,249	78,249	81,457	114,530	94,236	94,638	100,092
Services	64,801	60,296	69,041	78,970	46,850	45,047	47,397	55,082

Source: DJEI 2014.

[15] Lawless, McCann, and McIndoe-Calder (2012).

[16] This is supported by findings published in the Global Entrepreneurship Monitor (2013: Appendix Table D), which showed that 59 per cent of entrepreneurs who had exited business in the previous twelve months had reported as their reason that 'business was not profitable', compared to only 10 per cent who reported 'problems getting finance' as their reason.

[17] Global Entrepreneurship Monitor (2010: Table 1.2, 2013: Table 2). These data refer to owners of businesses between 4 and 42 months old.

[18] The agencies referred to are Enterprise Ireland and Industrial Development Agency (IDA) Ireland. International Financial Services Centre (IFSC) firms are also included.

[19] Table 4.10 shows the data on permanent employment. In 2014, there were an additional 20,000 temporary jobs in both the foreign and the indigenous segment.

Table 4.11. Regional employment dynamics, 2007–15

	Percentage Change in Employment	
	2007–12	2012–15
Border	−21	12
Midland	−16	12
West	−12	0
Dublin	−14	9
Mid-East	−10	4
Mid-West	−13	2
South-East	−18	12
South-West	−12	4
State	−14	7

Source: CSO, Quarterly National Household Survey.

Although the detailed data upon which we have relied in the chapter thus far are currently available only up to 2014 at the latest, we can use macroeconomic data to complete the picture. Having been in continuous decline since 2009, public net current spending grew for the first time in 2013. Private consumer spending followed in 2014 and investment rebounded strongly. For the first time in many years domestic sources were now making a significant contribution to growth, suggesting that the effects of the recovery are likely to be spread more evenly across sectors and across size classes of firms in the coming years.[20]

Aggregate employment has grown at an average rate of more than 2 per cent over the last three years, and unemployment finally fell below 10 per cent in 2015.[21] The recovery has also been more broadly based geographically than is generally recognized. As seen in Table 4.11, the regions that suffered the greatest proportionate employment losses over the downturn have tended to register the greatest percentage gains over the recovery. Of the more marginalized regions (the border, midland, and west), only the west has shown no evidence of employment recovery up to 2015. It is true, however, that since the recovery began Dublin has captured a disproportionate share of IDA-assisted foreign-MNC employment (DJEI 2014).

It is clear from Table 4.11 that aggregate employment is still well below its 2007 peak. What of other indicators? By 2014, Germany and the USA had surpassed their 2007 levels of real GDP per head, the UK had just about regained its previous level, while Ireland remained about 4 per cent below its

---

[20] This does not contradict the 'export base' model outlined in the Introduction. That model would indeed suggest that prior recovery in the export base was necessary for sustainable recovery in the components of domestic demand.

[21] ESRI Quarterly Economic Commentary, spring 2016. Available at: <http://www.esri.ie/publications/quarterly-economic-commentary-spring-2016/> (accessed 3 July 2016).

2007 peak.[22] The problems with using GDP as an indicator for Ireland are well known and have been reprised in the Introduction. While GNI or GNP are preferable—and these also registered strong growth in 2014 and 2015—they too have been growing increasingly opaque as measures of Irish performance (FitzGerald 2013b). It is telling that Irish real consumption per head in 2014, and aggregate employment in 2015, remained almost 9 per cent below their 2007 peaks, having recovered by then only to around their 2004–5 levels. There remains a good deal of ground to be regained.

CONCLUSION

This chapter has focused on the performance of the Irish business sector over the cycle, from the 1990s to the present. Ó Gráda (2011) has shown that the recent crisis has been the deepest since the foundation of the state, though obviously the margin above hardship is wider today (2016). Unsurprisingly, given the severity of the Irish contraction, export sectors fared much better than those oriented towards the domestic market, while, because of their home-market orientation, SMEs fared much worse than larger firms.

The recovery began to take hold in 2012–13 but was initially unevenly balanced. The distribution of IDA-assisted foreign-MNC jobs favoured the Dublin region, while employment growth was concentrated in jobs for graduates (Fitz Gerald 2014). The recovery has become much more broadly based in occupational terms since then, particularly as the construction sector rebounded.

Austerity held Irish wages down. The recovery in competitiveness was significantly amplified, however, by the decline of the euro against the currencies of major Irish trading partners. This latter effect, their earlier recoveries, and the general buoyancy in demand for the types of goods and services that Ireland exports, are key drivers of the recovery.

Barry and Bergin (2012: 1291) offered the opinion that: 'the country's prospects depend on whether the engine [of export growth] will be sufficiently powerful to outweigh the drag of the anchor of national public and private debt'. That engine does indeed appear to have been remarkably powerful.

There are numerous dangers on the horizon, however, some with particular resonances for Ireland. Given not just the extent but also the employment intensity of exports to the UK, a British withdrawal from the EU could be hugely damaging (Barrett et al. 2015). Ireland's corporation tax regime furthermore—which has been key to export-led growth—remains the focus

---

[22] IMF, World Economic Outlook database.

of criticism of a number of EU member states. It took the International Monetary Fund (IMF) to keep at bay their demands that the regime be changed in return for bailout assistance in 2010.

There are significant domestic threats as well. Having remained remarkably low over the austerity period, strike activity is on the increase, while pay demands seem to be responding to the exaggerated growth figures projected by the increasingly opaque national income or output data. The country needs some system to manage expectations. The uncertain international environment makes it imperative that earlier lessons about the dangers of pro-cyclical fiscal policy not be forgotten. Few of the political parties in the recent general election seem to have taken this point to heart.

REFERENCES

Barrett, A., Bergin, A., FitzGerald, J., Lambert, D., McCoy, D., Morgenroth, E., Siedschlag, I., and Studnicka, Z. 2015. 'Scoping the Possible Economic Implications of Brexit on Ireland'. *ESRI Research Series No. 48.*

Barry, F. and Bergin, A. 2012. 'Inward Investment and Irish Exports over the Recession and Beyond'. *The World Economy*, 35(10): 1291–304.

Barry, F. and Van Egeraat, C. 2008. 'The Decline of the Computer Hardware Sector: How Ireland Adjusted'. *ESRI Quarterly Economic Commentary*, spring, 58–72.

Bergin, A., Kelly, E., and McGuinness, S. 2013. 'Evidence on the Pattern of Earnings and Labour Costs over the Recession'. In *Using Evidence to Inform Policy*, ed. Pete Lunn and Frances Ruane. Dublin: Gill & Macmillan.

Brazys, S. and Regan, A. 2015. 'These Little PIIGS went to Market: Enterprise Policy and Divergent Recovery in the European Periphery'. Geary Working Paper 2015/17. Dublin: UCD Geary Institute for Public Policy.

Byrne, S. and O'Brien, M. 2015. 'The Changing Nature of Irish Exports: Context, Causes and Consequences'. *Central Bank of Ireland Quarterly Bulletin*, 2, April.

CSO (Central Statistics Office). 2012. *Business in Ireland*. Dublin: Central Statistics Office.

De Grauwe, P. 2013. 'Design Failures in the Eurozone: Can They Be Fixed?' *European Economy, Economic Papers* 491.

Department of Finance. 2014. *Economic Impact of the Foreign-Owned Sector in Ireland*. Dublin: Department of Finance.

DJEI (Department of Jobs, Enterprise and Innovation). 2014. *Annual Employment Survey*. Dublin: Department of Jobs, Enterprise and Innovation.

FitzGerald, J. 2013a. 'The Effect on Major National Accounting Aggregates of the Ending of Pharmaceutical Patents'. *ESRI Quarterly Economic Commentary*, autumn, 51–60.

FitzGerald, J. 2013b. 'The Effect of Redomiciled PLCs on GNP and the Irish Balance of Payments', ESRI Research Note 2013/1/2. Dublin: Economic and Social Research Institute.

FitzGerald, J. 2014. 'Ireland's Recovery from Crisis'. *CESifo Forum*, 2, June: 8–13.

Forfás. 1995. *Annual Employment Survey*. Dublin: Forfás.

Forfás. 2007. *Annual Employment Survey*. Dublin: Forfás.

Forfás. 2012. *Annual Business Survey of Economic Impact* (ABSEI). Dublin: Forfás.

Forfás. 2013. *Annual Business Survey of Economic Impact* (ABSEI). Dublin: Forfás.

Global Entrepreneurship Monitor. 2010. *Annual Report for Ireland*. Available at: <http://www.gemconsortium.org> (accessed 3 July 2016).

Global Entrepreneurship Monitor. 2013. *Annual Report for Ireland*. Available at: <http://www.gemconsortium.org> (accessed 3 July 2016).

Krugman, P. 1997. 'Good News from Ireland: A Geographical Perspective'. In *International Perspectives on the Irish Economy*, ed. A. Gray. Dublin: Indecon.

Lawless, M., McCann, F., and McIndoe-Calder, T. 2012. 'SMEs in Ireland: Stylised Facts from the Real Economy and Credit Market'. *Central Bank of Ireland Quarterly Bulletin*, 2, April: 99–124.

O'Brien, M. 2007. 'Building for the Future? Interpreting an "Irish" Current Account Deficit'. *ESRI Quarterly Economic Commentary*, winter: 80–103.

OECD (Organisation for Economic Co-operation and Development). 2010. *Measuring Globalisation*. Paris: OECD.

O'Farrell, R. 2015. 'Wages and Ireland's International Competitiveness'. *Economic and Social Review*, 46(3): 429–58.

Ó Gráda, C. 2011. 'Five Crises'. Central Bank of Ireland Whitaker Lecture, 29 June.

O'Toole, C., Gerlach-Kristin, P., and O'Connell, B. 2013. 'Measuring Credit Constraints for Irish SMEs', ESRI Research Notes 2013/1/3. Dublin: Economic and Soaicla Research Institute.

Walsh, K. 2012. 'Wage Bill Change in Ireland During Recession: How Have Employers Reacted to the Downturn?' *Journal of the Statistical and Social Inquiry Society of Ireland*, 41: 39–65.

5

The Financial Sector

Gregory Connor, Thomas Flavin, and Brian O'Kelly

INTRODUCTION

During the years 2003 to 2008, the Irish domestic financial sector experienced a very fast and poorly controlled expansion, followed by a dramatic collapse. The causes of the Irish credit bubble and bust have been exhaustively examined; see, for example, Connor, Flavin, and O'Kelly (2012), Honohan (2010), Nyberg (2011), Regling and Watson (2010), and additional references therein. Over the next six years, from late 2008 to 2014, the Irish financial sector went through a painful restructuring and slow, modestly successful, recovery. This chapter provides an economic analysis of the Irish financial sector's restructuring and recovery period. The chapter considers both domestic and foreign banks operating in Ireland, household and corporate debt, property and other asset markets, and business investment. We analyse what the Irish experience tells us about the economic theory of post-crisis financial sector restructuring and recovery strategies.

One can divide recent Irish economic history into three periods: the 'Celtic Tiger' period of strong export-led economic growth from about 1990 to roughly 2003; the 'financial bubble' from 2003 to early September 2008; and the 'austerity period' from mid-September 2008 to December 2014. For our purposes, the appropriate start date for the austerity period is clear: on 15 September 2008, Lehman Brothers went bankrupt, interbank borrowing markets froze, and the global credit-liquidity crisis began in earnest. The emerging difficulties in Ireland's financial and property markets were evident to some observers as early as mid-2007, but it was only after the September 2008 failure of Lehman Brothers that the true magnitude of the Irish financial crisis was widely recognized.

On 30 September 2008, following meetings on the previous night between senior government officials, representatives of the Irish banks, the Department

Table 5.1. Chronology of key events

Chronology	Date
Lehman Brothers file for bankruptcy	September 2008
Irish Government guarantee of bank liabilities	September 2008
Anglo chairman and CEO resign after revelation of loan scandals	December 2008
Chief executive of the Financial Regulator, Patrick Neary, resigns	January 2009
Irish Government announce nationalization of Anglo Irish Bank	January 2009
Garda Fraud squad raid Anglo Irish buildings	February 2009
Government announce €7bn capital injection for BOI and AIB	February 2009
Central Bank of Ireland (CBI) launch first version of code of conduct on mortgage arrears	February 2009
Standard & Poor's (S&P) downgrade Irish sovereign debt; loss of AAA-rating	March 2009
Government propose establishment of NAMA	April 2009
NAMA established	December 2009
CBI and Financial Regulator publish methodology for PCAR exercise; results for AIB, BOI, and EBS	March 2010
Anglo Irish Bank announce largest loss in Irish corporate history	March 2010
Anglo and Irish Nationwide Building Society (INBS) promissory notes issued	March 2010
First tranche of loans transferred to NAMA	May 2010
CEBS announce results of EU-wide stress tests	July 2010
Second tranche of loans transferred to NAMA	August 2010
PCAR results for Irish Life and Permanent (IL&P)	September 2010
Ireland agrees bailout programme with Troika	November 2010
Bulk transfer of remaining loans to NAMA	December 2010
CBI announces FMP results	March 2011
Anglo announce loss of €17.7bn for year 2010—a new record	March 2011
Moody's cut ratings on all Irish banks to junk status	April 2011
Creation of IBRC—merger of Anglo and INBS	July 2011
Irish deal to replace promissory notes with long-dated bonds	March 2012
Personal Insolvency Act becomes law	December 2012
Liquidation of IBRC	February 2013
Ireland complete return to bond markets	March 2013
Anglo Tapes released	June 2013
CBI launch fourth version of code of conduct on mortgage arrears	July 2013
Ireland exits Troika bailout programme	December 2013
BOI is first Irish bank to announce return to profit	August 2014

of Finance, and the Central Bank of Ireland,[1] the Irish Government decided to guarantee all the liabilities of the Irish domestic banking sector. The rationale for the state guarantee was twofold: to help Irish banks to access short-term funding markets; and to remove the uncertainty surrounding the future of Irish banks, which it was feared might lead to capital outflows. This extravagant act created a perilously large contingent liability of €440 billion for the

---

[1] Lyons (2014) provides a detailed account of those meetings on 29 September 2008.

Irish taxpayer, more than double Irish gross domestic product (GDP). The Irish domestic banks effectively changed from private enterprises to sickly wards of the state. For the next six years, the restructuring of the financial sector in Ireland was one of the key goals of public policy.

The section 'Imbalances in the Domestic Banking Sector' describes the key imbalances in the domestic financial system at the beginning of the restructuring-recovery period. This is followed by the section 'Sale and Liquidation of Distressed Loan Portfolios', which considers the sale and liquidation of distressed loan portfolios of the banks, particularly by the National Asset Management Agency (NAMA). The section 'The National Asset Management Agency' examines banking sector recovery strategies, including the Financial Measures Programme (FMP), a collection of directives imposed on the domestic banks by the Central Bank of Ireland to guide them towards more acceptable levels of capital adequacy and stable liquidity funding. 'The Recovery Strategy for the Surviving Domestic Banking Sector' section describes the explosive growth and slow retrenchment of Irish household and business debt, and the related problem of loan payment arrears and default. The 'Conclusion' sums up the chapter. The chapter is organized thematically rather than chronologically; Table 5.1 provides a guide to the chronology of some of the key events.

IMBALANCES IN THE DOMESTIC BANKING SECTOR

This section examines the key imbalances in the Irish domestic banking sector, which arose during the 2003–8 credit bubble period and slowly dissipated thereafter. The 2003–8 Irish growth-and-collapse episode is a classic example of a credit-fuelled property bubble and bust. Calvo, Leiderman, and Reinhart (1993, 1994) and Reinhart and Reinhart (2009) note that financial bubbles are often linked to large inflows of foreign capital. Such inflows are called 'capital bonanzas' and they are often, but not always, linked to financial bubbles and busts.[2]

During the years 2003–8, Ireland experienced a spectacular capital bonanza. The domestic banking sector in Ireland grew explosively, with a total growth of assets of 245 per cent over a five-a-half-year period, equivalent to 25 per cent per annum. This was not financed from domestic sources; rather, the funding was borrowed from overseas via the interbank borrowing market, bank bond market, and via foreign corporate deposits in Irish domestic banks. Figure 5.1 gives the asset (Panel A) and liability (Panel B) composition of the

---

[2] Using a large panel dataset, Calvo, Leiderman, and Reinhart (1994) estimate that a capital bonanza (suitably defined) increases the probability of a national banking crisis in the following year by a factor of seven.

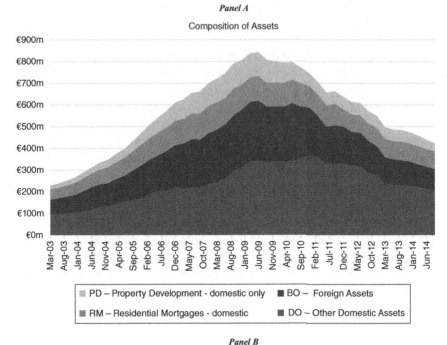

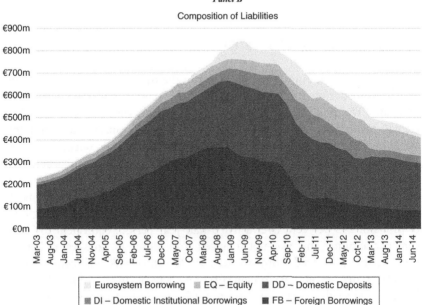

Figure 5.1. Composition of domestic banking sector balance sheet

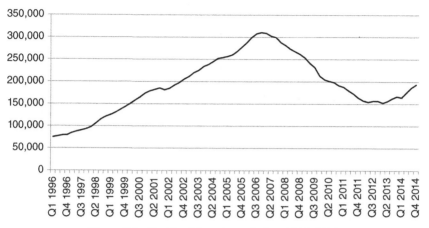

Figure 5.2. Residential property index: 1996–2014

aggregate balance sheet of the domestic banking sector.[3,4] On the asset side, the very fast growth of property development lending is notable—it grew by 502 per cent between Q1 2003 and Q3 2008.[5] Mortgage lending also grew quickly, by 172 per cent over the same period. On the liability side, the growth in net foreign borrowing is critical to explaining the banking crisis: it grew by 353 per cent over this same five-and-a-half-year period. In September 2008, the Irish domestic banks had €113 billion of net foreign liabilities, equivalent to 63 per cent of 2008 GDP. The growth of more stable sources of bank funding, such as domestic demand deposits, was more muted. Clarke (2016) describes how this excessive banking sector growth was related to regulatory failures in the oversight of the Irish banking system.

Linked to the growth of bank lending was a construction boom and property price bubble. Figure 5.2 shows a residential Property Price Index, which grew by 311 per cent between Q1 1996 and its peak in Q1 2007; it subsequently fell 51 per cent to its trough in Q1 2013. Also, it is worth noting that residential property prices understate the magnitude of the property price bubble, which was even more spectacular for development land. Ireland does not have a statistical index of development land prices.

---

[3] The aggregate balance sheet of the domestic banking sector is found by summing the asset and liability entries of each domestic bank and cancelling intra-bank items such as interbank lending from one bank to another within the domestic banking sector. See Central Bank of Ireland (2013) for details.

[4] All data used in the charts and figures in this chapter is available at <https://www.maynoothuniversity.ie/economics-finance-and-accounting/working-papers>.

[5] This statistic refers to domestic property development only. Including foreign property development (most of which was led by Irish-based developers) gives an even larger growth figure; see Connor and O'Kelly (2012).

SALE AND LIQUIDATION OF DISTRESSED LOAN PORTFOLIOS

At the beginning of 2009, the Irish banking system, and the Irish Government as guarantor of that system, was in a deep, existential crisis. The global Great Recession had begun, with the worst four consecutive quarters of worldwide economic contraction since the beginning of the Great Depression in 1929 (see Almunia et al. 2010). Although the government liability guarantee provided some short-term relief, serious funding problems continued to plague the Irish banking sector.

The Nationalization and Liquidation of Anglo Irish Bank and Irish Nationwide

The two most distressed Irish domestic banks were Irish Nationwide and Anglo Irish Bank. Within a few months of the September 2008 bank liability guarantee, it became obvious that both banks were essentially in the process of liquidation, although at first there was some hope that a rump institution might survive. Irresponsible corporate governance policies and accounting irregularities were discovered at both institutions; the extremely poor quality of their loan books also became quickly evident. In January 2009, the Irish Government nationalized Anglo Irish Bank with a view to an orderly wind-down of its operations. Later, in July 2011, Irish Nationwide was also officially nationalized after merging with Anglo Irish Bank to form the Irish Bank Resolution Corporation (IBRC).[6] This institution was finally declared bankrupt, and liquidated, in February 2013.

The European Central Bank (ECB) stood ready to provide liquidity funding to Eurozone banks, but only if backed by eligible collateral assets. The institutional bank run against Anglo Irish Bank was so severe that the bank did not have sufficient eligible collateral to obtain adequate emergency funding from the ECB. In the absence of suitable collateral, there was an additional fall-back source of Central Bank liquidity. The ECB Council had an extra funding channel by which it could allow direct lending from the bank's member-state Central Bank (i.e. the Central Bank of Ireland) to individual banks, in a programme called Emergency Liquidity Assistance (ELA). The risk from any potential default on ELA lending by the bank falls on the member Central Bank rather than on the ECB. Since the Central Bank of Ireland is guaranteed by the Irish sovereign, its ELA lending adds to Irish sovereign risk.

---

[6] It could be argued that Irish Nationwide was already nationalized upon receiving a capital injection of €5.4 billion from the Irish Government in 2010, which gave majority shareholding to the state.

By March 2010, Anglo Irish Bank needed large additional equity capital injections if it was to avoid technical insolvency (which would also trigger an immediate demand for repayment of its massive outstanding liquidity support from the ECB and Central Bank of Ireland). The ECB was reticent to allow a Eurozone bank to enter bankruptcy during this tumultuous period for the Eurozone financial system. The Irish Government did not have the fiscal resources to fully pay the creditors of Anglo Irish Bank, but having guaranteed the liabilities of these banks, an alternative funding arrangement had to be found. (One problem was the breadth of the guarantee. Honohan (2010) argues that the inclusion of existing long-term bonds and some subordinated debt was unnecessary to improve the liquidity position of the sector.) A compromise was struck between the ECB, Irish Government, and Central Bank of Ireland. The Irish Government gave a series of so-called 'promissory notes' to Anglo Irish Bank and Irish Nationwide, promising to pay the banks (or their creditors) €30 billion plus interest over a twenty-year period. The transaction increased the two banks' assets and (on the liability side of the balance sheet) equity capital by €30 billion. This capital injection kept Anglo and Irish Nationwide eligible for continued ECB and Central Bank of Ireland funding access. The promissory notes were then accepted as collateral for 'liquidity funding' from the Central Bank of Ireland (this acceptance was pre-agreed as part of the transaction).

Neither the Central Bank of Ireland nor the ECB could directly bail out Anglo Irish Bank or Irish Nationwide since this would represent debt monetization, which is forbidden under the ECB charter. Examined critically, this liquidity assistance could still be interpreted as *indirect* debt monetization since, in effect, the Central Bank of Ireland was creating new money for a member government unable to fund its claims, or rather for the claims of its private bank liability holders.

The promissory note transaction was widely criticized within Ireland since it involved Irish taxpayers taking on additional debt to pay off the private creditors of failed banks in liquidation. Unlike the capital injections into the surviving banks, where the Irish populace clearly benefited from the banks' survival, Anglo Irish Bank and Irish Nationwide were in full-scale liquidation and the injected money was only used to pay off private bank liabilities. A strategic decision to pay off private bank liabilities had been made earlier, in the September 2008 bank liability guarantee, but the promissory notes made this manifest.

The valuation of the promissory notes is quite subtle due to the budgeting relationship between the Central Bank of Ireland and Irish Government: the Central Bank of Ireland's investment surplus including interest earned is paid to the Irish Government. (See Whelan (2012) for a careful valuation analysis of the promissory note.) The promissory note valuation was made even more byzantine on the bankruptcy of IBRC in February 2013. As part of the IBRC bankruptcy, the Irish Government announced that it was altering the payment structure of the promissory notes, replacing the notes with long-term government bonds. Due to the circularity of interest payments between the Central Bank of Ireland and Irish Government, this debt swap substantially lowered the true cost of the debt to the Irish Government (see Whelan 2013). In an unusual move, the ECB Governing Council did not approve or disapprove of this change in the terms of the deal; rather, it announced that it 'took note' of the changed terms, without endorsing or rejecting the change. The Irish promissory note drama is a minor but fascinating episode in the evolving history of the Eurozone financial system.

THE NATIONAL ASSET MANAGEMENT AGENCY

The nationalization and planned liquidation of Anglo Irish Bank and Irish Nationwide still left unanswered the question of the best solution for the other, surviving domestic banks. Bacon (2009), in a report commissioned by the National Treasury Management Agency, proposed solutions to the domestic bank sector's credit and liquidity crisis. The report evaluated options for resolving property loan impairments and associated capital adequacy. The Bacon Report considered three alternative approaches:

1. A recapitalization programme, which injects sufficient capital into the banks to absorb likely losses;
2. An asset guarantee scheme, which would see the state guarantee the loan assets which would remain on bank balance sheets; and
3. An asset management arrangement which would remove the assets from the banks and place them in a separate vehicle.

The first approach (1) is least disruptive to the activities of the banks, since the bad loans remain under the banks' direct control, but the approach risks the banks becoming 'zombie banks' which focus only on dealing with past bad lending decisions and not engaging in new lending. The guarantee scheme (2) has the advantage of not creating the need for the state to finance the purchase of the assets or for the banks to write down their asset values. This has the disadvantage that it creates misaligned incentives for banks and borrowers since the taxpayer is liable for loan losses. The report argued for the bad bank approach (3). It concluded:

> when considered in the context of characteristic features of the Irish situation, in particular taking account of the contingent liability aspect; the implications of loans remaining on bank balance sheets and the continuing capital requirements of property related projects, it appears that the asset management approach has

the potential to offer greater assistance to achieving resolution of the impairment issue upfront and maximising taxpayer returns, over the longer term. (Bacon 2009: 6)

NAMA was established in December 2009. In a report outlining its functions (NAMA 2010) NAMA's founding goal is stated as striving to achieve the best possible return for the taxpayer on the acquired assets. These assets covered both performing and non-performing property development loans. The inclusion of performing loans was an effort to reduce the size of banks' balance sheets and to lower the capital that banks were required to hold against these large, and relatively illiquid, loans. At inception, NAMA was given a target to liquidate its entire portfolio (through loan rundowns, loan sales, and the sale of underlying collateral) within a seven- to ten-year period.

The government faced challenges in correctly pricing the loan assets to be transferred from the banks to NAMA. The government had to ensure that the prices paid were 'fair value', not containing a hidden subsidy to the selling banks, since an overpriced sale would constitute a national government subsidy to private industry; such subsidies are not permitted (or are very circumscribed) under European Union (EU) competition law. At the same time, the government was aware that if the loan pricing was low, the realized loss on the sale of these loans could devastate the banks' capital bases. The government took a compromise position, in which the loans were fairly valued by an objective outside party, and then a premium was added to this current-market valuation, to take account of the loan's long-term holding value. The approach was approved by the EU Competition Commission under the circumstances. In retrospect, the NAMA loan-pricing policy seems to have been about right. By the end of 2014, NAMA had unwound the majority of its portfolio with a small profit margin.

During 2009, as NAMA was being developed and launched, the Irish Government was in the midst of a fiscal crisis. The government could not afford the additional borrowing required to fund NAMA's purchase of loan assets. It was crucial that NAMA borrowing be treated as off-balance-sheet funding by national-income-accounting authorities; this meant that NAMA had, to satisfy criteria, be designated a privately controlled corporate entity rather than a government agency. Such a designation would ensure that the money borrowed to fund NAMA would not be recorded as Irish sovereign borrowing. The ownership structure of NAMA consisted of a 51 per cent stake owned by private investors and the remainder held by the Irish state. Originally, the private stake was equally divided among three domestic investors, namely: New Ireland Assurance, Irish Life investment managers, and Allied Irish Banks (AIB) investment managers. However, the holding of the latter two entities had to be sold off when the Irish Government became the majority shareholder in their parent banks. One share was bought by a South African firm, Prestige, with the other being acquired by an undisclosed client.

Ninety-five per cent of the amount which NAMA paid for the transferred property loans was paid with government-guaranteed securities. These so-called 'NAMA bonds' paid a floating rate of interest tied to the Libor rate and were deemed to be eligible collateral for obtaining funding from the ECB. The participating Irish domestic banks, who received the NAMA bonds in exchange for distressed loan assets, were able to convert the NAMA bonds to cash, courtesy of the ECB lending facility. The very low interest rate on NAMA bonds, together with their eligibility as collateral for extremely low-rate bank funding from the ECB, had the effect of creating a hidden borrowing-rate subsidy for NAMA and the participating banks from the ECB. These funding subsidies did not violate EU competition laws. The remaining 5 per cent of NAMA funding was in the form of subordinated securities and equity, which allowed the entity to qualify as a private enterprise, not a government agency.

NAMA acquired the first tranche of loans from the participating institutions (AIB, Bank of Ireland (BOI), Anglo Irish Bank, EBS, and Irish Nationwide) in May 2010. Over the following two years, it acquired approximately 12,000 loans with a par value of €77 billion for €30 billion. Hence, the participating banks suffered a par-value loss of €47 billion on the sale of the loan assets. Table 5.2 shows the composition of the NAMA portfolio by loan type and region.

By the end of 2014, NAMA had redeemed €16.6 billion of senior bonds, 55 per cent of the total senior debt originally issued (see NAMA 2015b), which placed it over two years ahead of its target redemption schedule (with an original target of 50 per cent redemption by 2016). NAMA is essentially an asset-disposal business with a limited lifespan, so its aggregate profitability depends critically upon the sale prices received on asset disposals over coming years. As of end 2014, NAMA seems on target to terminate with a modest positive profit (see NAMA 2015a).

It is very difficult to evaluate NAMA's risk-adjusted performance as a 'for-profit' entity. NAMA was financed 95 per cent by government-guaranteed senior bonds and 4.7 per cent by subordinated debt, with a mere 0.3 per cent of equity finance. The 300-times leverage implicit in this equity/debt capital structure is not capable of being obtained in normal markets. Given the tiny sliver of common equity, the subordinated debt is, in effect, an equity-like security, but is paid a debt-like return. Furthermore, the ECB agreed to accept the NAMA senior bonds as collateral for repurchase agreements with the Irish banks, thereby substantially lowering the carrying cost of these bonds for the banks.

NAMA was aided by three external factors: first, it had an extremely valuable borrowing subsidy provided by its indirect access to cheap ECB funding; second, it was able, as intended in its design, to take a long-term holding strategy for most assets and 'ride out' the poor market conditions of

Table 5.2. Composition of NAMA portfolio by asset and region

	Ireland	Dublin	Northern Ireland	Britain	Rest of World	Total	% of NAMA
Office	2.66	2.44	0.22	2.10	0.27	5.25	16.5%
Retail	2.91	1.51	0.22	1.16	0.15	4.44	14.0%
Other Investment	2.41	1.30	0.34	1.23	0.50	4.48	14.1%
Total Investment	*7.98*	*5.25*	*0.78*	*4.49*	*0.92*	*14.17*	*44.6%*
Residential	3.70	2.31	0.13	1.29	0.16	5.28	16.6%
Hotels	0.93	0.56	0.01	1.81	0.28	3.03	9.5%
Total Completed	*12.61*	*8.12*	*0.92*	*7.59*	*1.36*	*22.48*	*70.7%*
Development	1.13	0.52	0.06	1.33	0.33	2.85	9.0%
Land	4.17	2.42	0.28	1.85	0.16	6.46	20.3%
Total L&D	*5.30*	*2.94*	*0.34*	*3.18*	*0.49*	*9.31*	*29.3%*
Grand Total	**17.91**	**11.06**	**1.26**	**10.77**	**1.85**	**31.79**	**100.0%**
% of NAMA	56.3%	34.8%	4.0%	33.9%	5.8%	100.0%	

Note: Unless indicated, figures are in billions of euro.
Source: 'About NAMA Information Guide. Available at <http://www.nama.ie/publications>.

the first few years after its establishment; and third, it was indirectly aided by the quantitative easing and monetary expansion policies of the USA, British, and Eurozone Central Banks, which pushed down long-term interest rates to historic lows for long periods. These low long-term rates in all three currency zones (US dollar, British pound, and euro) made the potential yields on NAMA's property portfolio very attractive to outside investors.

THE RECOVERY STRATEGY FOR THE SURVIVING DOMESTIC BANKING SECTOR

The EU–IMF–ECB Programme and Bank Sector Stabilization

As of the last quarter of 2010, the Irish Government's attempts to restore the domestic banking system to health had not succeeded. Despite the nationalization of Anglo Irish Bank and several government-funded capital injections into banks, the markets remained unconvinced that the banking system was stabilized. Increasingly, wholesale deposits and bank bonds in domestic institutions began to be withdrawn on maturity, despite being protected by the government guarantee (Central Bank of Ireland 2011: 3). During this period, the Irish banking sector absorbed an enormous quantity of liquidity support from the Central Bank of Ireland and ECB (€136 billion at peak in November 2010). Particularly troubling were the ELA funds provided by the Central Bank of Ireland (see Figure 5.3). These funds were guaranteed by the Irish Government, but the ECB began to worry about the credit quality of this guarantee. The sharp economic downturn in Ireland following the banking collapse induced a very large Irish fiscal deficit, exacerbated by the high costs of capital injections into the banks. The ECB put pressure on the Irish Government to enter an International Monetary Fund (IMF)-led sovereign borrowing and restructuring programme. The Irish Government agreed to enter a programme in November 2010. There were three agencies involved in running the programme: the IMF, EU, and ECB, aptly named 'the Troika'.

The collapse of the Irish banking system caused the fiscal failure of the Irish sovereign and necessitated the sovereign bailout programme. This order of causality (banking crisis causing fiscal crisis) was not the case uniformly in the Eurozone crises; for some financially troubled countries in the Eurozone, the opposite causality applied. Greece's financial crisis, for example, began with a fiscal crisis, which then spread to the banking system. One of the design weaknesses in the single currency area was this perverse interaction between banking and fiscal uncertainty—the so-called 'doom loop' of interconnected banking sector and sovereign crises in the Eurozone monetary system (see De Grauwe 2013).

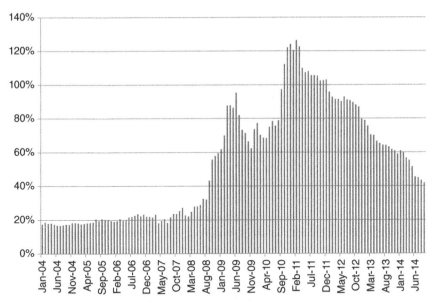

Figure 5.3. Liabilities of the Central Bank of Ireland relative to GDP

The Troika set the restoration of confidence in the banking system as one of the key goals of the programme. The Troika required €10 billion be immediately invested in the banks and set aside a further €25 billion as a contingency sum to address potential future capital needs.

BANK SECTOR STRESS TESTS

The establishment of NAMA, and the transfer of distressed property loans to it from the banks, generated a €47 billion realized capital loss for the domestic banks. The Irish Government and Central Bank of Ireland, together with the Troika, were forced to develop and implement a strategy to restore capital adequacy and public confidence in the Irish banking sector.

For several years after the 2008 US credit-liquidity crisis, a lack of confidence in the banking sector was widespread in the developed world, not just in Ireland. In an attempt to restore confidence in European banks, the Committee of European Bank Supervisors (CEBS) undertook a stress test in 2009. The test was applied to the twenty-two largest banks in Europe based on their balance sheet at the end of 2008, and projected the capital position of the banks two years forward. The test claimed to show that all the banks in the sample were adequately capitalized to withstand the assumed stresses. In July the following year, CEBS repeated the stress test, now covering ninety-one banks over the two-year period until the end of 2011. BOI and AIB were included in the sample and both passed the test, while seven non-Irish banks failed. The credibility of the stress tests was called into question when, just months after passing the 2011 stress test, a number of banks, including Dexia and Bankia, required substantial restructuring.

The CEBS stress tests of European banks had inconsistent goals, which may explain their lack of credibility. Their main objective was to restore confidence in European banks; producing a test finding that there were few if any serious problems in the region's banks could contribute to this goal, if the test finding was believed. CEBS had the authority to recommend capital injections or restructuring of failing banks, but was aware that making such recommendations, without any obvious sources of new capital, might cause funding chaos. The resulting tests were eventually seen as a failed public relations exercise rather than a serious attempt to measure bank sector stability.

Starting in March 2010, the Central Bank of Ireland undertook its own stress tests, the Prudential Capital Assessment Review (PCAR). It had learned from the public criticism of the CEBS stress tests and was very careful and explicit about ensuring the rigour of the tests. The PCAR exercise was preceded by a forensic asset quality review of all the domestic banks. Then, the participating banks were required to develop pro forma bank losses (and capital positions) linked to a base-case scenario and worst-case scenario for key loss-linked variables such as property prices and interest rates. In March 2010, BOI, AIB, and EBS, the three surviving institutions which had sold loans to NAMA, were subjected to PCAR. The PCAR covered a three-year period, 2010–12, and set a target level of 8 per cent Core Tier 1 capital in the base case scenario and a 4 per cent target in the stress scenario. Permanent TSB undertook the PCAR in September that year. The PCAR was repeated the following year, this time supervised by BlackRock Solutions and covering the period 2011–3. The target level of Core Tier 1 was raised to 10.5 per cent in the base scenario and 6 per cent in the adverse scenario. Arising from the tests, all four institutions, AIB, BOI, Permanent TSB, and EBS, were deemed to require additional capital.

Prior to 2008, the traditional approach to bank risk regulation focused upon capital risk with considerably less attention to liquidity risk. The US credit-liquidity crisis had made regulators more conscious of the importance of liquidity risk, in addition to capital risk. Reflecting this change in approach, the Central Bank of Ireland undertook a Prudential Liquidity Assessment Review (PLAR) as a supplement to the PCAR. The PLAR focused on trying to put the banking sector on a more stable funding footing. The purpose was to shrink the banking sector's dependence on volatile sources of bank funding, particularly short-term wholesale and interbank borrowing, which was also mostly foreign-sourced funding. This was to be either replaced by stable funding sources, such as domestic deposits, or, more realistically, matched by an offsetting shrinkage in the banks' assets.

THE FINANCIAL MEASURES PROGRAMME

The FMP was the collection of directives to the domestic banks based on the outcomes from the PCAR and PLAR tests. Although prepared by the Central Bank of Ireland, the FMP represented the banking element of the Troika rescue package. There were two main recommendations of the plan—capital injections and funding rebalancing—corresponding to the output from the PCAR and PLAR risk measurement tests.

The FMP required new capital injections into the banks; the capital amount needed was well within the funds allocated in the Troika support programme. The more difficult part of the FMP was the need for funding rebalancing in response to the PLAR findings. The PLAR set a clear target for the banks: each of the banks individually needed to reach a loan-to-deposit ratio of 122.5 per cent by December 2013. The purpose of this target was to return the Irish banks to a more appropriately leveraged and more stable funding position. To ensure smooth progress towards this 2013 target, the FMP also set interim six-monthly targets for the loan-to-deposit ratio.

The need to shrink assets in order to eliminate volatile funding created a difficulty in the PLAR recommendations. Forcing the banking sector to shrink its assets might incentivize the sector against new lending, which in turn might starve the economy of investment and lengthen the economic downturn. Selling the banks' existing assets was also problematic. The market for bank loan assets seemed poor at the time that the PLAR was undertaken. There was a risk that any forced sale of bank assets might attract 'fire-sale' prices and generate bigger than necessary capital losses for the banks.

The FMP shaped the deleveraging plan to minimize disruption to domestic bank lending and to avoid fire sales of assets. Banks were required to divide their existing lending operations into 'core' activities (chiefly, domestic lending) and 'non-core' (chiefly, foreign lending). The banks were then tasked with deleveraging by shrinking the non-core business while focusing solely on core activities for future lending growth.

The FMP forecast that losses of €27.7 billion would be incurred on bank portfolios and a further €13.2 billion of losses would arise from sales of non-core portfolios. This produced a capital shortfall of €18.7 billion, to which Irish Central Bank added a €5.3 billion conservatism buffer, creating a requirement for a €24 billion capital injection.

CORPORATE AND HOUSEHOLD DEBT OVERHANG
AND DELEVERAGING

The section 'Imbalances in the Domestic Banking Sector' looked at the explosive growth in bank lending through analysis of the banking sector balance sheet. This section returns to the same phenomenon, but now from the perspective of the borrowers: Irish households and businesses.

Figure 5.4 shows the growth and then decline of Irish household and private enterprise debt as a proportion of annual GDP. The run-up of household debt before 2008 was mostly but not entirely due to the fast growth in mortgage lending during the bubble period. To a considerable extent, the fast increase in private enterprise debt during the credit bubble was also due to property-related lending. During the Irish credit bubble, Irish private enterprises were very active as part-time property investors, both for commercial properties and buy-to-let (BTL) investment properties (see McCann and McIndoe-Calder 2014). Because of this, the collapse in property values created a very large unrealized capital loss for many Irish private enterprises. This large property investment loss, together with a sharp drop in business activity throughout the economy, contributed to widespread business distress and a lack of new investment by Irish businesses.

Figure 5.5 presents a breakdown by sector of the recipients of credit from Irish banks. It illustrates the banking sector's increasing exposure to property

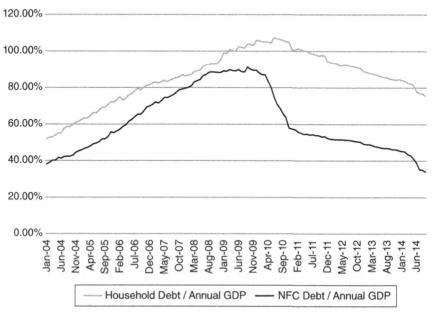

Figure 5.4. Household and private enterprise debt to GDP ratios

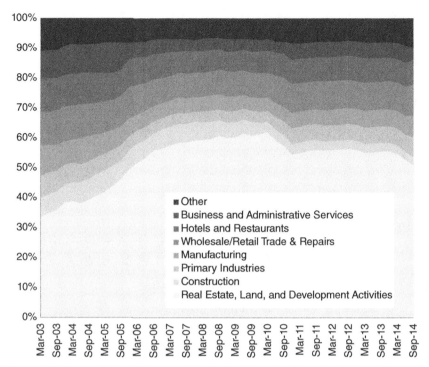

Legend:
- Other
- Business and Administrative Services
- Hotels and Restaurants
- Wholesale/Retail Trade & Repairs
- Manufacturing
- Primary Industries
- Construction
- Real Estate, Land, and Development Activities

Figure 5.5. Sectoral breakdown of Irish banking lending (excluding financial intermediation)

development and construction firms over the pre-crisis period, 2003–8. By 2008, this represented approximately 60 per cent of the combined banking loan book to private enterprises—a 20 percentage point increase over the start of our sample. This imbalance was still evident at the end of 2014, but the trend is towards a more stable ratio of property and construction debt to other sources of bank debt.

The large cumulative increase in property prices and mortgage debt prior to 2008, followed by the sharp fall in property prices after the banking crisis, led to an enormous increase in negative equity for mortgage holders, in both the primary residence and BTL categories. This negative equity, together with increasing unemployment and household income falls, led to a very sharp increase in mortgage arrears. Figure 5.6 shows the default rates (that is, percentage of mortgages with arrears of 90 days or more) for residential and BTL mortgages.

Widespread mortgage default is conventionally followed by property repossession, but this was not the case in Ireland after the banking crisis. Soon after the banking crash, in 2009, the Irish Government enacted the Land and Conveyancing Law Reform Act 2009, which inadvertently had the effect

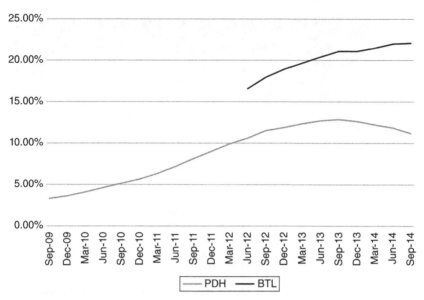

Figure 5.6. Default rates of residential and investment mortgages

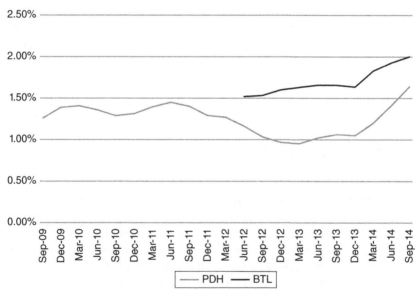

Figure 5.7. Repossession rates for defaulted mortgages

of making most repossession proceedings impossible following the discovery of an error, a 'lacuna' in legal jargon, by Ms Justice Dunne in July 2011. The judiciary ruled that the law, as written and passed by parliament, legally banned virtually all repossessions in most circumstances. Although not the stated intention of the law, the blanket ban on repossession was politically convenient at the time, and the law was not amended to correct the 'lacuna' for almost two years. Eventually, under intense pressure from the Troika, amending legislation was passed in 2013, allowing repossession of defaulted properties. In any case, repossession rates have remained extremely low in Ireland throughout the recovery period so far (see Figure 5.7). Connor and Flavin (2015) analyse how Ireland's very high mortgage arrears rate and extremely low property repossession rate interact and reinforce one another. This is one financial sector imbalance which has not yet been resolved as of 2016; there is still a large overhang of defaulted mortgages, with only slow and limited progress towards reducing this overhang.

CONCLUSION

During the period from late 2008 to the end of 2014, the Irish financial sector undertook a slow and painful restructuring and recovery from the financial excesses of the 2003–8 Irish credit bubble. During the credit bubble, the domestic banking sector had grown extremely quickly, building up a large, narrow exposure to property-related lending. The banks had financed this excessively fast growth using unstable sources of foreign funding. After the banking crash of September 2008, Irish policymakers were faced with a banking sector with massive prospective losses due to failed property loans, and an urgent need to replace quickly disappearing foreign funding. At the same time, the Irish household and business sectors were threatened by an overhang of property-related debt whose underlying collateral value had dropped precipitously. The economy suffered a deep recession, while the government entered a fiscal crisis due to falling tax revenues and unsustainable spending levels.

Policymakers implemented a range of corrective measures. A large quantum of property development loans were moved to a dedicated 'bad bank' called the NAMA. An IMF–EU–ECB financial rescue package was negotiated, mostly to deal with the government's fiscal crisis, but also to provide capital infusions to the domestic banking sector. A forensic analysis of banks' loan books was undertaken by the Central Bank of Ireland, followed by a stress test of their capital levels and funding stability. This in turn led to a series of Central Bank of Ireland directives to the domestic banking sector, requiring substantial new capital infusions and a slow rebalancing of funding (mostly by shrinking the size of the banking sector asset base) towards more stable funding ratios.

Given the dire initial conditions of late 2008, the restructuring and recovery of the Irish financial sector has proceeded reasonably well. NAMA seems on course, if conditions remain favourable, to liquidate its portfolio by the original target date and with a modest profit. The banking sector has regained the confidence of the domestic and international financial community, restored safe capital ratios, and made progress towards a stable funding model. Only the problem of long-term arrears on property debt in the household and small business sector remains mostly unresolved.

During the latter part of the period, the restructuring and recovery process was aided by foreign events favourable to the plan. In response to the Great Recession, the Central Banks of the USA, UK, and Eurozone set interest rates at unprecedentedly low levels; the US and UK Central Banks also undertook quantitative easing programmes, buying up long-term assets in order to revive their financial systems. These conditions helped to make the loan assets of the Irish banking system tempting for foreign purchasers.

The ECB was criticized in Ireland for its preference for domestic bank capital support (funded by the Irish Government) as opposed to allowing private-sector Irish banks to fail. On the other hand, some of the actions of the ECB were instrumental in the eventual recovery of the Irish financial system. It provided an enormous amount of funding support, both directly and through the Central Bank of Ireland, pushing the limits of its charter in terms of the ban on any indirect financial support for member governments. With hindsight, the insistence of the ECB that the Irish Government accept an IMF–EU–ECB support package was the correct decision, and it helped to restore confidence in the Irish financial system. The low financing rate provided to NAMA and the participating banks by the EU and ECB contributed to the profitability of NAMA's business strategy.

The poor performance of Irish business leaders, politicians, and financial regulators during 2003–8, when they allowed the Irish credit bubble to inflate unchecked, damaged Ireland's business reputation. The restructuring and recovery period was long and painful, but its relative success may have repaired some of the reputational damage arising from the Irish credit bubble and financial crash. Given the structure of the Irish economy, with its very strong reliance on international trade and its dependence on foreign direct investment, restoring Ireland's business reputation was critical for economic recovery and long-term growth.

Were enough new safeguards put in place during the restructuring and recovery period to ensure a similar credit bubble cannot occur again in Ireland? The answer is yes: the type of credit bubble and bust which devastated the Irish economy is extremely unlikely to reoccur in the new regulatory environment. The Basel III bank regulations include restrictions on the ratio of net stable funding to risky lending, and this restriction rules out the fast-growth strategies used by the Irish banking sector during the boom (which relied on volatile, foreign-funding vehicles such as interbank borrowing as the main sources of liability growth). Additionally, the risk regulation of the Irish domestic banks is now overseen by the ECB, and the ECB-based regulators will not allow any bank to adopt a narrow, unbalanced exposure to property development lending as was done by several Irish banks during the bubble. The Central Bank of Ireland has also changed drastically, taking a much stricter and more cautious approach to financial risk regulation.

ACKNOWLEDGEMENTS

We wish to acknowledge support from the Science Foundation of Ireland under grant 08/SRC/FM1389.

REFERENCES

Almunia, M., Bénétrix, A. S., Eichengreen, B., O'Rourke, K. H., and Rua, G. 2010. 'From Great Depression to Great Credit Crisis: Similarities, Differences and Lessons'. *Economic Policy* 25(62): 219–65.

Bacon, P. 2009. 'Evaluation of the Options for Resolving Property Loan Impairments and Associated Capital Adequacy of Irish Credit Institutions: Proposal for a National Asset Management Agency (NAMA)'. Available at: <https://www.nama.ie/fileadmin/user_upload/NAMAsummary.pdf> (accessed 15 April 2016).

Calvo, G., Leiderman, L., and Reinhart, C. R. 1993. 'Capital Inflows and Real Exchange Rate Appreciation in Latin America: The Role of External Factors'. *IMF Staff Papers* 40(1): 108–51.

Calvo, G., Leiderman, L., and Reinhart, C. R. 1994. 'The Capital Inflows Problem: Concepts and Issues'. *Contemporary Economic Policy*, 12: 266–80.

Central Bank of Ireland. 2011. *The Financial Measures Programme Report*. Dublin. Available at: <http://www.centralbank.ie/regulation/industry-sectors/credit-institutions/documents/the%20financial%20measures%20programme%20report.pdf> (accessed 15 April 2016).

Central Bank of Ireland. 2013. 'Money and Banking Statistics Explanatory Notes'. Dublin. Available at: <https://www.centralbank.ie/polstats/stats/cmab/Documents/Money%20and%20Banking%20Statistics%20Explanatory%20Notes_January2016.pdf> (accessed 15 April 2016).

Clarke, B. 2016. 'Banking Regulation'. In *Austerity and Recovery in Ireland: Europe's Poster Child and the Great Recession*, ed. B. Roche, P. O'Connell, and A. Prothero. Oxford: Oxford University Press.

Connor, G. and Flavin, T. J. 2015. 'Strategic, Unaffordability and Dual Trigger Default in the Irish Mortgage Market'. *Journal of Housing Economics*, 28: 59–75.

Connor, G. and O'Kelly, B. 2012. 'Sliding Doors Cost Measurement: The Net Economic Cost of Lax Regulation of the Irish Banking Sector'. *World Economy* 35(10): 1256–76.

Connor, G., Flavin, T. J., and O'Kelly, B. 2012. 'The U.S. and Irish Credit Crises: Their Distinctive Differences and Common Features'. *Journal of International Money and Finance*, 31(1): 60–79.

De Grauwe, P. 2013. 'Design Failures in the Eurozone: Can They Be Fixed?', LSE 'Europe in Question' Discussion Paper No. 57/2013. London: London School of Economics.

Honohan, P. 2010. 'The Irish Banking Crisis: Regulatory and Financial Stability Policy 2003–2008'. Report produced by the Governor of the Central Bank of Ireland for the Minister for Finance.

Lyons, T. 2014. 'What the Bankers Knew on the Night of the Bank Guarantee...'. *Irish Times*, 19 April. Available at: <http://www.irishtimes.com/news/politics/what-the-bankers-knew-on-the-night-of-the-bank-guarantee-1.1767215?page=1> (accessed 15 April 2016).

McCann, F. and T. McIndoe-Calder. 2014. 'Property Debt Overhang: The Case of Irish SMEs'. Central Bank of Ireland Research Technical Paper No. 14R14. Dublin: Central Bank of Ireland.

NAMA (National Asset Management Agency). 2010. 'The National Asset Management Agency: A Brief Guide'. Available at: <https://www.nama.ie/fileadmin/user_upload/NAMABriefGuide30March2010.pdf> (accessed 15 April 2016).

NAMA (National Asset Management Agency). 2015a. 'Key Financial Figures'. Available at: <https://www.nama.ie/financial/key-financial-figures/> (accessed 15 April 2016).

NAMA (National Asset Management Agency). 2015b. 'NAMA Issues End of Year Review for 2014'. Available at: <https://www.nama.ie/about-us/news/news-detailed-view/news/nama-issues-end-of-year-review-for-2014-45554-kb-pdf-format/> (accessed 15 April 2016).

Nyberg, P. 2011. *Misjudging Risk: Causes of the Systemic Banking Crisis in Ireland*. Dublin: Department of Finance.

Regling, K. and Watson, M. 2010. *A Preliminary Report on the Sources of Ireland's Banking Crisis*. Dublin: Stationery Office.

Reinhart, C. R. and Reinhart, V. 2009. 'Capital Flow Bonanzas: An Encompassing View of the Past and Present'. In *NBER International Seminar in Macroeconomics 2008*, ed. Jeffrey Frankel and Francesco Giavazzi. Chicago: Chicago University Press for NBER.

Whelan, K. 2012. 'ELA, Promissory Notes and All That: The Fiscal Costs of Anglo Irish Bank'. *Economic and Social Review*, 43(4): 653–73.

Whelan, K. 2013. 'Ireland's Promissory Note Deal', *Karl Whelan Blog*, 12 February. Available at: <http://karlwhelan.com/blog/?p=797> (accessed 15 April 2016).

6

Banking Regulation

Blanaid Clarke

INTRODUCTION

In response to the 2007 global financial crisis and the frailties in banking regulation which it exposed, there has been an extensive programme of financial regulatory reform both at a national and supranational level. In late 2014, Mark Carney, the chairman of the Financial Stability Board indicated, in his update to the G-20 leaders, that the task of agreeing measures to fix 'the fault lines that led to the global financial crisis is now substantially complete' (Carney 2014: 1). Indeed, the European Commission (EC) in September 2015 published a call for evidence on unnecessary regulatory burdens and rules, giving rise to unintended consequences (EC 2015b). This does not mean that the pendulum should swing back towards a 'light-touch' regulatory regime or even that the regulatory reform agenda has been completed. Carney emphasized the need to build on the regulatory successes to provide a safer and more resilient financial system. However, it is an appropriate time to take a step back to analyse the changes which have been introduced, and to assess the ability of the new regulatory regime to avoid the mistakes of the past and respond more efficiently to the new risks which will inevitably emerge.

In Ireland, where the blanket deposit guarantee effected in September 2008 by the Credit Institution (Financial Support) Act 2008 and the Credit Institutions (Financial Support) Scheme 2008 might be viewed as a tipping point in the Irish banking crisis, it is evident that the country has experienced a paradigm shift in regulatory approach since then, with significant reforms in banking regulation and supervision. Both macro- and micro-prudential regulation have been strengthened. (Though outside the scope of this chapter, it should be noted that a number of macro-prudential policy tools, including mortgage rules, counter-cyclical capital buffers, and other systemically important institutions buffers have also been introduced since the crisis.) An important element of improving regulation and supervision in this context was a strengthening of the Irish Central Bank's legal mandate, and the manner in which this has been done is examined in this chapter. It is argued that the changes made will have a positive impact, promoting greater financial stability and consumer protection. The section 'Brief Outline of the Banking Crisis in Ireland' of the chapter provides a brief introduction to the Irish banking crisis. Although it bore a resemblance in some ways to crises in many other jurisdictions such as the USA and the UK, it was characterized by a number of uniquely Irish features. The next section, 'Pre-Crisis Banking Regulation and Supervision', sets out the weaknesses in bank regulation and supervision revealed by the crisis in order to explain the rationale behind the various reforms. 'The Prism Model' section examines the new risk-based framework for the supervision of regulated entities introduced by the Central Bank and explores the impact of the single supervisory mechanism (SSM) on prudential supervision. The section 'Corporate Governance Reform' focuses on the crucial area of corporate governance and outlines the changes which have been introduced to remedy the deficiencies which undermine board effectiveness and oversight, strong risk management, and a responsible board culture. The 'Enforcement' section examines the Central Bank's new enforcement strategy and the enforcement tools at its disposal. Finally, the 'Conclusion' section considers the extent to which reforms in banking regulation and corporate governance have contributed to recovery.

One important point needs to be made at the outset. With the exception of the European Union (EU) banking union reforms discussed in 'The Prism Model' section, the significant majority of the reforms described could be classified as endogenous reforms emerging out of Ireland's own identification of regulatory failings, a belief on the part of the Financial Regulator and the legislature that change was a prerequisite to economic growth and financial stability, and a sometimes resigned acceptance by stakeholders that reform was inevitable. Christine Lagarde, managing director of the International Monetary Fund (IMF), acknowledged that many of the measures of the joint EU–IMF Programme of Financial Support ('Troika Programme') had already been agreed by the Irish Government and were at various stages of development when it commenced in November 2010. She therefore complemented the Irish response to the crisis on 'the sense of ownership' displayed (Lagarde 2013). Government action prior to November 2010 included: the nationalization of Anglo Irish Bank; the injection of capital into the larger domestic banks; the establishment of the National Asset Management Agency (NAMA); and the introduction of the eligible liabilities guarantee scheme. As discussed in 'The Prism Model' section, work had already commenced on developing a new regulatory infrastructure and a new supervisory system for credit institutions. The Troika Programme thus referred to 'continuing' the efforts to strengthen banking supervision (para.15) and the Financial Measures Programme (FMP), which implemented the Central Bank's obligations under the Troika Programme, referred to intensifying 'existing policy' (FMP 2011: 3). Before examining these developments, however, it is useful to consider the regulatory structures and systems which existed in the run-up to the crisis.

BRIEF OUTLINE OF THE BANKING CRISIS IN IRELAND

The Financial Crisis Inquiry Commission charged with determining the domestic and global causes of the crisis in the USA attributed it to: 'widespread failures in financial regulation; dramatic breakdowns in corporate governance; excessive borrowing and risk-taking by households and Wall Street; policy makers who were ill prepared for the crisis; and systemic breaches in accountability and ethics at all levels' (Financial Crisis Inquiry 2011: 27). If one were to replace the reference to 'Wall Street' with a reference to Irish credit institutions, this explanation would serve to explain many of the causal factors of the Irish crisis. However, it has been convincingly argued that 'Ireland's banking crisis bears the clear imprint of global influences, yet it was in crucial ways "home-made"' (Regling and Watson 2010: 5).

Reports were commissioned by the government from banking experts into: the conduct of the banking sector (Regling and Watson 2010); the performance of the Central Bank and Financial Regulator (Honohan 2010); and the policies, practices, and linkages that contributed to the Irish crisis (Nyberg 2011). The latter report, which focused on the reasons why a number of public and private institutions had acted in an imprudent or ineffective manner in the run-up to the crisis, was entitled *Misjudging Risk: Causes of the Systemic Banking Crisis in Ireland*. The title provides an immediate insight into the report's findings and epitomizes the crux of the crisis. In early 2016, a parliamentary Joint Committee of Inquiry into the Banking Crisis ('the Banking Inquiry'), charged with establishing the reasons Ireland experienced a systemic banking crisis, published its report having heard oral evidence from 131 witnesses and reviewed over half a million pages of documentation. It concluded that there were in reality two crises, a banking crisis and a fiscal crisis, and that they were caused by key failures in banking, regulation, government, and Europe.

Ireland was not, of course, the only country whose banks needed financial support. Support programmes for banks entailed non-recovered fiscal costs of about 5 per cent of gross domestic product (GDP) or more in Belgium, Greece, Luxembourg, the Netherlands, Austria, and the UK (EC 2015a: 9). Unusually, however, Ireland's enormous banking exposure was almost entirely related to property speculation, fuelled by the greater availability to the Irish banks of cheap European finance and to the unchecked domestic housing bubble of the preceding ten years (Clarke and Hardiman 2012). Between 2002 and 2008, domestic property-related lending had increased by almost €200 billion, representing 80 per cent of all growth in credit. This raised the share of property-related lending from below 45 per cent of total credit in December 2002 to above 60 per cent in December 2008 (Nyberg 2011: 14). This level of expansion and concentration was facilitated, according to Nyberg, by 'silent observers' (2011: 6), in the form of external auditors, and by the public authorities acting as 'enablers' (2011: 7). There was evidence of widespread failings in corporate governance over and above the poor risk management and inappropriate remuneration structures also found in banks in other countries. Regling and Watson found that lending guidelines and processes appeared to have been quite widely circumvented and that there were 'very specific and serious breaches of basic governance principles concerning iden-tifiable transactions in specific institutions that went far beyond any question of poor credit assessment' (2010: 35). The Banking Inquiry too attributed the banking crisis to decisions of bank boards, managers, and advisors to pursue risky business practices with a view either to protecting their market share or growing their business and profits.

The aforementioned three expert reports into the Irish crisis in 2010 and 2011 reflected a widespread acknowledgment that the banking system was broken and that, in order to affect the changes necessary to stimulate economic growth, credit would have to be restored and Ireland's image as the 'Wild West of European finance' (O'Toole 2010) transformed. One positive consequence of this introspection and national reflection was that the mistakes made were acknowledged and addressed at an early stage.

PRE-CRISIS BANKING REGULATION
AND SUPERVISION

The Central Bank and Financial Services Authority of Ireland Act, 2003, established the Central Bank of Ireland and Financial Services Authority (CBIFSA) in the form of two separate entities: a monetary authority carrying out functions related to the European System of Central Banks and a regula-tory authority entitled the Irish Financial Services Regulatory Authority (IFSRA) responsible for the supervision of financial services firms. Honohan has suggested that 'the division of responsibilities between the Governor, the CBFSAI and IFSRA was novel and contained the hazard of ambiguous lines of responsibility especially in the event of a systemic crisis' (2010: 36). It also encouraged the establishment of institutional silos, leading to poor coordination and communication between economists and supervisors.

An issue even more problematic than the flawed structure of regulation was the manner in which supervision was implemented in practice (Regling and Watson 2010: 36). Like many other jurisdictions at the time (Black 2010), the Irish regulatory regime was founded on 'principles-based regulation'. This phrase is generally understood as referring to a reliance on high-level, broadly stated rules or principles as a means of setting conduct of business standards for regulated entities, thus eschewing more detailed prescriptive rules. The attraction of such an approach was that it promised to provide greater flexibility to the regulated entities whilst promoting a high ethical standard of behaviour. IFSRA's regulatory approach was not to be prescriptive in terms of product design, pricing, and the specific risk decisions of regulated firms but to trust each firm to determine its own governance structure and control system (Honohan 2010: 44). Supervisors focused on verifying these structures and systems rather than making their own independent assessment of risk. The difficulty with this system of supervision is that it depends very much on the competence and probity of the directors and managers of the regulated entities. The aforementioned weaknesses in the Irish governance system left the Irish institutions particularly exposed in this regard. A further problem identified by Honohan, which was perhaps not so commonplace in other countries, was that the philosophy of trust led to 'the emergence of a somewhat diffident attitude on the part of the regulators so far as challenging the decisions of firms was concerned' (2010: 44). Reflecting one aspect of regulatory capture, this created what was described as a 'very accommodating' supervisory approach (Regling and Watson 2010: 38). This was compounded by an unduly hierarchical CBFSAI culture, discouraging challenge. One significant consequence of this was that quantitative assessment was neglected and insufficient focus was placed on ensuring that banks' capital could meet their property-related risks (Honohan 2010: 16).

Honohan also described unwillingness on the part of the CBFSAI to acknowledge the real risk of a looming crisis and to pre-empt it. This was attributed in part to a fear that 'rocking the boat' would lead to a potential adverse public reaction (Honohan 2010: 16). This fear may have been accentuated by the fact that section 5A(1)(b) of the Central Bank Act 1942 as amended, set out as one of the CBIFSA's statutory duties as the duty 'to promote the development within the State of the financial services industry (but in such a way as not to affect the objective of the Bank in contributing to the stability of the State's financial system)'. Despite the bracketed caveat, this encouragement to push the 'green jersey agenda' was unhelpful and clearly created a potential conflict with CBIFSA's financial stability objective. The Banking Inquiry strongly criticized regulators for underestimating and not responding fully to the systemic risk.

THE PRISM MODEL

A significant and innovative regulatory response was envisaged to address the problems identified. In July 2010, the Central Bank Reform Act, 2010 ('the 2010 Act'), established the Central Bank of Ireland as a new single unitary body, ensuring that the central banking and financial regulation roles are integrated and coordinated. The Central Bank is charged under this Act with ensuring inter alia Eurosystem effectiveness, financial stability, proper and effective regulation of the financial institutions and markets, independent high-quality economic analysis and markets, consumer protection, and the resolution of financial difficulties in credit institutions. It is no longer required to promote the financial services industry and so this potential conflict of interest is eliminated. The 2010 Act also serves to enhance the system of regulatory control and to confer additional powers on the Central Bank, as discussed in the paragraphs below.

Even before the 2010 Act, the approach to supervisory engagement with the banks had fundamentally changed. Since the commencement of the blanket deposit guarantee, site inspections had increased, there was a greater focus on the quality of governance structure, and regulatory resources were augmented. In June 2010, a new strategy on banking supervision in Ireland was announced, which articulated these changes and marked a departure from the principles-based regulatory approach. It involved a broadening of the approach to financial stability and changes to supervisory structures, supervisory culture and approach, corporate governance, and international supervisory cooperation. Although this strategy, like its predecessor, was described as 'outcome focused', it was envisaged as a more systematic risk framework which would serve as 'the engine of [the Central Bank's] supervisory strategy' (Brady 2010) and would be 'challenging, and where necessary, intrusive' (Central Bank 2010). Matthew Elderfield, the then head of Financial Regulation, explained:

> I am asking our supervisors to ask firms difficult questions, to be sceptical, to challenge established truths and to not necessarily take the first answer they are given. I wish them to be assertive...I will support our supervisors in being robust where they need to be robust in the face of obfuscation. (2011b)

The terms 'difficult', 'sceptical', 'challenge', and 'robust' are in stark contrast to earlier descriptions of the previous regime as 'trusting', 'diffident', and 'accommodating'.

In 2011, the Central Bank introduced its new model the Probability Risk and Impact System (PRISM). The title refers both to the supervisory tool introduced to make the risk assessments and also to the software application employed. The innovative model involves a number of quantitative impact metrics which allows the Central Bank to attribute an empirically driven score to each financial firm it supervises, which approximates to the ability of the firm to negatively impact financial stability and consumer welfare if it experienced problems, and also the probability of such problems arising. The objective of PRISM is not only to facilitate the adoption by supervisors of a consistent way of thinking about risk across all supervised firms but also to enable the Central Bank to allocate scarce supervisory resources appropriately. Under PRISM, the most significant firms which are capable of having the greatest impact on financial stability and consumer welfare receive a high level of supervision with structured engagement plans, leading to early interventions to mitigate potential risks. Risk mitigants include internal controls, organizational changes, ownership structures, and access to capital. Regulated firms which have the lowest potential adverse impact are supervised reactively and through thematic assessments. A further benefit of the PRISM tool is that it allows the Central Bank to identify patterns emerging across the different sectors within financial services more easily and more quickly. This is crucial in light of the fact that the apparent failure by the CBFSAI to grasp the scale of the potential exposure of the banks in the Irish market was a major contributor to the crisis (Honohan 2010: 9). The Central Bank has emphasized that the ultimate goal is not the prevention of failure:

> Firms will and must be allowed to fail in a functioning market economy—the direct costs of staffing the Central Bank to guarantee absolutely no failures ever would be prohibitive. Because economic dynamism and growth in the economy call for a degree of risk taking, the indirect damage to the economy that such a style of regulation would cause would be greater still. What PRISM does is to focus attention on the firms with the highest impact, making it materially less likely that they will fail in a disorderly fashion. (Central Bank 2016b: 2)

In November 2014, following a comprehensive EU-wide assessment of the credit institutions that were likely to fall under direct European Central Bank (ECB) supervision, the SSM came into operation. The SSM Council Regulation (EU) No 1024/2013 and SSM Framework Regulation (EU) No 468/2014 (insofar as was necessary) have been implemented further by the European Union (Single Supervisory Mechanism) Regulations 2014. The SSM, one of the twin pillars of banking union, involves the prudential supervision of all credit institutions in participating member states, including Ireland. Its primary objectives are to ensure the soundness of the European banking system; to increase financial integration and stability; and to ensure consistent supervision. Like the PRISM system, the supervisory practices of the SSM are proportionate to the systemic importance and risk profile of the credit institutions under supervision. The ECB now directly supervises the four Irish institutions classified by the ECB as 'significant', namely Bank of Ireland (BOI), Allied Irish Banks (AIB), Permanent TSB, and Ulster Bank, together with about 1,200 other credit institutions in the Eurozone, covering close to

85 per cent of total banking assets. Supervision is carried out by joint supervisory teams led by the ECB but comprising staff from the ECB and the national competent authorities. In practice, most of the supervision is carried out in the member states where the institutions are located, but the substantive decisions are made in ECB headquarters in Frankfurt. The Central Bank remains responsible for the supervision of activities defined in the Regulation underpinning the SSM as 'non-core', which includes anti-money laundering and consumer protection. For the 3,500 or so smaller institutions in the EU described as 'less significant supervised entities', supervisory responsibility has remained with the national competent authorities. Supervision for all the institutions is conducted in accordance with European law, national law as applied by the Central Bank, European Banking Authority technical standards, the European Banking Authority's European Supervisory Handbook, and harmonized standards and processes developed by the SSM. The overall approach to supervision has continued to be risk-based and to take into account both the impact and likelihood of an institution failing (Central Bank 2015a). In response to the establishment of the SSM, the Central Bank also created a three-divisional supervisory function with responsibility for: banking supervision; onsite inspections supervision; and banking supervision analytics.

The Credit Institutions (Stabilisation) Act 2010 was introduced with the express objective of giving the Minister for Finance the necessary powers to effect the restructuring and stabilization of the banking sector that the government committed to in the National Recovery Plan (NRP) 2011–14. It provided for: direction orders requiring institutions to take or refrain from taking any action in support of the government's banking strategy; transfer orders relating to institutions' assets and liabilities to facilitate the restructuring of the banking sector; and, under certain conditions, subordinated liabilities orders to achieve appropriate burden-sharing by subordinated creditors in institutions which have received state support.

An effective supervisory system must operate in conjunction with an effective resolution system for failing institutions. The Troika Programme identified the need for a permanent resolution regime (2010: para.14) and this was subsequently introduced in the form of the Central Bank and Credit Institutions (Resolution) Act 2011 ('the 2011 Act'), which empowers the Central Bank to resolve authorized credit institutions. It provided for the establishment of the Credit Institutions Resolution Fund, financed both by the institutions and the Minister for Finance, to fund the resolution of financially unstable credit institutions. The 2011 Act empowers the Central Bank to establish a 'bridge bank' to hold assets and liabilities transferred from a distressed institution, to seek a High Court transfer order to compel a distressed credit institution to transfer its assets and liabilities to another entity, to present a petition to wind up a credit institution, and to appoint a special manager to take over its management and operate it within defined terms. The fund has been used for four resolution cases concerning credit unions, constituting three transfers of business to other institutions and one winding-up order. The resolution component of banking union, the EU Bank Recovery and Resolution Directive 2014/59 ('BRRD'), was implemented by means of the European Union (Bank Recovery and Resolution) Regulations 2015 ('2015 Regulations') and applies to all banks licensed to operate in Ireland. Since the introduction of BRRD, all member states of the EU have to apply a single rulebook for the resolution of banks and large investment firms. If an institution subject to the SSM faces serious difficulties, its resolution will be managed through the Single Resolution Mechanism and resolution decisions will be made by the Single Resolution Board. The BRRD and the 2015 Regulations superseded the 2011 Act for banks and required the establishment of the Bank and Investment Firm Resolution Fund. The 2011 Act will continue to apply only to credit unions.

CORPORATE GOVERNANCE REFORM

Honohan identified three specific areas in the lead-up to the crisis where IFSRA failed to implement sufficiently robust requirements to underpin its supervisory approach. These were: corporate governance; fitness and probity; and directors' compliance statements. Changes to the legal rules in all three of these areas have been introduced since then. These changes reflect the fact that boards of directors and senior management are acknowledged to be 'the first line of defence in ensuring that a bank is well managed, with systems and controls, appropriate to the nature, scale, complexity and risk of its operations' (Elderfield 2011a); weaknesses in these areas, as we have seen, may be extremely costly.

Prior to the commencement of the Troika Programme in 2010, the Central Bank drafted and introduced its own *Corporate Governance Code for Credit Institutions and Insurance Undertakings* in 2010. The Code was revised, renamed as *Corporate Governance Requirements* ('Requirements') and divided into two separate documents for credit institutions and insurance undertakings in 2015. Unlike the vast majority of corporate governance codes across the world which are applied on a 'comply or explain' basis, the Requirements, like the Code before it, have statutory effect. The decision to adopt a higher governance standard here was explained by Matthew Elderfield on the basis that 'Ireland has suffered more than most countries in the financial crisis and now needs to get to grips with the home grown elements of that crisis' (2010). The Requirements seeks to ensure that the boards of banks and insurance companies are composed of suitably qualified and committed individuals who are in a position to advise, monitor, and challenge executive management on key issues such as strategy, internal controls, risk management, and remuneration. Mandatory rules prescribe the role and composition of the board and its committees. More onerous requirements are imposed on high-impact-designated institutions and credit institutions which are deemed significant for the purposes of the Capital Requirements Directive 2013/36/EU. The Central Bank monitors adherence to the Requirements through ongoing supervision of the institutions and it also requires each institution to submit an annual compliance statement and to alert it promptly if it becomes aware of a material deviation from the Requirements during the year, advising of the background and the remedial action it proposes to take. One of the advantages of a statutory code over a self-regulatory one is that formal sanctions are available for breaches. Contraventions of the Requirements may lead to the imposition of administrative sanctions, prosecutions, the refusal to appoint a proposed director to any pre- approval controlled function, or the suspension, removal, or prohibition of an individual from carrying out a controlled function, as described in the next paragraph.

Pursuant to the Central Bank Reform Act 2010, the Central Bank introduced a statutory fitness and probity regime for directors and senior management of financial institutions, including credit institutions, in 2011, and the Central Bank issued a Code setting out the relevant standards of fitness and probity. This Code was amended in 2014. The regime involves the classification of a number of senior positions as controlled functions or pre-approval controlled functions, the latter requiring the prior approval of the Central Bank before an individual can be appointed. Section 2.1 of the Code requires that the Central Bank provides that an individual performing a pre-approval controlled function or a controlled function is required to be: competent and capable; honest, ethical, and to act with integrity; and financially sound. In relation to the first criteria, the Central Bank advises that 'the person shall have the qualifications, experience, competence and capacity appropriate to the relevant function' (2014: 3.1). This specifically requires the person to have 'a clear and comprehensive understanding of the regulatory and legal environment appropriate to the relevant function' (2014: 3.2(e)). Defining the rather general standard of ethics and integrity is always going to be difficult, and the examples provided by the Central Bank refer to the absence of a restriction or disqualification order, a complaint to the Financial Services Ombudsman, disciplinary proceedings, a dismissal for breach of trust, and so on. The Central Bank has a range of powers available to it under Part 3 of the Central Bank Reform Act 2010 to investigate, suspend, or prohibit individuals from pre-approval controlled functions and controlled functions in order to ensure that those entering the industry are fit and proper. Since November 2014, the ECB has had exclusive competence for the fitness and probity assessments of the boards of significant credit institutions and all credit institutions applying for authorization. These assessments are carried out on the basis of the provisions of the Capital Requirements Directive 2013/36/EU in accordance with the suitability assessment guidelines produced by the EBA. Article 91(1) of Directive 2013/36/EU requires member states to ensure that board members will 'at all times be of sufficiently good repute and possess sufficient knowledge, skills and experience to perform their duties'.

Although the Companies (Auditing and Accounting) Act 2003 introduced the concept of a mandatory wide-ranging directors' compliance statement, the relevant section was never commenced. Following a recommendation of the Company Law Reform Group, published in 2005, the Companies Act 2014 required directors of public limited companies and other companies meeting certain size thresholds to make a statement in their Directors' Report acknowledging their responsibility for securing the company's compliance with specified relevant obligations under companies and tax legislation. They are also required to set out the company's policies in respect of its compliance with these obligations, to confirm that the company has appropriate arrangements or structures in place to provide a reasonable assurance of material compliance, and to review these arrangement and structures annually. In an effort to make compliance more practical, the Companies Act 2014 specifically provides that the arrangements can include reliance on the advice of a suitably qualified employee or service provider.

ENFORCEMENT

Regulators have been criticized not only for failing to supervise and enforce the rules that did exist but also for not ensuring that an appropriate enforcement framework was in place. The Banking Inquiry concluded that the Financial Regulator had sufficient powers to deliver their prudential supervision of the banking sector in a more intrusive manner and that it could have imposed conditions on banking licences, revoked or suspended licences, and, after late 2005, imposed administrative sanctions for breaches, including breaches of lending limits (Joint Committee of Inquiry into the Banking Crisis 2016: 158). However, the excessively deferential regulatory approach adopted by IFSRA, together with its apparently limited appetite for legal challenge, led to a failure to move 'decisively and effectively enough against banks with governance issues' (Central Bank 2010: 9).

Although a persistent pattern of breaches of regulations in certain credit institutions occurred (Honohan 2010: 72), no administrative sanctions were imposed before 2008 on a credit institution in relation to a prudential matter. One egregious case made public involved a detailed report by an IFSRA supervisor recommending 'tough action' in response to 'severe governance deficiencies' and 'failings at every level' in a particular bank (Honohan 2010: 73). Instead, eight years of correspondence ensued in a vain endeavour to correct the problem. Honohan noted that this 'protracted engagement approach to dealing with a series of serious issues was by no means atypical' (2010: 73). He concluded that 'the seeming lack of a credible threat of action by the Financial Regulator reduced the urgency of dealing with issues (by all parties)' (2010: 74).

As has been evidenced from the earlier examination of reform in the area of corporate governance, a substantial number of regulations have been introduced since the crisis in order to incentivize and encourage appropriate behaviour. These are part of the Central Bank's commitment to operate a risk-based supervisory model of regulation 'underpinned by a credible threat of enforcement'. The most important change in this context has been the Central Bank (Supervision and Enforcement) Act 2013, which provides enhanced powers under its administrative sanctions regime, including increased financial penalties. The quantum of the penalties which may be levied against individuals and regulated entities is doubled to €1 million and €10 million respectively, and it may be based now on the turnover of the regulated entity. The Central Bank was given stronger powers in relation to investigations, including the very valuable power to require the production of a skilled person's report into possible contraventions. It was also authorized to give a direction to allow it recover the costs of an investigation and to require a regulated entity to make appropriate redress to customers that have suffered or will suffer loss as a result of its widespread or regular defaults. It was described by the Minister for Finance as 'not a piece of crisis legislation' but one which provides a long-term regulatory framework for supervision and enforcement.

As earlier experience indicates, strong enforcement depends not only on the availability of enforcement tools but also on the readiness of the regulator to employ them. In this respect too, there has been a marked change in approach. In early 2010, the Enforcement Directorate was established as a separate and distinct directorate with an overarching objective of safeguarding stability and protecting consumers. The Central Bank acknowledged that a failure to establish such an independent entity in the past suggested 'the lack of use and lack of value placed on the role of enforcement as a necessary component of an efficient and effective regulatory framework' (Rowland 2014). A new enforcement strategy was published in 2010, and between 2010 and 2014 there were sixty-two administrative sanctions procedure cases against regulated entities for breaches of prudential and consumer obligations arising from a mix of pre-defined themes and reactive actions. These cases led to the imposition of approximately €27.5 million in monetary sanctions and a number of disqualifications (Rowland 2014). All these administrative sanctions cases settled, making this an efficient means of resolving disputes. Public disclosure of the outcomes brings a reputational cost to the firm sanctioned in addition to the fine levied. It also makes firms, individual managers, and regulators more accountable. The Central Bank correctly anticipated that a referral of two administrative sanction procedure cases to inquiry stage would lead to legal challenge, and its acceptance that this is 'an unavoidable part of the refining and maturing of the procedure'(Rowland 2014) is to be welcomed. The contrast between this approach and the timid and reluctant pre-crisis approach is stark.

The allocation of enforcement and sanctioning powers between the ECB and the Central Bank under the SSM is dependent on the nature of the alleged contravention, the person responsible, and the measure to be adopted. In the case of significant institutions, the ECB may adopt enforcement measures in respect of breaches of relevant directly applicable EU law. For less significant institutions, the ECB may pursue breaches of ECB regulations or decisions that impose obligations on such institutions vis-à-vis the ECB. It may also request the Central Bank make use of its enforcement powers under national law or open proceedings as a means of ensuring that appropriate penalties are available. It may do this, for example, in the case of penalties to be imposed on natural persons, non-pecuniary penalties, or breaches of Irish law transposing relevant EU directives.

CONCLUSION

The legal response to the crisis in Ireland has been strong and sustained. Attempts were made at an early stage to address the significant problems identified with the previous system of bank regulation and supervision. Lessons seem to have been learned and innovative solutions introduced and, in many cases, reviewed and developed. Rather than relying on the EU to drive legal change, the Central Bank's PRISM model and its fitness and probity regime saw Ireland provide leadership in the regulatory field. Honohan has described the smooth transition of the prudential aspects of Ireland's supervision of banks to the SSM as a testament to the credibility of the transformation that was achieved in the Central Bank in regulatory and supervisory staffing, methodology, and culture in the years from 2009 to 2013 (2015: 9).

Banking union too has brought its own challenges in terms of application and coordination. At this early stage, the SSM is still bedding down and although the initial signs are positive, the scale of the task involved in ensuring a consistent and effective system of regulation should not be underestimated. There has been some complaint in Ireland about what is seen as an over-reaction to the crisis and the introduction of excessive regulation. A not infrequent observation is that current participants in the financial services industry are being forced in this way to 'pay for the mistakes of the bankers'. This, it is submitted, is a skewed view of the reforms described in this chapter and it is more correct to view them as the product of efforts to learn from the mistakes of the bankers. Regulation should not be resisted as an inhibitor to growth and development but rather as a stimulant to them.

As this chapter indicates, the majority of the initiatives discussed were already underway by the time the Troika Programme was published. Chalking up these reforms as successful outcomes of the Troika is thus open to challenge. It is clear, however, that the follow-through of many of the actions planned were updated to reflect the FMP (Central Bank 2016a: 323). The latter facilitated the reorganization of the banking sector and the recapitalization of the main banks and was itself described by Kevin Cardiff, former secretary general at the Department of Finance, as 'a key turning point in the rescue of the Irish banking system' (Joint Committee of Inquiry into the Banking Crisis 2016: 301).

A related issue is the extent to which the reforms in banking regulation and corporate governance discussed in this chapter contributed to economic recovery. The correlation is clear but proving causation is always more difficult. It might be argued that the fact the remaining banks have been able to access the capital markets is evidence of market confidence in their governance structures and the quality of their supervision. However, our recent experience has taught us the fallibility of the markets. A further measure of success might be the fact that there has been no disorderly failure of an Irish financial service provider under the Central Bank's prudential supervision and the aggregate transitional total capital ratio of the banks active in the Irish retail sector has improved (Central Bank 2016c: 17). The Central Bank has indicated that:

> significant progress has been made by Bank supervisors identifying areas of risk in regulated firms and conclusively mitigating these areas of risk. Bank supervisors have now conducted inspections and assessed the risks of Higher Impact regulated firms over multiple assessment cycles and this has allowed supervisors to progressively focus on new areas of weakness which were of a lower priority in previous years. Significant changes are apparent in the culture and compliance of firms across a broad range of areas including prudential requirements, corporate governance and conduct of business. (Central Bank 2015b: 9)

The ECB Comprehensive Assessment has concluded and is continuing to drive the continued resolution of financial difficulties. In addition, the IMF upon completion of its 2016 Financial Sector Assessment Program Mission to Ireland reported that the authorities have been 'effective and vigorous in strengthening prudential regulation and supervision' (IMF 2016). However, while domestic banks have returned to profitability, the sector remains weak and non-performing loans and related provisions remain elevated (Central Bank 2016d: 3). The economic uncertainty which follows the UK vote in favour of Brexit will place significant pressure on this exposed sector.

The Central Bank has acknowledged that, despite a new and more robust regulatory infrastructure, no amount of regulation, supervision, or enforcement can prevent breaches or 'change behaviours on their own' (Rowland 2014). It has thus added its voice to calls for a real and substantive industry-wide cultural change. While the role of corporate culture in organizations has been increasingly recognized as central to good governance, defining what exactly this concept means, reshaping those institutions, and creating the desired ethos, remains, for the moment at least, a work in progress.

NOTE

The views set out in this chapter are the views of the author and do not represent the views of any other person or body.

REFERENCES

Black, J. 2010. 'The Rise, Fall and Fate of Principles Based Regulation', Working Paper No. 17/2010. London: LSE Legal Studies.

Brady, P. 2010. 'Central Bank Publishes New Strategic Approach to Banking Supervision', Press Release, 21 June. Available at: <http://www.centralbank.ie/press-area/press-releases/Pages/CentralBankPublishesnewStrategicapproach.aspx> (accessed 27 August 2015).

Carney, M. 2014. 'Financial Reforms: Completing the Job and Looking Ahead', Letter to G20 Leaders, Financial Stability Board, 7 November.

Central Bank. 2010. *Banking Supervision: Our New Approach*. Available at: <http://www.centralbank.ie/publications/Documents/Banking%20Supervision%20-%20Our%20New%20Approach.pdf> (accessed 1 March 2016).

Central Bank. 2011. *Financial Measures Programme*. Available at: <https://www.centralbank.ie/regulation/industry-sectors/credit-institutions/Pages/FinancialMeasures Programme.aspx> (accessed 1 March 2016).

Central Bank. 2014. *Fitness and Probity Standards (Code issued under Section 50 of the Central Bank Reform Act 2010)*. Available at: <http://www.centralbank.ie/regulation/processes/fandp/serviceproviders/Documents/Fitness%20and%20Probity%20 Standards%202014.pdf> (accessed 27 August 2015).

Central Bank. 2015a. 'Supervision Process for Credit Institutions'. Available at: <http://www.centralbank.ie/regulation/industry-sectors/credit-institutions/Pages/supervision.aspx> (accessed 22 March 2016).

Central Bank. 2015b. *The Central Bank's Annual Performance Statement (Financial Regulation) 2014–2015*. Available at <https://www.centralbank.ie/press-area/press-

releases/Documents/Annual%20Performance%20Statement%202014.pdf> (accessed 23 June 2016).

Central Bank. 2016a. 'Core Books 8 and 12'. In *Report of the Joint Committee of Inquiry into the Banking Crisis*, vol. 3. Available at: <https://inquiries.oireachtas.ie/ banking/hearings-evidence/core-documents/> (accessed 22 March 2016).

Central Bank. 2016b. *PRISM Explained*. Available at <http://www.centralbank.ie/ regulation/processes/prism/Documents/PRISM%20Explained%20Feb%202016.pdf> (accessed 22 March 2016).

Central Bank. 2016c. *Central Bank's Annual Performance Statement (Financial Regulation) 2015–2016*. Available at <http://www.centralbank.ie/publications/ Documents/Annual%20Performance%20Statement%20(Financial%20Regulation)% 202015-2016.pdf> (accessed 20 June 2016).

Central Bank. 2016d. *Macro Financial Review H1 2016*. Available at: <https://www. centralbank.ie/publications/Pages/MacroFinancialReviews.aspx> (accessed 23 June 2016).

Clarke, B. and Hardiman, N. 2012. 'Crisis in the Irish Banking System', UCD Geary Institute Discussion Paper Series WP2012/03. Available at: <http://ssrn.com/ abstract=2008302> (accessed 27 August 2015).

Company Law Reform Group. 2005. *Report on Directors' Compliance Statement*. Available at: <http://www.clrg.org/publications/clrg-report-on-directors-compliance. pdf> (accessed 20 June 2016).

EC (European Commission). 2015a. *Staff Working Document: Economic Analysis*, SWD 183 final. Available at: <http://ec.europa.eu/finance/capital-markets-union/ docs/building-cmu-economic-analysis_en.pdf> (accessed 22 March 2016).

EC (European Commission). 2015b. *Call for Evidence: EU Regulatory Framework for Financial Services*. Available at: <http://ec.europa.eu/finance/consultations/2015/ financial-regulatory-framework-review/docs/consultation-document_en.pdf> (accessed 22 March 2016).

Elderfield, M. 2010. 'The Regulation Agenda: Update on Bank Recapitalisation and New Corporate Governance Requirements'. Presentation to the Association of Compliance Officers in Ireland, 22 November. Available at: <http://www.financial regulator.ie/press-area/speeches/Pages/AddressbyMatthewElderfield,HeadofFinancial RegulationtotheAssociationofComplianceOfficersinIreland-22November2010.aspx> (accessed 27 August 2015).

Elderfield, M. 2011a. 'Raising Standards in Banking'. Presentation to the Foresight Business Group, Trinity College Dublin, 22 March. Available at: <http://www. centralbank.ie/press-area/speeches%5CPages%5CAddressbyHeadofFinancialRegulation, MatthewElderfieldtoForesightBusinessGroupMarch222011.aspx> (accessed 20 June 2016).

Elderfield, M. 2011b. 'Risk Based Supervision in Ireland'. Presentation to Association of Chartered Certified Accountants, Dublin, 1 December. Available at: <http://www. bis.org/review/r111202e.pdf> (accessed 27 August 2015).

Financial Crisis Inquiry. 2011. *Commission Financial Crisis Inquiry Report*. Available at: <http://fcic.law.stanford.edu/report/> (accessed 27 August 2015).

Honohan, P. 2010. *The Irish Banking Crisis: Regulatory and Financial Stability Policy 2003–2008, a Report to the Minister for Finance from the Governor of the Central Bank*. Dublin: The Central Bank.

Honohan, P. 2015. *Statement by Patrick Honohan to the Banking Inquiry*. Available at: <https://inquiries.oireachtas.ie/banking/wp-content/uploads/2015/06/25062015-Opening-Statement-Patrick-Honohan.pdf> (accessed 27 August 2015).

IMF (International Monetary Fund). 2016. *Press Release: IMF Staff Completes 2016 Financial Sector Assessment Program (FSAP) Mission to Ireland*. Available at <https://www.imf.org/external/np/sec/pr/2016/pr16113.htm> (accessed 22 June 2016).

Joint Committee of Inquiry into the Banking Crisis. 2016. *Report of the Joint Committee of Inquiry into the Banking Crisis*. Available at: <https://inquiries.oireachtas.ie/banking/volume-1-report/> (accessed 1 March 2016).

Lagarde, C. 2013. 'Ireland and the European Union: Shared Determination, Shared Destiny'. Presentation, Dublin Castle, 8 March. Available at: <http://www.imf.org/external/np/speeches/2013/030813.htm> (accessed 22 March 2016).

Nyberg, P. 2011. *Misjudging Risk: Causes of the Systemic Banking Crisis in Ireland*. Reports of the Commission on Investigation into the Banking Sector. Available at: <http://www.bankinginquiry.gov.ie/Documents/Misjuding%20Risk%20-%20Causes%20of%20the%20Systemic%20Banking%20Crisis%20in%20Ireland.pdf> (accessed 27 August 2015).

O'Toole, F. 2010. *Ship of Fools: How Stupidity and Corruption Sank the Celtic Tiger*. London: Faber and Faber.

Regling, K. and Watson, M. 2010. *A Preliminary Report on the Sources of Ireland's Banking Crisis*. Dublin: Government Publications Office.

Rowland, D. 2014. 'Enforcement at the Central Bank of Ireland'. Presentation at Compliance Ireland Seminar, 12 December. Available at: <https://www.centralbank.ie/press-area/speeches/Pages/RemarkspreparedbyDirectorofEnforcementDervilleRowlandfortheComplianceIrelandSeminar.aspx> (accessed 22 March 2016).

7

Consumption

Marius C. Claudy, Andrew Keating, and Andrea Prothero

INTRODUCTION

The extent to which the recession affected Irish consumers across all social strata and socioeconomic backgrounds took most people by surprise. While the effects of the recession are well documented on the macro-level, there has been little exploration about the impact the downturn has had on consumers and consumption practices. This chapter addresses this theme, and aims to shed light on how Irish consumers adjusted to this new austere reality. In particular, the chapter summarizes key consumer indicators that reflect changes in spending and consumption habits during the years of recession and subsequent recovery. While much has been written on impoverished consumers and the strategies people have utilized to cope with poverty (Hamilton 2009; Hill 2001; Hill and Stamey 1990), little is understood about how (previously affluent) consumers adjust their consumption practices when their disposable income is suddenly reduced. Further, this chapter discusses whether the observed changes in consumption patterns and consumer values brought about by the recession are likely to continue during the recovery and beyond. The chapter draws on national statistics, attitudinal survey data, and in-depth qualitative interviews to provide insight into how people adjusted their consumption and spending habits.

CONSUMPTION: THE RECESSION AND RECOVERY

During the so-called 'Celtic Tiger Years' (1994–2007) the Irish economy had grown at an average annual rate of 6 per cent, while unemployment fell from 14 per cent in 1994 to 4.7 per cent in 2007. During the same period, the average disposable income increased by 132 per cent, while poverty levels dropped from 14.5 per cent to 5.1 per cent of the population (CSO 2014). As a result, consumption during the Celtic Tiger years increased dramatically.

In 2008, the collapse of the Irish economy led to a drastic reversal of these trends. A study conducted by the National Economic and Social Council (NESC 2014) showed that most households experienced a drop in wealth and/or income, while data from the Central Statistics Office (CSO 2014) suggests average disposable income fell by about 16 per cent between 2007 and 2012. These figures closely coincide with a drop in consumer spending. Specifically, data from the quarterly consumer market monitor (Lambkin 2016) shows that, for the same period, personal spending declined by almost 13 per cent in current terms (Figure 7.1).

According to the CSO, in 2011, 79 per cent of Irish households cut back their spending (CSO 2012). In particular, these cutbacks happened mainly in areas such as clothing and footwear (64 per cent), socializing (57 per cent), groceries (56 per cent), and/or holidays abroad (48 per cent). Moreover, people made cutbacks in areas such as health insurance (15 per cent) and pension contributions (11 per cent). The decrease in spending is most notable in the Irish Retail Sales Index (Figure 7.2), which shows a 13 per cent decline in volume and 17 per cent decline in value between 2007 and 2012.

A detailed breakdown of retail sales shows that some sectors were affected more than others. In line with the CSO data, sectoral retail figures (Lambkin 2016) show that the value of clothing and footwear sales declined by 29 per cent between 2007 and 2013. Interestingly, however, the volume of sales only declined by about 6.5 per cent, suggesting that people sought out value, and bought more products on discounts and promotions. Likewise, over half of Irish consumers stated they had reduced spending on socializing, which is most notable in the figures for Ireland's bar trade. For the recession years,

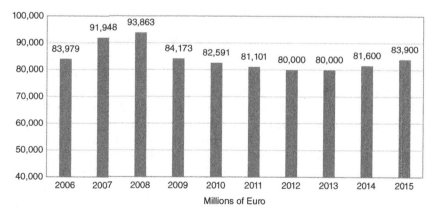

Figure 7.1. Personal spending on goods and services in Ireland, 2006–15

Source: Lambkin, M. 2016. Consumer Market Monitor. Quarterly Report, Quarter 4, 2015. Ed. Dublin: University College Dublin & Irish Marketing Institute.

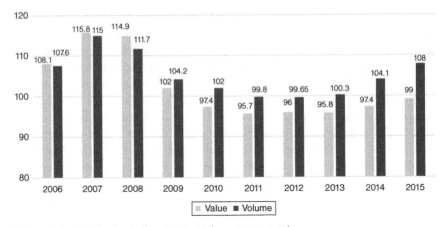

Figure 7.2. Retail sales index: 2006–15 (Base 2005=100)

Source: Lambkin, M. 2016. Consumer Market Monitor. Quarterly Report, Quarter 4, 2015. Ed. Dublin: University College Dublin & Irish Marketing Institute.

volume sales of bars decreased by 33 per cent, while the value of sales dropped by over 30 per cent. Food sales were affected, but not as drastically as some other areas. According to Lambkin (2015: 26), 'food sales increased steadily between 2005 and 2008 along with most other retail categories, increasing by 16 per cent in volume, an average annual growth rate of 5.3%'. However, sales only dropped by just under 3 per cent in both volume and value between 2007 and the end of 2012. Most notably, and not surprisingly, Irish consumers cut spending on big-ticket items such as holidays and private cars. For example, the overall number of outbound holiday trips made by Irish residents declined by 31 per cent between 2007 and 2012, while the average estimated spending per trip decreased by over 42 per cent during the same period (CSO 2015a). Likewise, sales of new private cars, which increased dramatically during the Celtic Tiger era, declined by more than 60 per cent.

While the emergence of the recession and the resulting rise in unemployment and fall in average disposable income would explain this dramatic fall in spending, it has been observed that the 'decline in consumer spending is more pronounced than can be explained by changes in current income' alone (NSDO 2009: 13). For example, data from the CSO (2015b) show that the level of net personal saving in Ireland increased from 0 per cent of personal income in 2007 to 9 per cent in 2012. Importantly, the net savings ratio has remained high, indicating that consumers have been concerned to restore their finances, and repay loans and credit card debts (Lambkin 2016). However, the most significant factor is the sharp decline in consumer confidence, which reached an all-time low in 2008 (Figure 7.3), and remained low throughout the International Monetary Fund (IMF)/European Union (EU) bailout in 2010, and the Eurozone crisis of 2011–12 (Lambkin 2016). The Consumer Confidence Indicator reflects (changes in) consumers' assessment

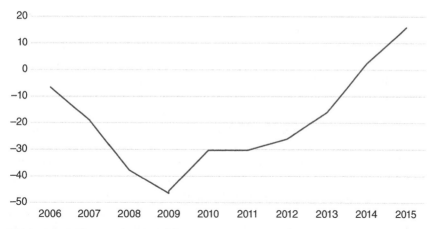

Figure 7.3. Irish consumer confidence, 2006–15

Source: Lambkin, M. 2016. Consumer Market Monitor. Quarterly Report, Quarter 4, 2015. Ed. Dublin: University College Dublin & Irish Marketing Institute.

of their: (i) personal financial situation; (ii) general economic situation; (iii) unemployment situation; and (iv) personal savings, over the next twelve months.[1] Importantly, the steep drop in consumer confidence was directly attributable to the economic collapse, the subsequent rise in unemployment, and the corresponding decrease in income, including pensions. Further, the prospect of future tax increases and/or earnings reductions could have had a significant impact on consumers' confidence (NESC 2009).

While most households made significant cutbacks in spending, estimates suggest that, in the case of 38 per cent of households, expenditure exceeded disposable income during the recession years (NESC 2014). Further, the same study suggests that 23 per cent of Irish households were in arrears with at least one bill or loan. While mortgage arrears of more than ninety days were practically zero in 2004, they stood at 12 per cent for principal private dwellings in 2012. People most likely to be in mortgage arrears included those who had lost their jobs, took out mortgages in the 2000s, and/or younger mortgage holders (NESC 2014).

Further, the proportion of people in consistent poverty increased from 4.2 per cent in 2008 to 7.7 per cent in 2012. The number of people who were deprived (i.e. lacking at least two basic necessities) increased from 11.8 per cent in 2007 to 26.9 per cent in 2012 (CSO 2014). According to the same study, the types of deprivation experienced most commonly related to consumers' inability to replace worn-out furniture (24.5 per cent), afford a morning/

---

[1] More details on the Consumer Confidence Indicator and how it is constructed can be found here: <http://ec.europa.eu/economy_finance/db_indicators/surveys/documents/bcs_user_guide_en.pdf>.

afternoon/evening out (23.3 per cent), or to have family/friends over for a meal/drink (16.1 per cent).

However, it is important to note that the years of recovery (2012–15) have seen a slow reversal of some of these trends. For example, Figure 7.3 illustrates that consumer confidence is higher than at the peak of the Celtic Tiger in 2007, and that consumer spending (Figure 7.1) and retail sales value (Figure 7.2) have increased by 5 and 3 per cent, respectively. While these trends are positive signs for economic recovery, 'much of this reflects "pent up demand" in the economy following a long period of stagnation, and this can be seen most clearly in growing sales of "big ticket" items—homes and home furnishings, new cars, clothing and other consumer durables' (Lambkin 2016: 1). Another indicator that Ireland has not (yet) returned to the spending habits of the Celtic Tiger is the continuing decline in the number of personal credit cards and the value of credit card debt. The number of credit cards in circulation has fallen by 10 per cent since 2012, and over 27 per cent since its peak in 2008 (Central Bank of Ireland 2015). Concurrently, Irish consumers' credit card debt peaked in 2009, and has since fallen by over 38 per cent (Lambkin 2016), suggesting that consumers continue to consume more prudently.

CONSUMERS' EXPERIENCES AND COPING STRATEGIES DURING THE RECESSION

While the statistics provide a detailed profile of the extent to which the recession and subsequent recovery affected spending and consumption, they say very little about how Irish consumers coped with these changes. In industrialized countries, consumption is an activity that enriches people's lives, gives them meaning (Belk 1988), and helps construct their identity (Arnould and Thompson 2005). Consumer research has emphasized that consumption plays an important role during periods of transition, and suggests consumption may help people to cope with and reduce uncertainty (Andreasen 1984; Schouten 1991; Price, Arnould, and Curasi 2000). It is less clear what happens when people transition from a period of personal affluence into one of material deprivation, and by definition, cannot use consumption as a strategy of coping in the same way due to their new circumstances. Research has shown that transitioning into deprivation, or worse into poverty, is often accompanied by a feeling of 'losing control' over a situation (Hill 2001; Baker, Gentry, and Rittenburg 2005), and of people feeling 'trapped, alone, and unable to manoeuvre their way back to their previous consumer lives' (Hill 2001: 375). The literature has identified different coping strategies (Adkins and Ozanne 2005; Baker, Gentry, and Rittenburg 2005) that consumers have availed themselves of in situations of impoverishment and/or deprivation. It is apparent in the Irish case that many consumers were forced to significantly change their spending and consumption habits. The second half of this chapter seeks to shed light on the personal experiences and behavioural changes that Irish consumers used to cope with their changed circumstances. Furthermore, it addresses the question of whether the recession is likely to have altered patterns of consumption in more lasting ways that will prevail beyond economic recovery.

In order to explore how Irish consumers managed the transition from abundance to austerity at a more micro-level, twenty-six people were interviewed between 2012 and 2013. During the in-depth interviews, which lasted on average between sixty and ninety minutes, participants gave detailed accounts of their personal experiences and consumption practices before and during the recession. All had been adversely affected by the recession by, for example, reductions in wealth or income, significant mortgage debt, and/or negative equity. Furthermore, close to half of the participants (twelve) were affected by sustained periods of unemployment and job insecurity. All were Irish citizens who had lived in Ireland throughout the Celtic Tiger years as well as the recession. The participants' age ranged from 28 to 65 years old, and, according to their education and occupation, the majority (twenty-one) could be classified as middle class, while the remaining five were working class. The participants interviewed were drawn from the four provinces of the Republic of Ireland. The majority (sixteen) lived in towns or cities, while ten lived in villages or isolated rural areas.

While all participants had experienced some loss of income and/or wealth, consumers' coping strategies differed significantly. In the following we outline the most commonly mentioned adjustments in consumption and spending practices that occurred during the transition from (relative) prosperity to austerity. When asked about their experiences and feelings towards the Celtic Tiger years, all consumers vividly recalled their personal expenditure and consumption habits during that time. Many remembered and reminisced about unique experiences such as exotic holidays, expensive nights out, and/or the purchase of big-ticket items such as houses, luxury cars, or designer clothing. A common theme was that most participants did not used to worry about the consequences of their consumption habits. As one recalls: 'I didn't care, I had the money . . . it was there for the spending.' However, it needs to be noted that, for many, expenditure and consumption were partly financed by borrowing.

Despite a sense of material excess and indulgence that many interviewees engaged in during the Celtic Tiger era, the majority stated they felt comfortable but not wealthy during that period. Most recalled that they experienced a sense of material security, absence of financial worries, and a feeling of freedom and limitlessness in regard to buying and spending. As one participant recalls, 'I would never have been worried about not being able to pay a bill or not being able to pay my rent. I was never concerned that we didn't have enough to get by on.'

Experiences during the recession provided a stark contrast to consumer spending habits during the Celtic Tiger years. Feelings of security and exuberance were replaced by anxiety and frustration, often accompanied by (involuntary) shifts in consumption practices. One participant explained that 'it's frustrating not having disposable income—the frustration would be lack of job prospects, lack of money in my pocket'. Another voiced similar feelings: 'I'm resigned to sort of existing for the next five years, rather than living, you know. That's probably the sad thing for me.'

Cutting Back and Changes in Shopping Habits

A common theme that emerged was the immediate change in spending habits as a result of reductions in wealth and income. The extent of cutbacks ranged from discontinuing certain consumption practices completely, to reductions in spending, and/or availing of alternatives. Across almost all forms of consumption, participants reported some level of change or modification in overall expenditure, in frequency of consumption, in amounts consumed, and in types of consumption.

Cutbacks in spending ranged from essential items such as food or utility bills, to discretionary/luxury items like holidays or beauty products. In regard to the former, for most participants one of the first and most lasting changes in consumption habits occurred in grocery shopping. Almost all interviewed consumers mentioned low-cost multiples (Lidl and Aldi), and described how they had partially or fully transferred their shopping to discounters. For example, one participant declared that 'we do all our shopping in Aldi now. Without them we'd be starving because you couldn't afford to buy food in the likes of Superquinn [a high-end retailer that was taken over in 2014 by the Supervalu chain] now.' The personal accounts thus mirror market trends, which show that discounters' share of the Irish grocery market grew from 5.4 per cent in 2005 to 11.6 per cent in 2013. Importantly, this trend seems to be continuing, with latest figures showing that, as of August 2015, Aldi and Lidl's market share accounted for about 17.8 per cent (Kantarworldpanel 2015).

Consumers' behavioural changes also affected the shopping process. A large proportion of participants reported they had changed from an ad hoc, spontaneous shopping behaviour, towards more carefully planned shopping, which often included detailed shopping lists, the collection and use of coupons, as well as actively seeking special offers. A 2014 shopper survey, which was conducted with a representative sample of the Irish population, revealed that 52 per cent of consumers claimed they buy more goods on special offer than they did before the recession (Beere 2014). The same survey revealed that

66 per cent of shoppers plan their grocery shopping more, while 71 per cent claim to purchase more own brand/private labels than they did before the recession. For example, one participant stated that: 'you go to the reduced section first... because you can pick up a salad and it's like two euro and then you go over the reduced section and it's like thirty cent and you know you're going to consume it within that night'. A number of those interviewed also explained how they had cut back expenditure on clothing and shoes, and that impulse purchases had been drastically reduced. Most claimed they had reduced overall spending, but also had shifted towards cheaper retailers like TK Maxx, Penneys, or H&M, as well as doing more of their shopping online and/or only during the 'sales'. For example, one participant said, 'I would try and wait until they have some sort of mid-season sale or a Christmas sale... summer sale.' Again, these personal accounts correspond with survey data, showing that 78 per cent of shoppers actively sought out cheaper ways of living (Beere 2014).

Cutbacks also affected personal transportation and travel. While many delayed buying new cars, or rationed their use to cut petrol consumption, others traded down or sold their car(s) altogether. For example, one participant explained how she had to give up her car, and was now no longer able to drive her elderly father to church on Sunday. Others reported they had switched completely or partially to alternative modes of transport such as cycling or buses. Similarly, most participants gave up or scaled back on holidays abroad. For example, one stated: '2007, 2008 was a very, kind of, financially restrained time. We didn't have any holidays for four years. The whole travelling thing stopped.' Survey data reveals that, in 2014, a large proportion of consumers (46 per cent) claimed they were unlikely to make a big-spend purchase in the next twelve months (Beere 2014).

Shifting from Public Spaces and Being More Thrifty

The majority of participants reported they were forced to make cuts that affected their social lives. While some, mainly the younger group, reduced the frequency of their nights out with friends and/or family, almost all reported they had cut down on eating in restaurants and/or visiting pubs. For many, their social life had shifted from public spaces (e.g. restaurants, bars, nightclubs) into their private homes or those of their family and friends. As one of our participants explains: 'I wouldn't deny myself a bottle of Pinot Grigio on a Friday night, with a DVD. So, that would be my idea of socializing, as in getting my friends up or go to theirs... but nothing like going to a club.' Again, the personal accounts of consumers mirror trends in the market, which, as a result, forced many bars and pubs in Ireland to close. Data from the Irish drinks industry indicates that the number of pub licences plunged by 13 per cent between 2007 and 2012 (Lambkin 2016).

For the majority of people, economic cutbacks meant they had to be more frugal and make do with limited financial means. However, some participants said they had fully embraced the new lifestyle, and found some gratification in saving money across different consumption contexts. For example, one participant stated that 'even if I'd had the money, I wouldn't have gone out and replaced it . . . no, I just don't think you have to . . . sell on or replace something which is still working'. Many said they had delayed replacing cars or electrical and home entertainment equipment as well as mobile phones or clothing. The interviews also pointed towards some potentially longer-lasting changes in people's mindsets, which in some instances had changed from a 'throwaway mentality' to a more frugal approach.

The trend towards simpler forms of consumption has been popularly termed 'voluntary simplicity' (Shaw and Moraes 2009). While many Irish consumers were 'forced' to adopt more prudent and frugal consumption decisions, others said that it was a deliberate lifestyle choice. The findings seem to tie in with findings from a nationally representative online survey (n=600), which was conducted by the Irish Food Board, suggesting that 66 per cent of Irish consumers are now actively looking for ways to simplify their lives (Bord Bia 2015).

Being Creative and Innovative

While embracing a more frugal lifestyle was one way of coping with involuntary cutbacks, some participants actively explored different ways to consume. Indeed, many of these aimed to be (financially) 'less dependent' on their consumption habits. For example, one participant explained how she had bought a sewing machine in order to alter her existing clothes: 'I'm saving all that money on, you know, altering clothes . . . Instead of bringing them to the dressmaker and paying twenty euro a pop, to get a hem turned up.' Others explained how they had begun to invest more effort and time 'sourcing' (cheaper) alternatives, like one individual who described how he replaced oil with wood: 'So, I have been cutting down the forest bit by bit and that's my source of heating. . . . I'm saving probably . . . forty euro a week by not having to buy oil.' This trend towards more self-reliance has been partly driven by a growing decline in trust towards businesses. Survey findings suggest that 72 per cent of Irish consumers are sceptical of claims made by big brands (Bord Bia 2015).

While many of the changes made by consumers involved avoiding and being less dependent upon big institutions, such as brands, retailers, and/or utilities, other consumption practices appeared to verge towards the unlawful. One participant explained that she was no longer able to afford the subscription fees for her cable network. However, instead of reducing television consumption, she downloaded codes from the Internet, which unscrambled all signals 'for free'. Likewise, some participants talked about downloading and streaming of music, television series, and movies for 'free'. For example, a widely reported study by Ignite Research for Core Media suggests that, on average, about 36,806 Irish adults illegally download media content every day (Taylor 2015).

Many alternative ways of consumption developed in social contexts, and involved an element of sharing. For example, some female participants took part in clothes swapping parties with their friends in order to update their wardrobes, and exchanged outfits for work, day-to-day wear, and special occasions, which they otherwise could no longer afford. As one participant stated 'I don't worry about my clothes anymore because . . . we're swapping all our clothes around . . .' The personal accounts of participants seem to reflect a more global trend, which has received growing attention in the media and has been widely labelled as 'the sharing economy' (Friedman 2013). Further, the in-depth interviews tie in with the nationally representative survey data, which suggests that a growing proportion of Irish consumers are seeking fulfilment from things other than (materialistic) consumption (Bord Bia 2015).

Reconnecting

During the interviews, many participants, particularly the older ones, explained how they felt they had lost touch with certain values, people, and activities throughout the Celtic Tiger era, and how the recession had given them an opportunity to 'reconnect'. Indeed, many participants described how they had engaged in or experienced more altruistic and collaborative behaviours: 'Everyone's giving out a little bit to get by . . . everyone scratches everyone else's back . . .'. In this way, participants explained how reconnecting with activities and people that they had valued, but had somewhat neglected throughout the Celtic Tiger years, helped them to cope during this difficult time of transition. For example, many emphasized the importance of reconnecting with family. One participant, for example, explained how his wife lost her job and how they struggled financially, but how he felt their circumstances had partially improved because they spent more time together as a family. Survey research shows that 92 per cent of Irish consumers now view being a dutiful member of their family as a sign of success in life (Bord Bia 2015).

Many participants said this feeling of reconnecting had extended into the wider community:

I think . . . that there's a stronger sense . . . community. I can even see it with my brother, after his business failed . . . there were other people whose businesses failed, as well but they...all go out of their way to help each other. Like, if something comes up or someone hears of someone looking for something, they're more than willing to recommend or...they kind of go out of their way to help...

Again, the Bord Bia (2015) findings suggest that people have reconnected with their local communities, with 74 per cent believing that groups of individuals making small changes in their behaviour can make a big difference in the world.

Our qualitative research revealed that many participants had taken up volunteering roles in their local communities, for example, helping people who had been affected by the recession. One stated that: 'I volunteer...in a mental health organisation...we go on retreats and take all the youths—the teenagers—out and we're taking them up to Offaly, in a couple of months' time and it was Killarney only recently, so...going for the whole weekend.'

According to survey research, 94 per cent of Irish consumers believe that being physically fit and in good health is a sign of success in life, compared to 17 per cent who believe they would be happier if they had more material possessions (Bord Bia 2015). One participant recalls: 'I actually sat down and started to read books again, you know, something that had been lost on me.' Another described how growing potatoes and reconnecting with nature had helped him cope with a drastic drop in income:

> I suppose the growing of the potatoes is almost like a spiritual thing because the piece of ground that I decided to plant the potatoes in last year, is bog land, literally and we ploughed it last year and we turned it over and it was so rough and it was very frustrating and I was a lot heavier than I am now and I was unfit and in bad humour and so many things wrong...but we got potatoes in there and we got potatoes out of the ground, so the first day, it was like a big celebration here...

However, for others, the economic downturn had more detrimental effects on their social relationships with friends and family. One participant explains how many of his friends emigrated due to lack of job prospects in Ireland: 'Our (GAA) football team has been damaged because of the players leaving...that actually makes me feel quite emotional about it because some very close friends of mine are in Australia now and I won't see them for some time. Some of them may not return.' Some participants found it incredibly difficult to cope at all, and either surrendered to their bleak circumstances or were actively seeking support.

Struggling and Seeking Support

People with particularly constrained financial circumstances and debt struggled to find ways and mechanisms to deal with their new circumstances. In particular, people who felt they were being chased for outstanding loans, bills, mortgages, or other repayments often found it very difficult to cope. While some managed to negotiate smaller loan repayments, others were faced with giving up essential items such as health insurance or pension plans. For example, a participant who was in a very difficult financial position stated that: 'the worst one, because I am a diabetic, was losing my VHI [private health insurance]', while another participant described the worry he felt after having to give up health insurance even though his wife had a serious heart condition. Others described how being hounded by banks made them ignore most phone calls and bills, as they were simply unable to cope with the mounting pressure, particularly in situations where participants felt the looming threat of potential repossessions of family homes.

Continual economic cutbacks had serious implications for some people's physical and mental well-being. Commonly mentioned symptoms were depression, depressive thoughts, anxiety attacks, strains and breakdown of personal relationships, and excessive use of alcohol. For example, one of our participants, playing on a well-known advertising slogan at the time for Orange Mobile, stated about his own future that 'Well, I can say to you, my mantra, of late, has been *the future is grim, the future is grey.*'

While the recession put additional stress on people with pre-existing mental health problems, those with no previous mental health issues were also affected. Other studies of how people coped during the recession reported similar conclusions: 'Some of these individuals may have little previous experience of coping with hardship (some may have been quite well off materially) and may be at greater risk of mental health problems that others who are "inured" to financial insecurity' (Mental Health Commission 2011: 9).

In response to such stress, some participants actively looked for emotional and material support. Some were, in part, being supported financially by family members, while others sought advice and support from debt agencies and support groups such as Money Advice and Budgeting Service (MABS), the Phoenix Project (support for distressed borrowers), and/or charities such as St Vincent de Paul. MABS reported: 'a 10 per cent increase in the number of people accessing their service in 2010 compared to 2009 and figures for 2011 show a further increase' (Mental Health Commission 2011: 9). One participant recalls how she sought support when she had no other options left:

Well, my personal friends would say to me, 'Why are you so proud? Why don't you ask?' and I said—at one stage, I was very much at breaking point and I did have to contact St Vincent de Paul's myself. I did. I didn't have a choice... everything was on top of me. The bills were on top of me. Everything was just out of control and I just couldn't take it.

HAVE PATTERNS OF CONSUMPTION CHANGED?

While the recovery has seen consumer confidence in Ireland steadily return-ing, many spending habits and consumption practices that altered during the recession have been normalized for Irish consumers and are unlikely to change soon. On a general level, many of the participants interviewed, in retrospect, expressed ambivalent feelings towards consumption during the Celtic Tiger years, as well as during the recession. Participants felt positive about the boom years, particularly about having job security and disposable income. When thinking back on the Celtic Tiger years, one explains 'Oh, I think it was a great time—I do. I felt great, purely because of financial reasons. If you lose a job, you'll get another one tomorrow...', while another recalled that the positive aspect of the pre-recession era was that: 'you had money to spend... and the freedom to do whatever you wanted... but you're actually trapped [in the recession]'.

However, consumers also saw negative features of the Celtic Tiger years, and many discussions revolved around how consumption and materialism had spiralled out of control, most notably in the property market. As one person recalls: 'When property got more expensive in Dublin than in London or New York, you'd kind of see that there is something broken.' Others recalled how even socializing had become lavish, and that excessive spending was driven by social pressures and conspicuous consumption, and one remembers that 'there probably was an element of keeping up with the Joneses, people put pressure on themselves. I think Irish people kind of lost a bit of identity...'.

While losses in income and wealth, and the fear of losing their job, forced participants to cut their spending, this was mirrored by more general changes in consumption practices during the recession. These were most notable in a more price-conscious and measured approach to consumption and shopping, as well as a move away from 'big brands'. For example, one person said that '[if] we do, eventually, get out of this... I'll always be more price-aware and always kind of look at little bit more at what the different prices are'. Another made a similar statement, saying that, 'You're more careful with consumption. So, you're more conscious of what you spend, you're more conscious of value for money, you're more conscious of what you might have to sacrifice.'

Importantly, these austere shopping behaviours have been normalized. While, during the recovery, consumer spending has seen a significant increase, much of it reflects pent-up demand and market figures indicate that Irish consumers are unlikely to return to the conspicuous and lavish consumption patterns of the Celtic Tiger years. Findings from the Retail Ireland Shopper Attitude Survey (Beere 2014) show that consumers 'remain very price con-scious, with savvy shoppers buying more goods on special offers and "own brand" products'. For example, in the automobile market, mid-market brands like Kia, Hyundai, and Skoda, which are considered as 'good value for money' by consumers, have seen the most substantial increase in market share (SIMI 2016). Likewise, budget retailers like Aldi and Lidl continue to grow their share in a post-austerity market environment (Kantarworldpanel 2015).

Some of these changes seem to be grounded in disillusionment and distrust in institutions, and a general strive towards consuming less (material things). In this way, it appears that not only spending patterns changed, but that the meaning of consumption may have significantly been altered over the course of the recession. For example, one of the older participants critically reflected that the recession had a positive aspect in that it forced people 'to absolutely abandon that fast-lane, consumeristic lifestyle they were just getting a taste for...'. This sentiment was reflected in nationally representative survey research, which suggested a greater desire among many (particularly younger) consumers for more simplified lifestyles and consumption.

This trend is most notable in the rapid growth of the 'sharing economy'. For a growing number of consumers, temporary access to products and services is now (economically) more desirable than actually buying and owning them outright. The rapid diffusion of so-called 'access-based solutions' in entertainment (e.g. Spotify, Tidal, Netflix), accommodation and travel (e.g. Airbnb, Homestay, Couchsurfing), transportation (e.g. GoCar, Zipcar, Dublin Bike), or food (e.g. EatWith, Kitchensurfing) indicates that, for many people, the benefits of sharing and access-based solutions are greater than those of material possessions.

Finally, the qualitative research presented in this study suggests that the recession led many Irish consumers to reassess their values, and their relationships with material possessions. As a result, many consumers claim to have reconnected with the activities and people that they cherished but had neglected before the recession. As one participant reflects: 'I think families become more important, a little bit because people, during the Celtic Tiger, were just becoming fixated on money and power and moving on and "where can we go next?" whereas now, they're maybe looking more towards the family and things that count for them.'

The findings correspond with attitudinal research, which shows that 92 per cent of Irish people believe that being a dutiful member of their family is a sign of success, implying that a shift towards non-consumerist values is likely to continue (Bord Bia 2015). This is further supported by market data, which show that the sales of household goods like lighting (+18.7 per cent), electric goods (+10 per cent), and hardware, paints, and glass (+5 per cent) have increased significantly (Lambkin 2016), suggesting that people focus more on their 'inner circle' like family and home, and that they seem to care less about conspicuous aspects of consumption. While economic cutbacks, deprivation, and in some cases poverty had a significant and very painful impact on many participants' lives, the refocus on values such as family and community might be one of the few positive aspects of Ireland's recession which has continued into the period of recovery.

CONCLUSION

The aim of this chapter was to describe key changes in spending and consumption that were brought about by the recession, while also reflecting on consumption during the subsequent recovery. Therefore, it went beyond macro-trends and gave a voice to consumers affected by the recession, thus offering micro-level insights into changes in Irish consumerism. In particular, this chapter investigated the strategies that a cross-section of Irish consumers adopted to cope with significant losses in income and wealth. Some struggled during this time of transition, particularly when faced with significant problems such as repossession of houses, loss of health insurance, and the inability to purchase even basic necessities. Some experienced severe financial difficulties, and in some cases saw their physical and mental well-being suffer. However, many participants managed to cope via changes to their lifestyle and through the help of friends, family, and/or external organizations. Key changes often revolved around making economic cutbacks as well as finding more frugal and/or creative ways to consume. However, other behaviours that were adopted appeared to reflect a deeper re-evaluation of the 'meaning of consumption'. In particular, people reconnected with values that many felt had partially been lost during exuberant times. The findings presented in this chapter suggest that many spending habits and consumption practices that altered during the recession are now normal for Irish consumers. The observed shifts in shopping behaviour, as well as the trends towards non-consumerist and family values are continuing beyond the recession and are likely to influence consumption in the years to come. While the recovery has coincided with an increase in consumer confidence and spending, the surge in consumption is most likely attributable to pent-up demand. Indeed, consumers continue to be more prudent and less conspicuous in their consumption. Furthermore, consumers continue to save more and to repay loans and credit card debts, and it therefore seems unlikely that the lavish and excessive consumption patterns Ireland experienced during the Celtic Tiger years will return any time soon.

REFERENCES

Adkins, N. R. and Ozanne, J. L. 2005. 'The Low Literate Consumer'. *Journal of Consumer Research*, 32(1): 93–105.

Andreasen, A. 1984. 'Life Status Changes and Changes in Consumer Preferences and Satisfaction'. *Journal of Consumer Research*, 11(3): 784–94.

Arnould, E. and Thompson, C. 2005. 'Consumer Culture Theory (CCT): Twenty Years of Research'. *Journal of Consumer Research*, 31(4): 868–82.

Baker, S. M., Gentry, J. W., and Rittenburg, T. L. 2005. 'Vulnerable Consumers: Building Understanding of the Domain of Consumer Vulnerability'. *Journal of Macromarketing*, 25(2): 128–39.

Beere, B. 2014. 'Retail Ireland Shopper Attitude Survey, Report Prepared for Retail Ireland', *RetailIreland*. Available at: <http://www.retailireland.ie/IBEC/Press/PressPublicationsdoclib3.nsf/wvRINewsByTitle/recession-prompts-major-shift-in-shopping-trends—survey-14-09-2014?OpenDocument> (accessed 30 July 2015).

Belk, R. W. 1988. 'Possessions and the Extended Self'. *Journal of Consumer Research*, 15(2): 139–68.

Bord Bia. 2015. 'The Irish Consumer 2015: From Recession to Recovery: The New Consumer Agenda', Consumer Insight Team Report, July.

Central Bank of Ireland. 2015. 'Quarterly Financial Accounts for Ireland, Quarter 1, Report', Dublin.

CSO (Central Statistics Office). 2012. *Quarterly National Household Survey: Responses to the Economic Downturn—Pilot Module Quarter 2 2011*. Available at: <http://www.cso.ie/en/media/csoie/releasespublications/documents/labourmarket/2011/qnhsdownturnq22011.pdf> (accessed 30 July 2015).

CSO (Central Statistics Office). 2014. 'Quarterly National Household Survey: Quarter 4'. Available at: <http://www.cso.ie/en/releasesandpublications/er/qnhs/quarterlynationalhouseholdsurveyquarter42014/#.VPSzgfmsVJk> (accessed 30 July 2015).

CSO (Central Statistics Office). 2015a. 'Household Travel Survey'. Available at: <http://www.cso.ie/px/pxeirestat/Database/eirestat/Household%20Travel%20Survey/Household%20Travel%20Survey_statbank.asp?SP=Household%20Travel%20Surve&Planguage=0y> (accessed 30 July 2015).

CSO (Central Statistics Office). 2015b. 'Quarterly Institutional Sector Accounts, Quarter 4'. Available at: <http://www.cso.ie/en/releasesandpublications/er/isanf/institutionalsectoraccountsnonfinancialquarter42015/> (accessed 30 July 2015).

Friedman, T. 2013. 'Welcome to the Sharing Economy'. *New York Times*, 21 July. Available at: <http://www.nytimes.com/2013/07/21/opinion/sunday/friedman-welcome-to-the-sharing-economy.html?_r=0> (accessed 30 July 2015).

Hamilton, K. 2009. 'Low-Income Families: Experiences and Responses to Consumer Exclusion'. *International Journal of Sociology and Social Policy*, 29(9/10): 543–57.

Hill R. P. 2001. 'Surviving in a Material World: Evidence from Ethnographic Consumer Research on People in Poverty'. *Journal of Contemporary Ethnography*, 30, August: 364–91.

Hill, R. P. and Stamey, M. 1990. 'The Homeless in America: An Examination of Possessions and Consumption Behaviors'. *Journal of Consumer Research*, 17(3): 303–21.

Kantarworldpanel. 2015. 'SuperValue Gains Ground as Aldi and Lidl Continue to Increase', Press Release, 28 October. Available at: <http://www.kantarworldpanel.com/ie/Press-Releases/SuperValu-gains-ground-as-Aldi-and-Lidl-continue-to-increase> (accessed 30 July 2015).

Lambkin, M. 2015. *Consumer Market Monitor: Quarterly Report*, Quarter 4, 2014 edn. Dublin: University College Dublin & Irish Marketing Institute.

Lambkin, M. 2016. *Consumer Market Monitor: Quarterly Report*, Quarter 4, 2015 edn. Dublin: University College Dublin & Irish Marketing Institute.

Mental Health Commission. 2011. *The Human Cost: An Overview of the Evidence on Economic Adversity and Mental Health and Recommendations for Action.* Available at: <http://www.mhcirl.ie/file/hcpaper.pdf> (accessed 30 July 2015).

NESC (National Economic and Social Council). 2009. *Ireland's Five Part Crisis: An Integrated National Response*, Report 118 (March). Available at: <http://files.nesc.ie/nesc_reports/en/NESC_118_2009.pdf> (accessed 30 July 2015).

NESC (National Economic and Social Council). 2014. *The Social Dimensions of the Crisis: The Evidence and its Implications*, Report 134. Available at: <http://files.nesc.ie/nesc_reports/en/NESC_134_The_Social_Dimensions_of_the_Crisis_Main_%20Report.pdf> (accessed 30 July 2015).

Price, L. L., Arnould, E. J., and Curasi, C. F. 2000. 'Older Consumers' Disposition of Special Possessions'. *Journal of Consumer Research*, 27(2): 179–201.

Schouten, J. W. 1991. 'Selves in Transition: Symbolic Consumption in Personal Rites of Passage and Identity Reconstruction'. *Journal of Consumer Research*, 17(4): 412–25.

Shaw, D. and Moraes, C. 2009. 'Voluntary Simplicity: An Exploration of Market Interactions'. *International Journal of Consumer Studies*, 33(2): 215–23.

SIMI (The Society of the Irish Motor Industry). 2016. National Vehicle Registrations 2016. Available at: <http://www.simi.ie/Statistics/National+Vehicle+Statistics.html> (accessed 30 May 2016).

Taylor, C. 2015. 'Study Shows over 36,000 Irish Adults Downloading Illegally', *Irish Times*, 22 January. Available at: <http://www.irishtimes.com/business/media-and-marketing/study-shows-over-36-000-irish-adults-downloading-illegally-1.2075451> (accessed 30 July 2015).

8

Ireland and the 'GIPS' Countries

Paul Teague

INTRODUCTION

One of the main side effects of the Great Recession was to expose the economic and institutional weaknesses of the Eurozone. An important argument gaining influence is that the fragility of the Eurozone is not simply tied to a series of institutional design weaknesses such as the absence of fully fledged fiscal or banking unions, but to deep-seated differences in economic structure and performance between its core and periphery members (Iversen and Soskice 2013). On this account, the Great Recession exposed a wide schism within the Eurozone between a group of Northern European countries led by Germany that had generated economic growth through exporting large volumes of tradable goods and services, and a group of countries largely on the European periphery that had secured growth during the early 2000s through consumption-led, credit-financed booms (see Hassel 2014). The Great Recession not only exposed the unsustainability of the development pathway taken by the European periphery, but also the deeply flawed nature of the Eurozone as a currency area.

Greece, Ireland, Portugal, and Spain, which became known as the GIPS countries, were seen as the countries that pursued full-throttle consumption-led growth. When the financial crisis erupted in 2008, the ability of these countries to save their banks and wider financial systems was severely questioned by international money markets. As a result, what started off as a financial crisis in most GIPS countries quickly mutated into a sovereign debt crisis, which called into question the capacity of these economies to remain solvent without external help. On paper, the GIPS countries could have been rescued by Eurozone member states devising some form of European Keynesian macroeconomic regime to increase aggregate demand across the Continent. At the beginning of the crisis, there were signs that the member states might actually follow such a pathway, as fiscal policy was initially relaxed almost everywhere in the European Union (EU) in response to the economic crisis (Grahl and Teague 2013).

But, relatively quickly, this stance was fully reversed due to serious political and economic objections emerging across Northern European member states. Instead, under German leadership, a double-barrelled strategy was adopted to restore stability to the Eurozone. On the one hand, the economic governance of the Eurozone would be improved by introducing a battery of institutional innovations, most notably the creation of a banking union and a new surveillance procedure to guide public expenditure in EU member states. On the other hand, the Eurozone members considered to have been economically reckless would be provided with financial support to help them address their sovereign debt problems and, in return, these countries would enact internal fiscal consolidation and structural adjustment. Thus, Euro-austerity trumped Euro-Keynesianism as the strategy adopted to make the Eurozone a better functioning currency area (De Grauwe and Ji 2013).

The purpose of this chapter is to compare the fiscal consolidation and structural adjustment policies pursued in Ireland with those implemented in other GIPS countries. In doing so, the twofold aim is to assess the usefulness of viewing the GIPS countries as a homogeneous group and to gauge whether the Eurozone has been strengthened by requiring these countries to enact far-reaching retrenchment policies. The chapter is organized as follows. The section, 'Fiscal Retrenchment in the GIPS Countries', sets out the nature and scale of the fiscal retrenchment policies that GIPS countries have had to implement at the behest of the Troika. The following section, 'The Consequences of Fiscal Consolidation', assesses the economic impact of these austerity measures. Then, in 'Labour Market Flexibility in the GIPS Countries', an assessment is made of the labour market flexibility programmes each GIPS country had been obliged to implement. The penultimate section, 'Ireland: Between the Core and the Periphery', contrasts Ireland's experience with those of the other GIPS countries. The 'Conclusions' bring together the arguments of the chapter.

FISCAL RETRENCHMENT IN THE GIPS COUNTRIES

A tripartite committee known as the Troika, which involved the European Central Bank (ECB), the European Commission (EC), and the International Monetary Fund (IMF), was established to design and implement economic adjustment programmes across the GIPS countries. The first country to seek assistance was Greece in early 2010, when it received a €110 billion package, consisting of loans from the IMF and some core Eurozone countries. Later in 2010, Ireland requested and received financial support to the tune of

€85 billion, made up from loans from the IMF and EU. The following year Portugal received a financial support package of €78 billion to stabilize public finances. In 2012, a second IMF/EU rescue package amounting to €130 billion was put in place for Greece as the economic situation in the country remained precarious despite the initial support programme. At the end of 2012, a financial package only consisting of loans from EU sources and not involving the IMF was put together for Spain. The package provided a €100 billion loan facility specifically to recapitalize and restructure the Spanish banking sector, which had been badly affected by the collapse of the country's housing market bubble. Thus, Spain was not formally under a Troika programme, but it came under considerable external pressure to enact fiscal retrenchment nevertheless. In the end, Spain only needed €41 billion of the €100 billion loan facility to stabilize its banking sector. Finally, a third bailout programme consisting of €86 billion had to be devised for Greece in 2015 to help the country arrest sharply deteriorating economic conditions. Securing these financial support packages came with a heavy price for all recipient countries. Each country agreed to enact large-scale fiscal retrenchment programmes, principally through slashing public expenditure. The aim of these cutbacks was to cut government deficits quickly and decisively: Greece was committed to reducing government deficits from 13.6 per cent of gross domestic product (GDP) in 2009 to 3 per cent in 2014; Ireland from 12.2 per cent in 2012 to 3 per cent in 2015; and Portugal 9.1 per cent in 2010 to 3 per cent in 2013.

But the Troika viewed its task as not simply orchestrating fiscal consolidation in the indebted GIPS countries, but also aiding with structural adjustment. In all programmes, structural adjustment was viewed as enhancing the competiveness of the economy. The adjustment programmes for Greece and Portugal encouraged wide-ranging reforms to the domestic business environment: far-reaching privatization programmes; measures to liberalize the professions; initiatives to promote entrepreneurship and the development of small businesses; and so on. In contrast, the programme for Ireland was relatively silent on these matters. Overall, the theme that dominated Troika discussions of structural adjustment was labour market flexibility reforms. An IMF working paper systematically set outs the scope and nature of the macro- and micro-oriented labour market reforms demanded of the GIPS countries, considered necessary to improve their ability to withstand macroeconomic shocks in the future and to enhance the competiveness of firms (Blanchard, Jaumotee, and Loungani 2013). Policies that were to be introduced included streamlining employment protection legislation (EPL), not only to improve the economy-wide movement of workers, but also to improve enterprise-level profitability by weakening legal rules governing internal labour markets. Other policies involved the reduction of social benefits and minimum wage levels, as well as the reorganization and weakening of collective bargaining systems to ensure that employee behaviour was more responsive to market conditions and that wages fluctuated in line with patterns of demand. The broad thrust of the reforms was to deregulate labour markets, using supply-side measures to address unemployment because any increase in aggregate demand was ruled out by the restrictive macro-policy regime that had been imposed. Behind this policy goal was the belief that labour market rigidities were widespread in these countries, causing economic sclerosis. Thus, across the GIPS countries, the quid pro quo for receiving large financial assistance was the adoption of widespread measures aimed at reducing government expenditure and promoting labour market flexibility (De Grauwe 2011).

THE CONSEQUENCES OF FISCAL CONSOLIDATION

On the surface, just before the crisis public finances in Ireland appeared to be in a strong position. Public debt was 24 per cent of GDP and the government was running a budget surplus. But behind this positive veneer, a less healthy fiscal situation was fermenting in the country (Keane 2015). In particular, Irish Governments had become too reliant on asset-based taxes—stamp duties, capital gains tax, and capital acquisitions tax—from the booming construction industry, rather than income tax, to finance public expenditure. When the Great Recession started in 2008, the Irish Government experienced a sharp decline in tax revenue due to the virtual collapse of the construction sector. The result, of course, was an immediate deterioration in the government deficit, ballooning to near 32 per cent of GDP in 2010, mostly as a result of the government's €64 billion bank bailout programme. No other GIPS country experienced such a sharp rise in the deficit.

Overall, fiscal consolidation in Ireland involved €11.5 billion of new tax revenue being generated and £25.5 billion being slashed from public expenditure programmes, which together roughly amounted to 20 per cent of GDP. Other GIPS countries enacted more or less the same balance between public expenditure cuts and tax increases: in Portugal, the consolidation programme was 40 per cent increased taxes and 60 per cent expenditure reductions. Spain followed a similar ratio as Portugal, whereas fiscal consolidation in Greece was evenly split between revenue and expenditure measures. The consensus is that Greece had to implement more stringent retrenchment policies than the other three countries.

The nature of the fiscal retrenchment programmes was broadly similar across the GIPS countries. Table 8.1 shows that all countries apart from Spain have cut and frozen public-sector pay. Similarly, all countries have cut and frozen public-sector pensions. Civil service jobs have been reduced everywhere. Unemployment benefits have been cut across the board as have welfare and education budgets. Early retirement schemes have been made less

Table 8.1. Social consequences of fiscal consolidation in GIPS countries

	Public-Sector Pay		Public-Sector Pensions		Civil Service	Retirement Age	Unemployment Benefits	Minimum Wage		Reduced Budgetary Expenditure	
	Freeze	Cut	Freeze	Cut	Reduction	Retirement	Reduction	Freeze	Cut	Welfare	Education
Greece	✓	✓	✓	✓	✓	✓	✓		✓	✓	✓
Ireland	✓	✓	✓	✓	✓	✓	✓		✓	✓	✓
Spain	✓	✓	✓		✓	✓	✓	✓		✓	✓
Portugal	✓	✓		✓	✓	✓	✓	✓		✓	✓

Source: Compiled by author from multiple sources.

generous and minimum wages have either been reduced or frozen. Education and welfare budgets were also cut back in all countries. Thus, the systems of social protection in all GIPS countries were a big casualty of the Troika economic assistance programmes. In addition to the squeeze on social protection, Greece and Portugal were required to launch far-reaching privatization programmes as part of the wider drive for structural economic adjustment. In Spain, the emphasis was more on financial reform, and in Ireland the Troika appeared to be particularly exercised by the government's active labour market policies (ALMPs), which were considered wholly inadequate.

The immediate first-order effects of the tough austerity programmes that the GIPS countries were obliged to follow have been predictable enough. As Figure 8.1 shows, living standards declined immediately, with fiscal consolidation triggering a sharp fall in GDP growth across the GIPS countries. Greece has been the most acutely affected, with national income falling by over 20 per cent since 2008: austerity has shrunk the economy by more than a fifth. The picture has been less bleak since 2012 as economic contraction has abetted. But the outlook in terms of economic growth remains bleak, with GDP levels almost static in nearly all countries. The only exception is Ireland where the figure shows national output increased by 4.6 per cent in 2014 and 5.6 per cent in 2015. With growth faltering, all GIPS countries experienced significant increases in joblessness. Figure 8.2 highlights that unemployment rates now stand around 25 per cent in Greece and Spain, while the figures for Portugal and Ireland are just dipping below 10 per cent,

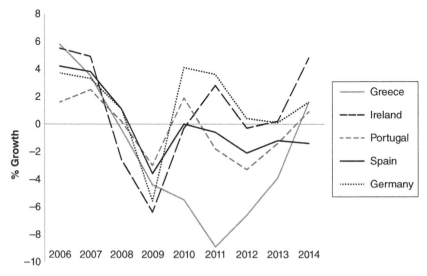

Figure 8.1. GDP growth in GIPS countries, 2006–14
Source: Annual Macro-Economic Database, EC.

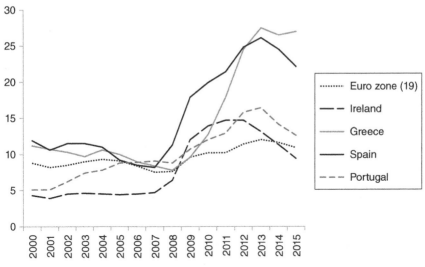

Figure 8.2. Unemployment in GIPS countries
Source: Annual Macro-Economic Database, EC.

having been nearer 20 and 15 per cent per cent a few years ago. Young people have suffered the most from the lack of job opportunities: youth unemployment stands at a shocking 53 per cent in both Spain and Greece, while the figures are 35 and 24 per cent respectively for Portugal and Ireland. In all these countries, including Ireland, emigration has provided a safety valve for labour market pressures. Unsurprisingly, all GIPS countries have experienced sharp falls in public-sector employment due to the huge scaling back in government expenditure.

Falling national output alongside increasing unemployment not only reduces living standards, but is also likely to have an adverse impact on the fiscal position of governments. For a start, social protection budgets will have to increase massively in response to big increases in unemployment. Thus, although the fiscal consolidation programmes led to countries moving towards primary budgetary surpluses, Figure 8.3 shows that the weight of public-sector indebtedness relative to GDP increased sharply across the GIPS countries—it now stands at a massive 180 per cent of GDP in Greece. As a result, these countries remain far from fiscal stability. Fiscal retrenchment has also triggered—as was intended—internal devaluation in most of the GIPS countries. Figure 8.4 shows that unit labour costs have fallen in all countries. This is due more to falling wages than improved productivity, which, in the short run, can improve competitiveness, but whether it adds up to a sustainable development model is another matter entirely. It can be clearly seen that Ireland experienced the sharpest fall in unit labour costs. On paper, this suggests that the country has been the most aggressive in realigning its wage structure to

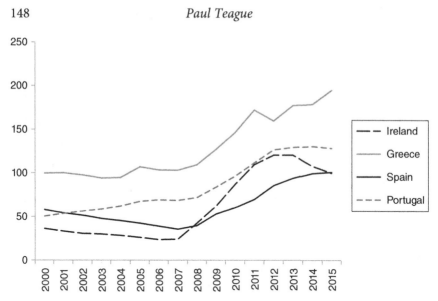

Figure 8.3. Gross public debt as per cent of GDP at market prices
Source: Annual Macro-Economic Database, EC.

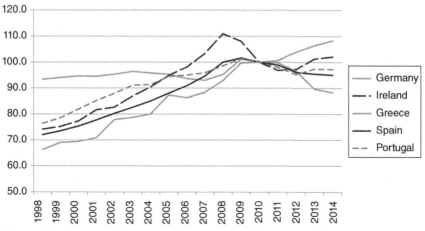

Figure 8.4. Unit labour costs in GIPS countries, 1998–2014
Source: Annual Macro-Economic Database, EC.

prevailing Eurozone economic conditions, but careful work done by McDonnell and O'Farrell (2015) suggests that the decline can be almost entirely attributed to the collapse of the construction sector during the recession.

The worst years of the Great Recession for all GIPS countries were 2008–11. Since 2012, bleak economic times have started to ease, at least to some extent, apart perhaps for Greece. Figure 8.1 shows that the decline in national output bottomed out in 2012 and all countries have started the climb back to positive economic growth rates since then, with Ireland's performance notably better than other countries. Current account balances also started to improve everywhere. Exports from all GIPS countries increased, although the rate of improvement was relatively modest, apart from Ireland, where the increase was huge. A more important factor behind improvements in current account balances in GIPS countries, apart from Ireland, was a decline in imports as a share of GDP, caused largely by depressed domestic demand. Better terms of trade have been accompanied by the rise in unemployment halting, although joblessness remains high across GIPS countries. The competitive position of the GIPS countries has also improved relative to the core member states of the Eurozone (see Hardiman et al. 2016). Improved economic conditions have led all GIPS, apart from Greece, exiting from their Troika economic adjustment programmes: Ireland was the first country to exit at the end of 2013, followed quickly by Spain in January 2014, and then by Portugal in May 2014. Greece is the only exception: political and economic conditions remained turbulent during most of 2014 and the first half of 2015, which led to the country entering into a third bailout programme.

It is starkly evident that the economic situation in Ireland has improved markedly compared to other GIPS countries. A number of chapters in the book, particularly Chapters 3 and 4, discuss at length two interrelated factors widely seen as behind the standout performance of the Irish economy. One was Ireland's deeper economic ties with non-Eurozone countries such as the UK and USA, where economic conditions were more buoyant than inside the Eurozone area. The other was the strong export performance of the Irish economy throughout the recession apart from the beginning, a factor that would be critical to the performance of any small open economy. A growing consensus is emerging that it is these two factors and not the fiscal consolidation/internal devaluation measures that are responsible for Ireland's stronger bounce back from the economic recession than other parts of the Eurozone periphery (see Chapter 1, this volume). A great deal of evidence can be found in support of this consensus. The trade structure of the Irish economy contrasts sharply with other GIPS countries. Figure 8.5 shows that exports from Ireland stood in 2015 at 120 per cent of GDP, whereas the comparable figures for the other GIPS countries are Portugal 41.1 per cent, Spain 33.1 per cent, and Greece 31.9 per cent. Figure 8.5 also shows that the export performance of the Irish economy was much superior to the rest. While all this evidence is very persuasive, it might be too strong to say that the bailout programme had no influence on the turnaround of the performance of the Irish economy. It can be plausibly argued that Ireland required some level of internal devaluation to correct for the huge unit labour cost misalignment that had opened up in the early to mid-2000s with the European core, as highlighted in Figure 8.4.

Two key conclusions arise from this assessment. One is that economic recovery from the Great Recession has been more pronounced in Ireland

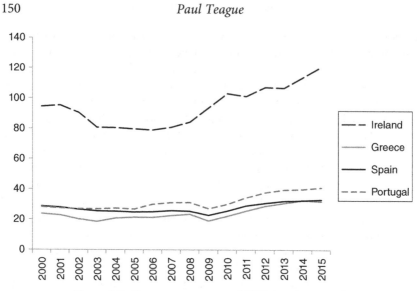

Figure 8.5. Exports as per cent of GDP (market prices)
Source: Annual Macro-Economic Database, EC.

than any other GIPS country. The other is that Greece has performed notably worse than the other GIPS countries. Greece remains in a perilous economic state and it is hard to see how it can recover when the government is obliged to service a huge deficit at the same time as repaying loans to the EU and the IMF. Spain and Portugal are in-between Ireland; economic times have been harsh for both countries, but in each case there are signs that a slow recovery is starting. Overall, the Troika-imposed fiscal consolidation programmes have put GIPS countries through severe economic hardship. But the Troika has not only been concerned with fiscal retrenchment, it has also been trying to engineer greater labour market flexibility across the GIPS countries. In the next section, 'Labour Market Flexibility in the GIPS Countries', we set out the Troika-inspired institutional changes each country has made to their labour markets.

LABOUR MARKET FLEXIBILITY IN THE GIPS COUNTRIES

Ireland

The economic recession, which commenced in 2008 in the wake of the credit crunch and the international financial crisis, is widely regarded as the most serious in Ireland's history as an independent country, and the Irish crisis has been among the worst of all developed economies. In terms of labour market reform, successive governments, in response to the crisis, have not launched any systematic or noteworthy legislative programme to reshape the governance of the labour market (Roche et al. 2013). To a large extent, the absence of labour market deregulation measures can be explained by the Irish employment system already being highly flexible. In other words, *initial conditions* separated Ireland from Greece, Portugal, and Spain, in that the Troika, for the most part, did not view the country as possessing institutional rigidities that required a radical labour market deregulation programme.

Thus, the Troika did not exert any significant pressure on Irish governments to ease employment protection rules. Indicative of the attitude adopted by the Troika on the matter was the reform of Registered Employment Agreements and Joint Labour Committees, statutory instruments to legally extend pay agreements in (mostly) low wage sectors. In its initial economic programme, the Troika signalled that these arrangements should be radically scaled back. But once it realized that the government had already initiated a reform of these bodies, it relaxed this demand and allowed the domestic reform programme to run its course. Of more concern to the Troika was the need for Ireland to adopt a new ALMP regime for the employed. In particular, the Troika sought greater efficiency in the administration of unemployment and related social benefits, more stringent conditions regarding availability to work rules, the development of customized activation plans of the unemployed, and more comprehensive monitoring of job-seeking activities by the unemployed. For the most part, Ireland has complied with these demands (see Chapter 13, this volume).

For the most part, the labour market adjustment that has occurred in Ireland in response to the economic recession has focused on arranging wage reductions in the public sector and changing the institutional contours of wage bargaining both nationally and in the public sector. One of the first casualties of the Irish crisis was the 'social partnership' model, which collapsed at the end of 2009 (Teague and Donaghey 2015). As highlighted in Chapter 11, after the collapse of social partnership, pay determination and industrial relations underwent a process of orderly decentralization in the private sector. At the same time, the government quickly moved to adjust downwards public-sector pay and pensions in a similarly orderly manner. To this end, in 2010, as documented in Chapter 12, it concluded, with various public-sector trade unions and professional associations, a four-year centralized Public Service Agreement, which became known as the Croke Park Agreement. An important innovation made by the Croke Park Agreement was the introduction of a third-party compulsory arbitration system into organizational change programmes for the public sector.

Assessments of this new arbitration system suggest that it has had a decisive impact on public-sector collective bargaining. Before the economic crisis, trade union and management relations in many parts of the public sector were characterized by arm's-length accommodation, which involved management not pushing for radical organizational change and trade unions not pushing too strongly for improved wages and working conditions. The introduction of arbitration has disrupted this compromise, leading to accelerated public-sector organizational change. Whether this new industrial relations climate will endure when more buoyant economic times return remains to be seen. Overall, Irish Governments have engineered a significant internal devaluation. But even in the context of far-reaching internal devaluation, vast swathes of the institutional architecture of Irish industrial relations have remained untouched.

Greece

Under the Troika economic adjustment programme, the Greek Government was required to introduce even more extensive and rapid changes to the country's labour law and collective bargaining systems (EC 2011a). Greece traditionally had a multilayered system of wage bargaining, with sector-level bargaining predominating over bargaining at national, occupational (national or local level), and company levels. The coverage of collective agreements is high, despite relatively low union density (24 per cent of employees in 2008 before the recession). High coverage is secured through the administrative extension of agreements to those firms not involved in the negotiations (with no opt-out possible). Moreover, firm-level wage bargaining could not lower, only increase, wages established by higher collective agreements (the so-called favourability principle). Wage setting was also traditionally influenced by the arbitration system in a way that favoured trade unions. In particular, only trade unions had recourse to arbitration when a deadlock existed between trade union and employer positions in sector-level or occupational collective bargaining negotiations; over the years, arbitration decisions normally favoured trade unions (Voskeritsian and Kornelakis 2011).

Legislative action at the end of 2010 introduced a series of reforms to this traditional collective bargaining system. Effectively, the law abolished the favourability principle associated with firm-level collective agreements and offered non-negotiating firms an opt-out from the administrative extension of collectively agreed wages. The law also reformed the arbitration system so that both trade unions and employers could resort to arbitration. In addition, the legislation required mediators and arbitrators, when dealing with a dispute, to take into consideration the competitiveness and economic performance of both the firm and the sector in which it was located (Ioannou and Papadimitriou 2013). In particular, an additional type of collective agreement was introduced—the Special Firm-Level Collective Agreement (SFLCA)—that allows employers and employees to agree wages levels less favourable than those stipulated in sectoral collective agreements. Collective bargaining was subject to further legal reform in 2012 when the *metenergeia* system, which allowed sectoral collective agreements that had reached the end of their time period to continue operating for six months, was terminated. In addition, individualized forms of bargaining on pay and working conditions were made legally permissible for the first time. Salary increases linked to length of employment service, that were sanctioned by collective bargaining, were also suspended until unemployment had dropped once again below 10 per cent.

Although EPL in Greece is around the Organisation for Economic Co-operation and Development (OECD) average, legal reforms have been introduced to relax some of the rules. First of all, the notice period prior to dismissal of white collar workers was substantially reduced: for those on long tenure, it has been shortened to six from twenty-four months. The new legal provisions also lowered total severance costs for white collar workers with long tenure, in some cases by a half. No changes, however, were made to notice periods or severance payments for blue collar workers. Collective dismissals rules were also diluted to increase the threshold above which dismissals are characterized as collective—up from 4 to 6 employees for enterprises with 20–150 employees and 5 per cent (up from 2–3 per cent) or 30 employees (whichever is smaller) for those with more than 150 employees. The probationary period in a job was extended from two months to one year, and permitted fixed-term contracts for employees hired through temporary work agencies were extended to thirty-six months from eighteen months, with renewal limits abolished, thus effectively eliminating indefinite contracts for newly hired workers.

Further labour market deregulation was introduced to increase the flexibility of working time arrangements. Legislative action was taken to reduce overtime pay by 20 per cent across the board and to amend downwards pay for part-time workers. Legal changes were also made to allow firms to introduce short-time working and various forms of annualized working hours schemes (Papadimitriou 2013). Minimum wage levels have been significantly lowered. In 2014, yet more reforms were introduced, aimed at reducing salary levels and scales, as well as pension provision for certain categories of public-sector workers. In addition, across-the-board changes were introduced to make working hours in the public sector more flexible (EC 2014).

Portugal

A key element of the Troika economic adjustment programme for Portugal was reforms to increase labour market flexibility (EC 2011b). These reforms were introduced in agreement with the social partners through the Tripartite Agreement (Compromisso para o Crescimento, Competitividade e Emprego) reached in January 2012. This agreement gave the green light to wide-ranging reforms. First of all, the collective bargaining system was reformed. Traditionally, wage levels were set through sector-level collective bargaining, which government extended as a matter of routine to other firms in the same sector that did not participate directly in the process. The reform measures sought to revamp this arrangement by decentralizing collective bargaining from the sector to the firm level. In addition, the extension of collective agreement by government was heavily constrained (under the new measures, government was only permitted to extend agreements when the involved employers' associations employed more than 50 per cent of employees in a sector). As well as fragmenting sector-level bargaining, the 2012 reforms froze minimum wages until a full economic recovery had been secured. Far-reaching changes were introduced to shorten the duration and limit unemployment benefits. In particular, the maximum duration of unemployment benefits was reduced from thirty-eight to twenty-six months and the level of benefits was reduced by about 16 per cent on average. The aim of these changes was to encourage early return to employment, thus reducing the risk of long-term unemployment (LTU).

A series of reforms were introduced to encourage micro-level flexibility. Measures were enacted to weaken the insulated status of permanent employees. Regulation governing working time arrangements was also scaled back: in terms of overtime, employees were previously paid 50 per cent extra for the first hour of overtime worked, 75 per cent extra for additional hours, and 100 per cent extra for overtime on holidays and Sundays. These rates were reduced to 25 per cent, 37.5 per cent, and 50 per cent respectively. Further legislation encouraged firms to adopt annualized working schemes to reduce the need for overtime in the first place (Ramalho and do Rosário 2013).

Thus, as part of the wider economic adjustment programme developed by the Troika, the Portuguese government introduced a comprehensive labour market flexibility programme. Since it was first enacted in 2012, there has been some rowing back on particular facets of the programme, especially in the area of collective bargaining (OECD 2014a). In particular, a legislative measure relating to the functioning of sector-level collective bargaining may curtail decentralized firm-level collective bargaining, and an additional piece of legislation rescinded the more stringent criterion for extending collective agreements introduced in 2012. Overall, however, the labour market flexibility programme has been implemented effectively and the first signs are emerging that it may be influencing labour market behaviour (OECD 2014a).

Spain

Although a formal Troika economic adjustment was not developed for Spain, the government nevertheless committed itself to labour market reform in return for EU bailout finance to rescue Spanish banks. As a result, in 2012, a newly elected Conservative Government gave effect to this programme when it adopted the Real Decreto Ley 3/2012, which contained a hefty catalogue of labour market flexibility initiatives. The 2012 reform programme sought to increase macro-flexibility of the labour market by decentralizing collective bargaining from the sector level to firms (Molina and Miguélez 2013). In addition, the new law made it easier for firms to opt out of established collective agreements, enabling them, for the first time, to introduce unilateral changes to work organization and working conditions; in other words, firms were given greater freedom to pursue internal flexibility measures. These collective bargaining reforms brought to an end the last vestiges of the national social pact system that had existed in the country before the crisis, which involved trade unions, employers, and government concluding tripartite agreements.

In addition to recasting the institutional architecture of the country's collective bargaining system, the 2012 reform programme introduced substantial changes to its employment dismissal rules. The law made it easier for firms to dismiss employees and also significantly reduced the monetary compensation employees received for unfair dismissal (Wolf and Mora-Sanguinetti 2011). These micro-flexibility reforms to employment protection regulations were aimed at reducing what was widely perceived as endemic levels of labour market segmentation in the country.

The 2012 labour market reform programme was significant, as it simultaneously sought to improve the macro- and micro-flexibility of the employment system (OECD 2014b). Initially, trade unions mounted a campaign of strong opposition to this campaign, which culminated in a general strike in May 2012. However, a more pragmatic stance now seems to prevail amongst unions. Although still firmly opposed to the direction of labour market reform, trade unions have actively sought to conclude national bilateral collective agreements with employers. For example, in an effort to maintain an autonomous national social dialogue with employers, trade unions signed up to the Inter-Confederal Agreement on Employment and Collective Bargaining, which effectively sanctioned decentralized collective bargaining and encouraged firms to use collective bargaining processes to develop internal flexibility plans.

IRELAND: BETWEEN THE CORE AND THE PERIPHERY

All in all, the Troika's insistence on 'structural adjustment' to the governance of labour markets appears to be having a greater impact on some GIPS countries than others. It is difficult to argue that the Troika's labour market adjustment programme has uprooted established industrial relations institutions in Ireland. Although the country has undergone a serious bout of internal devaluation, which delivered a knockout blow to the eighteen-year regime of social partnership, the Troika's austerity regime has left the country's industrial relations, rules, and traditions more or less intact. Ireland escaped from having to implement the far-reaching labour market flexibility reforms required of other GIPS countries. For the most part, this is because the Troika did not consider the country as possessing the segmented 'Mediterranean' employment systems institutions that were seen to be embedded in the labour markets of Greece, Portugal, and Spain.

A 'Mediterranean' employment system is widely seen—and not simply by the Troika—as dividing the labour market into 'insiders' and 'outsiders', with highly distortionary effects. Extensive employment protection for those on permanent contracts is seen as leading to wage rigidity, as insider employees become insulated from wider economic conditions (Bentolila, Boeri, and Cahuc 2010). Labour mobility, which facilitates economic adjustment from old to new economic activity, is considered impaired, as insider employees stay with their existing employees. Training too is seen to be harmed, as firms have little incentive to upskill employees on temporary contracts and employees on these contacts have little motivation to engage in training (Cabrales, Dolado, and Mora 2014). Finally, labour market dualism makes it difficult to integrate young people properly into work (Bentolila, Dolado, and Jimeno 2012).

The concerted drive by the Troika to disrupt these insider/outsider labour markets by weakening collective wage-setting processes and employment regulation is motivated by a desire to create national industrial relations systems that are compatible with monetary union in Europe. To move closer towards an optimal currency area, the Eurozone needs its institutionally heterogeneous national employment systems to function in a manner that ensures the alignment of wages with productivity growth as well as wider labour market adaptability. Insider/outsider labour markets are considered to do neither and thus contribute to macroeconomic asymmetries inside the Eurozone by aggravating real exchange-rate misalignments between core and periphery members. Reform efforts to curtail the functioning of Mediterranean labour markets have had a telling, yet uneven, impact. Although reforms are corroding mechanisms for employment protection and social solidarity, it is unlikely that they are fully dismantling established industrial relations systems. The only possible exception is Greece, where ongoing institutional and economic upheavals are immense.

At the same time, the Troika-imposed reforms have been strong enough to trigger widespread resentment amongst citizens in the European periphery towards the battery of regressive economic and social policies which they consider are being imposed upon them from the outside in a highly undemocratic manner. As a result, a new dualism has opened between the core and periphery inside the Eurozone, with the only common ground tying the two together being the idea that the unravelling of the Eurozone would be an even greater calamity than its continuation.

Ireland stands apart from the other GIPS countries in that its employment relations system is more institutionally aligned with the demands of Eurozone membership. A standout feature of the country's response to the Great Recession was the ability of the collective bargaining system in the public sector to deliver a large-scale fiscal retrenchment programme in an orderly manner. In the private sector, the break-up of national social partnership and the return to decentralized pay bargaining was achieved in a similarly orderly fashion. Although employers were obliged sometimes to enact uncomfortably large-scale organizational adjustment programmes, there was little attempt to take advantage of the recession to marginalize unions. These developments suggest that Ireland's collective bargaining system functions in a manner that is broadly consistent with the country's highly open model of economic development, including membership of the Eurozone. An abiding sense emerges from the period that trade unions, employer organizations, and government recognized that they had to act, both on their own and in their interactions with each other, in a manner that did not compromise the credibility of the country's model of economic development, or Eurozone membership. Thus, Ireland has an industrial relations system with the internal capacity to respond more quickly to unanticipated economic shocks than other GIPS countries.

CONCLUSIONS

Two standout features emerge from this chapter. One is that the Troika-imposed large-scale fiscal consolidation and large-scale labour market flexibility programmes on the GIPS countries has brought the Eurozone short-term relief, but its long-term stability is in no way assured: the Eurozone still faces an existentialist threat. The incapacity of the member states to govern the Eurozone in a manner that is tolerable to all means that industrial relations systems everywhere within the EU, but particularly in GIPS countries, are likely to be placed under even more stress. The other is that Ireland stands out from the other GIPS countries in terms of the quicker, more robust manner it has been emerging from the Great Recession. The better fortunes of Ireland are not only due to its extensive economic ties with countries outside the Eurozone, but also to the close alignment between domestic industrial relations institutions and the highly open nature of the economy. This assessment suggests the prevailing tendency to lump together different groups of countries inside the Eurozone should not be pushed too far. Each member state has its own idiosyncratic features and a Eurozone that cannot accommodate these is likely to remain precarious.

REFERENCES

Bentolila, S., Boeri, T., and Cahuc, P. 2010. 'Ending the Scourge of Dual Labour Markets in Europe'. *Vox*, 1 July.

Bentolila, S., Dolado, J. J., and Jimeno, J. F. 2012. 'Reforming an Insider–Outsider Labour Market: The Spanish Experience'. *IZA Journal of European Labor Studies*, 1: 4.

Blanchard, O., Jaumotee, F., and Loungani, P. 2013. 'Labor Market Policies and IMF Advice in Advanced Economies during the Great Recession', IMF Staff Discussion Paper, Washington, 29 March.

Cabrales, A., Dolado, J. J., and Mora, R. 2014. 'Dual Labour Markets and (Lack of) On-the-Job Training: PIAAC Evidence from Spain and Other EU Countries', CEPR Discussion Paper 10246. London: Centre for Economic Policy Research.

De Grauwe, P. 2011. 'The Governance of a Fragile Eurozone', CEPS Working Documents, Economic Policy, May.

De Grauwe, P. and Ji, Y. 2013. 'Panic-Driven Austerity in the Eurozone and its Implications'. Available at: <http://voxeu.org/article/panic-driven-austerity-eurozone-and-its-implications> (accessed 11 April 2016).

EC (European Commission). 2011a. *The Economic Adjustment Programme for Greece. Fourth Review, Spring 2011*. Brussels: European Commission.

EC (European Commission). 2011b. 'The Economic Adjustment Programme for Portugal', European Economy Occasional Papers No. 79. Brussels: European Commission.

EC (European Commission). 2014. 'The Second Economic Adjustment Programme for Greece: Fourth Review', European Economy Occasional Papers No. 192. Brussels: European Commission.

Grahl, J. and Teague, P. 2013. 'Reconstructing the Eurozone: The Role of EU Social Policy'. *Cambridge Journal of Economics*, 37(3): 677–92.

Hardiman, N., Blavoukos, S., Dellepiane-Avellaneda, S., and Pagoulatos, G. 2016. 'Austerity in the European Periphery: The Irish Experience', Geary Institute Working Paper 2016/4. Dublin: University College Dublin.

Hassel, A. 2014. 'Adjustments in the Eurozone: Varieties of Capitalism and the Crisis in Southern Europe', LEQS Working Paper No. 76, May., London: Lndon School of Economics.

Ioannou, C. and Papadimitriou, K. 2013. *Collective Negotiations in Greece during 2011–2012: Trends, Changes and Prospects*. Athens: OMED.

Iversen, T. and Soskice, D. 2013. 'A Structural-Institutional Explanation of the Eurozone Crisis', Unpublished Manuscript, Harvard University, Department of Government, Cambridge, MA.

Keane, C. 2015. 'Irish Public Finances through the Financial Crisis'. *Fiscal Studies*, 36 (4): 475–97.

McDonnell, T. and O'Farrell, P. 2015. 'Internal Devaluation and Labour Market Trends during Ireland's Economic Crisis', Working Paper 2015/No. 28. Dublin: Nevin Economic Research Institute.

Molina, O. and Miguélez, F. 2013. 'From Negotiation to Imposition: Social Dialogue in Austerity Times', Working Paper No. 51. Geneva: International Labour Organization.

OECD (Organisation for Economic Co-operation and Development). 2014a. *Economic Survey of Portugal 2014*. Paris: OECD.

OECD (Organisation for Economic Co-operation and Development). 2014b. *Economic Survey of Spain 2014*. Paris: OECD.

Papadimitriou, G. 2013. 'The Greek Labour Law Face to the Crisis: A Dangerous Passage towards a New Juridical Nature', Working Paper 3/2013. Brussels: European Labour Law Network.

Ramalho, P. and do Rosário, M. 2013. 'Portuguese Labour Law and Industrial Relations during the Crisis', Governance Working Paper No. 54. Geneva: International Labour Organization.

Roche, W. K., Teague, P., Coughlan, A., and Fahy, M. 2013. *Recession at Work: HRM in the Irish Crisis*. London: Routledge.

Teague, P. and Donaghey, J. 2015. 'The Life and Death of Irish Social Partnership: Lessons for Social Pacts'. *Business History*, 57(3): 418–37.

Voskeritsian, H. and Kornelakis, A. 2011. 'Institutional Change in Greek Industrial Relations in an Era of Fiscal Crisis', Hellenic Observatory Papers on Greece and East Europe, Greece Paper No. 52. London: London School of Economics.

Wolf, A. and Mora-Sanguinetti, J. 2011. 'Reforming the Labour Market in Spain', Working Paper No. 845. Paris: OECD Economics Department.

9

Political Reform

David M. Farrell

INTRODUCTION

Austerity has had more than economic implications for Ireland: there have been significant political consequences too, as shown, first, in the dramatic election of the Fine Gael/Labour Coalition in 2011 and, most recently, in the 2016 election that saw both parties lose significant support and ushered in an uncertain political outcome. Throughout this period there has been an unprecedented interest in political reform. The purpose of this chapter is to set this in context. The principal finding is that while political reform has indeed occurred, many of the actual reforms that have taken place have been to a large degree 'distractive' rather than 'constructive'—that is, in many instances they haven't amount to much real change to how politics operates in Ireland. There was, however, one significant innovation—in the form of the Irish Constitutional Convention—that is attracting international interest.

The chapter is arranged in four parts. It starts with a brief outline of the extent of democratic transformation that has been visited on most of the world's established democracies, a transformation that until recently appears to have largely passed Ireland by. We then review the context of the 2011 election, which was to see political reform come to the top of the political agenda. The next section, 'Political Reforms in Ireland 2011–16', examines the reforms that were implemented by the Fine Gael/Labour government between 2011 and 2016, a large portion of which have done little to change how politics operates. In the section 'Ireland as a Trailblazer: The Irish Constitutional Convention, 2012–14', the focus shifts from content to method in the form of the Irish Constitutional Convention, a deliberative 'mini-public' method of discussing constitutional reform. We conclude with a discussion of the 2016 general election and its ramifications for the state of Irish democracy.

DEMOCRATIC TRANSFORMATION

Democracies are transforming before our very eyes (Cain, Dalton, and Scarrow 2003; Saward 2010). In most of Europe's established democracies the experience for today's citizens is very different from that of previous generations. Consider these examples:

- Austria's decision in 2008 to reduce the voting age to 16;
- Belgium's long road to federalization;
- Finland's 2000 reforms to reduce the power of the presidency;
- Reforms in France (2008) and the Netherlands (2004) introducing the right for citizens to petition for referenda;
- Italy's various stages of electoral reform;
- The ongoing devolution agenda in the UK.

The most comprehensive evidence of these institutional reforms is provided by Bedock, Mair, and Wilson (2012), who examined the trends across seven main dimensions of institutional reform in eighteen established European democracies over a twenty-year period from 1990 to 2010. Summary indicators are provided in Table 9.1, showing a total of 173 reforms across the period, 51 of which were deemed 'substantial'—defined as: 'significantly alter [ing] the balance of power and/or the nature of the relationship between parties...citizens and elites' (Bedock, Mair, and Wilson 2012: 9). As they note, this amounts to an average of 9.5 reforms (3 of them substantial) per country. The evidence is emphatic: 'institutional reform is far from a rare occurrence and indeed occurs quite frequently' (Bedock, Mair, and Wilson 2012: 17).

Ireland has not been entirely immune from these pressures for change—or so it may appear. There have been many referendums to change the Constitution—thirty-nine to date, putting Ireland in third position (behind

Table 9.1. Institutional reforms in Europe: 1990–2010 (number)

	Total	Substantial
Decentralization	58	20
Electoral Reform	29	7
Public Subsidies	28	2
Parliament Reform	23	10
Suffrage Access	16	1
Direct Election	13	8
Direct Democracy	6	3
Total	173	51

Source: Bedock, Mair, and Wilson 2012: Figure 1.

Switzerland and Italy) for the regularity of referendums in Europe.[1] And there have been no shortage of weighty constitutional reviews proposing all manner of constitutional and institutional reforms, most notably: the 1967 Committee on the Constitution, the 1996 Constitution Review Group, the 1996–2002 All-Party Committees on the Constitution, and the 2007–11 Joint Committee on the Constitution (see Coakley 2013).

It would seem that the Irish experience fits the wider European picture of reform. But does it? The fact is that none of the worthy Irish constitutional reviews actually resulted in constitutional change: the proverbial 'dusty shelf' became their final resting place. And only a minority of the referendums to date have made changes to how Ireland's political institutions operate; instead, most focus has been on moral issues such as abortion and divorce (and most recently marriage equality), on treaty reforms to meet Irish obligations as an European Union (EU) member state, or on changes relating to the Northern Ireland agenda. The list of institutional reforms resulting from national referendums is pretty short, amounting to the following:

- The failed electoral reform referendums of 1959 and 1968;
- Reducing the voting age to 18 (1972);
- Seanad votes for graduates from all Irish universities (passed in 1979 but to date never implemented);
- Votes for (certain) non-citizens (1984);
- Constitutional recognition to local government and regularization of local government elections (1999).

The fact is that, for the past ninety years or so, unlike most of its European counterparts, the picture Ireland has presented is one of relatively little reform: the original 1937 Constitution drafted by Éamon de Valera has stood the test of time, its fundamentals for the most part remaining unaltered. Indeed, it is somewhat ironic to note just how steadfastly the 'Westminster tradition' remains unaltered on this side of the Irish sea despite some pretty fundamental institutional reforms in the UK over the past twenty years or so (e.g. Hazell et al. 2001): Brian Farrell's (1988) description of the Irish political system as 'more British than the British themselves' was never more true.

EARTHQUAKES AND REVOLUTIONS?

In the wake of the Great Recession, starting in 2008, and the economic havoc it wreaked on Ireland, all this looked set to change. The stage was seemingly set

---

[1] <http://www.c2d.ch/index.php>.

with the outcome of the 2011 general election, which, in comparative terms, was one of the most dramatic ever witnessed: only two other elections (the Italian election of 1994 and the Dutch election of 2002) surpassed it in terms of inter-party volatility in established democracies (Mair 2011).

Whatever way one looks at it, the Irish general election of 2011 appeared exceptional. The various accounts of it competed to find the most appropriate metaphor: 'watershed moment', 'perfect storm', or 'electoral earthquake' (Gallagher and Marsh 2011; though for more recent treatment of this election, see Marsh, Farrell, and McElroy forthcoming). The most notable outcome of the election was the collapse of Fianna Fáil, one of the world's most enduring and successful parties. In comparative terms, Fianna Fáil's defeat was among the largest experienced by a major party in the history of parliamentary democracy. Fianna Fáil—in government between 1997 and 2011 and widely blamed for Ireland's economic collapse—went from being the largest party in the state (a position it had held since 1932) to being a bit player in Irish political life; it had never received so few seats (12 per cent in the lower house) or such a small vote share (17.4 per cent) as in 2011.

Fine Gael and Labour were swept to power on a promise to radically overhaul politics in Ireland. Their 2011 Programme for Government spoke breathlessly of a 'democratic revolution'. The potential for real political reform looked good. There was a strong sense that politics needed to change in the light of the country's economic collapse. To that end, an agenda for radical political reform was pushed by all the parties bar none in their election manifestos (Suiter and Farrell 2011), and this coincided with a clamour from wider civil society groups for change. The newly elected government was in the envious position of holding the largest majority in the history of the state, elected with a mandate for radical reform, and faced by a divided and somewhat cowed (at least then) opposition. There was every reason to expect a large-scale overhaul of the political system: the circumstances could not have been more perfect.

POLITICAL REFORMS IN IRELAND 2011–16

Before examining the Irish case we need to clarify terms: in particular, what do we mean by 'political reform'? In its essence this is a change to a political institution (or practice) that is intended to make it operate differently. There are two dimensions to this (see Renwick and Pilet 2014 for more): the size (or extent) of the reform and the mechanism of reform. In terms of size we have, at one extreme, major reforms that have the potential of changing how politics in this area operates, of producing a 'cultural' shift in behaviour. A prominent example of this would be the process of federalizing the Belgian system since the 1970s. Minor reforms, by contrast, generally involve small changes to an existing institution that may have little if any tangible impact (e.g. a small reduction in the size of a parliament). As we might expect, there are likely to be reforms that lie somewhere between these two extremes. There is also the potential that a series of small coterminous reforms may be 'bundled' together in such a way that, in combination, they could have major impact (Bedock 2014).

A second dimension of variation in reforms is over the mechanisms of (or approaches to) reform, which again range between two extremes (Renwick and Pilet 2014). On the one hand, we have constructive approaches to reform that are genuinely and unambiguously aimed at improving the operation of the democratic system; in this instance, the general consensus among the reforms' observers would be that these are reforms aimed at resolving an identified problem (e.g. the introduction of gender quotas to bring more women into politics). By contrast, distractive reforms are changes that are intended to distract public attention, usually by making reforms that do not (and were not intended to) actually change how things operate. Much like a parent may seek to distract a child's attention by jangling a set of keys, governments are adept at raising red herrings so as to avoid making changes that could affect their hold over power (e.g. shortening parliamentary summer vacations). A variant of the distractive approach is to push a populist agenda that may satisfy public anger without actually changing how politics operates (e.g. reducing politicians' pay).

So what was it that needed to be fixed in Ireland? Views on the precise details always differ, but what is apparent from a review of the posts on the Political Studies Association of Ireland's 'Irish Politics Forum' blog (<http://www.politicalreform.ie>) around the time of the 2011 election is that there was a large degree of consensus on the part of the academic community that reforms were needed most of all to address two major problems in Irish politics: a highly centralized system of government and a serious lack in openness and transparency. In combination these were seen to have contributed to the clear failings in the Irish political system in the lead up to the economic crash (more generally, see Hardiman 2012; Farrell 2015a).

The lack of openness and transparency manifested itself in weak freedom-of-information (FOI) legislation, lack of protection to whistle-blowers, and no regulation of lobbyists. When combined with poor regulation of party finance, Ireland had all the ingredients for a political system open to abuse: images of certain 'Galway tents' spring to mind.[2] In its turn, the excessive centralization of Irish Government is seen to have a number of features, but most prominent among these are the weakness of the Dáil vis-à-vis government, the fact that TDs (MPs) are distracted from their legislative scrutiny roles due to their

---

[2] These were receptions held during the annual Galway race meetings by Fianna Fáil and reputably attended by major builders and developers.

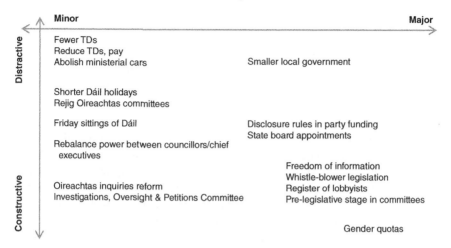

Figure 9.1. Irish political reforms, 2011–

Source: Compiled by author

zealous focus on constituency concerns (Farrell et al. 2016a), and a weak system of local government.

There is no disputing the fact that a lot of reforms were implemented between 2011 and 2016: Figure 9.1 summarizes the main ones (though this is certainly not the full list[3]). Clearly many of these were relatively minor and fall on the 'distractive' end of the scale. But there was a grouping of reforms which—if 'bundled' together (à la Bedock)—are potentially system changing: gender quotas (which opens up access to politics), the pre-legislative stage (which gives a greater role to Oireachtas committees in scrutinizing draft legislation), and the reforms relating to open government (FOI, whistle-blowers, and register of lobbyists).

For the purposes of this chapter, if we focus on the two key concerns identified—open government and overly centralized government—the reform record of the 2011–16 Fine Gael/Labour Coalition Government was, at best, pretty mixed. On the one hand, there was undoubted progress on the open government agenda, in large part driven by Brendan Howlin as Minister for Public Expenditure and Reform. After a long process of consultation—its longevity at one point sparking concerns over the government's seriousness of intent—the relevant legislation appeared in a series of steps, the first of which was the passing of the Protected Disclosures Act in July 2014, introducing statutory protection for whistle-blowers. While a welcome move, the extent to which this legislation has been matched by a cultural shift in the

[3] For more, see <http://www.villagemagazine.ie/index.php/2016/02/report-card-accountability-and-transparency/>.

senior echelons of the public service has yet to be seen. Major public and political controversy over the treatment of whistle-blowers in the Garda (the Irish police force) suggests that much remains to be done in this area.

Within a few months of the passing of the whistle-blowing legislation, the government passed a new Freedom of Information Act that reversed the serious watering down of FOI by the Fianna Fáil–Progressive Democrat Coalition in 2003. The third main plank of the open government regime was the Regulation of Lobbying Act in early 2015, a core feature of which is the creation of a register of lobbyists. Whereas it could be said of FOI and whistle-blowing legislation that Ireland is playing catch up with its European counterparts, the register of lobbyists places Ireland somewhat more at the vanguard (Chari, Hogan, and Murphy 2010). Overall, these three pieces of legislation place Ireland on a par with open government trends in other European democracies (Cain, Dalton, and Scarrow 2003), with the government's intent in this regard buttressed by its active engagement, since July 2014, in the international Open Government Partnership programme (<http://www.opengovpartnership.org>) that is operating in over sixty countries around the world.

One additional plank of the open government agenda was a tightening up of regulatory controls relating to party finance—in this instance a reform introduced by Phil Hogan in 2012 when he was the Minister for the Environment. A series of damning findings in costly judicial tribunals investigating Irish party finance raised serious concerns over political corruption in high places (Byrne 2012a), prompting the newly elected government to pass fresh legislation that, in principle, was designed to plug serious gaps in the regulation of party funding. But whatever the government's intent, many problems remain, to the extent that its most recent annual report, as in every annual report that preceded it, the Standards in Public Office Commission (SIPO)—the body responsible for monitoring party finance—called for greater clarity in party accounts:[4] many of the details of the income and expenditure of Irish parties remain unknown and unmonitored.

If the news on the open government agenda is generally good, the same cannot be said for reforms relating to reducing the excessive centralization of Irish Government. For all the rhetoric around Oireachtas reform, the situation remains that Ireland has one of the weakest parliaments in Europe. The bulk of the reforms implemented—for example, relating to Dáil hours, ministerial pay, and numbers of committees—were more cosmetic than substantial, more key-jangling distractive (or populist) than the constructive reforms needed to address the imbalance between executive and legislature that characterizes politics in Ireland. The singular exception to this has been the introduction of

---

[4] <http://www.sipo.gov.ie/en/reports/annual-reports/2014-annual-report/>.

a 'pre-legislative' stage in the scrutiny of legislation, giving parliamentarians greater scope to persuade the Minister to take on board suggestions for amendment. This is a reform that has long been called for (e.g. MacCarthaigh and Manning 2010) and already it is making a difference in giving parliamentary committees greater influence over the fine-tuning of draft legislation.

In addition, there were some last-minute changes—passed in the dying days of the Dáil session—that were to presage a fresh round of Dáil reforms in the subsequent parliament elected in early 2016. The government held a vote to change parliamentary standing orders to make two key changes, namely: that the next Ceann Comhairle (Speaker) of the Dáil will be elected by secret ballot (modelled on the procedure used in the UK House of Commons), and that committee chair positions should be allocated proportionally using the d'Hondt formula (similar to the process used in the European Parliament). Both of these changes wrest power from the Taoiseach and the governing parties. The precise reason for these late reforms is unclear, but it is speculated that one factor may have been a desire on the part of the Fine Gael Party to pre-empt moves by others to wrong-foot them on this agenda in the lead up to the election.[5]

In general, then, the 2011–16 Fine Gael/Labour Coalition Government did produce some reforms, but was they enough? Certainly one feature that stood out was the government's proclivity to pat its own back with annual statements on progress in implementing its Programme for Government.[6] But once we drill down into what actually changed, things were not as impressive as they may seem. Apart from the pre-legislative stage and the last-minute changes relating to the Ceann Comhairle and the committee chairs, little was done to address the serious power imbalance between government and parliament: Irish political power remains as highly centralized at the top as it has always been (Döring 2002; MacCarthaigh 2005).

In short, a large portion of the reforms was towards the distractive end of the scale (Figure 9.1). In some instances, the reform process was started so late that there was little chance of it being concluded before the end of the government's term of office: a prominent example of this was the move to establish an electoral commission. This form of election management body, which is common to most democracies (Massicotte, Blais, and Yoshinaka 2004), is something that successive Irish Governments have promised, but never delivered (Farrell 2015b). All this was supposed to change with the election of the Fine Gael/Labour Government, but nothing transpired until after the Irish Constitutional Convention (discussed in the next section of this

---

[5] <http://www.irishtimes.com/opinion/noel-whelan-government-had-no-option-but-to-embrace-dáil-reforms-1.2488637>.

[6] As an illustration, see <http://www.taoiseach.gov.ie/eng/Work_Of_The_Department/Programme_for_Government/>.

chapter) recommended that an electoral commission should be established, thus putting it back on the political agenda. But by the time the government got around to addressing this it was in the closing months of the government's term, meaning that the issue never got any further than the preliminary phase of a parliamentary report. In short, the government quite deliberately ran out the clock on this reform.

Another feature that stands out about the government's reform agenda was the distinct lack of joined-up thinking, as manifested in a number of respects: the fact that some ministers (most notable among them Brendan Howlin) were more proactive on the reform agenda than others; reforms that moved in differing directions (e.g. a supposed agenda of decentralizing government coinciding with efforts to kill off one of the houses of the legislature) or haven't done what they say on the tin (a local government reform agenda whose ambition to bring local government closer to the people actually resulted in a drastic reduction in the number of councillors); or inexplicable differences in the routes taken to progress reforms (a good example being the insistence of the government to call a referendum on Seanad abolition without allowing any prior consultation, very different from the intense consultation on its open government agenda).

The 2011–16 government's record on introducing substantial reforms to Irish politics was, at best, mixed. But in one important respect there was an undoubted innovation over the creation of a new type of citizen-oriented forum to discuss a series of reform measures: this was the Irish Constitutional Convention.

IRELAND AS A TRAILBLAZER: THE IRISH CONSTITUTIONAL CONVENTION, 2012–14

In late 2012, the Irish Government took the long-anticipated step of establishing the Irish Constitutional Convention (<http://www.constitution.ie>), whose first formal session was held on the weekend of 26–27 January 2013. Internationally there have been plenty of examples over the years of the involvement of citizens in debates over constitutional reform, whether by giving them a voice in referendums or public initiatives, or by allowing them to run for election as members of a convention (a recent example being Iceland's constitutional council of 2011). Ireland's Constitutional Convention also included citizens as members, but it is the nature of how these citizens were selected to participate and how the process was run that is of particular interest. There are a small but growing number of cases in which governments have opted to follow 'deliberative principles', selecting citizens at random rather than by election and managing the discussions along deliberative lines (Farrell 2014).

Irish policymakers were influenced by the citizens' assemblies on electoral reform in the Canadian provinces of British Columbia (2004) and Ontario (2007), and the Dutch citizen's forum (BürgerForum) of 2006 (Fournier et al. 2011). In all these cases the citizen members were selected at random rather than running for election, and deliberation was the modus operandi. This is constitutional reform by 'mini-public'.

The Irish Constitutional Convention emerged out of a compromise between Fine Gael and Labour, both of which had included in their 2011 election manifestos proposals for establishing citizen-oriented forums to discuss possible constitutional reforms in a number of areas. In Fine Gael's case the proposal was specific: for a British Columbia-style citizens' assembly to consider electoral reform. Labour's plan was more ambitious: it proposed the establishment of a Constitutional Convention (made up of equal proportions of politicians, experts, and ordinary citizens) to consider a root and branch review of the Irish Constitution.

In forming the coalition government, the parties sought to marry their sometimes quite disparate manifesto promises, resulting in the promise to establish a Constitutional Convention to examine eight specific issues:

- Reduction of the presidential term of office to five years;
- Reduction of the voting age to 17;
- Review of the Dáil electoral system;
- Irish citizens' right to vote at Irish embassies in presidential elections;
- Provisions for marriage equality;
- Amendment to the existing clause in the Irish Constitution on the role of women in the home and encouraging greater participation of women in public life;
- Increasing the participation of women in politics; and
- Removal of the offence of blasphemy from the Constitution.

This somewhat eclectic mix of items, from the relatively mundane issue of the length of office of the Irish President to the potentially explosive issue of marriage equality, merely reflected the decision of the inter-party negotiators to 'park' certain matters in their respective election manifestos that were unlikely to be resolved easily during their febrile and intense negotiations. They were up against the (largely media-driven) clock to conclude the negotiations and establish a government, so what better way to deal with these matters then wrap them all together and give them to the Constitutional Convention to consider.

It was to take a further eighteen months before the Constitutional Convention was finally established—at the end of 2012—with its work programme starting in early 2013. It was given a small budget and a deadline of one year to conclude its work. Chaired by Tom Arnold (the former chief executive of the development charity Concern), the other ninety-nine members of the convention consisted of sixty-six citizens and thirty-three elected legislators. Whereas the parties could determine by themselves how to select their members (with the parties' allocations proportionate to their representation in parliament), the citizen members were selected at random by a survey company, which had the brief of ensuring that the membership was a fair reflection of the population in terms of gender, age, region, education, and socioeconomic status.

Analysis of the *process* of discussion and deliberation of the convention reveals a high degree of success (Suiter et al. 2016), but how might we judge the convention in terms of its *outcomes*?

A core criticism of the convention from the outset was its agenda, which was seen, at the same time, as too limited and overly crowded (e.g. Byrne 2012b). More to the point, specific matters of constitutional reform that were also on the government political reform agenda (e.g. children's rights, or abolition of the upper house of parliament) were not included on the list of items. While the latter is undoubtedly true—speaking once again to the lack of joined-up thinking on the reform agenda discussed in the previous section, 'Political Reforms in Ireland 2011–16'—the former complaint over the constrained agenda was in large part dissipated by the inventiveness with which convention members interpreted their agenda. As Table 9.2 shows, the agenda of eight specified topics was to ultimately result in no less than forty-one separate recommendations for reform.

But for all that effort, ultimately it was up to the government to determine how it would respond to these recommendations, and it proved slow to do so— responding to the final reports on the eve of the 2016 election. In the end, the government formally accepted just seven of the recommendations—the most prominent of which was the strong endorsement by the convention of a proposed referendum on marriage equality. It was the furore around the convention endorsement that forced the hand of a socially conservative Taoiseach (Collins 2015), and the strong degree of cross-party support engendered by having representatives of all the parties in the membership,[7] that ensured that this referendum question was asked and that it received all party backing.

---

[7] As Alan Shatter (who, as Minister for Justice, had formally announced to the Dáil the government's decision to accept the convention's recommendation) observed in a radio interview: 'The constitutional convention, which produced a recommendation that all parties in the Oireachtas supported, which took—if I could put it this way—the party politics out of this, meant that we had a conversation about the real human dilemmas of individuals affected by our laws. I think that was the key to the outcome of the referendum' (interview on RTÉ, *Morning Ireland*, 25 May 2015). Similarly, the Minister for Foreign Affairs, Charlie Flanagan, was of the view that the referendum campaign would have been 'much more divisive' but for the convention (quoted in Mullally 2014: 243).

Table 9.2. Assessing the ICC in terms of outcomes

Topic	ICC Output	Government Reaction	Action?
1. Reduction of Presidential Term	Three recommendations	Government accepted two; rejected one	Referendum defeated May 2015
2. Reduce Voting Age	One recommendation	Government accepted this	Referendum was promised for 2015; now 'deferred'
3. Role of Women in Home/Public Life	Two recommendations	Ministerial task force to investigate further	Task force 'in progress'
4. Increasing Women's Participation in Politics	Three recommendations	Ministerial task force to investigate further	Task force 'in progress'
5. Marriage Equality	Two recommendations	Government agreed to referendum and to supporting legislation	Referendum passed (May 2015) and legislation passed
6. Electoral System	Ten recommendations	Government promised to establish an electoral commission and to task it with addressing four of the other recommendations; remaining five recommendations rejected	Oireachtas Committee on the Environment published a report (January 2016) supporting electoral commission establishment
7. Votes for Emigrants/ N. Ireland Residents in Presidential Elections	One recommendation	To be investigated further	Still in progress
8. Blasphemy	Two recommendations	Government has agreed to principle of referendum, but no date set	No action taken
9. Dáil Reform	Thirteen recommendations	Government accepted three; rejected two; and gave ambiguous responses to the rest	Standing order changes were made relating to the three accepted recommendations
10. Economic, Social and Cultural Rights	Two recommendations	To be investigated further	Still in progress

Note: For more details see: Farrell, Harris, and Suiter 2016; <http://politicalreform.ie/2016/01/23/final-report-card-on-the-governments-reactions-to-the-irish-constitutional-convention/>.

In both of those senses the convention proved decisive. And, in one other respect, the convention was also to prove important: that was over the decision of voters to vote in favour on polling day. Multivariate analysis of survey data gathered in an opinion poll directly after the referendum shows a statistically significant association between knowledge of the convention and the decision to vote Yes (Elkink et al. 2015).

But the significance of the Irish Constitutional Convention is less over the reforms it may or may not manage to get through the political system. The bigger point is the very fact that it was established, how it was designed, and how it operated. Apart from Canadian provincial and the Dutch cases, this is a world first as a mini-public form of Constitutional Convention. And, in the light of the marriage referendum result, it is certainly the first time in the world that a process of deliberation involving at its heart a random selection of ordinary citizens has resulted in actual constitutional change. For this at least the government deserves some plaudits.

CONCLUSION

The coalition government elected in 2011 was presented with an historically unprecedented opportunity to introduce real and sustained reforms to how politics operates in Ireland. It was elected with the largest majority in the history of the state, on an agenda of large-scale political reform, facing a divided opposition (that nevertheless included parties that also favoured reform), and with a strong mood in the country that politics needed to change. The government appeared to rise to the challenge, promising a 'democratic revolution'. Its much-trumpeted Programme for Government set out an ambitious agenda for change and renewal. The Irish people were told that:

> [N]ew ways, new approaches and new thinking will form the constant backdrop to the coalition's style of governance. In all the major areas of public life this determination to modernise, renew and transform our country will be evident over time as our shared programme is implemented.... [T]here is a clear need for our political system to embrace change, share the burden and lead by example. Every section of our society is facing hardship. Our political system, if it is to regain credibility and relevance, must change too.[8]

As we have seen throughout this chapter, in some important areas progress was made, notably on the implementation of the 'open government' agenda, the introduction of gender quotas, and some facets of the parliamentary reform programme. The establishment of the Irish Constitutional Convention

---

[8] <http://www.merrionstreet.ie/en/About/Programme-for-Government/>.

was also a bold move—even if the subsequent follow through was far less bold. These are undoubted examples of constructive reforms, the intent behind them being to improve how politics and the political system operate in Ireland.

But after that the list starts to look rather threadbare. As a result of five years of government reforms Ireland now has a Dáil that sits for slightly longer hours (but does little more with that time than it did before). It has ministers using private chauffeurs instead of state cars to ferry themselves around (yet the state still picks up the tab for the chauffeurs). Ireland has seen a cut in politicians' pay, a slight reduction in their number in the Dáil, a large reduction in their number at local level, and a failed attempt to kill off one of the houses of parliament that would have reduced their number still more. What all these examples—and more—share in common is that they are distracting attention from the true reforms that are needed, and that had been promised. Ireland continues to have one of the weakest parliaments and one of the least accountable systems of government among Europe's established democracies. The weaknesses that were inherent in the Irish political system in the lead up to the economic crisis remain to this day. Given the unprecedented circumstances the government found itself in, this is especially regrettable. In its Programme for Government, the coalition could not have been clearer in expressing the view that if the political system 'is to regain credibility and relevance, [it] must change too'. The fact that it did not may well have been one of the factors behind the coalition's poor electoral performance in 2016.

As we have seen (in the section entitled 'Earthquakes and Revolutions?'), the 2011 general election proved costly for the Fianna Fáil/Green Coalition Government, but the outcome was only to be expected given the economic crisis that was unfolding at that time and the clear finger of blame that could be pointed at the outgoing administration. But there was reason to believe that things would be different in 2016.

Throughout 2011–16, one of the conundrums that puzzled outside observers of the Irish scene was the lack of social unrest, the reluctant yet stoical willingness of Irish citizens to take the hard medicine of austerity that was a core requirement of the EU/International Monetary Fund (IMF) bailout programme, and the cross-party consensus among all the established parties over the need to implement the austerity programme (even if there were differences over the details). Ireland was to become the poster child for austerity: the Taoiseach was lauded from Berlin to Davos for his leadership in steering his country out of its economic mess. With all the main economic indicators falling nicely into place (economic growth, declining unemployment, bumper tax receipts, debt starting to fall back towards sustainable territory) there seemed good reason for the government to expect a strong performance in the election. Certainly the poll trends were good for Fine Gael; the party was in striking distance of its 2011 vote and the momentum was in the right direction. For

Labour, the polls were more worrisome, but the government parties expected that voters would flock back to them as polling day drew near.

The predictions proved very wrong: both parties lost heavily—with Fine Gael's vote plummeting by 10 percentage points to just over 25 per cent (barely 1 percentage point more than a resurgent Fianna Fáil), and Labour barely managing to hold enough seats to remain politically relevant. What is apparent is that the government badly misjudged the political mood. They (most particularly Fine Gael) fought a campaign focused on tax cuts that left them open to criticism by economic commentators that they were damaging their brand as prudent managers of the economy. The proposal was also out of step with public opinion. An exit poll for the national broadcaster, Radio Telefís Éireann (RTÉ), revealed that voters attached more importance to greater expenditure on social services than to tax cuts.

The outcome of the election was political stalemate: the two established parties that have long dominated Irish politics—Fine Gael (with 25 per cent of the vote) and Fianna Fáil (24 per cent)—remain the largest parties in the Dáil, but neither has enough to form a government without the other and neither want to form a coalition together. The forces ranged against them—the largest of them Sinn Féin (at just under 14 per cent)—are too divided and in any event have insufficient seats to form a government. The outcome, after an unprecedentedly long period of inter-party negotiations, was the creation of a minority Fine Gael government including some independent TDs as members and reliant on the support of Fianna Fáil for votes on 'supply and confidence' matters. The expectation (at the time of writing) is that this government is unlikely to last long.

ACKNOWLEDGEMENTS

I am grateful to the editors for their comments and feedback on earlier drafts of this chapter.

REFERENCES

Bedock, C. 2014. 'Explaining the Determinants and Processes of Institutional Change'. *French Politics*, 12: 357–74.

Bedock, C., Mair, P., and Wilson, A. 2012. 'Institutional Change in Advanced European Democracies: An Exploratory Assessment', EUI Working Papers RSCAS 2012/11. Florence: European University Institute.

Byrne, E. 2012a. *Corruption in Ireland, 1922–2010: A Crooked Harp*. Manchester: Manchester University Press.

Byrne, E. 2012b. 'The Democracy of a Republic'. In *Up the Republic!*, ed. F. O'Toole. Dublin: Faber and Faber.

Cain, B., Dalton, R., and Scarrow, S. (eds.) 2003. *Democracy Transformed? Expanding Political Opportunities in Advanced Industrial Democracies*. Oxford: Oxford University Press.

Chari, R., Hogan, J., and Murphy, G. 2010. *Regulating Lobbying: A Global Comparison*. Manchester: Manchester University Press.

Coakley, J. 2013. *Reforming Political Institutions: Ireland in Comparative Perspective*. Dublin: Institute of Public Administration.

Collins, S. 2015. 'Big Parties Vie for Credit for Yes Vote'. *Irish Times*, 25 May.

Döring, H. (ed.) 2002. *Parliaments and Majority Rule in Western Europe*. Available at: <http://allman.rhon.itam.mx/~emagar/ep3/rules/doring.ed.parliamentsAndMajRule 1995.pdf> (accessed 11 April 2016).

Elkink, J., Farrell, D., Reidy, T., and Suiter, J. 2015. 'The 2015 Marriage Referendum: Conservative Ireland Is Dead and Gone'. Draft paper.

Farrell, B. 1988. 'Ireland. The Irish Cabinet System: More British than the British Themselves'. In *Cabinets in Western Europe*, ed. J. Blondel and F. Mueller-Rommel. Basingstoke: Macmillan.

Farrell, D. 2014. '"Stripped Down" or Reconfigured Democracy'. *West European Politics*, 37: 439–55.

Farrell, D. 2015a. 'Public Policy in Parliamentary Democracies: Evidence to the Committee of Inquiry into the Banking Crisis, March 11 2015'. Available at: <https://inquiries. oireachtas.ie/banking/hearings/david-farrell-public-policy-in-parliamentary-democ racies/> (accessed 11 April 2016).

Farrell, D. 2015b. 'Conclusion and Reflection: Time for an Electoral Commission for Ireland'. *Irish Political Studies*, 30: 641–6.

Farrell, D., Harris, C., and Suiter, J. 2016. 'Bringing People into the Heart of Constitutional Design: The Irish Constitutional Convention of 2012–14'. In *Participatory Constitutional Change: The People as Amenders of the Constitution*, ed. X. Contiades and A. Fotiadou. Aldershot: Ashgate.

Farrell, D., Mair, P., Ó Muineacháin, S., and Wall, M. 2016. 'Courting But Not Always Serving: Perverted Burkeanism and the Puzzle of Irish Parliamentary Cohesion'. In *Parties, Structure and Context*, ed. R. Johnston and C. Sharman. Vancouver: University of British Columbia Press.

Fournier, P., van der Kolk, H., Carty, K., Blais, A., and Rose, J. 2011. *When Citizens Decide: Lessons from Citizen Assemblies on Electoral Reform*. Oxford: Oxford University Press.

Gallagher, M. and Marsh, M. 2011. *How Ireland Voted 2011: The Full Story of Ireland's Earthquake Election*. Basingstoke: Palgrave Macmillan.

Hardiman, N. (ed.) 2012. *Irish Governance in Crisis*. Manchester: Manchester University Press.

Hazell, R., Russell, M., Croft, J., Seyd, B., Masterman, R., and Sandford, M. 2001. 'The Constitution: Rolling out the New Settlement'. *Parliamentary Affairs*, 54(2): 190–205.

MacCarthaigh, M. 2005. *Accountability in Irish Parliamentary Politics*. Dublin: Institute of Public Administration.

MacCarthaigh, M. and Manning, M. 2010. 'Parliamentary Reform'. In *The Houses of the Oireachtas: Parliament in Ireland*, ed. M. MacCarthaigh and M. Manning. Dublin: Institute of Public Administration.

Mair, P. 2011. 'The Election in Context'. In *How Ireland Voted 2011: The Full Story of Ireland's Earthquake Election*, ed. M. Gallagher and M. Marsh. Basingstoke: Palgrave Macmillan.

Marsh, M., Farrell, D., and McElroy, G. (eds.) Forthcoming. *A Conservative Revolution? Electoral Change in 21st Century Ireland*. Oxford: Oxford University Press.

Massicotte, L., Blais, A., and Yoshinaka, A. 2004. *Establishing the Rules of the Game: Election Laws in Democracies*. Toronto: University of Toronto Press.

Mullally, U. 2014. *In the Name of Love: The Movement for Marriage Equality in Ireland —an Oral History*. Dublin: The History Press Ireland.

Renwick, A. and Pilet, J.-B. 2014. 'Populist Democratic Reform: Is It Anything More than Talk?' Paper presented at the ECPR Joint Sessions, Salamanca, April.

Saward, M. 2010. *The Representative Claim*. Oxford: Oxford University Press.

Suiter, J. and Farrell, D. 2011. 'The Parties' Manifestos. In *How Ireland Voted 2011: The Full Story of Ireland's Earthquake Election*, ed. M. Gallagher and M. Marsh. Basingstoke: Palgrave Macmillan.

Suiter, J., Farrell, D., Harris, C., and O'Malley, E. 2016. 'The Irish Constitutional Convention: A Case of "High Legitimacy"?' In *Constitutional Deliberative Democracy in Europe*, ed. M. Reuchamps and J. Suiter. Colchester: ECPR Press.

10

International Actors and Agencies

Brigid Laffan

INTRODUCTION

An assessment of the role of international bodies is essential when seeking to explore and analyse the Irish experience of austerity. It is important to define what 'international' represents in this context. Clearly the International Monetary Fund (IMF) is a classical international organization but the European Union (EU) cannot be classified as purely 'international'. Ireland is a member of the EU and the Eurozone, and thus Ireland's political, constitutional, and public policy system is part of a multilevel governance architecture that extends beyond Ireland but includes it. Irish ministers, civil servants, and central bankers are fully part of day-to-day policymaking in the EU, representing Ireland but also wearing a collective European hat. Irish ministers and officials were part of the Economic and Financial Affairs Council (ECOFIN) and Eurogroup in their capacity as representatives of Ireland. That said, from November 2010 until December 2013, Ireland was transformed from a member state into a programme country with all that this implied for domestic autonomy.

Three European institutions played a particularly important role in the Irish experience, ECOFIN and its subset, the Eurogroup, the European Commission (EC), and the European Central Bank (ECB). The EC and ECB together with the IMF formed the Troika, an institutional innovation that was developed to manage country programmes. The objective of this chapter is to analyse both the role of international and EU bodies during the course of the Irish crisis and Ireland's response to Troika governance. The analysis is contained in four sections. First, the chapter addresses the significance for Ireland of how the crisis was framed by the EU. Second, the role of the Union and the ECB in the 'bank bailout' and its aftermath is explored, together with an exploration of the role of the EU and its institutions in the lead-up to the bailout and the negotiations of the programme in November 2010. The role of the ECB was particularly important in the process that led the Irish Government to formally request official assistance in November 2010. Third, the role of the Troika in the governance of austerity between 2010 and 2013 is analysed. In the fourth section, 'Ireland's State Capacity: Managing Asymmetry', the lens switches to an exploration of how Irish actors and institutions engaged with these international agencies.

The issues addressed in this chapter are highly contested and unlikely ever to be the subject of a consensus interpretation (Donovan and Murphy 2013; Ó Riain 2014; Thorhallsson and Kirby 2012; Whelan 2013a). There are different perspectives within Ireland, varying institutional views among the Troika and Ireland's partners, and a range of political views generated by party competition. Among the many contested issues associated with this period, the two most controversial are the roles that President Trichet and US Treasury Secretary Timothy Geithner played in preventing haircuts on senior bondholders, and the position adopted by President Trichet in the lead-up to the November 2010 bailout.

The study of politics was, for a long time, divided into two subfields, domestic and comparative politics, on the one hand, and international relations, on the other—a distinction which continues to have significance today. From the 1970s onwards, however, scholars of complex interdependence began to address the permeability of borders and the divisibility of sovereignty (Gourevitch 1992; Keohane and Nye 1977). The study of European integration also focused attention on the links between the domestic and the external by characterizing the EU as a system of multilevel governance and by developing a literature on Europeanization. Windhoff-Héritier (2001: 3) defines Europeanization as 'the process of influence deriving from European decisions and impacting member states' policies and political and administrative structures'. This definition highlights the capacity of European decisions to have an effect on policy choice, on the development of political and administrative structures, and on the behaviour of policymakers; in particular, the concept 'influence' denotes the power of European decisions to shape the domestic sphere. A key argument in this chapter is that the Europeanization associated with bailouts and rescue differed from the impact of the EU in normal times for three reasons. First, the crisis gave rise to policymaking in a state of emergency. The pressure of the financial markets and the fragility of Europe's financial systems had a major impact on the timing and nature of policy responses. Second, the crisis gave rise to a major cleavage between creditors and debtors, and the latter were in an extremely vulnerable position with weak negotiating capital. Each troubled country negotiated with the system on their own, not as a bloc. In fact, troubled countries were at pains to say that they were not the worst or the most vulnerable; 'we are not Greece' was a constant refrain during the crisis. Third, as a consequence of vulnerability there was a high level of 'conditionality' associated with the bailouts.

Day-to-day policymaking in the EU is non-hierarchical, and highly fragmented with multiple entry points. In contrast, policymaking in the Eurozone crisis, particularly in relation to the bailouts, was hierarchical and asymmetrical. For Ireland, becoming and being a programme country marked a shift from interdependence within the Union to dependence. Although Ireland became 'semi-sovereign' as a programme country, its political and institutional actors retained a margin of manoeuvrability, an ability to influence Troika governance. The crisis was a major test of Ireland's state capacity, of the ability of its institutions to adapt to a politics of asymmetry and to navigate the challenges of a severe economic, financial, social, and political crisis. The management of asymmetry may well have demonstrated some of the inherent strengths of the Irish system of public policymaking.

THE EU FRAMING THE CRISIS

Political actors do not just respond to a crisis but, crucially, identify and define it though framing a crisis narrative and discourse (Hay 1996; Schmidt 2008). Framing through language is a crucial part of crisis management because 'those who are able to define what the crisis is all about also hold the key to defining the appropriate strategies for resolution' (d'Hart 1993: 41). Masking may also play an important role in crisis management as political actors seek to downplay the extent of the problems or keep aspects of the crisis off the public agenda (d'Hart 1993). The framing of a crisis is a crucial part of the politics of policymaking and has consequences for how problems are understood and addressed.

Initially, following the Lehman collapse, the crisis was interpreted as a problem of the Anglo-Saxon model of capitalism rather than one that might call into question the design and survival of the single currency. It was not until May 2010 that the Heads of Governments (HoGs) acknowledged that there was a 'crisis' when they issued a statement following the first Greek bailout on the 7 May. One month later, in a European Council conclusion, they referred again to the 'worldwide financial crisis' rather than acknowledging that the global crisis had assumed a distinctive Eurozone character. There was an initial period of denial as the Euro states and the ECB grappled with a rapidly evolving situation (Laffan 2014a). Throughout the crisis, the President of the ECB, M. Trichet, was adamant that this was not a crisis of the euro, rather, 'There are important problems at present which are related to bad public finances, by way of consequence, to financial stability. But these problems are the responsibility of the governments in question. Each government must keep its own house in order' (ECB 2011a).

The meta-crisis narrative both from the ECB and the HoGs was that of a crisis of public finances or sovereign debt. Because the focus was on Greece from autumn 2009 onwards, sovereign debt was the core crisis narrative. The first storyline identified fiscal profligacy as the underlying cause of the crisis, attributed blame to the peripheral states, particularly Greece, and assigned primary responsibility to the Euro states themselves. In response to the systemic threat, responsibility was elevated to a shared one within the Eurozone. The narrative was characterized by a strong emphasis on core/periphery and north/south divergence of economic and fiscal performance; Club Med profligacy in contrast to northern prudence. If the cause of the crisis was fiscal profligacy, then the cure was fiscal balance and consolidation. Responsibility for redemption was assigned to individual Euro states but they were to be encased in a set of institutions and rules that would sanction the transgressors.

The meta-narrative of the crisis, however, served to mask a significant dimension of the crisis. States with excessive sovereign debt did not borrow all of the money from their own citizens or banks. And for countries such as Spain and Ireland, the underlying problems were in the banking system not the sovereign signature. For every debtor there was a lender, and in the case of Greece, Ireland, Italy, Portugal, and Spain (GIIPS), the lenders included banks in the core. From the outset, the problem was an interlinked sovereign debt and banking crisis, a crisis of interdependence and financial integration. Banks owe primary responsibility to their shareholders not to taxpayers either of creditor or debtor states. Like all commercial organizations, banks did not want to face losses, and if those losses could be offloaded, they would protect their balance sheets. Governments in Europe had just come through a phase, following Lehman Brothers, of injecting capital into troubled banks. This was deeply unpopular with their citizens and they did not want to face another period of recapitalizing banks. Moreover, the core countries could shift some of the burden of maintaining the financial system and their banks to the taxpayers on the periphery. The problems in the European banking system were disguised in two rounds of limited stress tests (in summer 2010 and 2011). It took until the collapse and rescue of the state-owned Belgian bank Dexia in September 2011, which had passed a stress test in July 2011, for the acute problems in Europe's financial system to be acknowledged. Furthermore, it took until the 29 June 2012 for the Euro Area Summit to acknowledge 'the imperative to break the vicious circle between banks and sovereigns' (EU 2012: 1). This statement signalled the launch of negotiations on a banking union. Eurozone did not have any instruments to deal with a financial crisis. It was every government and state for itself.

FROM THE BANK BAILOUT TO
PROGRAMME COUNTRY

The Bank Bailout: A Unilateral Move

The collapse of Northern Rock in 2007 and Bear Stearns in March 2008 were harbingers of what would follow in September 2008 following the collapse of Lehman Brothers, a seismic event that triggered a global financial crisis and a freezing of the inter-bank market in the Eurozone. The exogenous shock of Lehman Brothers ultimately exposed the vulnerability of Ireland's financial system. Faced with a deteriorating situation and in an atmosphere of acute crisis, the Irish Government opted for a blanket guarantee of the liabilities of the Irish banking system on 30 September 2008 (Houses of the Oireachtas 2016). The decision to do so was predicated on the belief that the banks faced a liquidity squeeze not an underlying problem of solvency (Honohan 2010; Nyberg 2011; Regling and Watson 2010). The bailout decision was taken by a small group of senior politicians and their advisors, in an atmosphere of extreme urgency and panic, and later agreed by the Cabinet and ratified by the Oireachtas (lower and upper houses of the Irish Parliament). Concern about the Irish banks led ECB President Trichet to contact the Irish Finance Minister Brian Lenihan over the weekend of 27/28 September. The scope of the discussion between Trichet and Lenihan is not in the public domain but it is reasonable to conclude the ECB President stressed the dangers lurking in the global financial system and the importance of preventing another Lehman Brothers event. It is unlikely that they discussed the measures that the Irish Government might take to address the evolving stress in the financial system. During the evening and night of 29 September, the Irish authorities did not contact the ECB or the Euro Group to discuss the interventions that they were considering in relation to the Irish banking system. In other words, they did not consider nor attempt to 'Europeanize' the problem, to call on the resources of the EU and not just Irish exchequer and taxpayer.

It is highly likely that the advice by the ECB and Euro Group would have favoured protecting the financial system but perhaps not in the form that it took. The blanket guarantee was a domestic decision taken under duress. Given the ultimate cost of the guarantee, it would have been wiser to at least engage with Ireland's partners and not embark on a 'dangerous gamble' in a unilateral manner. The ECB, in its official Q&A on the role of the ECB in relation to the Irish bank bailout, maintains that 'guarantee was introduced by the Irish government without any coordination with European partner' (ECB 2010). Former ECB President Trichet reiterated this at his engagement with the Banking Enquiry on 30 April 2015 in the following terms: 'it is also important that the guarantee was introduced by the Irish Government without any co-ordination with the ECB or with any other European partners, and I was the witness of that, or any other international partner' (Houses of the Oireachtas 2016(2): 6). The implications of the decision unfolded over the next years as the Irish state was faced with injecting unprecedented capital into the Irish banks. The Irish authorities were caught in a pincer movement between the increasing costs of the bank bailout and deteriorating public finances, notwithstanding severe cuts, because of the crisis in the real economy. The vicious cycle ended in Ireland becoming a programme country.

Becoming a Programme Country: ECB Pressure

If the blanket guarantee was a unilateral play by Ireland, the role of EU institutions was very significant in Ireland's transition from a country in trouble to one requesting assistance. As the toxic link between the Irish sovereign and its banks deepened, the actions of EU institutions and European leaders had a major impact on Ireland's freedom of manoeuvre. The cost of the banking collapse began to weigh ever more heavily on the Irish sovereign in the latter half of 2010, leading to a vicious cycle of rising borrowing costs and market pressure. From August onwards, the rating agencies began to downgrade Ireland, which in turn triggered an increase in spreads. By October 2010, the ECB was increasingly concerned about its exposure to the Irish banking system and decided formally to intervene in the form of a letter, dated 15 October 2010, from ECB President Trichet to the Irish Finance Minister, Brian Lenihan. The message that President Trichet intended to convey is emphasized by the use of italics in the original letter. Of clear concern was 'the extraordinarily large provision of liquidity by the Eurosystem to Irish banks', and the blunt message was that the support from the Eurosystem and the Irish Central Bank to banks such as Anglo Irish Bank should 'not be taken for granted as a long-term solution' (ECB 2010). Ireland's position worsened following a bilateral meeting at Deauville between President Sarkozy and Chancellor Merkel on 18 October, when the two leaders discussed a transition from bailout to bail-in. This had a very unsettling impact on the financial markets because of the discussion on private sector involvement. The Irish Finance Minister did not reply to the October letter but did send a letter to the ECB on the 4 November because of the widening spread between Irish Government bonds and the German bund.

ECB concern about its exposure to the Irish financial system did not abate. In a letter, dated 17 February 2015, to Matt Carthy MEP, Trichet's successor Mario Draghi outlined the scale of ECB support to Ireland in the following terms:

> In the case of Ireland, the level of liquidity provided by the Eurosystem in support of the Irish banking system had reached about Euro 140 billon (including ELA) or

around 85 per cent of Irish GDP, by November 2010. This represented about one-quarter of the ECB's total lending at the time—an unprecedented level of exposure to any country, not least in the light of the fact that Ireland's share in the capital of the ECB was about 1 per cent. (ECB 2015)

The decisive letter from Trichet came on 19 November, and included the following four stipulations: (a) that the Irish authorities would request financial support; (b) that they would commit to decisive action in relation to fiscal consolidation, structural reforms, and financial sector restructuring; (c) that the restructuring of the Irish financial system would draw on external funding and the reserves of the Irish state; and (d) that the Irish government would fully guarantee all Emergency Liquidity Assistance (ELA) issued by the Irish Central Bank (ECB 2010a).

Without agreement to these four stipulations in writing, the Governing Council of the ECB would not authorize further provision of ELA to Irish financial institutions. The ECB effectively powered Ireland into a programme because of the reliance of the Irish financial system on emergency funding. The Irish Finance Minister's reply on 21 November stated that the Irish Government had taken the decision to seek external support from the EU and the IMF (Ireland 2010a). In autumn 2010, the two most controversial aspects of the Irish experience of austerity came together. First, was the question of Ireland entering a bailout programme. The actions of the ECB and the French and German political leaders made it impossible for Ireland to stay out of a programme. There is no doubt that the Trichet letter of 19 November was decisive in the timing of the request for financial assistance; the government was left with no choice other than to request assistance. Governments resist having to ask for international support, fully understanding the consequences for their room for manoeuvre and the likely domestic political consequences. It is doubtful in any case that Ireland could have avoided a bailout given the toxic link between the banks and the sovereign in a Eurozone that lacked the policy instruments to deal with the depth of the crisis. The key objective of the ECB was financial stability and the avoidance of overexposure to the Irish banking system. Its primary concern for the stability of the European-wide financial system also influenced its policy preference concerning the imposition of losses on senior bondholders both in autumn 2010 and spring 2011. The ECB and EC were at odds with the IMF and the Irish Government on this central question. This led, in the words of the Irish Banking Inquiry, 'to the inappropriate placing of significant banking debts on the Irish citizen' (Houses of the Oireachtas 2016(1): 17). The sense of injustice and moral outrage that flowed from these negotiations has left a lasting legacy in Ireland. The absence of burden-sharing on banking debt made it more difficult for the Irish public to accept the level of cutbacks in public expenditure, tax increases, and the reduction of services that were part of the experience of austerity. The legacy is seen in opposition to water charges, the rise of independents who are not attached to a party, and the fragmentation of political representation.

THE TROIKA

Act One in the life of a programme country is the negotiations of the terms of the bailout—the Memorandum of Understanding (MoU) that provides the legal framework for the deal. Official assistance comes with a high level of conditionality attached and the *demandeur* is in a vulnerable and dependent position. One of the key programme documents was entitled *Ireland Memorandum of Understanding on Specific Economic Policy Conditionality* (Ireland 2010b). The creditors hold the stronger cards in these negotiations, which in the Irish case ended on 28 November when agreement at a technical level was agreed on a *Programme for Financial Assistance* (Ireland 2010c). The EC and IMF issued a statement on the 28 November in support of the Irish programme in the following terms: 'We strongly support the economic programme announced today by Ireland. It is a forceful response to vulnerabilities in the banking system imposing a heavy cost on the budget and, in turn, hurting the prospects for growth that Ireland needs for an enduring solution to the crisis' (EU 2010). The technical agreement had to be translated into MoUs and decisions by the EC, the Council, and the IMF on financial support. Three documents formed the core of the programme: (a) the Memorandum of Economic and Financial Policies (7 December 2010); (b) Memorandum of Understanding on Specific Economic Policy Conditionality (3 December 2010); and (c) Technical Memorandum of Understanding (7 December 2010). These documents set out the financial envelope of the programme, its policy goals, specific policy actions, and the processes associated with being in a programme. The substantive content encompassed three areas, the downsizing and reorganization of the banking system, a programme of fiscal consolidation, and structural reform designed to renew growth.

Becoming a programme country comes with a world of programme monitoring, surveillance, and precise timetables: performance criteria, indicative targets, and structural benchmarks. In the initial MoU, the performance criteria, targets, and structural benchmarks were very specific for 2010–11. Monitoring and the disbursement of financial assistance were subject to quarterly programme reviews by the Troika. The MoU on Policy Conditionality stated that the 'Release of instalments will be based on observance of quantitative performance criteria', and that 'If targets are (expected to be) missed, additional action will be taken' (Ireland 2010b: 16). The Troika became a central part of Irish governance and public policymaking, with a specific mandate to ensure compliance and certify that Ireland was fulfilling the terms of the agreement. Fifteen pages of the MoU on Policy Conditionality specified the actions that had to be achieved by each review from the beginning of the programme to the end. Irish governance entered a period in which choice was heavily circumscribed by the programme and its requirements. The speed of the negotiations was attributable to the fact that the government had developed a domestic four-year economic plan to run from 2011 to 2014, the National Recovery Plan (NRP), which already contained targets for budgetary adjustments, including a large front-loaded adjustment of 6 billion in 2011, and structural economic reforms (Ireland 2010d). Ireland's fiscal consolidation was not imposed from the outside but was central to the government's strategy from 2008 onwards; by autumn 2010, fiscal adjustment of approximately 15 billion had already been implemented and a further 15 billion was foreseen in the NRP. Given the importance of framing in any public policy process, the NRP shaped the negotiations with the Troika by providing them with an already articulated strategy of fiscal consolidation and some areas of structural reform. Thus, although Ireland became semi-sovereign it had some capacity to influence the terms of engagement. This also added to the 'ownership' of the programme by the Irish public policy system.

Act Two unfolded as the government that negotiated the programme collapsed and an election was called for February 2011. It would have been impossible for the government, particularly a two-party coalition, to have survived accepting a bailout, particularly a government that had agreed the bank guarantee in the first place. The chaotic handling of the communication with the Irish public about the bailout severely undermined already weak public confidence in the government. The election was an earthquake election for the incumbent parties, particularly for the strongest party in Irish electoral competition since the 1930s, Fianna Fáil, whose vote fell 41.6 per cent in 2007 to 17.4 per cent, a drop of just over 24 points (Little 2011; Marsh and Mikhaylov 2012). Inevitably, because of the link between the bailout and the collapse of the government, the election was dominated by the economy. Outright opposition to the bailout and its conditions was found to the left of the political spectrum, the United Left Alliance and Sinn Fein who promised to 'burn the bondholders' and repudiate the EU/IMF package (Hutcheson 2011: 9–10). The two main opposition parties, Fine Gael and Labour, emerged as the available coalition, and had to take over the unpalatable role of governing with the Troika and through the crisis.

Their Programme for Government (2011–16) was billed as a Programme of National Recovery (PNR). The Labour Party depicted itself during the campaign as the party most likely to be in a position to renegotiate the bailout package, underlined by a quip from the then leader Eamon Gilmore that it would be 'Frankfurt's Way or Labour's Way', a quip that followed him throughout his time in government (Hutcheson 2011). Fine Gael used its membership of the European People's Party (EPP) (particularly a photo opportunity with Chancellor Merkel), to depict its candidate for Taoiseach, Enda Kenny, as a statesmen capable of influencing events in Ireland's favour. At a press conference on 3 February 2011, ECB President Trichet was asked about the Irish election and the fact that some of the opposition parties had suggested that they might be able to renegotiate the package. President Trichet's reply was circumspect but telling:

> Let me only say that Ireland has a medium-term plan approved by the international community, namely the IMF, and by the European Union, with the positive judgement of the Commission in liaison with the ECB. The implementation of the plan is absolutely essential, in the opinion of the ECB, for the credibility of the country. (ECB 2011b)

This did not suggest that there would be much leeway for a new government. However, the government's overwhelming majority and electoral mandate gave it the legitimacy to seek changes and improvements in programme conditions.

In the PNR, the new government agreed to maintain the objectives of the EU/IMF programme but said that they had secured a strong mandate from the Irish electorate 'to renegotiate a more credible package that is better for both Ireland and Europe' (Ireland 2011).[1] Governments and parliaments sign up to legally binding MoUs in order to access programme funding, and the question is: How bound are subsequent governments by these commitments? A new government may be squeezed between its responsibility to its creditors and its desire, given its electoral mandate, to be responsive to its electorate (Laffan 2014b). In addition, the asymmetric relationship between a programme country and its creditors imposes limits on what might be achieved. The strategy of the Fine Gael–Labour Government was to treat its relationship with the Troika as a series of iterative negotiations during which concessions would be extracted. The dominant negotiating style was to focus on repairing Ireland's reputation and to buttress key bilateral and institutional relationships using official and political channels as appropriate. Below-the-radar diplomacy was preferred to public diplomacy and overt politicization. This was in line with a deeply rooted political and administrative culture of pragmatism.

The Fine Gael–Labour Government came to power in the heat of a deep economic, political, and social crisis. It had to manage the interface between policymaking within Ireland and the relationship with the Troika and Ireland's partners. The government achieved a number of changes in the rescue package during the first year following their election. These were: a reversal in the cut in the minimum wage, a negotiated reduction in the interest rates (which were punitive) associated with the financial support package, and agreement from the Troika that the proceeds from the sale of state assets

---

[1] The role of elections in programme countries is, to date, under-researched.

could be invested in job creation (Ireland 2012: 9–10). The strategy of the government was to hit the target numbers required by the programme and to introduce changes through a form of 'fiscal equivalence'. The focus of negotiations with the Troika during the second year of the programme concerned changes related to the promissory notes.

Promissory notes were one of the most contentious issues associated with the Irish banking crisis. During 2012, the Irish authorities, particularly Finance Minister Noonan and Central Bank Governor Honohan, engaged in a prolonged negotiation to alter the terms of the so-called promissory notes which were issued to the Irish Bank Resolution Corporation (IBRC), the amalgam of the insolvent Anglo Irish and Irish Nationwide Building Society (INBS). The promissory notes represented an IOU for over 30 billion euros, which involved the state agreeing to pay IBRC 3.06 billion each year to 2023 and smaller amounts after that. IBRC used the promissory note as collateral for Central Bank of Ireland ELA, which must have the agreement of the ECB. The core objective of the ECB was to prevent 'monetary financing', the printing of money by governments. The promissory notes represented a very heavy annual charge on an already indebted sovereign. Finding a means to alter the terms of the promissory notes was challenging because of ECB sensitivity on monetary financing, illegal under the Treaty of Maastricht. Following tortuous negotiations, the Irish Government and the ECB agreed to replace the promissory notes with long-term government bonds with maturities of between twenty-six to forty years in February 2013 (Whelan 2013b). The agreement had a significant impact on Ireland's short-term borrowing needs at a time of acute fiscal pressure; instead of a payment of over 3 billion, the government had to borrow less than 1 billion per year. As part of the agreement, the Central Bank had to agree to sell off the bonds over a prescribed time frame. The promissory note deal represents the most significant agreement with the creditors that the Irish authorities secured during the life of the programme.

IRELAND'S STATE CAPACITY: MANAGING ASYMMETRY

The Eurozone crisis created a high level of tension among the member states and European institutions because the crisis had very different impacts across Europe and there were very significant and diverse material interests at stake. The issue of 'who pays' was at the core of the conflict: Who was to pay for the losses arising from a bubble—public or private sectors? And if public which taxpayers? A related issue was which countries and social groups were to pay for the cost of adjustment, given the scale of the Great Recession, and whose money was to be risked to maintain the euro. Given the fragility of the global financial system and the likely consequences of an implosion of the single currency, political actors both in government and at EU level were in 'rescue' and 'muddling-through' mode. A politics of fear—unknown unknowns—kept the euro alive notwithstanding the severity of the crisis. From an Irish perspective, the 'who pays' question was and remains deeply contested, particularly in relation to the cost of bailing out the Irish financial system. The Irish taxpayer injected 64 billion euros into its banks, a sum that was ten times that of Sweden when it bailed out its banks in the early 1990s (Frisell 2015). Although the final cost of the bank guarantee will not be known for some time, it will represent a major cost to Irish taxpayers. According to Frisell, 'the bailout decision will still go down in Irish history as a very costly mistake' (Frisell 2015). This mistake was made by an Irish Government, albeit within an environment of acute fear that the failure of any bank might trigger serious instability in the wider financial system. The decision was, however, essentially a unilateral one. Thereafter, when the full consequences of the guarantee unfolded, it proved impossible for the Irish authorities to unravel the guarantee and to reduce the cost of the bailout to the Irish tax payers. The debate in Irish public discourse was one of 'burning' or 'not burning the bondholders'. At issue was the treatment of senior bondholders once the initial two-year period of the guarantee ended. The ECB was strongly of the view, and its views carried considerable weight, that bailing-in the senior bondholders was an 'extremely risky' option for Ireland (Trichet 2015). Uncertainty about the rules and high volatility in the financial markets formed part of ECB's justification for this stance. Successive Irish Governments considered bailing in senior unsecured bondholders in autumn 2010 and again in spring 2011 but did not do so given pressure from Ireland's creditors, the USA and ECB.[2] The Fine Gael–Labour Government weighted the trade-off following their election and opted for caution. Minister Noonan in the Dáil in November 2011 outlined the views of the European institutions, particularly the ECB:

> After my meeting with the President of the ECB, Mr. Trichet, and the Commis-
> sioner for Economic and Monetary Affairs, Mr. Rehn, last month, our European
> partners expressed strong reservations about burden sharing with senior bond-
> holders in IBRC. Mr. Trichet voiced his opinion that he is against such actions for
> two reasons. First, private sector involvement carries very significant contagion
> risk and may be inconsistent with encouraging private investors to return to
> markets. Second, he said Ireland had done particularly well over the summer. He

---

[2] Michael Noonan, the Finance Minister, said in a reply to a question on whether or not the ECB prevented Ireland from burning bondholders: 'Jean [Claude] Trichet is a very subtle, refined, cultivated Frenchman and he would never make a threat like that—but he would not allow me to burn the senior bondholders' (Smyth 2013).

mentioned the narrowing of bond spreads and indicated his view that anything to do with senior debt burden sharing might knock the confidence of the market in the absolute commitment of the Government to take, once again, its place in normally functioning markets. The result of that might be a further widening of bond yields and a loss of the ground we have gained. (Houses of the Oireachtas 2011)

Ajai Chopra, the former head of the IMF mission to Ireland, argued afterwards that unsecured bondholders in the two failed financial institutions, Anglo Irish and INBS, should not have been paid (Breaking News.ie 2013). For a country experiencing significant fiscal retrenchment and a costly bank bailout, not bailing in senior unsecured bondholders was deeply unpopular at the domestic level and 'difficult to understand' according to a non-Irish advisor to the Irish Governor of the Central Bank (Frisell 2015).

The acute phase of the Irish crisis lasted from 2008 to December 2013, when Ireland formally exited the rescue and ceased to be a programme country. During this period, Ireland's political, institutional, and public policy capacity was severely tested. Successive Irish Governments had to navigate between the domestic, the European, and the international. The Fianna Fáil–Green Government was in crisis mode from autumn 2008 onwards as the full effects of the bank guarantee became apparent. The government that assumed power in spring 2011 governed in the toughest times, but had the advantage of not being responsible for the bank guarantee nor having asked for financial assistance. The new Irish Government, state agencies, and diplomatic service were transformed into a task force to prosecute the MoU and take Ireland out of acute crisis. A key part of the strategy was repairing the reputational damage that Ireland experienced as a result of the collapse of its economy (NESC 2009). This involved changes in personnel, multiple multilateral and bilateral meetings with counterparts in other member states and beyond, a well-run EU presidency in 2013, and leveraging the Irish diaspora. There was a rapid change in senior personnel at the head of the Irish Central Bank, the Financial Regulator, and the Finance Ministry. Within the Irish core executive, the Finance Ministry was divided into a Finance Department and a Department of Public Expenditure and Reform, and problems in the Finance Ministry that had contributed to poor fiscal and financial oversight were brought sharply into focus (Wright 2010). The second part of the strategy was to hit the headline goals of the programme but seek to alleviate Ireland's debt burden by continuously working with the external actors. The Department of Finance was the lead ministry in managing relations with the Troika; an External Programme Compliance Unit (EPCU) was established to coordinate formal relations with the institutions. Within the Taoiseach's department, an Economic Management Council (EMC), a Cabinet subcommittee was established. The nerve centre of the crisis response, particularly under the Fine Gael–Labour Coalition, was the EMC, which was the key institutional device to manage relations with the Troika, deliver the MoU, and manage the coalition. Having failed to identify and prevent the bubble in the first place, Irish Central Government proved adept at managing the demands of the MoU and delivering on the terms of the bailout. The periodic reviews on the Irish programme by the Troika were replete with references to strong implementation and a high level of domestic ownership.

CONCLUSIONS

International actors and agencies played a pivotal and contested role in the Irish experience of austerity as a result of the Great Recession. In analysing their role, it is important to distinguish between the interconnected dynamics of the two bailouts—the bank bailout in September 2008 and the bailout of the sovereign in November 2010. International agencies, particularly the ECB, were pivotal to Ireland entering a programme and repaying unsecured senior bondholders. The ECB's 'hard power' stemmed from the fragility of the Irish financial system and dependence on Emergency Liquidity Support (ELS) funding. The bank bailout was a unilateral decision of the Irish Government taken under duress in crisis conditions. As the depth of the problems in the Irish banking sector became apparent following the bank bailout, the Irish banking system became more and more reliant on emergency liquidity from the European System of Central Banks, and thus the ECB became the most powerful player in autumn 2010 and effectively insisted that the Irish sovereign apply for a programme. The Trichet letters demanded that Ireland enter a programme. Ireland's acute economic vulnerability and the reliance on ELA funding gave the Irish Government no choice. Pressure on Ireland did not just come from the EU but also the markets, which had shut down as a source of funding. The ECB was also very instrumental in Ireland's dealings with unsecured bondholders; it was the strong preference of the ECB, clearly understood by Brian Lenihan and Michael Noonan, that the ECB was against non-payment of senior bondholders because of a fear of the implications for financial stability. This has left a toxic legacy, given the cost to Irish society of the bank bailout and the societal consequences of austerity. The political costs are still being felt in the body polity.

REFERENCES

Breaking News.ie. 2013. 'IMF: Ireland Could Have Saved Billions by Burning Anglo Bondholders', 19 December. Available at: <http://www.breakingnews.ie/ireland/

imf-ireland-could-have-saved-billions-by-burning-anglo-bondholders-617688.html> (accessed 11 April 2016).

D'Hart, P. 1993. 'Symbols, Rituals and Power: The Lost Dimensions of Crisis Management'. *Journal of Contingencies and Crisis Management,* 1(1): 36–50.

Donovan, D. and Murphy, A. E. 2013. *The Fall of the Celtic Tiger: Ireland and the Euro Debt Crisis.* Oxford: Oxford University Press.

ECB (European Central Bank). 2010. 'Letter of the ECB President to the Irish Minister for Finance dated 15th October 2010 on the Large Provision of Liquidity by the Eurosystem and the Central Bank of Ireland to Irish Banks and the Need for Ireland to Agree to an Adjustment Programme'. Available at: <http://www.ecb.europa.eu/press/html/irish-letters.en.html> (accessed 11 April 2016).

ECB (European Central Bank). 2011a. 'President Trichet Interview with Financial Times Deutschland', 18 July. Available at: <https://www.ecb.europa.eu/press/inter/date/2011/html/sp110718.en.html> (accessed 11 April 2016).

ECB (European Central Bank). 2011b. 'Introductory Statement to the Press Conference (with Q&A)'. Available at: <https://www.ecb.europa.eu/press/pressconf/2011/html/is110203.en.html> (accessed 11 April 2016).

ECB (European Central Bank). 2015. *Letter from the ECB President to Mr Matt Carthy, MEP.* Available at: <https://www.ecb.europa.eu/pub/pdf/other/150218letter_carthy.en.pdf> (accessed 11 April 2016).

EU (European Union). 2010. 'Commission–IMF Joint Statement on Ireland'. Available at <http://ec.europa.eu/economy_finance/articles/eu_economic_situation/2010-11-28-js-ireland_en.htm> (accessed 11 April 2016).

EU (European Union). 2012. *Euro Area Statement, 29 June 2012.* Brussels: European Union.

Frisell L. 2015. 'Address by Advisor to the Governor, Lars Frisell, to the Financial Safety Net Conference in Stockholm, 19 May 2015'. Available at: <https://www.centralbank.ie/press-area/speeches/Pages/AddressbyAdvisortotheGovernorCentralBankofIrelandLarsFriselltoTheFinancialSafetyNetConferenceStockholmSweden19May2015.aspx> (accessed 11 April 2016).

Gourevitch, P. 1992. *Politics in Hard Times: Comparative Responses to Economic Crises.* New York: Cornell University Press.

Hay, C. 1996. 'Narrating Crisis: The Discursive Construction of the "Winter of Discontent"'. *Sociology,* 30(2): 253–77.

Honohan, P. 2010. *The Irish Banking Crisis: Regulatory and Financial Stability Policy 2003–2008: A Report to the Minister for Finance by the Governor of the Central Bank.* Dublin: Government Publications.

Hutcheson, D. S. 2011. 'The February 2011 Parliamentary Election in Ireland', Working Papers in British-Irish Studies No. 109. Dublin: IBIS.

Houses of the Oireachtas. 2011. *Dail Debates,* 15 November. Dublin: Houses of the Oireachtas. Houses of the Oireachtas. 2016. *Report of the Joint Committee of Inquiry into the Banking Crisis,* 3 vols. Dublin: Houses of the Oireachtas.

Ireland. 2010a. 'Letter from Finance Minister Lenihan Signalling that Ireland Would Ask for a Bailout. Available at: <http://www.ecb.europa.eu/press/html/irish-letters.en.html> (accessed 11 April 2016).

Ireland. 2010b. *Ireland Memorandum of Understanding on Specific Economic Policy Conditionality,* 3 December. Available at: <http://ec.europa.eu/economy_finance/

articles/eu_economic_situation/pdf/2010-12-07-mou_en.pdf> (accessed 11 April 2016).

Ireland. 2010c. *Programme of Financial Assistance*. Available at: <http://www.finance. gov.ie/sites/default/files/euimfrevised.pdf> (accessed 11 April 2016).

Ireland. 2010d. *National Recovery Plan*. Available at: <http://www.budget.gov.ie/The% 20National%20Recovery%20Plan%202011-2014.pdf> (accessed 11 April 2016).

Ireland. 2011. 'Programme for Government 2011–2016'. Available at: <http://www. taoiseach.gov.ie/eng/Work_Of_The_Department/Programme_for_Government/> (accessed 11 April 2016).

Ireland. 2012. 'Programme for Government Review'. Available at: <http://www.taoiseach. gov.ie/eng/Work_Of_The_Department/Programme_for_Government/> (accessed 11 April 2016).

Keohane, B. and Joseph, N. 1977. *Power and Interdependence: World Politics in Transition*, 2nd edn. Boston, MA: Little.

Laffan, B. 2014a. 'Framing the Crisis, Defining the Problems: Decoding the Euro Area Crisis'. *Perspectives on European Politics and Society*, 15(3): 266–80.

Laffan, B. 2014b. 'Testing Times: The Growing Primacy of Responsibility in the Euro Area'. *West European Politics*, 37(2): 270–87.

Little, C. 2011. 'The General Election of 2011 in the Republic of Ireland: All Changed Utterly?' *West European Politics*, 34(6): 1304–13.

Marsh, M. and Mikhaylov, S. 2012. 'Economic Voting in a Crisis: The Irish Election of 2011'. *Electoral Studies*, (31)3: 478–84.

NESC (National Economic and Social Council). 2009. 'Ireland's Five-Part Crisis: An Integrated National Response', NESC Report No. 118. Dublin: National Economic and Social Council.

Nyberg, P. 2011. *Misjudging Risks: Causes of the Systemic Banking Crisis in Ireland, Report of the Commission of Investigation into the Banking Sector in Ireland*. Dublin: Government Publications.

Ó Riain, S. 2014. *The Rise and Fall of Ireland's Celtic Tiger: Liberalism, Boom and Bust*. Cambridge: Cambridge University Press.

Regling, K. and Watson, M. 2010. *A Preliminary Report on the Sources of Ireland's Banking Crisis*. Dublin: Government Publications.

Schmidt, V. 2008. 'Discursive Institutionalism: The Explanatory Power of Ideas and Discourse'. *American Review of Political Science*, 11: 303–26.

Smyth, J. 2013. 'Ireland Unfairly Treated Over Bondholders in Bust Banks'. *EU Economy*, 19 December. Available at: <http://www.ft.com/intl/cms/s/0/71cfb9c6-68d7-11e3-bb3e-00144feabdc0.html#axzz3d2SuYMre> (accessed 11 April 2016).

Thorhallsson, B. and Kirby, P. 2012. 'Financial Crisis in Iceland and Ireland: Does European Union and Euro Membership Matter?' *Journal of Common Market Studies*, 50(5): 801–18.

Trichet, J. C. 2015. 'Statement in the Context of the Irish Banking Inquiry', 30 April. Available at: <https://inquiries.oireachtas.ie/banking/hearings/jean-claude-trichet-iiea-event-not-an-official-inquiry-hearing/> (accessed 11 April 2016).

Whelan, K. 2013a. 'Ireland's Economic Crisis: The Good, the Bad and the Ugly'. *Journal of Macroeconomics*, 39(Part B): 424–40.

Whelan, K. 2013b. 'Ireland's Promissory Note Deal'. Available at: <http://karlwhelan. com/blog/?p=797> (accessed 11 April 2016).

Windhoff-Héritier, A. 2001. *Differential Europe: The European Union Impact on National Policymaking*. Lanham, MD and Oxford: Rowman & Littlefield.

Wright, R. 2010. *Strengthening the Capacity of the Department of Finance: Report of the Independent Review Panel*. Dublin: Department of Finance.

11

Workplaces

William K. Roche

INTRODUCTION

The Great Recession was without precedent in Irish workplaces. Employers across a wide front implemented retrenchment programmes. Unions traded concessions on pay and conditions for enhanced job security. Those employees who managed to retain their jobs experienced increases in insecurity and work pressure. The state retreated from the tripartite social partnership system that had shaped so much of the world of industrial relations for more than twenty years. What occurred in workplaces is the subject of this chapter.[1] The chapter begins by considering features of the austerity programme that might have been expected to impact on workplaces, and examines views on the effects of recessions, especially the Great Recession, on employment relations. Subsequent sections examine empirical data on the postures and experiences of employers, unions, and employees. The final section offers a series of conclusions on the effects of the recession and austerity programme on workplaces in Ireland.

WORKPLACES IN AUSTERITY AND RECESSION

While the term 'internal devaluation' was seldom used by Irish policymakers (McDonnell and O'Farrell 2015: 3), the government and the Central Bank appeared to advocate generalized reductions in pay to restore competitiveness as the recession took hold (see Central Bank of Ireland 2009: 10; Department of Finance 2009: 7). The austerity programme agreed between the Troika and

---

[1] The focus is on workplaces employing the dependent workforce, which comprised 82 per cent of all people at work at the outset of the recession in 2008.

the government and an associated National Recovery Plan (NRP) focused on achieving competitively sustainable unit labour costs rather than general reductions in pay levels. A cut in the national minimum wage (which took effect in 2011 and was soon reversed) and a commitment to review and streamline sectoral pay fixing arrangements, contained in the programme, targeted pay levels in low-wage, labour-intensive sectors, heavily dependent on the domestic market (Department of Finance 2010: 20; Government of Ireland 2010: 10). While across-the-board cuts in private-sector pay levels did not occur, reductions in absolute and relative Irish unit labour costs were achieved and met with approval from policymakers (Department of Finance 2010; Government of Ireland 2010: 35). Otherwise, the austerity programme and the recovery plan made reference to the need for knowledge and innovation-driven improvements in productivity, for high value-added employment, for investment in human capital, and for repositioning Ireland as a 'global innovation hub'. These objectives carried clear implications for work and employment arrangements (Department of Finance 2010; Government of Ireland 2010). Public service workplaces were to be impacted by agreed reductions in salaries and cuts in numbers employed. 'Public service transformation' was also intended to deliver administrative efficiencies, changes in work practices, measures to redeploy public servants, and more rigorous performance management systems (Department of Finance 2010: 19–24; Government of Ireland 2010: 53–60).

Beyond Ireland, international commentary and research on workplaces during the recession has focused on whether nominal wage rigidity had been sustained and how retrenchment programmes varied both within and across different countries (see Barrett and McGuinness 2012; Bergin, Kelly, and McGuinness 2012; Doris, O'Neill, and Sweetman 2014; Eurofound 2014a; Roche et al. 2013: 30–6). Echoing commentary on the 1980s recession (see Cappelli 1999a, 1999b), attention also focused on whether employers had sought to change underlying work and employment regimes or models: commentators differing between those who claimed that work regimes had become more 'market driven' (Briner 2010; Towers-Watson 2010); more reliant on the commitment, skills, and 'high performance' of workforces (Mohrman and Worley 2009; Ulrich, reported in Brockett 2010); or were marked by essentially improvised, pragmatic, and eclectic changes (Brown and Reilly 2009; Roche and Teague 2014a; Roche et al. 2013; van Wanrooy et al. 2013: 191–2). Commentary had also focused on trade unions, especially on the rate of unionization, commonly known as 'trade union density', and on the nature of collective bargaining with employers during the recession (Chaison 2012; Roche, Teague, and Coughlan 2015). Finally, research in Europe has also examined the work experiences of employees during the recession. Here the focus was on the trend in work pressure or intensity, and in employees' levels of influence over the conduct of their jobs and over decision-making in the organizations for which they worked (Eurofound 2014a; Gallie 2013).

These major themes of both the austerity programme and international commentary provide a framework for examining the effects of the Great Recession on work and employment in Ireland. Data on the effects of the recovery are also considered. The next section considers the actions of employers, and subsequent sections examine trade unions and employees.

EMPLOYERS: RETRENCHMENT AND CONTINUITY

Private-Sector Firms

Significant numbers of employers in the private sector made cuts to employment, working hours, and basic pay during the years after 2008. Table 11.1 presents the trend in basic pay in member firms of the Irish Business and Employers' Confederation (IBEC). The overall pattern during the recession was dominated by pay freezes. Significant minorities of firms cut basic rates at the peak of the recession. The numbers of employers indicating that they had increased basic rates rose from 2012 as the trough of the downturn passed. From 2014, most firms awarded basic pay rises as recovery set in.

Most IBEC members are larger employers. Data from the Central Statistics Office (CSO) provide a more representative picture of changes in pay and other components of firms' pay bills during the recession. Around the trough of the recession in 2009, 23 per cent of private-sector firms cut basic pay, 29 per cent cut hours worked, and 34 per cent cut staff numbers (Barrett and McGuinness 2012: 32; Bergin, Kelly, and McGuinness 2012: 28). As shown in Table 11.2, over the three-year period between the third quarters of 2008 and 2010, the proportion of enterprises cutting pay bills peaked at 67 per cent in

Table 11.1. Developments in basic rates of pay in IBEC member firms, 2009–15

Year	Basic Rates Decreased %	Basic Rates Increased %	Basic Rates Frozen %
2009	22	12	54
2010	11	13	72
2011	7	18	72
2012	4	33	63
2013	5	38	58
2014	2	51	47
2015	0	61	39

Source: Irish Business and Employers' Confederation, *Business Sentiment Reports* and *HR Updates*.

Table 11.2. Cuts in pay bills and their components in private-sector enterprises

Period	% Firms Cutting Pay Bill	% Cuts in Employment	% Cuts in Average Hours	% Cuts in Average Hourly Earnings
2008–9	67	52	39	36
2009–10	54	43	22	27
2010–11	41	29	18	18

Notes: Periods shown extend from Q3 to Q3 of each year. Data pertain to firms reducing pay bills by more than 2 per cent.
Source: Walsh 2012. Data for 2010–11 generously provided by Kieran Walsh.

2008–9, and then declined over successive twelve-month periods from 54 per cent to 41 per cent. Pay-bill reductions depended least on cuts in hourly earnings. Over the three years from 2008, successively 36 per cent, 27 per cent, and 18 per cent of firms cut hourly earnings—an indicator of cuts in basic rates, premiums, bonuses, and allowances. More firms cut working hours: over the three-year period, successively 36 per cent, 27 per cent, and 18 per cent of firms implemented reduced working time. Firms relied mainly, however, on reductions in numbers employed to cut pay bills. More than one in two firms making cuts to pay bills in 2008–9 cut employment. The proportions of firms cutting jobs fell to 43 per cent and 29 per cent over the following two years.

While these data point to substantial pay and pay-bill flexibility during the downturn, they also show that no *generalized* rounds of reductions in nominal basic pay and salary *levels* occurred across the private sector during the recession (Barrett and McGuinness 2012; Bergin, Kelly, and McGuinness 2012; Walsh 2012). To the degree to which 'internal devaluation' can be said to have occurred, this took the form of reductions in nominal unit labour costs and improvements in Irish unit labour costs relative to important competitor countries. From the early 2000s to the advent of the crisis, Ireland's labour cost competitiveness had declined significantly relative to major trading partners. In interpreting the post-2008 trend shown in Figure 11.1, it needs to be borne in mind that the collapse of employment in the low-productivity construction sector significantly affected the improvement in Irish unit labour costs (McDonnell and O'Farrell 2015).

Other than introducing retrenchment programmes, did employers seek to transform workplaces by reconfiguring different work and employment practices in a consistent manner, suggesting some underlying blueprint or direction of travel? A detailed empirical study conducted in 2010 showed that human resource (HR) managers across a range of multinational and Irish firms were concerned mainly with short-term or day-to-day measures aimed at cost-cutting while maintaining morale and commitment—their work activities marked by what has been described as the 'tyranny of the short-term' (Roche and Teague 2014a: 273–5; Roche et al. 2013). Much of the work of

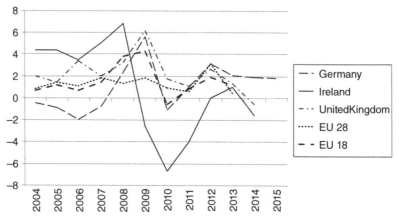

Figure 11.1. The trend in nominal unit labour costs in Ireland and the EU
Source: Eurostat.

these HR *consigliere* involved 'working the pumps' to respond to immediate pressures and challenges (Roche and Teague 2012). There was little evidence that they had been involved to any significant degree in longer-term strategic activity aimed at reconfiguring underlying work and employment models. Case studies of firms deemed by peers and expert commentators to have responded to the recession in innovative and effective ways pointed to the same conclusion. All were found to have engaged in pragmatic responses to different types of recessionary pressures. Often their focus was on preserving pre-recession models of work and employment rather than seeking to exploit the opportunity presented by the recession to make path-breaking or path-accelerating changes (Roche et al. 2013: 130–97). With economic recovery, employers' priorities have begun to shift towards emerging skills gaps, problems in recruiting and retaining staff, talent management, and employee engagement—concerns reflecting renewed business buoyancy (see IBEC 2014).

Public Service Organizations

Cuts in public service pay and reductions in employment preceded the austerity programme, but reductions in the public service pay bill and associated measures were central to fiscal consolidation measures agreed with the Troika. Three pay cuts were implemented across the public service in 2009, 2010, and 2013 (see Chapter 12, this volume). Cuts were progressive and successively involved average salary reductions of 7 per cent, 6 per cent, and 6 per cent. Overtime rates and other premium salary payments were reduced. Lower salary scales were introduced for new entrants to the public service.

Service-based increments continued to be paid until 2013, when increments became subject to freezes of varying durations (LRC 2013: 7–8). Performance-based pay systems for senior public service managers were suspended in 2009. Pensions for new entrants were changed from final-salary to career-average payment, and pension levels were decoupled from future changes in public service salaries (Higgins 2011a).

Strict controls were imposed on recruitment to the public service and on promotions, and voluntary early retirement was incentivized. Over the period from 2008 to 2013, the numbers working in the public service fell by 10 per cent (DPER 2014a: 7), while between 2009 and 2013 the public service pay bill was cut by about 17.7 per cent (DPER 2014a: 7). The reductions in employment occurred against the background of a significant rise in the demand for public services, particularly in the areas of social welfare, health, and education (DPER 2014a: 5). From 2013, public servants undertook to work longer hours, involving an addition to capacity of almost 15 million working hours (DPER 2014a: 8). An agreement with public service unions in 2010 provided for higher levels of staff mobility across and within workplaces. A series of rolling sectoral action plans across different parts of the public service contained further agreed measures to increase work flexibility and improve productivity.

The performance management system for public servants, known as the Performance Management and Development System (PMDS), was revamped: setting higher performance thresholds for the payment of service-based increments and for entitlement to be considered for promotion, and introducing a more rigorous procedure for managing underperformance (DPER 2013). Further measures were introduced to promote external appointments to top-level public service posts (Higgins 2011b). A 'senior public service' cadre was created to strengthen senior management, foster leadership, and promote greater mobility at senior levels (Higgins 2011c). Restrictions on promotions in the civil service were removed to allow people with suitable skills and experience to apply for posts at any grade (Frawley 2014a). Measures were introduced to encourage staff exchanges between the civil service and the private sector (Frawley 2013). Senior management sought to accelerate outsourcing, particularly with respect to 'non-critical' functions of departments and agencies (Higgins 2012). In 2015, against a backdrop of significant improvement in the fiscal position and outlook, the government and public service unions negotiated the Lansdowne Road Agreement, which makes provision for the phased restoration of public service salaries over the period to 2018. Demands have also emerged from some public service unions for improvements in allowances and pay premia, and this may presage wider public service union pressure for pay rises over and above those agreed under Lansdowne Road (Roche and Teague 2016).

A more robust bargaining relationship was established with public service unions, marking a departure from more than a decade of what was intended as 'workplace partnership', involving the creation and operation of structures for

cooperation and consultation between management and unions in the civil
service, local government, health, and, to lesser degrees, other areas of the
public service (Roche and Teague 2014b). New binding dispute resolution
arrangements were also agreed in 2010, greatly facilitating the introduction
of agreed changes, particularly in the health service, where earlier attempts
to revise work and employment practices often became bogged down in
lengthy negotiations and protracted conflict resolution processes (Teague
et al. 2015: ch.10).

During the trough of the recession, the main priority was to reduce public
service employment and to cut the pay bill. Following the establishment of the
Department of Public Expenditure and Reform in 2011 more attention was
devoted to the future shape of public service delivery, including work and
employment arrangements (see DPER 2011). Two documents contain a
blueprint for future public service work and employment arrangements. *The
Public Service Reform Plan 2014–2016* and *The Civil Service Renewal Plan*
envisage an employment model retaining the core elements of a 'career-based'
public service in which people, to be recruited in the main through designated
recruitment grades, will pursue long-term generalist professional careers.[2]
A strong emphasis is also found on reinforcing reforms introduced or developed during the fiscal crisis: more rigorous performance management, better
accountability, senior management leadership, greater use of open recruitment for specialist and for top-level positions, higher internal staff mobility,
and merit-based promotion (DPER 2014a, 2014b). The emerging work and
employment blueprint envisages a performance-driven and primarily career-
based public service. The direction of travel is marked less by transformation
than by continuity with work and employment reforms pursued—often
with limited success—over two decades since the launch of the Strategic
Management Initiative (SMI) in the mid-1990s.[3]

TRADE UNIONS: ACCELERATED DECLINE AND CONCESSION BARGAINING

The social partnership model in place for more than twenty years was an early
casualty of the Great Recession. Under social partnership, employers, unions,

---

[2] A report by the Independent Panel on Strengthening Civil Service Accountability recommended that continuation of permanent tenure but with greater flexibility in employment
arrangements (DPER 2014c: 25). This recommendation was not, however, explicitly endorsed
in the Civil Service Renewal Plan or the Public Service Reform Plan.

[3] One observer commented, with respect to the Civil Service Renewal Plan: 'most of the...
actions start off with the words "expand", "strengthen" or "improve", indicating that much of the
plan is simply re-asserting what has been included in previous reform plans' (Frawley 2014b: 20).

farming organizations, the state, and (from 1997) a range of civil society organizations, were party to seven agreements or 'programmes' covering pay increases and pledges on economic, social, fiscal, monetary, and tax policies (Roche 2007).

Talks between the erstwhile 'social partners' on measures for tackling the crisis were conducted during 2009 but agreement could not be reached. Unions sought support for a 'social solidarity pact' containing a series of measures, which, in their view, spread the burden of adjusting to the crisis equitably across different social groups. They also sought public spending measures to stimulate economic activity and to reduce the deficit to a sustainable level over a period of about eight years. Employers looked for urgent measures for tackling the deficit, particularly a sharp reduction in public spending, and supported a competitive devaluation of pay to restore competitiveness. The government aimed to curb the deficit by 2013 and determined on large cuts in public spending and increases in taxation. The final straw for social partnership was a failure by public service employers and unions to reach accord in December 2009 on proposed cuts in the public service pay bill for 2010 and successive years (Roche 2013). Following the collapse of centralized collective bargaining, unions negotiated with individual firms in the private sector, while governments bargained over measures to reduce the pay bill with public service unions. The transition to a more decentralized pattern of bargaining was highly orderly.

Union density, or the proportion of employees at work who are members of trade unions, had been in decline in Ireland since the early 1980s. After 2008, the decline in density accelerated. The trend in union density is portrayed in Figure 11.2. Panel (a) reports the overall pattern of decline. Panel (b) reveals near even, continuous decline in the private sector from the onset of the downturn.[4] While public service union density held up during the early years of austerity, as revealed in panel (c), it began to fall from 2011. While no data are available on the trend in public service union density prior to the early 2000s, this was probably the most significant and sustained decline in public service unionization in living memory.

'Concession bargaining' between trade unions and employers is likely to have contributed to declining density in the private sector and public service. For much of the period after 2008, unions in many firms faced demands from employers for concessions over pay, working conditions, and work practices in return for general or specific assurances that remaining jobs would be made more secure, or worse job losses avoided (Roche et al. 2013:

---

[4] Trends for the private sector and public services need to be interpreted with caution. Private-sector data include those working in state-owned commercial companies and workers in private schools and health providers may appear in the available aggregate public service data (see Walsh 2014).

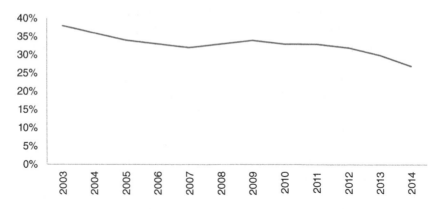

Panel (a) The Overall Trend in Trade Union Density

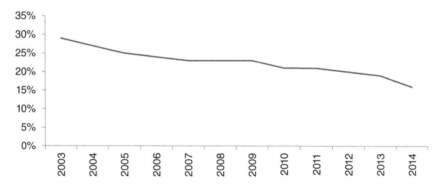

Panel (b) The Trend in Trade Union Density
in the Private Sector

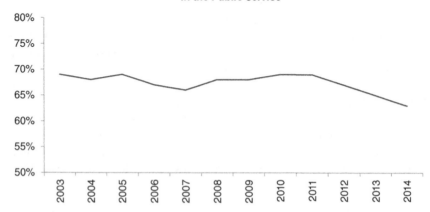

Panel (c) The Trend in Trade Union Density
in the Public Service

Figure 11.2. The trend in trade union density 2003–14

Notes: Data pertain to Q2 of all years. The public service data comprise public administration, defence, compulsory social security, education, and human health activities.
Source: Based on CSO, Quarterly National Household Survey micro-data (Walsh 2014).

102–29). So-called 'ultra-concession bargaining', where employers challenge union recognition, or seek formally to rescind or narrow the scope of collective bargaining, was not prominent in Ireland post-2008 (Roche et al. 2015). Groups of employers, however, mounted successful constitutional challenges to collective bargaining arrangements in low-pay industries, and in construction. Reforms to wage-fixing arrangements in these sectors incorporated the new flexibilities covered in the Troika programme and procedural changes required to copper-fasten their constitutionality.

Most private-sector employers pursued narrower pragmatic objectives focused around winning concessions on pay, conditions of employment, and work practices. It has been estimated that only about 12 per cent of unionized employers engaged in what has been termed cooperative or 'integrative' concession bargaining, where they actively engaged with unions and their members when responding to the recession, and offered reciprocal concessions, such as access to financial information, review mechanisms that might trigger the restoration of pay and conditions, or supports to union representation (Roche et al. 2014). Most employers' bargaining postures showed strong affinities with pre-recession collective bargaining, offering few reciprocal concessions, other than assurances with respect to enhanced employment security. Some engaged with unions and employees in a cursory or minimal way, or sought to bypass them when developing and implementing measures for responding to the recession (Roche and Teague 2014a; Roche et al. 2014).

In the public service, concession bargaining also dominated dealings between employers and unions. The 2009 salary cut, in the form of a so-called 'pension levy', was imposed unilaterally and without negotiation. A second unilateral cut in salaries was imposed in January 2010. The Croke Park Agreement in March 2010 marked a new phase of negotiated accommodation. Unions for different public service grades agreed to changes in work practices that facilitated the redeployment of staff within and across workplaces, making it possible for public services to be delivered with significant reductions in staff numbers. In return for these concessions, there were no compulsory job losses and no further pay cuts were to be made for the duration of the agreement. In the event, in 2013, the government sought further pay-bill savings, before the expiry of the Croke Park Agreement. Following difficult and complex negotiations, the parties concluded the Haddington Road Agreement, providing for further salary cuts for higher-paid public servants and for increased working hours, while unions pledged cooperation with changes in work practices and measures to reform the public service. The 2015 Lansdowne Road Agreement on public service pay restoration was concluded quickly and with little ceremony.

While public service unions were able to influence the details of retrenchment measures, pay cuts, coupled with cycles of concessions on working time and work practices, inevitably contributed to declining union density (Sheehan 2014). The incentivized exit of large numbers of older public servants, more likely to have been union members than younger colleagues, was a further contributor.

One of the notable features of collective bargaining during the recession was how little industrial conflict occurred. In the private sector, the absence of industrial disorder can be attributed to a combination of the sheer magnitude of the reversal in the labour market after 2015 and people's fears for their jobs, the absence of generalized rounds of cuts in nominal pay rates and employers' pragmatism in reaching accommodation with unions in firm-level pay bargaining. In the public service, where pay cuts were universal, industrial peace was secured through reaching accommodation with unions in successive public service agreements.

With economic revival, rounds of pay increases began to emerge in relatively buoyant sectors such as pharmaceuticals, food manufacturing, and retail multiples. In 2014 and 2015, as gross domestic product (GDP) growth exceeded 5 per cent, a growing number of pay agreements involving average pay increases of around 2 per cent developed—unions negotiating pay rises on a widespread basis for the first time since 2008. Towards the end of 2016, this pay norm began to drift upwards as a rising number of pay agreements involved annual pay rises of between 2.5 to 3 per cent.

EMPLOYEES: DECLINING EARNINGS AND MORE PRESSURIZED WORK

Reflecting data on employers' pay practices examined in the section on private sector firms, many employees were affected by reductions in earnings, especially during the trough of the downturn. Table 11.3 presents the trend in average weekly earnings for employees in the private sector. The data reflect changes in the composition of the private-sector workforce, as well as changes in hours worked and rates of pay, but they point towards significant falls in average weekly earnings, especially in the early years of the crisis, and show that average earnings had only returned to their 2008 level in 2015. Overall, median annual earnings in the private sector declined by 1.6 per cent over the period 2008–11—but the average masks significant variations in the fortunes of employees during the recession (Doris, O'Neill, and Sweetman 2014).

The effects of the public service pay cuts are examined in Table 11.4. Both the scale and the progressive nature of salary cuts across lower to higher public service grades are evident. The cumulative effect of the three public service pay

Table 11.3. Developments in earnings in the private sector

	Average Weekly Earnings €	% Change
2008	636.9	
2009	622.7	−2.2
2010	616.6	−1.0
2011	613.7	−0.5
2012	619.7	1.0
2013	620.1	0.1
2014	623.5	0.5
2015	637.1	2.2

Source: Data for 2011–15 compiled from CSO, Earnings, Hours and Employment Costs Survey. Data from 2008–10 from O'Connell 2013.

Table 11.4. Reductions in the gross salaries of public service grades, 2009–13

Grade	Total % Reduction	
	Grade Minimum	Grade Maximum
Principal Officer	19.25	20.52
Assistant Principal	13.36	18.96
Higher Executive Officer	11.55	12.65
Executive Officer	8.83	11.75
Clerical Officer	6.82	10.30
Staff Nurse	8.75	11.27
Garda	8.21	11.51

Source: Reply by the Department of Public Expenditure and Reform to query by *Industrial Relations News* on public service pay reductions, 2018–14 (*Industrial Relations News*, unpublished).

cuts on gross salaries ranged from under 7 per cent at junior clerical grades to over 20 per cent at senior management grades.

A survey of over 5,000 employees asked about a series of changes at work during the two years up to 2009. Thirty-four per cent reported a decline in employment security. More than 50 per cent of those working in the private sector reported reductions in numbers employed in their organizations and 44 per cent reported that their workplaces had undergone reorganization. In the public sector, 57 per cent reported reductions in numbers employed and 49 per cent reported that workplaces had been reorganized (Russell and McGinnity 2014: 294–6). This was before the moratorium on public service recruitment and the large contraction in public service numbers that followed in subsequent years (O'Connell 2013).

The same study examined work pressure, understood as a combination of working very hard, working under a great deal of pressure, never seeming to

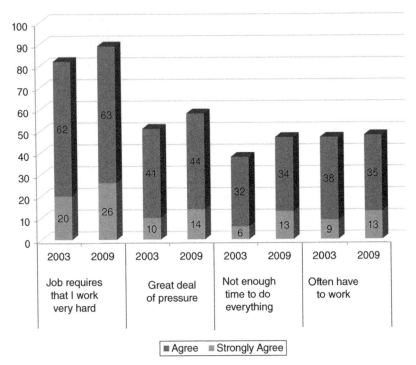

Figure 11.3. Work pressure, 2003 and 2009

Source: Russell, H. and McGinnity, F. (2014), 'Under Pressure: The Impact of Recession on Employees in Ireland.' British Journal of Industrial Relations, 52 (2). John Wiley & Sons). © 2013 John Wiley & Sons Ltd/ London School of Economics.

have enough time to get everything done, and often having to work extra time to get through the job or to help out. Over half reported an increase in work pressure. As revealed in Figure 11.3, all aspects of work pressure increased significantly when compared with a survey conducted during the boom in 2003.

Work pressure in 2009 was greater where there had been staff reductions and workplace reorganization and where jobs were very insecure. Large reductions in pay, increases in job responsibility, and closer monitoring of work were also associated with higher work pressure (Russell and McGinnity 2014: 298–300). A measure of 'work intensity' included in the European Social Survey and presented in Figure 11.4 reveals a similar, albeit less pronounced, upward trend between 2004 and 2010.

Data for Ireland collected in the 2004 and 2010 waves of the European Social Survey allow for a comparison between people's sense of how much control they exercised over the performance of their jobs and decisions in the organizations where they worked at the height of the economic boom and in the trough of the recession. The measure of 'job control' asked people to rate the degree to which management allowed them: (1) to decide how their own

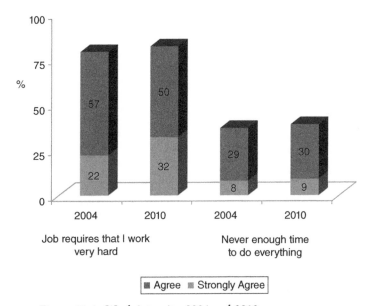

Figure 11.4. Work intensity, 2004 and 2010

Source: European Social Survey, Ireland data files for 2004 and 2010 waves.

daily work was organized; (2) to influence policy decisions about the activities of the organization; and (3) to choose or change their pace of work (see Gallie and Zhou 2013: 117). Each question was answered on a scale ranging from 1 = no influence to 10 = complete control. Figure 11.5 shows that the distributions of job control levels in 2004 and 2010 coil around each other, suggesting no significant differences across these time points. This is confirmed by the near identical mean values for the scale in each of these years.

A more rigorous assessment of whether employees' levels of job control were impacted by the recession and austerity—either negatively, as would be expected if work regimes had become more market driven, or positively as might have occurred had work regimes shifted in a high-performance direction—would require data on *changes* in levels of job control experienced by employees during the period of recession and austerity. No such data are available. A second-best strategy involves examining whether any association existed between *levels* of job control during the recession and the severity of the impact of the recession on workplaces. This can be attempted using 2010 European Social Survey data for Ireland. The measure of job control has already been detailed. Two indicators of retrenchment are available. The first is a question asking employees to indicate the degree of financial difficulty experienced by the organizations for which they worked in the last three years, using a four-point scale ranging from 'a great deal of financial difficulty' to

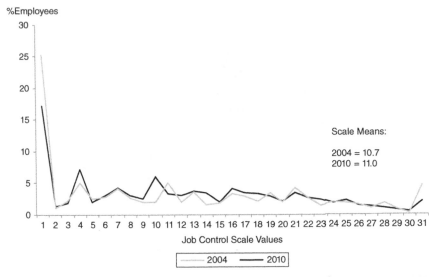

Figure 11.5. Employees' influence over decisions in the job and organization, 2004 and 2010

Source: European Social Survey, Ireland data files for 2004 and 2010 waves.

Table 11.5. Effects of recessionary financial difficulty and changes in employment on levels of job control (OLS regression results)

Independent Variables	Whole Economy	Private Sector	Public Service
Financial Difficulty	0.278	0.140	1.473**
Changes in Employment	0.041	−0.258	0.504
R^2 Change	0.001	0.000	0.029**
N	741	509	230

Notes: Private sector includes employees working in commercial state-owned firms.   ** = Significant at 0.05 level (two tailed t tests for coefficients of independent variables).   Controls included for industry sector, occupational categories, size of employing organization, gender, whether employed on a temporary or permanent contract, union membership, and incumbency of jobs requiring supervision of work of others. *Source*: Ireland data file, 2010 wave of European Social Survey, archived at <http://www.europeansocialsurvey.org/>.

'no financial difficulty'. The second indicator is a question that asked whether the number of people employed by the organization over the last three years had changed. The response options ranged along a five-point scale from 'decreased a lot' to 'increased a lot'.

Table 11.5 examines whether commercial or fiscal retrenchment measured in these ways had affected the levels of work control of people doing otherwise broadly similar jobs. The results for the economy as a whole indicate that neither financial pressures nor the scale of employment losses were associated with higher or lower levels of job control. The same result is obtained for the private sector (including state-owned commercial firms). In the case of the public service, higher levels of job control are associated with the scale of financial pressure affecting organizations. It could, of course, be the case that those organizations severely affected by financial retrenchment had always afforded employees higher levels of job control.

The broad picture that emerges of employees' experiences of work after 2008 is one where many employees worked under more pressure. At the same time, work and employment regimes in the organizations in which most of them worked were not reconfigured in any major way. There appears to have been a modest overall decline in employees' level of job control, but no compelling evidence is available from the 2010 European Social Survey that job control was consistently positively or negatively impacted by the recession—public service organizations appearing to be an exception. Overall, it seems reasonable to suggest an underlying picture in which many employees found themselves having to deal with more pressurized and demanding work in organizations where work and employment regimes had undergone little formal work reorganization either to incorporate more market-like controls or their converse: empowerment and more influence and decision-making power for employees.

CONCLUSIONS

The onset of recession and fiscal crisis in 2008 had very significant effects on workplaces in Ireland. The austerity programme agreed with the Troika in the main affected the private sector indirectly through enshrining policies that were expected to depress the domestic economy significantly. The direct effects of the programme were much more pronounced in public service workplaces. Many firms in the private sector and all agencies across the public sector reduced pay bills by implementing retrenchment programmes involving combinations of job losses, reduced working hours, cuts or freezes in pay and salaries, changes to pension arrangements, lower pay and salaries for new recruits, and changes in work practices. Tripartite social partnership collapsed and collective bargaining was decentralized for the first time in over twenty years. Unions commonly engaged in concession bargaining with employers—trading concessions on pay, conditions, and work practices for pledges regarding enhanced employment security or fewer job losses. The rate of decline in union density accelerated, and the level of unionization fell in the public service for the first time in living memory, having held up during the early years of austerity. Many employees suffered reductions in earnings, increased insecurity, and higher levels of work pressure or intensity.

Internal devaluation, in the sense of general rounds of cuts in basic pay and salaries, was not evident in the private sector, but nominal unit labour costs declined significantly both absolutely and relative to Ireland's main trading partners. This was an outcome of both declining pressure for pay advances against the background of deep job insecurity and structural change in the economy, especially the collapse of the construction sector. Data on the trend in unit labour costs may thus exaggerate competitive gains across the economy and the contribution of pay restraint to economic recovery. The contribution of pay reductions in the public service to fiscal consolidation is clear and beyond doubt. The absence of any general pressure by private-sector employers, concerted or otherwise, on basic pay levels and their refusal to countenance ultra-concession bargaining, as well as the accommodation reached with unions in three public service agreements, explain how so little industrial conflict occurred during the period of recession and austerity. Otherwise, the story for employees was often one of reduced earnings, higher job insecurity, accommodation to changes in work practices, and increased work pressure.

Employers' and unions' postures towards retrenchment in the private sector revealed a great deal of improvisation as the parties sought to respond to short-term pressures—often in unfamiliar ways or by adopting measures that would have been inconceivable a few years earlier. The focus of employers in the private sector, as of the HR specialists who advised them, was squarely on responding to immediate pressures by reducing or controlling pay-bill costs. There was little appetite among employers for radical systemic change in underlying work and employment regimes or models. The austerity programme and NRP made reference, albeit in soft focus, to objectives such as investment in human capital and innovation-driven improvements in productivity and high value-added employment, which seemed to endorse a 'high road' skill- and knowledge-intensive vision of workplace regimes based on high commitment or high perform-ance. However, data on employers' postures and employees' experience of job and organizational decision-making revealed no recession- or austerity-induced shift in the centre of gravity in work regimes—either towards a 'high road' or conversely a 'low road', involving deeper and more extensive market-focused flexibilities. Overall, workplaces in Ireland thus remain posi-tioned competitively much as they had been prior to the crisis and austerity programme.

In the public service, the focus during much of the fiscal crisis was on cutting pay-bill costs, reducing headcount, and gaining flexibilities in work practices and staff deployment that allowed productivity to rise at a time when demand for public services expanded. The scale of the adjustment achieved was very significant. While the austerity programme and the NRP aimed to achieve 'public service transformation', in practice radical changes to work and employment arrangements were not a priority. Many of the reforms introduced revisited innovations of pre-crisis vintage—seeking to make these more effective (e.g. performance management and open appointments to top-level positions). By 2014, a vision or blueprint had emerged for the public service, which embedded multiple reforms, mainly of pre-crisis vintage, within a public service model of work and employment that showed strong affinities with the established career-based public service model.

REFERENCES

Barrett, A. and McGuinness, S. 2012. *The Irish Labour Market and the Great Recession*. Munich: CESifo DICE Report.

Bergin, A., Kelly, E., and McGuinness, S. 2012. 'Explaining Changes in Earnings and Labour Costs during the Recession', Renewal Series Paper 9. Dublin: Economic and Social Research Institute.

Briner, R. 2010. 'Deal Breakers'. *People Management*, 29 July.

Brockett, J. 2010. 'See HR as a Professional Services Firm, Says Ulrich'. *People Management*, 25 March.

Brown, D. and Reilly, P. 2009. *HR in Recession: What are the Prospects and Priorities for HR Management in 2009?* London: Institute for Employment Studies.

Cappelli, P. 1999a. *The New Deal at Work: Managing the Market-Driven Workforce*. Boston MA: Harvard Business School Press.

Cappelli, P. 1999b. 'Career Jobs are Dead'. *California Management Review*, 42: 146–66.

Central Bank of Ireland. 2009. *Quarterly Bulletin: October*. Dublin: Central Bank of Ireland.

Chaison, G. 2012. *The New Collective Bargaining*. New York: Springer.

Department of Finance. 2009. *Supplementary Budget*. Dublin: Department of Finance.

Department of Finance. 2010. *EU/IMF Programme of Financial Support for Ireland*. Dublin: Department of Finance.

Doris, A., O'Neill, D., and Sweetman, O. 2014. *Recession: The Response of the Irish Labour Market*. Maynooth: Maynooth University, Department of Economics, Finance and Accounting.

DPER (Department of Public Expenditure and Reform). 2011. *Public Service Reform*. Dublin: Department of Public Expenditure and Reform.

DPER (Department of Public Expenditure and Reform). 2013. *Performance Management and Development System 2013 Phase 2 Changes: Overview of revised System*. Dublin: Department of Public Expenditure and Reform.

DPER (Department of Public Expenditure and Reform). 2014a. *Public Service Reform Plan 2014–2016*. Dublin: Department of Public Expenditure and Reform.

DPER (Department of Public Expenditure and Reform). 2014b. *Civil Service Renewal Plan*. Dublin: Department of Public Expenditure and Reform.

DPER (Department of Public Expenditure and Reform). 2014c. *Strengthening Civil Service Accountability and Performance*. Dublin: Department of Public Expenditure and Reform.

Eurofound (European Foundation for the Improvement of Living and Working Conditions). 2014a. *Impact of the Crisis on Industrial Relations and Working Conditions in Europe*. Dublin: Eurofound.

Frawley 2013. 'Pilot Exchange for Managers Between Private and Public Sectors', *Industrial Relations News*, 13 February.

Frawley 2014a. 'Civil Servants Can Now Apply for Promotions Beyond Traditional Boundaries', *Industrial Relations News*, 15 January.

Frawley, M. 2014b. 'Howlin Steers Away from "Head of Civil Service", Opts for Collectivity', *Industrial Relations News*, 6 November.

Gallie, D. 2013. 'Economic Crisis, the Quality of Work and Social Integration: Issues and Context'. In *Economic Crisis, Quality of Work and Social Integration: The European Experience*, ed. D. Gallie. Oxford: Oxford University Press.

Gallie, D. and Zhou, Y. 2013. 'Job Control, Work Intensity and Work Stress'. In *Economic Crisis, Quality of Work and Social Integration: The European Experience*, ed. D. Gallie. Oxford: Oxford University Press.

Government of Ireland. 2010. *National Recovery Plan 2011–2014*. Dublin: Government Publications.

Higgins, C. 2011a. 'Public Pension Reform to Slash Costs – But Only for Distant Future', *Industrial Relations News*, 5 October.

Higgins, C. 2011b. 'Top Civil Service Group Now Has Outsider Majority', *Industrial Relations News*, 13 April.

Higgins, C. 2011c. 'Senior Public Service Cadre Now Initiated in Civil Service', *Industrial Relations News*, 26 January.

IBEC (Irish Business and Employers' Confederation). 2014. *HR Update: Spring*. Dublin: Irish Business and Employers' Confederation.

LRC (Labour Relations Commission). 2013. *LRC Proposals: Public Service Stability Agreement 2013–2016*. Dublin: Labour Relations Commission.

McDonnell, T. and O'Farrell, R. 2015. *Internal Devaluation and Labour Market Trends in Ireland during the Crisis*. Dublin: Nevin Economic Institute.

Mohrman, S. and Worley, C. G. 2009. 'Dealing with Rough Times: A Capabilities Development Approach to Surviving and Thriving'. *Human Resource Management*, 48(3): 433–45.

O'Connell, P. 2010. *The Changing Workplace: A Survey of Employees' Views and Experiences*. Dublin: National Centre for Partnership and Performance.

O'Connell, P. 2013. 'Cautious Adjustment in a Context of Economic Collapse: The Public Sector in the Irish Crises'. In *Public Sector Shock: The Impact of Policy Retrenchment in Europe*, ed. D. Vaughan-Whitehead. London: Edward Elgar.

Roche, W. K. 2013. 'Human Resource Management and Public Service Reform'. *Administration*, 60(3): 211–18.

Roche, W. K. 2007. 'Social Partnership in Ireland and New Social Pacts'. *Industrial Relations: A Journal of Economy and Society*, 46(3): 394–425.

Roche, W. K. and Teague, P. 2012. 'Business Partners and Working the Pumps: Human Resource Managers in the Recession'. *Human Relations Journal*, 65(10): 1333–58.

Roche, W. K. and Teague, P. 2014a. 'Do Recessions Transform Work and Employment? Evidence from Ireland. *British Journal of Industrial Relations*, 52(2): 261–85.

Roche, W. K. and Teague, P. 2014b. 'Effective but Unappealing: Fifteen Years of Workplace Partnership in Ireland'. *International Journal of Human Resource Management*, 25(6): 781–94.

Roche, W. K. and Teague, P. 2016. 'The Workplace Relations Environment and Outlook', Unpublished report prepared for the Workplace Relations Commission.

Roche, W. K., Teague, P., and Coughlan, A. 2015. 'Employers, Unions and Concession Bargaining in the Irish Recession'. *Economic and Industrial Democracy*, 36(4): 653–76.

Roche, W. K., Teague, P., Coughlan, A., and Fahy, M. 2013. *Recession at Work: HRM in the Irish Crisis*. Oxford and New York: Routledge.

Russell, H. and McGinnity, F. 2014. 'Under Pressure: The Impact of Recession on Employees in Ireland'. *British Journal of Industrial Relations*, 52(2): 286–307.

Sheehan, B. 2014. 'Union Membership Decline Now Hitting Public as Well as Private Sector'. *Industrial Relations News*, 1 October.

Teague, P., Roche, W. K., Gormley, T., and Currie, D. 2015. *Managing Workplace Conflict: Alternative Dispute Resolution in Ireland*. Dublin: Institute of Public Administration.

Towers Watson. 2010. *The New Employment Deal: How Far, How Fast and How Enduring?* New York: Towers Watson.

Van Wanrooy, B., Bewley, H., Bryson, A., Forth, A., Freeth, S., Stokes, L., and Wood, S. 2013. *Employment Relations in the Shadow of Recession*. London: Palgrave Macmillan.

Walsh, F. 2014. *Union Membership over Ireland's Recession*. Dublin: School of Economics, University College Dublin.

Walsh, K. 2012. 'Wage Bill Change in Ireland During Recession: How Have Employers Reacted to the Downturn'. *Journal of the Statistical and Social Inquiry Society of Ireland*, 41: 39–70.

12

Public Service Reform

Richard Boyle

INTRODUCTION

The financial crisis triggered by the collapse of the international banking system in the late 2000s has driven a new round of cutbacks and public service reforms in many countries. This wave of reforms is characterized by consolidation and recentralization (Gieve and Provost 2012; Thynne 2011). There is an emphasis on spending cuts, the need to do 'more with less', joined-up government, closer integration of policy formulation and implementation, more flexible public service labour markets, greater use of technology, building and maintaining public trust in public institutions, and accountability (Posner and Blöndal 2012; Van de Walle and Jilke 2014).

Despite these common themes, a review of academic studies (Raudla, Savi, and Randma-Liiv 2013) shows that government responses to the crisis have been diverse (Bideleux 2011; Kickert 2012; Lodge and Hood 2012; Peters 2011; Peters, Pierre and Randma-Liiv 2011; Pollitt 2010). Raudla, Savi, and Randma-Liiv (2013: 39) note that 'this means that the contextual factors that define the depth of the crisis and hence shape the response(s) to crisis are vastly different due to country specific features'.

Given the depth and the scale of the fiscal crisis in Ireland, it is of interest to examine the nature and scale of public service reform that has occurred in response to austerity. To what extent has the crisis resulted in short-term changes or will it lead to longer-term, more systemic structural and process changes in the way public services are provided? Has austerity resulted in more centralized or decentralized modes of decision-making? What has been the impact on the behaviour and attitudes of public servants working in challenging conditions? How does Ireland's response compare to that of other countries affected by the fiscal and economic crisis?

This chapter is divided into three main sections. In the first section, 'Reform in the Irish Public Service', the reforms which have taken place in public services are briefly described, covering three main time periods: (a) an overview of reform prior to the financial crisis, (b) immediate reform efforts post-crisis, focused on reduction in pay and numbers, and (c) reform initiatives which have occurred since a change of government in 2011. In the second section, 'Public Service Reform in Ireland: The Effects of Austerity', the impact of the reforms is analysed and assessed from four main perspectives: (a) the impact on numbers and pay, (b) the views of senior public executives on the impact of austerity and reform efforts, (c) the effect on the public service bargain, and (d) the effect on the public service landscape. Finally, a concluding section sets out some general thoughts on the likely longer-term implications of the public service reforms undertaken during the time of austerity.

REFORM IN THE IRISH PUBLIC SERVICE

A Brief Overview of Reform pre the Fiscal and Economic Crisis

Reform of the public service in Ireland has, as in many countries, been an episodic item on the political agenda for many years. In the 1960s, the report of the Public Service Organisation Review Group (1969), popularly known as the Devlin Report, recommended sweeping and controversial changes regarding the separation of policymaking and execution. As Barrington, Carpenter, and MacFeely (2015) note, this provoked extensive debate but ultimately had little effect. The 1980s saw the publication of a white paper titled *Serving the Country Better* (1985). The emphasis was predominantly on changing administrative process rather than more significant structural reform (Connaughton 2005) and had some positive albeit limited impact (Boyle 1997).

The Strategic Management Initiative (SMI) was launched in 1994 with the stated objective of improving the efficiency and effectiveness of the Irish public service. Two years later, the report *Delivering Better Government* (1996) set out a reform agenda. Over the ensuing decade, with varying degrees of emphasis and success, a range of initiatives, policies, guidelines, and new legislation was put in place. The Public Service Management Act 1997 was an important piece of legislation, setting out a formal structure for assigning authority and accountability within the civil service (Boyle and MacCarthaigh 2011).

In 2008, the Organisation for Economic Co-operation and Development (OECD) produced a landmark report on the Irish public service. It was the first time the OECD had benchmarked a national public service against good international practice. Their report broadly indicated that Irish public services were doing a good job but that there was a need for more integration and coordination of public services, better implementation of reform initiatives, and more of a focus on performance and value for money (OECD 2008). In response, the government produced a report titled *Transforming Public Services* (Department of the Taoiseach 2008) but the actions proposed here were rapidly overtaken by the impact of the fiscal and economic crisis.

Early Public Service Reform Efforts at a Time of Crisis: Reducing Pay and Numbers

The impact of the financial crisis on the public service was immediate and dramatic. In 2009, as a means of addressing the escalating public service wage bill and with considerable anti-public service sentiment in the media, the government introduced a public service pension levy of 7 per cent on average, and public service pay cuts of between 5 and 20 per cent depending on salary level.

In an initiative to reduce public service numbers and to further reduce the pay bill, incentivized early retirement (available to staff over 50 years) and career break schemes were also introduced, with staff availing of these programmes not being replaced. In December 2009, a further decision imposed new ceilings on total public service numbers to be achieved through the implementation of employment control frameworks (ECF) in respect of each organization. Administrative budgets for all organizations were cut.

The key enabler of these dramatic changes, post the introduction of the pension levy and immediate wage cuts in 2009, was the Public Service Agreement 2010–14, commonly known as the Croke Park Agreement from the location at which negotiations took place. This was an industrial relations agreement reached between the government and the trade unions. The agreement gave employees assurances that there would be no compulsory redundancies from the public service and, in as far as could be foreseen, no further pay cuts. In return, the government obtained agreement on significant restructuring and reorganization of the public service as a means of achieving cost reductions. The agreement also set out arrangements in respect of the redeployment of staff across the different sectors of the public service.

In assessing the impact of the agreement, Roche (2012: 1) states that 'the Croke Park Agreement has provided a framework for managing fiscal consolidation and public service retrenchment, and so avoiding the industrial conflict, general strikes and chaos often observed in other bailout countries and indeed in non-bailout countries like Italy, Spain, France and the UK'.

New Government, New Public Service Reform Agenda

The Irish Government collapsed in early 2011 in the aftermath of the European Union (EU)/International Monetary Fund (IMF) deal. Political and public-sector reform was a prominent issue in the subsequent election campaign. A new Fine Gael/Labour Party Coalition came into power in March 2011. Its Programme for Government, titled Government for National Recovery 2011–16 signalled the government's intention to introduce significant public service reforms.

The depth of the crisis had provoked many commentators to call for fundamental reform in Irish political and administrative structures, and indeed to suggest that the political and administrative system itself was in need of major reform (Hardiman 2009; Laffan 2010). One economic academic and commentator summed up the general view of many people: 'any programme of public service reform needs to pursue two objectives simultaneously. The system needs to work much better and it needs to cost much less. The record of the last decade has been one of missed opportunities, waffle, increased cost and reduced effectiveness' (McCarthy 2011).

The need for reform, particularly in relation to human resources (HR) management, was exemplified by the findings of an independent review of the Department of Finance and its role in the financial crisis, commissioned by the government, which found weaknesses with regard to the availability of specialist skills (Wright 2010: 35). These limitations had also been identified in an internal capacity analysis carried out in 2009 (Department of Finance 2009), and were consistent with the generalist and career-based nature of the civil service in Ireland. Compared to many OECD countries, the Irish civil service has remained at the more conservative end of the spectrum with regard to HR reform (O'Riordan 2008: 49).

Christensen (2013) and Wallis, Goldfinch, and Klein (2012) contrast the Irish experience with that of New Zealand. Christensen (2013: 566), for example, states that in New Zealand they recruited economists into the civil service who took an activist approach to policy advice. He compares this to the Irish situation where there was little economic expertise in the civil service, limited knowledge of microeconomic ideas about taxation, and a passive approach to policy advice.

An early action by the new government was the establishment of a new department, the Department of Public Expenditure and Reform, to manage reductions in public expenditure to sustainable levels while reforming and improving public services (Department of Public Expenditure and Reform 2011). The new department took over functions previously managed by the Department of Finance and the Department of the Taoiseach. The intention behind the establishment of the new department was that public service spending and reform should be managed together. The Department of Finance retained responsibility for overall budget, tax, and spending matters. New secretaries general, each with public- and private-sector experience, were appointed to lead the Department of Finance and the Department of Public Expenditure and Reform. Economists were recruited into the central departments.

Bringing in people with outside experience was seen as sending a message that the traditional ways of doing things needed to be changed, providing an opportunity to develop a new approach and culture. These personnel and institutional changes were aimed at creating a new dynamic at top levels at the centre of government regulatory and fiscal administration. They were intended in part to enhance the challenge function and strengthen independent advice.[1]

An Economic Management Council (EMC) was also created, with the status of a Cabinet committee, and membership of the Taoiseach (Prime Minister), Tánaiste (Deputy Prime Minister), Minister for Finance, and Minister for Public Expenditure and Reform. The council oversees economic policy. It is intended to give a strong political lead to the required budgetary adjustments and reforms. The creation of this EMC has generated some degree of debate as to its role, as some see it as usurping the role of the Cabinet in government (Whelan 2014). Other institutional reforms include the creation of a Fiscal Advisory Council and a Government Economic and Evaluation Service.

In November 2011, the government published the Public Service Reform Plan (Department of Public Expenditure and Reform 2011), a blueprint for public service reforms up to 2015. Revised targets for reductions in public-sector numbers were set out. Public service numbers were to be reduced by 37,500 from peak 2008 figures to 282,500 by 2015. Facilitated by an ageing public service, it was envisaged these reductions could be accommodated through retirements and voluntary departures. The plan also identified five priorities: customer service; maximizing new and innovative service-delivery channels; radically reducing costs to drive better value for money; leading, organizing, and working in new ways; and a focus on implementation and delivery. Issues such as the development of shared services, procurement, and outsourcing were emphasized. A review of progress (Boyle 2013) suggests that most actions identified in the plan have been implemented to some degree, but that significant challenges still remain.

In January 2014, the Department of Public Expenditure and Reform announced a further reform initiative. The Public Service Reform Plan 2014–16 (Department of Public Expenditure and Reform 2014) identifies four main reform themes: delivery of improved outcomes, reform dividend (using savings to invest in new or improved services), digitalization/open data, and openness and accountability.

---

[1] External appointments at senior levels in central government agencies were a more general feature of change at the time. In 2009, a new Governor of the Central Bank of Ireland was appointed, a well-respected professor of international financial economics, as well as a new Head of Financial Supervision in the Central Bank, a former Chief Executive of the Bermuda Monetary Authority. These appointments coincided with developing new regulatory structures for financial regulation.

These service-wide reforms have been accompanied by sectoral reform plans. For example Putting People First, the action programme for local government reform, set out a number of key objectives in relation to local government (Department of the Environment, Community and Local Government 2012). These objectives include the structural reform of local authorities such as mergers and rationalization; reorganization of political and executive structures; alignment of community and enterprise functions with the local government system; greater impact and involvement in local economic and community development; service efficiencies; and revised funding arrangements. The Civil Service Renewal Plan (Department of Public Expenditure and Reform 2014) was published in October 2014. This plan sets out changes to accountability and performance regimes in the civil service.

Important in maintaining the momentum of reform and cooperation of public servants was the negotiation of a successor to the Public Service Agreement, the Public Service Stability Agreement 2013–16 (LRC 2013), commonly known as the Haddington Road Agreement. The driver for the agreement was a government decision, in the light of the economic situation, to seek a further €1 billion savings in the cost of the pay and pensions bill. The agreement saw the introduction of initiatives such as more flexible and speedier redeployment, longer working hours, changes to overtime rates, and pay cuts for those earning over €65,000 per annum.

At the same time as the Public Service Stability Agreement was introduced, the government enacted the Financial Emergency Measures in the Public Interest (FEMPI) Act 2013. This legislation gave effect to reductions in pay and pension rates and enabled far-reaching changes to pay and working conditions for members of unions that had not signed up to the Public Service Stability Agreement. The legislation allows the Minister for Public Expenditure and Reform to impose further changes to working conditions by ministerial order.

The Public Service Stability Agreement, as with the preceding Public Service Agreement, provided a mechanism for securing the cooperation of staff for the reforms needed to ensure cost reductions. This included a continuation of the restriction on recruitment and promotion, the selective recruitment of appropriately skilled personnel from outside the public service at all grades if required, cooperation in respect of processes and systems to allow for shared services and e-government initiatives, commitment to the redesign of work processes, and the dismantling of barriers to a unified public service to be achieved through progress towards standardized terms and conditions of employment across the public service.

In a sign of the improving economic climate, in November 2015 the Minister for Public Expenditure and Reform formally signed the Commencement Order, bringing into law the FEMPI Act 2015. The Act gives effect to the provisions of the Lansdowne Road Agreement, negotiated between the government and trade union bodies in 2015 to follow on from the Haddington Road Agreement, and amends previous FEMPI legislation, which has underpinned the various public service pay and pensions reductions since 2009. The 2015 Act provides for a number of measures to begin a partial and phased restoration of the pay reductions of recent years. The bulk of the measures are focused on lower-paid public servants in the first instance.

PUBLIC SERVICE REFORM IN IRELAND: THE EFFECTS OF AUSTERITY

Effects on Numbers Employed and Pay

There have been dramatic reductions in public service numbers and pay, broadly in line with the proposed actions, as illustrated in Figure 12.1. From its peak in 2008, the total number of people employed in the public service dropped from 320,000 to 294,000 in 2015, a drop of 8 per cent. While numbers have fallen in all sectors since 2008, some have been affected significantly more than others. The biggest drop proportionally has been in local authorities (23 per cent). The smallest drop proportionally has been in the education sector (1 per cent) and civil service (7 per cent). Overall numbers employed rose slightly in 2015.

While public service employment levels have been dropping, the population has continued to increase. At 63.4 public service employees per 000 population in 2015 there were approximately 10 less public service employees per 000 people than there was in 2008 (Boyle 2015).

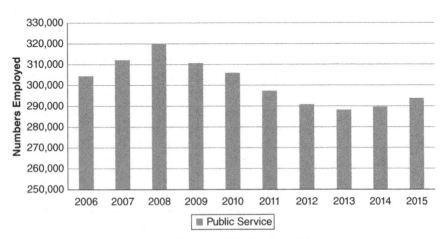

Figure 12.1. Numbers employed in the public service
Source: Department of Public Expenditure and Reform Databank.

Figure 12.2. Public service pay and pensions

Source: Department of Public Expenditure and Reform Databank. Separate data on pensions only available from 2011.

There is no doubt that the reduction in numbers employed in the public service will continue to have a major impact on working conditions over the coming years. Early staff retirements have also caused difficulties. For example, an independent review of the Department of Justice conducted to examine the performance, management, and administration of the department following a series of controversies, found, amongst other things, that: 'There is a failure to ensure effective knowledge transfer from retiring staff. A combination of retirements and the public service staffing moratorium, without a sufficient focus on succession planning, has led to loss of knowledge and expertise' (Report of the Independent Review Group on the Department of Justice and Equality 2014: 10).

Changes to public service pay and pensions are shown in Figure 12.2. The public service pay bill and pensions reached a peak of €18.7 billion in 2008. From 2008 to 2014, as the cutbacks in numbers and pay introduced by the government have taken effect, expenditure on public service pay and pensions decreased from its high of €18.7 billion to €16.8 billion in 2015.

What evidence there is to assess the impact these changes in numbers and pay have had on service provision suggests that provision has, overall, held up well to date. In terms of perception of quality of service provided, as assessed by surveys of business executives, Ireland's score on a Quality of Public Administration Index has actually increased slightly in recent years compared to European averages (Boyle 2015). There may, of course, be time lag issues which will manifest themselves in the future. In an examination of Irish health system performance, Burke and colleagues (2014) found that indicators of activity in the Irish health system during the economic crisis had shown a relatively resilient system (as measured by activity) from 2008 to 2012.

However, indicators from 2013 on demonstrated a system under increasing pressure that could no longer continue 'to do more with less'. The indicators revealed a system that had no choice other than 'to do less with less'.

The Views of Senior Public Executives on the Impact of Austerity on Reform

Coordinating for Cohesion in the Public Sector of the Future (COCOPS), a major comparative public management research project, provides a picture of the challenges facing the public service in European countries and explores the impact of new public management (NPM) style reforms in Europe. A cornerstone of the project is the COCOPS executive survey on public-sector reform in Europe: a large-scale survey of public-sector top executives, exploring executives' opinions and experiences with regard to public-sector reforms. In Ireland, the survey was carried out in September and October 2013. A total of 437 valid responses were received, giving a response rate of 27 per cent (see Boyle 2014 for details).

Figure 12.3 shows senior public executives perceptions of the impact of the fiscal crisis on power relations. Ireland is compared to the COCOPS average.[2] It can be seen that there is a strong view that the power of the Ministry of Finance has increased,[3] and that decision-making has been centralized in organizations. In other European countries there is also a view that greater centralization of power has occurred, particularly that of the Ministry of Finance, but not to the same extent as in Ireland. The relevance of performance information is seen as having increased, as has the role of budget-planning units in organizations. There are more mixed views as to whether the power of politicians has increased or if conflict between organizations has increased.

Irish officials feel they have a low level of management autonomy. The lowest degree of management autonomy is expressed with regard to hiring staff (78 per cent rather low autonomy), promoting staff (76 per cent rather low autonomy), and dismissing or removing staff (74 per cent rather low autonomy).[4] These levels of management autonomy are generally much lower than those expressed in the COCOPS sample. For example, only 13 per cent

---

[2] Here, Ireland is compared to the ten countries that were originally involved in the COCOPS project: Austria, Estonia, France, Germany, Hungary, Italy, the Netherlands, Norway, Spain, and the UK. The COCOPS survey has subsequently been applied in a number of other countries.

[3] In Ireland, this includes both the Department of Finance and the Department of Public Expenditure and Reform, which took over a number of functions of the Department of Finance in 2011, as discussed elsewhere in this chapter.

[4] 'Rather low' refers to a score of 1 or 2 on the 7-point scale. 'Rather high' refers to a score of 6 or 7.

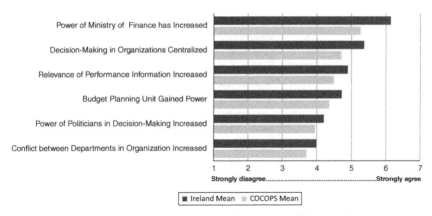

Figure 12.3. Senior Executives' Perceptions of the Impact of the Fiscal Crisis on Power Relations

Source: Boyle 2014.

feel they have a rather high degree of autonomy in hiring staff compared to 41 per cent in the COCOPS sample. This general picture of low management autonomy reflects the fact that, historically, the management of the Irish public service has tended to be relatively highly centralized, and also that, in response to the financial crisis, measures were introduced which further restricted managers with regard to issues such as staff recruitment or promotion.

With regard to reform trends more generally, 84 per cent of Irish senior public servants believe that public-sector downsizing has been an important reform, while a similarly high percentage see focusing on outcomes and results as one of the most important reforms. Collaboration and cooperation among different public-sector actors, transparency and open government, and digital or e-government are the next three most important ranked reforms. The reforms that Irish respondents thought least important are privatization, the creation of autonomous agencies, and extending state provision into new areas. When compared to the average results from the COCOPS sample, Irish respondents rate contracting out, a focus on outcomes and results, and transparency and open government as more important reform trends.

The vast majority of respondents (90 per cent registering points 1–5 on a 10-point scale) feel that the reforms have been more top down than bottom up. A high percentage also feel that the reforms have been more about cost-cutting and savings than about service improvement (80 per cent), and have tended towards no public involvement rather than high public involvement. Respondents are also more likely to see the reforms as crisis driven, partial, and contested by unions, than planned, comprehensive, and supported by unions. Views are relatively evenly split as to whether reforms are consistent or inconsistent, or too much versus not enough. A small majority feel that the reforms are more driven by politicians than by senior executives. A similar

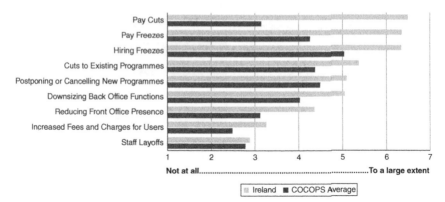

Figure 12.4. Cutback measures applied at organizational level in response to the fiscal crisis

Source: Boyle 2014.

small majority see the reforms as more unsuccessful than successful. Here, the Irish results are broadly in line with the COCOPS sample.

Figure 12.4 sets out the views of public executives on a range of cutback measures applied at the organizational level in response to the financial crisis. In the view of Irish public executives, the main cutback measures applied are pay cuts, pay freezes, and hiring freezes. This is to be expected given the government response to the fiscal crisis outlined in the section 'Early Public Service Reform Efforts at a Time of Crisis: Reducing Pay and Numbers'. Compared to the COCOPS sample, Irish public executives are much more likely to feel that all the listed cutback measures have been applied to a greater extent. For example, only 21 per cent of the COCOPS sample note pay cuts as being applied to a rather large extent, compared to 93 per cent of Irish respondents.

Irish public executives on the whole feel that public administration has got better over the five years to the end of 2013: 62 per cent feel that it has got better, and 38 per cent feel that it has got worse. Compared to the COCOPS sample, Irish respondents tend to be somewhat more positive in their assessment of how public administration has performed. Notably with regard to policy effectiveness, policy coherence and coordination, cost and efficiency, external transparency, and openness and ethical behaviour, a larger share of Irish respondents feel things have improved. Conversely, Irish executives are more likely to feel that things have deteriorated with regard to citizen trust in government, the attractiveness of the public sector as an employer, and staff motivation. These findings need to be interpreted in the context of the scale of cutbacks applied to the Irish public service over this period and the fact that, in most of the other countries in the COCOPS sample, cutback measures have not been applied to the same degree. To a significant extent this might be seen as a rather positive assessment by Irish senior public servants.

Overall, the results tend to underline the mixed managerialist/Weberian character of Irish public administration (Rhodes and Boyle 2012). There is also evidence of what Pollitt and Bouckaert (2011) describe as a new public governance (NPG) reform agenda, where outcomes, networks, and joined-up government receive more emphasis. The influence of the fiscal crisis has been strong and is reflected in aspects of reform such as the emphasis on downsizing, cost-cutting, and efficiency. Centralization of power in what was already a centralized control environment has increased. At the same time, Irish senior public executives have a broadly positive view of many aspects of public-sector reform.

Effect of the Crisis and Reform on the Public Service Bargain

Lodge and Hood (2012: 81) argue that austerity has impacted on the public service bargain, which they see as covering issues such as what kind of skills and competencies are required from public servants, how public servants are to be rewarded, and what kinds of responsibility or political stance is expected of them. However, they note that the effect is not uniform, and that different states have been affected in different ways. Not least because the financial crisis is only one of several major forces, including long-term demographic and environmental change, that can be expected to impact on governments in the coming years.

In Ireland, the reduction in numbers employed in the public service, reductions in pay, and changed terms and conditions of employment outlined in the section 'Early Public Service Reform Efforts at a Time of Crisis: Reducing Pay and Numbers' have resulted in significant changes to the public service bargain. The Public Service Agreement and Public Service Stability Agreement in particular have changed the nature of the public service bargain. But at the same time, some traditional characteristics of public service employment (security of tenure, a common grade and pay system, defined benefit pension) have remained intact. With regard to competencies and skills there is an increasing trend away from the generalist public servant working in a relatively closed environment to more use of specialist staff with more open recruitment. Nevertheless, traditional competencies and skills in areas such as policy analysis and HR management have been re-emphasized. The public service bargain is changing, but the extent and form of that change is still evolving.

Effect on Organization and Delivery of Public Services

On a very basic structural level, there have been significant changes in the public service landscape during the period of austerity. At central government level, the new Department of Public Expenditure and Reform, and initiatives such as the creation of the EMC, have changed the dynamic. As at early 2015, all bar three secretaries general of government departments have been appointed in 2011 or later, reflecting a significant change of personnel at the top. Shared services in areas such as HR management and payroll have been introduced. State agencies have been rationalized, and a programme of closure and consolidation implemented as part of the public service reform plans. Though, as Boyle (2016) notes, new agencies also continue to emerge.

At local government level, there has been the merger of city/county councils in Limerick, Tipperary, and Waterford; abolition of eighty town councils, replaced by a new system of municipal districts; new structures for community and economic development; and the establishment of a National Oversight and Audit Commission. The number of elected councillors has been reduced from 1,627 to around 950. The eight regional authorities and two regional assemblies have been replaced by three regional assemblies.

More generally, with regard to service provision there has been an emphasis on widening the mix of providers and using alternative service delivery mechanisms. Robert Watt, Secretary General at the Department of Public Expenditure and Reform, noted that a major challenge in developing new service models is to reallocate resources to try something new and different in an environment where rising demand for services means that it is unsustainable to provide services in the traditional way (McKeown 2013: 12). This is reflective of a view across many countries and management consultancies that, as well as being provided by directly employed state employees, services could equally well be provided, often at lower cost to the exchequer, by private-sector or third-sector organizations, working under contract (Pollitt 2014).

However, Pollitt (2014: 26–7) cautions that the increase in contracting out, which seems to be accompanying austerity in a number of countries including Ireland, may be storing up trouble for the future. Such caution is supported by Reeves (2013), in particular with regard to the development of public–private partnerships (PPPs).

CONCLUSION

Austerity has caused major change in the public service. Arguably, Ireland has seen the biggest change to its public services since the foundation of the state. Not least, the reduction in numbers employed has resulted in a much smaller public service, at a time of growing population and growing demand for services. Growth in demand in some areas has been facilitated by redeployment of staff, and in other cases by changed ways of working. In this broad context, it is possible to identify a number of reform themes and trends.

One trend is the increased centralization of power and control, both politically and administratively. A second trend is more of a role for 'outsiders', particularly in senior management positions, combined with more open recruitment and an increasing emphasis on specialization and professionalization. A third trend is more use of commissioning and contracting out of services, allied with rationalization and more use of shared services. A fourth trend is a greater use of new models of service delivery, and an increasing emphasis on what Dunleavy and colleagues (2006) call digital-era governance. And a fifth trend is a changing public service bargain, with changed terms and conditions of employment giving more flexibility to employers.

An inevitable question is whether these reform trends will be long-lasting or if they are likely to be temporary and alter as the economic environment stabilizes. The increased centralization of power, certainly at the administrative level, is likely to diminish as the effects of austerity reduce. As mentioned in the section 'New Government, New Public Service Reform Agenda' Ireland was already relatively highly centralized with regard to HR management in the public service and was subject to recommendations from the OECD (2008) that a more decentralized approach would be welcome. There are some early signs of moves to more decentralized decision-making, such as proposals in the Civil Service Renewal Plan (2014) that departments and state agencies be given more flexibility and accountability for managing staff resources within strict multi-annual pay allocations.

The use of more open recruitment, a greater role for 'outsiders', and more specialization and professionalization in the public service is likely to continue. Whilst having benefits and bringing about a more diverse and specialized skills base, this will bring its own challenges. In the UK, which has promoted open recruitment and employment of senior managers from outside the public service for a number of years, there have been issues around higher levels of turnover and difficulties for some outsiders in adjusting to the organizational culture and practice of the public service (Institute for Government 2013; Public Administration Select Committee 2010). Greater specialization and professionalization also brings with it the need for career structures and paths for such staff.

More commissioning and contracting of services, greater use of shared services, and the use of a wider variety of service delivery models is likely to be a continuing and increasing feature of public service reform. As resource constraints continue, and demands increase, it is inevitable that a more diverse set of delivery mechanisms and cheaper cost options will be a growing feature of reform, and innovation seen as a means of organizational change (O'Donnell 2006). Again there are both benefits and challenges associated with such a move. A more active role for individual citizens and communities in shaping public services can make services more responsive and help deliver desired outcomes. But commissioning and contracting of services requires public servants to acquire new skill sets, and may lead to challenges such as the potential for more misuse of public funds and more fragmentation of services.

Finally, changes to the public service bargain in Ireland look set to stay, and will likely continue to evolve. The 'deal' between elected politicians and public servants as to their respective roles and responsibilities, entitlements and duties has seen changes to such fundamentals as pay and pensions and working conditions more generally. While some of these changes, such as pay cuts, are being ameliorated as the economy improves, some are likely to remain and be further developed. The idea of the anonymous public servant providing frank advice to their ministers in return for security of tenure and an absence of public scrutiny is one that increasingly bears little resemblance to reality.

The Irish public service has been subject to significant and in many ways radical reform as a result of austerity. It would have been impossible to envisage proposals to cut pay and pensions, reduce numbers employed, increase working hours, introduce major redeployment and other wider reforms without the driving force of the financial crisis providing the catalyst for change. Some changes may have happened anyway, including more professionalization and specialization and more commissioning of services, but would likely have occurred over a much longer time frame.

Public service reform has been implemented in line with the commitments entered into in the austerity programme. The reform initiatives broadly conform to the prevailing international thinking on good practice with regard to public service modernization (OECD 2015). The inevitable question as to the extent these reforms have contributed to fiscal consolidation and economic recovery is a difficult if not impossible one to answer definitively. On the plus side, many of the issues identified as in need of being addressed have, to varying degrees, been tackled. A revised budgetary framework and greater use of alternative service delivery mechanisms are examples of reforms widely seen as necessary and useful. Irish public services are seen as relatively well managed compared to those of many other European countries (Boyle 2015). But challenges remain and initiatives such as shared services and centralized procurement bring their own difficulties if not managed well. Reform of the health service is a major area where significant problems remain to be tackled. There are difficulties in ensuring coordination and coherence in the revised budgetary landscape. Many services are increasingly under strain as a result of years of cutbacks. Providing good, evidence-informed, and independent advice to support long-term recovery remains a continuing challenge. The public service landscape is changed, but the resilience and results of these changes remains to be tested.

REFERENCES

Barrington, A., Carpenter, B., and MacFeely, S. 2015. 'Setting Out a Vision for the Civil Service in Ireland'. *Administration*, 62 (3): 65–92.

Bideleux, R. 2011. 'Contrasting Responses to the International Economic Crisis of 2008–2010 in the 11 CIS Countries and in the 10 Post-Communist EU Member Countries'. *Journal of Communist Studies and Transition Politics*, 27(3–4): 338–63.

Boyle, R. 1997. 'Civil Service Reform in the Republic of Ireland'. *Public Money & Management*, 17(1): 49–53.

Boyle, R. 2013. 'Fit for Purpose? Progress Report on Public Service Reform', Research Paper No. 9, State of the Public Service Series. Dublin: Institute of Public Administration.

Boyle, R. 2014. 'Public Sector Reform in Ireland: Views and Experiences from Senior Executives', Research Paper No. 13, State of the Public Service Series. Dublin: Institute of Public Administration.

Boyle, R. 2015. 'Public Sector Trends 2015', Research Paper No. 17, State of the Public Service Series. Dublin: Institute of Public Administration.

Boyle, R. 2016. 'Review of National Non-Commercial State Agencies in Ireland: 2011–2015', Research Paper No. 18. Dublin: Institute of Public Administration.

Boyle, R. and MacCarthaigh, M. 2011. *Fit for Purpose? Challenges for Irish Public Administration and Priorities for Public Service Reform*. Dublin: Institute of Public Administration.

Burke, S., Thomas, S., Barry, S., and Keegan, C. 2014. 'Measuring, Mapping and Making Sense of Irish Health System Performance in the Recession', Working Paper from the Resilience Project in the Centre for Health Policy and Management. School of Medicine, Trinity College Dublin.

Christensen, J. 2013. 'Bureaucracies, Neoliberal Ideas, and Tax Reform in New Zealand and Ireland'. *Governance*, 26 (4): 563–84.

Connaughton, B. 2005. 'The Impact of Reform on Politico-Administrative Relations in Ireland: Enlightening or Confusing Roles of Political and Managerial Accountability?' Paper presented at the 13th Annual NISPAcee Conference 'Democratic Governance for the XXI Century: Challenges and Responses in CEE Countries', Moscow, Russia, 19–21 May. Available at: <http://www.unpan.org/Portals/0/UNPAN/Conferences/conf_13nispaceemeeting04.asp> (accessed 10 December 2014).

Delivering Better Government: Second Report to Government of the Co-ordinating Group of Secretaries—A Programme of Change for the Irish Civil Service. 1996. Dublin: Stationery Office.

Department of Public Expenditure and Reform. 2011. *Public Service Reform*. Dublin: Department of Public Expenditure and Reform.

Department of Public Expenditure and Reform. 2014. *Public Service Reform Plan 2014–2016*. Dublin: Department of Public Expenditure and Reform.

Department of the Environment, Community and Local Government. 2012. *Putting People First: Action Programme for Effective Local Government*. Dublin: Department of the Environment, Community and Local Government.

Department of Finance. 2009. *Capacity Review*. Dublin: Department of Finance.

Department of the Taoiseach. 2008. *Transforming Public Services, Report of the Task Force on the Public Service*. Dublin: Stationery Office

Dunleavy, P., Margetts, H., Bastow, S., and Tinkler, J. 2006. 'New Public Management is Dead: Long Live Digital-Era Governance'. *Journal of Public Administration Research and Theory*, 16(3): 467–94.

Gieve, J. and Provost, C. 2012. 'Ideas and Coordination in Policymaking: The Financial Crisis of 2007–2009'. *Governance*, 25(1): 61–77.

Hardiman, N. 2009. 'The Impact of the Crisis on the Irish Political System'. Paper presented at Statistical and Social Inquiry Society of Ireland Symposium on Resolving Ireland's Fiscal Crisis, Dublin, 26 November.

Institute for Government. 2013. *Permanent Secretary Appointments and the Role of Ministers*. London: Institute for Government.

Kickert, W. 2012. 'State Responses to the Fiscal Crisis in Britain, Germany and the Netherlands'. *Public Management Review*, 14(3): 299–309.

Laffan, B. 2010. 'Accountability and Performance: Challenges to Ireland'. Available at: <https://politicalreformireland.files.wordpress.com/2010/07/accountability-and-performance-in-the-irish-public-sector.pdf> (accessed 20 June 2016).

Lodge, M. and Hood, C. 2012. 'Into an Age of Multiple Austerities? Public Management and Public Service Bargains across OECD Countries'. *Governance*, 25(1): 79–101.

LRC (Labour Relations Commission). 2013. *Public Service Stability Agreement 2013–2016*. Dublin: Department of Public Expenditure and Reform.

McCarthy, C. 2011. 'Don't Reform the Seanad, Scrap It', *Sunday Independent*, 9 January.

McKeown, K. 2013. *Reforming Social Services through Public Private Partnership*. Dublin: Genio.

O'Donnell, O. 2006. 'Innovation in the Irish Public Sector', Committee for Public Management Research Discussion Paper No. 37. Dublin: Institute of Public Administration.

OECD (Organisation for Economic Co-operation and Development). 2008. *Ireland: Towards an Integrated Public Service*. Paris: OECD.

OECD (Organisation for Economic Co-operation and Development). 2015. *Building on Basics*. Paris: OECD.

O'Riordan, J. 2008. *A Review of the Civil Service Grading and Pay System*. Committee for Public Management Discussion Paper No. 38. Dublin: Institute of Public Administration.

Peters, B. G. 2011. 'Governance Responses to the Fiscal Crisis: Comparative Perspectives'. *Public Money & Management*, 31(1): 75–80.

Peters, B. G., Pierre, J., and Randma-Liiv, T. 2011. 'Economic Crisis, Public Administration and Governance: Do New Problems Require New Solutions?' *Public Organization Review*, March: 13–28.

Pollitt, C. 2010. 'Cuts and Reforms: Public Services As We Move into a New Era'. *Society and Economy*, 32(1): 17–31.

Pollitt, C. 2014. *Future Trends in European Public Administration and Management: An Outside-In Perspective*. COCOPS Report Work Package 8. Available at: <http://www.cocops.eu/wp-content/uploads/2014/04/

FutureTrendsInEuropeanPublicAdministrationAndManagement.pdf> (accessed 18 December 2014).

Pollitt, C. and Bouckaert, G. 2011. *Public Management Reform: A Comparative Analysis—New Public Management, Governance, and the Neo-Weberian State*. Oxford: Oxford University Press.

Posner, P. and Blöndal, J. 2012. 'Democracies and Deficits: Prospects for Fiscal Responsibility in Democratic Nations'. *Governance*, 25(1): 11–34.

Public Administration Select Committee. 2010. *Outsiders and Insiders: External Appointments to the Senior Civil Service, Seventh Report of Session 2009–10*. London: Stationery Office.

Raudla, R., Savi, R., and Randma-Liiv, T. 2013. *Literature Review on Cutback Management*. COCOPS Work Package 7 Deliverable 1. Available at: <http://www.cocops.eu/wp-content/uploads/2013/03/COCOPS_Deliverable_7_1.pdf> (accessed 9 December 2014).

Reeves, E. 2013. 'Public–Private Partnerships in Ireland: A Review of the Experience 1999–2012'. Paper presented to the Nevin Economic Research Institute, Dublin, 23 January.

Report of the Independent Review Group on the Department of Justice and Equality. 2014. Dublin: Department of Justice.

Report of the Public Service Organisation Review Group. 1969. Dublin: Stationery Office.

Rhodes, M. L. and Boyle, R. 2012. 'Progress and Pitfalls in Public Service Reform and Performance Management in Ireland'. *Administration*, 60(1): 31–59.

Roche, W. 2012. 'Contribution to Panel Session on the Croke Park Agreement: Performance to Date and Future'. Presentation to 'The Future of HR in the Public Sector', Public Affairs Ireland Annual HR Conference, Westin Hotel, Dublin, 27 September.

Serving the Country Better: A White Paper on the Public Service. 1985. Dublin: Stationery Office.

Thynne, I. 2011. 'Symposium Introduction: The Global Financial Crisis, Governance and Institutional Dynamics'. *Public Organization Review*, 11: 1–12.

Van de Walle, S. and Jilke, S. R. 2014. 'Savings in Public Services after the Crisis: A Multilevel Analysis of Public Preferences in the EU27'. *International Review of Administrative Sciences*, 80(3): 597–618.

Wallis, J., Goldfinch, S., and Klein, A. 2012. 'The Challenge of Sustaining Respect in a Central Budget Agency: What can Ireland Learn from New Zealand?' *Public Money & Management*, 32(4): 281–8.

Whelan, N. 2014. 'How the Economic Management Council Undermines Cabinet and Government'. *Irish Times*, 22 December.

Wright, R. 2010. *Strengthening the Capacity of the Department of Finance: Report of the Independent Review Panel*. Dublin: Department of Finance.

13

Unemployment and Labour Market Policy

Philip J. O'Connell

INTRODUCTION

Unemployment has been one of the most serious and persistent manifest-ations of the Great Recession in Ireland. As the recession took hold, unemployment soared, particularly among men laid off from the imploding construction sector. As the recession deepened, long-term unemployment (LTU) mounted, posing particular challenges to policymakers, who were slow to develop appropriate policy responses to the crisis. This chapter begins with a review of the principal developments in the Irish labour market from the end of the boom period through the depth of the Great Recession and the recent years of recovery. It focuses in particular on the growth in unemploy-ment and long-term unemployment. It then discusses the policy response to unemployment and the shift in Irish policy from a passive to a more active approach to unemployment.

PRINCIPAL DEVELOPMENTS IN THE LABOUR MARKET

Table 13.1 shows summary data on some of the principal changes in the labour market between 2007, at the end of the boom, through 2012, in the depths of the crisis, and 2015, during the recovery. Indicators are measured at the end of each year in order to take account of seasonal variations in the labour market. Total employment fell by over 300,000 (14 per cent) between 2007 and 2012, but, with recovery, increased by over 7 per cent in the following three years. The employment rate—the percentage of the adult population aged 15–64 at work—fell from almost 69 per cent in 2007 to less than 60 per cent in 2012, and then increased to 63.9 per cent.

Table 13.1. Principal changes in the labour market, 2007, 2012, and 2015 (Q4)

	2007	2012	2015	% Change 2007–12	2012–15
Employment (000)	2,156.0	1,848.9	1,983.0	−14.2	7.3
Employment Rate (%)	68.8	59.3	63.9	−13.8	7.8
Participation Rate (%)	63.8	59.6	60.0	−6.6	0.7
Unemployment (000)	104.6	294.6	187.5	181.6	−36.4
Unemployment Rate (%)	4.6	13.7	8.7	197.8	−36.5
Long-term Unemployment (LTU) (000)	31.7	176.4	102.1	456.5	−42.1
LTU Rate (%)	1.4	8.2	4.7	485.7	−42.7
Men					
Employment Rate (%)	76.8	63.2	69.0	−17.7	9.2
Unemployment Rate (%)	5.2	16.6	10.4	219.2	−37.3
LTU Rate (%)	1.8	11.1	6.7	514.4	−39.7
Women					
Employment Rate (%)	60.7	55.4	59.0	−8.7	6.5
Unemployment Rate (%)	3.9	10.3	6.6	164.1	−35.9
LTU Rate (%)	0.9	4.7	2.8	432.8	−39.5

Source: CSO 2015.

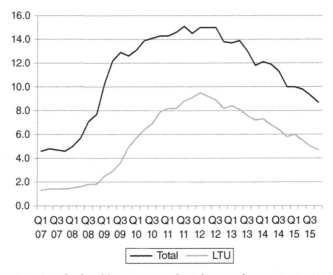

Figure 13.1. Standardized long-term and total unemployment rates, 2007–15
Source: CSO 2015.

The number unemployed increased from just over 100,000 in 2007 to 295,000 in 2012 before falling to 188,000 in 2015. Figure 13.1 shows the unemployment rate rising from 4.6 per cent of the labour force at the beginning of 2007, to 15 per cent during the first three quarters of 2012.

Over the following three years the unemployment rate fell steadily, to 8.7 per cent at the end of 2015. Of particular concern is the LTU rate, referring to those continuously unemployed for twelve months or more. LTU is regarded as particularly problematic as the long-term unemployed find it difficult to get back to work due partly to deterioration in skills, to discouragement and decline in job-searching, and to possible discrimination on the part of employers. The LTU rate increased from 1.4 per cent in 2007 to 9.5 per cent in Q1 2012, at which point LTU accounted for over 63 per cent of total unemployment. LTU fell to 4.7 per cent of the labour force at the end of 2015, still unacceptably high, but the fact that LTU fell more rapidly than total unemployment, and that the share of LTU in total unemployment fell to 54 per cent, is a reassuring element of the recovery.

Given the nature of the crisis, with severe job losses in construction and manufacturing, the brunt of unemployment fell upon men. Male unemployment increased from 5.2 per cent in 2007 to 16.6 per cent in 2012: among women the increase was from 3.9 per cent to 10.3 per cent. In 2012, two in every three unemployed people were men and, among males, LTU accounted for 67 per cent of total unemployment, compared to 45 per cent of women. The employment rate among men fell by 13 percentage points, from 76.8 per cent of the adult population in 2007 to 63.2 per cent in 2012, while the corresponding decline among women was from 60.7 to 55.4 per cent—5 percentage points. Men have benefited more from the employment recovery: between 2012 and 2015, the male employment rate increased by 6 percentage points, and the unemployment rate fell commensurately.

Young people were hit particularly hard by the Great Recession and they have benefited little from recovery. Table 13.2 shows that total employment of those aged 15–24 years fell by almost 180,000 between 2007 and 2012—a seismic contraction of almost 54 per cent. In sharp contrast, the decline in employment among those aged over 25 years was 128,000, or 7 per cent. As a consequence, the youth share of total employment fell from 15.5 per cent in 2007 to just over 8 per cent in 2012. This represents an extraordinary closing off of opportunities and labour market entry points for young people. Young people's employment rate declined from just under 50 per cent of the youth population in 2007 to 28 per cent in 2012.

The impact of the crisis on unemployment among young people was somewhat more muted, mainly because large numbers of young people stayed in, or returned to, education. This can be seen in the labour force participation rate, which dropped by almost 29 per cent among those aged 15–24 years, compared to a less than 7 per cent decline in the population as a whole. Accordingly, the number of those aged 15–24 years unemployed increased by 28,000 (or 90 per cent) while unemployment among those aged over 25 years increased by 162,000 (or 220 per cent). The unemployment rate among young people increased from an already high rate of

Table 13.2. Employment, unemployment, and labour force participation by age group, 2007, 2012, and 2015 (Q4)

	2007	2012	2015	% Change 2007–12	2012–15
Employment (000)					
15–24 Years	333.2	154.4	148.0	−53.7	−4.1
25 Years and Over	1,822.8	1,694.5	1,835.0	−7.0	8.3
All	2,156.0	1,848.9	1,983.0	−14.2	7.3
Youth Share (%)	15.5	8.4	7.5		
Employment Rate (%)					
15–24 Years	49.9	28.2	28.6	−43.5	1.4
All	68.8	59.3	63.9	−13.8	7.8
Unemployment (000)					
15–24 Years	31.1	59.0	34.5	89.7	−41.5
25 Years and Over	73.5	235.6	153.0	220.5	−35.1
All	104.6	294.6	187.5	181.6	−36.4
Youth Share (%)	29.7	20.0	18.4		
Unemployment Rate (%)					
15–24 Years	8.5	27.7	18.8	225.9	−31.8
All	4.6	13.7	8.7	197.8	−36.5
Labour Force Participation (%)					
15–24 Years	54.6	39.0	35.3	−28.6	−9.5
All	63.8	59.6	60.0	−6.6	0.7

Source: CSO 2015.

8.5 per cent of young labour force participants in 2007 to a peak of 33 per cent in Q2 of 2012.

During the recovery, employment among young people continued to fall by another 6,000, or 4 per cent, while employment among those aged over 25 years increased by 140,000, or 8 per cent. Unemployment among young people fell by 24,000 between 2012 and 2015 (−41 per cent) compared to a decline of 83,000 (−35 per cent) among those aged over 25 years. Young people's labour force participation also continued to fall, by another 10 per cent between 2012 and 2015, in contrast to the overall trend, which showed a slight increase in the labour force participation rate.

The impact of the recession has been highly stratified by education. Table 13.3 shows that all of the employment contraction was concentrated at the lower levels of education: employment of those with primary or lower secondary level education fell by over 220,000, a contraction of 46 per cent. Employment among those with upper secondary qualifications fell by another 134,000, a 23 per cent decline. Employment of those with post-Leaving Certificate (PLC) level qualifications increased marginally (5 per cent), and among those with third-level qualifications, by 10 per cent. After 2012,

Table 13.3. Employment and unemployment by education, 2007, 2012, and 2015 (Q4)

				Change	
	2007	2012	2015	2007–12	2012–15
Employment (000)					
Lower Secondary or Less	481.8	259.1	251.2	−46.2	−3.0
Upper Secondary	582.9	449.2	463.1	−22.9	3.1
PLC	221.9	233.4	236.1	5.2	1.2
Third Level	744.6	823.0	907.4	10.5	10.3
All	2109.0	1799.6	1919.3	−14.7	6.7
Unemployment (000)					
Lower Secondary or Less	40.6	86.0	48.2	111.8	−44.0
Upper Secondary	30.6	81.4	56.7	166.0	−30.3
PLC	8.2	54.0	28.1	558.5	−48.0
Third Level	20.7	66.4	47.5	220.8	−28.5
All	104.5	293.9	186.0	181.2	−36.0

Source: CSO 2015.

employment continued to decline among those with lower secondary qualifications, but increased at all other educational levels—most rapidly, by 10 per cent, among those with third-level qualifications.

Unemployment increased sharply across all educational attainment levels between 2007 and 2012. The greatest proportionate increase related to those with PLC qualifications—where unemployment increased by over 550 per cent. These are intermediate vocational qualifications intended to provide construction, industry, and routine services skills, and it is clear that these occupations and sectors contracted sharply in the recession. Figure 13.2 shows unemployment rates expressed as a proportion of the labour force. In 2007, we observe relatively low unemployment in a classic 'step pattern', in which the higher the education level the lower the unemployment. In 2012, unemployment rates soar, to 25 per cent in the case of those with lower secondary education, and while the unemployment rate is 10 percentage points lower in the case of those with upper secondary educations, the step pattern is disturbed by a higher level of unemployment (almost 19 per cent) among those with PLC qualifications. This is a very unusual pattern in which particular forms of additional education carry an unemployment penalty. The unemployment gap between upper secondary and PLC levels emerged in 2008 and persisted throughout the recession.

Unemployment among third-level graduates also increased by over 200 per cent between 2007 and 2012. Nevertheless, the rate of graduate unemployment has been consistently lower than the national average throughout the period under consideration.

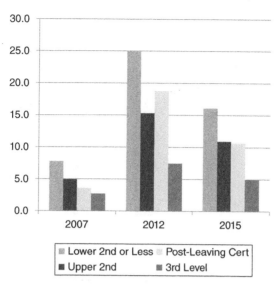

Figure 13.2. Unemployment rates by education, 2007, 2012, 2015 (Q4)
Source: CSO 2015.

It should be noted that these data on employment and unemployment by education tell us nothing about the quality of the jobs taken up by incumbents during the recession. In the context of the dramatic contraction in employment, we can expect that there was an increase in over-education, with many of those at work having taken jobs that required lower levels of qualification than they possessed. It should also be noted that there was substantial emigration during this period and that emigration was disproportionately undertaken by those with higher levels of education, although many emigrants were employed, rather than unemployed, immediately prior to emigration (see Chapter 16, this volume).

There was a significant influx of immigrants, particularly from the new European Union (EU) member states (NMS) after EU enlargement in 2004 to meet the demand for labour in the booming Irish economy. However, immigrants began to lose ground after 2007. While employment among Irish nationals fell by 13 per cent between 2007 and 2012, it fell by 21 per cent among non-Irish nationals (see Table 13.4). Employment among NMS nationals contracted by over 26 per cent between 2007 and 2012, and among UK nationals by 18 per cent.

In the more recent context of economic recovery, with total employment increasing by over 7 per cent between the end of 2012 and 2015, employment among Irish natives increased by 6.5 per cent and among non-Irish by almost 12 per cent. The rate of growth was greatest (36 per cent) among those from outside the EU, reflecting demand for skills in short supply among Europeans. Employment of nationals of the older EU countries (other than UK) continued

Philip J. O'Connell

Table 13.4. Employment and unemployment by nationality, 2007, 2012, and 2015

	2007	2012	2014	% Change	
				2007–12	2012–15
Employed (000)					
Irish	1,814.5	1,579.7	1,682.2	−12.9	6.5
Non-Irish	341.5	269.2	300.9	−21.2	11.8
Of which					
UK	56.8	46.5	53.5	−18.1	15.1
Old EU 13	32.4	29.1	17.5	−10.2	−39.9
New EU 12	171.3	125.9	137.9	−26.5	9.5
Rest of World	81.0	67.7	92.0	−16.4	35.9
Unemployed (000)					
Irish	83.4	241.2	152.8	189.2	−36.7
Non-Irish	21.2	53.4	34.7	151.9	−35.0
Of which					
UK	4.6	11.2	6.5*	143.5	−42.0
Old EU13**					
New EU12	10.3	25.7	14.3	149.5	−44.4
Rest of World	5.1	13.6	13.2	166.7	−2.9

* Estimate with wide margin of error due to small number of cases.
** Estimates too small to be considered reliable.
Source: CSO 2015.

Table 13.5. Unemployment rates by nationality, 2007, 2012, and 2015

	2007 %	2012 %	2015 %
Irish	4.4	13.2	8.3
Non-Irish	5.8	16.6	10.3
Of which			
UK	7.5	19.4	10.8*
Old EU13**			
New EU12	5.7	17.0	9.4
Rest of World	5.9	16.7	12.5
All	4.6	13.7	8.6

* Estimate with wide margin of error due to small number of cases.
** Estimates too small to be considered reliable.
Source: CSO 2015.

to decline, reflecting significant emigration of nationals of the 'old European' countries since the start of the crisis (O'Connell and Joyce 2015).

As shown in Table 13.5, at the end of 2007, the unemployment rate among Irish nationals was 4.4 per cent, compared with 5.8 per cent among non-Irish nationals: a gap of less than 1.5 percentage points. As the recession deepened,

Table 13.6. Employment by sector 2007, 2012, and 2015 (000)

	2007	2012	2015	% Change	
				2007–12	2012–15
Agriculture, Forestry, and Fishing	114.3	90.0	106.4	−21.3	18.2
Total Industry	**551.6**	**340.4**	**375.0**	**-38.3**	**10.2**
Industry	285.4	237.2	248.4	−16.9	4.7
Construction	266.2	103.2	126.6	−61.2	22.7
Total Services	**1,482.9**	**1,415.3**	**1,495.0**	**-4.6**	**5.6**
Wholesale and Retail Trade	316.8	273.4	279.4	−13.7	2.2
Transportation and Storage	98.0	89.0	93.8	−9.2	5.4
Accommodation and Food Service Activities	132.2	118.3	143.1	−10.5	21.0
Information and Communication	70.7	83.2	85.4	17.7	2.6
Financial, Insurance and Real Estate Activities	105.4	102.8	97.8	−2.5	−4.9
Professional, Scientific, and Technical Activities	114.6	102.2	119.3	−10.8	16.7
Administrative and Support Service Activities	81.5	63.2	67.1	−22.5	6.2
Public Administration and Defence; Compulsory Social Security	104.5	96.0	99.1	−8.1	3.2
Education	141.5	145.3	153.5	2.7	5.6
Human Health and Social Work Activities	222.1	245.7	253.7	10.6	3.3
Other NACE Activities	95.5	96.2	102.7	0.7	6.8
Not Stated	7.2	3.2	6.6	−55.6	106.3
Total	**2,156.0**	**1,848.9**	**1,983.00**	**−14.2**	**7.3**

Source: CSO 2015.

the gap in unemployment rates grew wider. Following substantial job losses in late 2008 and early 2009, the unemployment rate among non-Irish nationals was 5 per cent higher than among Irish nationals. Unemployment continued to grow until the end of 2012, although the gap between Irish and non-Irish nationals declined somewhat. Since then unemployment has trended downwards, and the gap in rates has fallen to 2 per cent.

Just before the property bubble burst in 2007, more than one in every five men at work in Ireland were employed in the construction sector. The folly of this disproportionate allocation of human resources to a single sector became apparent as the recession deepened: employment in construction fell by 163,000 between 2007 and 2012, a contraction of over 60 per cent. Manufacturing and wholesale and retail trade also contracted sharply. Employment growth in the recovery has been in accommodation and food services and in professional, scientific and technical services, with some recent growth also in construction.

With the dramatic contraction in economic activity, employment fell sharply and unemployment soared, followed by a surge in LTU. With the recovery, employment has increased and unemployment fallen. Unemployment was particularly high among males, partly due to the collapse of the construction sector. The labour market for young people was devastated by the recession and young people have not benefited from economic recovery. The dramatic increases in unemployment and LTU posed particular challenges to policy-makers, and their policy responses to the crisis are examined in the next section, 'Activation in Labour Market Policy'.

ACTIVATION IN LABOUR MARKET POLICY

In the last two decades, most industrial countries have shifted the balance from passive support of the unemployed, mainly through income mainten-ance, to more active measures to encourage and assist the unemployed to get back into work. Ireland's policy shift in this direction has been late, uncertain, insufficiently resourced, and often poorly thought out. The Organisation for Economic Co-operation and Development (OECD) argues that the core objectives of activation

> are to bring more people into the effective labour force, to counteract the potentially negative effects of unemployment and related benefits on work incentives by enforcing their conditionality on active job search and participation in measures to improve employability, and to manage employment services and other labour market measures so that they effectively promote and assist the return to work. (OECD 2013: 132)

There is considerable variation between countries and, arguably, that diversity can be better appreciated if we distinguish four key dimensions of activation systems: two relating to active labour market policies (ALMPs) themselves, the *nature of intervention* and the *scale of implementation*; and two relating to how activation interacts with the welfare state—the *level of support* and *condition-ality*. There is a great deal of variation in the *nature of interventions*: in terms of their orientation to achieving just any form of employment versus signifi-cantly enhancing skills; engaging in training versus employment subsidies; and in the effectiveness of such measures in improving the job prospects of their participants—a topic that has spawned a large research literature (see Martin and Grubb (2001) and Kelly, McGuinness, and O'Connell (2013) for reviews). The *scale of implementation* has direct implications for whether all those in unemployment can avail themselves of services to assist them to get back to work, and this can be a particular issue during periods of high unemployment. This dimension can also include differential access to services for different groups—for example, long-term unemployed, young people, women, immigrants. National variation in welfare state regimes gives rise to variation in the *level of support* in the form of unemployment welfare payments. Employment supports have long been of concern to economists who worry that the higher the replacement rate—the ratio of out-of-work welfare payments to expected earnings from employment—the lower the incentive to return to work. Finally, activation systems and welfare regimes may vary in terms of *condition-ality*—whether participation in ALMPs is voluntary or a compulsory condition for continued receipt of welfare payments. These welfare dimensions interact, so, for example, it is widely believed that a combination of high-level income support with low conditionality undermines incentives for unemployed people to find work, whereas low supports combined with high conditionality may force people to quickly accept any work available.

In terms of these dimensions, Ireland entered the Great Recession with a very passive approach to activation (Martin 2014), with a wide range of relatively ineffective ALMPs (McGuinness, O'Connell, and Kelly 2014), com-bined with relatively low levels of income support, oriented to keeping the unemployed out of poverty (NESC 2011), and virtually no conditionality over extended periods of unemployment (Grubb, Singh, and Tergeist 2009; McGuinness et al. 2011). In similar vein, NESC (2011) points to the paradox of high expenditure on ALMPs without an activation framework.

THE SHIFT FROM PASSIVE TO ACTIVE LABOUR MARKET POLICY

A 'preventative strategy' was introduced in 1998 under the National Employ-ment Action Plan (NEAP) developed in response to the European Employment Strategy. Under the NEAP, targeted groups—on either social insurance-based Jobseeker's Benefit (JB) or social assistance-based and means-tested Jobseeker's Allowance (JA)—were subject to intervention after a period of thirteen weeks on the Live Register—Ireland's official unemployment benefit claimant record. After this point, jobseekers were referred by the benefit agency, the Department for Social Protection (DSP), to the then national training and employment authority, Foras Áiseanna Saothair (FÁS), for an activation interview. At this time Ireland was one of a small number of OECD countries where the placement function of the Public Employment Service (PES) was separate from the benefit function (Grubb, Singh, and Tergeist 2009). The activation interview was to initiate a process whereby FÁS would assist unemployed individuals to reinte-grate into the labour market, via intensive engagement, guidance, and counsel-ling; establishment of action plans; provision of employment and/or training programmes; work placement; and/or job offers. Attendance at the initial inter-view was the benefit recipient's only *quasi-compulsory* contact with employment services under the NEAP (Grubb, Singh, and Tergeist 2009). Any subsequent activation measures were purely voluntary: refusal to participate beyond the interview stage or to actively seek employment would generally not be met with sanctions. Grubb, Singh, and Tergeist (2009: 85) argued that sanction rates in Ireland 'are either the lowest or close to the lowest in international comparative terms in three areas: sanctions for voluntary job leaving, refusal of work and refusal of an ALMP place'. Grubb, Singh, and Tergeist (2009) also highlighted that employment service staff numbers relative to the labour force fell well short of ratios in other countries, suggesting a capacity deficit in Ireland.

At the onset of the Great Recession, labour market policies in Ireland were clearly not fit for purpose. In their evaluation of the impact NEAP over the period 2006–8, McGuinness and colleagues (2011) found serious problems with the activation components of the programme. They found that only about half of unemployed clients who should have been eligible for assistance under the NEAP received help—about a quarter were not identified and referred for an activation interview, and another quarter were deemed ineligible for assistance because they had been interviewed in the course of a previous spell of unemployment. Both of these policy failures may have been due to capacity constraints on the part of the DSP and/or FÁS. However, the evaluation also discovered that those who received an activation interview were much less likely to become employed than a comparison group of unemployed people who did not participate. McGuinness and colleagues (2011) attributed this negative effect to the absence of systematic support for unemployed clients, leading to discouragement, and to clients learning that they were unlikely to face monitoring or sanctions for not searching actively for employment, leading to a decline in job search intensity.

The initial response to the labour market crisis emerging in 2008 was to expand capacity to provide social welfare payments to the growing numbers of unemployed: the claimant count on the Live Register increased from 170,000 at the end of 2007 to 460,000 in mid-2012. Given the scale of the crisis it was a significant achievement that all claims for income support were processed effectively. However, this response reinforced the emphasis on passive rather than active approaches to unemployment. It was not until the arrival of the European Central Bank (ECB)–EU–International Monetary Fund (IMF) Troika in December 2010 and the election of a new government in spring 2011 that a new policy was initiated to seek greater integration between activation and income maintenance functions.

Pathways to Work

One of the key areas of structural reforms agreed with the Troika in December 2010 was in the area of labour market activation. Under the Memorandum of

Understanding (MoU), Ireland undertook to tackle unemployment, reduce replacement rates, and reform activation measures by increasing monitoring of jobseekers' activities and applying sanctions for non-compliance with work search requirements (Department of Finance 2010). Pathways to Work (PTW), implemented by the DSP during the years 2012–15, represents a major reform in Irish labour market policy. PTW established the new Integrated National Employment and Entitlement Service (Intreo) to integrate employment and income maintenance services for the unemployed. Intreo services are delivered in one-stop-shop centres where newly unemployed clients are initially registered for both activation and income support services. Clients complete a profiling questionnaire that allows their probability of exit (PEX) to employment to be assessed using a nationally calibrated profiling system (see O'Connell, McGuinness, and Kelly 2012). The profiling drives the level and type of service. Clients with high PEX to employment are encouraged and assisted to search for work. Those with medium PEX are invited to group sessions to provide guidance on job search activities as well as training opportunities. Those with low PEX scores are referred for one-to-one support. PTW is organized around five strands:

1. More regular and ongoing engagement with people who are unemployed. This is mainly driven by the Intreo engagement process outlined in the previous paragraph.

2. Greater targeting of activation places and opportunities. This combines some increase in provision of employment, education, and training programme places as well as targeting via the profiling system to ensure that scarce resources are targeted towards those most likely to benefit.

3. Incentivizing the take-up of opportunities. This is to reduce the extent to which tax, welfare, health, and housing policies act as disincentives to employment. The main initiative is to replace housing subsidies that are withdrawn when unemployed people go to work with a Housing Assistance Payment (HAP) with an in-work element. HAP was piloted in 2014. Reductions in rates and duration of payment to young unemployed people in 2013 were also partially justified under this strand.

4. Incentivizing employers to provide more jobs for people who are unemployed. The main incentive is JobsPlus, an incentive for employers to hire long-term unemployed people.

5. Reforming institutions to deliver better services to the unemployed. This includes increasing numerical capacity for activation in the DSP, and substantial reform of institutions in the further education and vocation training sector.

In 2013, PTW was revised to provide for a greater emphasis on long-term unemployed, greater engagement with employers, and initial/pilot activities for young unemployed people under the EU Youth Guarantee programme.[1]

Implementation

The pace of change has been slow. Reforms to integrate the integration and income support functions in Intreo were initiated in 2011, more than three years after the onset of the crisis. Restructuring of services to the unemployed entailed a series of organizational mergers. During 2011, about 1,000 personnel from the Community Welfare Service (CWS) were transferred to the DSP, thus enhancing staff capacity for case management and activation in Intreo. FÁS, the national training and employment authority, was abolished, its functions dispersed, and about 700 staff transferred to DSP. These staff brought competencies in job placement and advice to the new activation regime. Several hundred civil servants were also transferred to DSP from other government departments in order to cope with the increased workload resulting from the unemployment crisis, with the result that total staff in DSP increased from about 4,900 in 2008 to almost 7,000 in 2012. This redeployment of staff and reorganization of work practices can be seen as one of the positive outcomes of the series of agreements between the state as employer and the public service trade unions that facilitated the development of a strategic response to the unemployment crisis.

Implementation of Intreo was sluggish: the establishment of over sixty Intreo one-stop-shops nationwide was not completed until 2015. Intreo, with its more intensive engagement, was rolled out mainly to new entrants to unemployment. By 2012, inflows to unemployment had slowed to a trickle, the labour market crisis had moved on, and the most pressing issue for labour market policy was LTU. However, systematic engagement with the long-term unemployed only began in 2014. Over the course of 2014, DSP engaged in one-to-one meetings with 56,000 long-term unemployed people, equivalent to about one-third of the total long-term unemployed on the Live Register at the beginning of the year.

Far-reaching reforms were also initiated in further education and training. The thirty-three regional vocational education committees, responsible for further education, were combined into sixteen Education and Training Boards (ETBs). In addition to provision of further vocational education (and adult

---

[1] In 2013, the EU adopted a Council Recommendation on a Youth Guarantee to: 'ensure that all young people under the age of 25 years receive a good-quality offer of employment, continued education, an apprenticeship or a traineeship within a period of four months of becoming unemployed or leaving formal education'.

education more generally) the ETBs also took over training of the unemployed following the abolition of FÁS, the discredited organization formerly responsible for training the unemployed, and the establishment of An tSeirbhís Oideachais Leanúnaigh agus Scileanna (SOLAS), an oversight and funding body for further education and training. The pace of change in the further education and training system, under the Department of Education and Skills, mirrors the sluggish rate of change in the DSP: the reforms were announced in 2011 but SOLAS was still developing its strategy in 2015. There is concern about whether SOLAS and the ETBs, with limited experience in the field, will be able to deliver cost-effective training to enhance the job prospects of the unemployed.

The slow rate of reform and limitations on the frequency of engagement with clients is partly due to capacity constraints in the DSP. In 2015, the DSP began implementing JobPath, an innovative programme to increase the capacity of Intreo to deal with the large numbers of long-term unemployed. Under this new programme, the DSP subcontracts re-employment services to private employment agencies under performance-related contracts, with payments made periodically on initial sign-up and after set periods of sustained employment. The programme is targeted mainly at the long-term unemployed. JobPath is innovative not just in Ireland but also internationally: there were significant teething difficulties with similar such programmes in Australia and the UK. JobPath is being introduced by the Irish authorities without a pilot that might identify design flaws and implementation difficulties. It is as yet not clear how JobPath will interact with the PES, and with the further education and training system run by SOLAS and the ETBs, who are also to remain active in supplying training services to the unemployed.

The Nature and Scale of Active Labour Market Programmes

There was a significant increase in engagement with new entrants to unemployment, and latterly, with long-term unemployed, under the Intreo system. However, the quality and frequency of interventions under Intreo are unclear. Many clients simply receive a group interview, others participate in monitoring/review meetings at two- or three-month intervals depending on the PEX estimate of their probability of an unaided exit to employment. Of considerable concern is that the Intreo system continues to lack a systematic and rigorous system of monitoring whereby jobseekers update their case workers on progress at frequent intervals. In other countries with more vigorous activation regimes, monitoring is fortnightly or monthly.

PTW also commits to increased provision of a 'suite of employment, education and training programmes that are relevant to labour market needs, that are attractive to unemployed people and that promote and assist in progression to paid open labour market employment' (Department of Social Protection 2013: 17). There has been little interest in the evaluation of the impact of ALMPs in Irish labour market policymaking over an extended period. Nevertheless, there are some indications of the types of programmes that have proved effective in enhancing the job prospects of their participants, from rigorous evaluations that were conducted in the 1990s (O'Connell 2002) and in the late 2000s (Indecon 2013; McGuinness, O'Connell, and Kelly 2014). While these evaluations may appear dated, innovation in programme development has been sluggish, so many of the programme evaluated in the 1990s and the early part of this century are still offered today.

Figure 13.3 presents the number of participants on ALMPs at end 2014, categorizing them in terms of a typology that distinguishes between programmes on the basis of their linkages to the labour market as well as dividing them into supply-side (e.g. education or training) versus demand-side (e.g. employment subsidies) measures. Previous Irish research found that programmes with strong links to the labour market (e.g. skills training for particular occupations or subsidies to support employment experience in real jobs in the economy) are more likely to enhance the subsequent employment prospects of their participants (McGuinness, O'Connell, and Kelly 2014; O'Connell 2002). Programmes with weak linkages are much less likely to.

There were a total of almost 90,000 participating in ALMPs in December 2014, equivalent about one-quarter of the total number on the Live Register that month. About two-thirds of participants were engaged in the types of programmes that previous research has found to be less effective in improving their job prospects. Thirty-five per cent participated in Direct Employment schemes, mainly in social-economy activities; however, these schemes have been found in the past, in Ireland and in international research, to have little impact on employment chances. Community Employment (CE), with over 23,000 participants, is the single largest ALMP implemented by DSP. It has been known for many years that CE does little to enhance the job prospects of its participants (O'Connell 2002). However, CE is popular with the voluntary sector, as a source of labour, and with politicians—it is regarded as essential to have at least one CE scheme in every political constituency. With regard to general education programmes, Kelly, McGuinness, and Walsh (2015) show that the employment prospects of participants on the Back to Education Allowance scheme are not improved compared to a similar group that did not participate. General education programmes accounted for over 30 per cent of programme participants in 2014.

On the other hand, programmes with strong links to the labour market— the type that have been found to be effective in enhancing employment prospects—accounted for just one-third of total participants at end 2014. There were 8,771 participants in FÁS full-time training for the unemployed. This category includes specific skills training, which has been found to

	Market Linkages			
	Weak		**Strong**	**Total**
Supply	**General Education/Training** • *Back to Education Allowance* • *Vocational Training Opportunities Scheme*	27,714 (31%)	**Skills Training** • *'FÁS Full Time Training for Unemployed'*	8,771 (10%)	36,485 (41%)
Demand	**Direct Employment** • *Community Employment* • *TUS* • *Part-Time Job Incentive*	31,323 (35%)	**Employment Supports** • *Back to Work Allowance Schemes* • *JobBridge* • *JobsPlus*	21,939 (24%)	53,462 (59%)
Total		59,237 (66%)		30,710 (34%)	89,947 (100%)

Figure 13.3. Number of participants in ALMPs, December 2014

Note: Includes an additional 3,902 on JobsPlus scheme not taken account of in the CSO data.
Source: CSO, *Live Register January* 2015.

enhance both employment and earnings, compared to a control group (O'Connell 2002). However, not all full-time training is in specific skills: the data reported by the Central Statistics Office (CSO) include other (less effective) training as well. Moreover, McGuinness, O'Connell, and Kelly (2014) show that, within the category of specific skills training it is training at medium- and higher-level skills that improves job prospects, and that this level of skills training accounts for less than half of all skills training. The number participating in FÁS full-time training for the employed has fallen since 2011: a decline that coincides with the demise of FÁS and the transfer of its activities to SOLAS and the ETBs.

Finally, there are almost 22,000 people receiving employment supports, about one-quarter of total ALMP provision, and these programmes have expanded somewhat over the recession. These types of programmes are expected to enhance employment prospects. They include subsidies to self-employment as well as internships. The self-employment subsidies account for about half of all employment supports (over 11,000 in 2014) and have been in existence for some time. They have not been formally evaluated although international research suggests that such programmes are prone to: (1) displacement (driving other (unsupported) small enterprises out of business); and (2) supporting low value-added enterprises unlikely to provide adequate incomes over the long term without continued subsidies. JobBridge, a six- to nine-month internship programme in which participants retain their jobseekers' payment, plus a €50 per week top-up, has been positively evaluated (Indecon 2013), although the evaluation was unable to compare outcomes for participants with a control group of non-participants. JobBridge has proved controversial, particularly in respect of reported exploitation of interns, lack of any payment by employers for work performed, and lack of opportunities to stay on with employers after the end of the internship (Murphy 2015). However, it would be possible to reform elements of Job-Bridge. JobsPlus, a new programme that pays subsidies to employers who recruit long-term unemployed individuals, which had almost 4,000 participants at the end of 2014, is another example of a type of programme with strong linkages to the labour market.

Support and Conditionality

One of the recommendations of the Troika in 2011, to reduce replacement rates, was based on an assumption that the ratio of out-of-work income to earnings from work was comparatively high in Ireland, particularly over longer durations of unemployment. However, recent work by Savage and colleagues (2014) shows that the proportion of those not in employment facing high replacement rates (70 per cent or more) are very similar in the UK and in Ireland, although the proportion facing very high replacement rates (over 90 per cent) are higher in Ireland. Savage and colleagues also argue that reductions in personal jobseeker payment rates would have quite a limited impact on replacement rates, given that many of those on jobseeker schemes are single and face low replacement rates. The key factors contributing to high replacement rates are rent supplement and payments relating to adult dependents. The base rate of jobseeker's payments was cut by 4 per cent in 2010 (from €196 to €188) and has been maintained at that level ever since. Young people's payment rates were cut in 2009 and in 2013 and rationalized on the grounds that lower payments would incentivize activation. In 2015, the maximum jobseeker's rate for those aged 18–24 was €100 per week. Payment periods for jobseeker's payments were also reduced.

International research suggests that continual monitoring, assistance, encouragement, and sanctions are key to successful reintegration to work. The use of sanctions has increased, but sanctions remain unusual in the case of Ireland and lower than in other countries such as Australia and the UK (OECD 2013). An average of less than 450 sanctions was initiated per month during 2014,[2] representing about 1 in 800 of those on the Live Register at the end of that year. Part of the lack of monitoring relates to the shortage of numerical capacity to perform intensive case management for the large numbers on the Live Register. There are also concerns about the skill levels of DSP officials, whose previous experience has been mainly in benefit administration, or who have been drafted in from other government departments to cope with the surge in demand for services.

Summing up the reforms, it is clear that there is both continuity and change. Over the course of the Great Recession, Irish labour market policy has developed a system that entails a greater emphasis on activation, albeit at insufficient scale, with a range of programmes whose effectiveness remains questionable, where income supports have been cut back, particularly for young people, and conditionality has been increased.

CONCLUSION

The Great Recession, entailing dramatic contractions in economic activity and employment, led to a very sharp increase in unemployment. LTU increased steadily—a particularly worrying development as the long-term unemployed find it very difficult to get back to work. Young people were hit very hard by the recession and they have not benefited from the recovery. Long-term and youth unemployment both pose particularly difficult challenges for policy.

The unemployment crisis was followed, several years later, by significant changes in labour market policy. In 2012 Ireland followed most of its neighbours, albeit belatedly, in integrating income support and employment services. Initially, that reform was targeted on new entrants to unemployment, and it was only in 2014 that attention was turned to the long-term unemployed, who at that stage accounted for about 60 per cent of total unemployment. The shift to a more active approach in PTW does represent a series of steps in the right direction, and Intreo seems set to deliver a great deal more activation than the previous approach under the NEAP. Nevertheless, there are concerns that the

---

[2] *Irish Times*, 3 August 2015.

Intreo system continues to lack a systematic and rigorous system of monitoring of job search—in this respect Intreo appears to fall short of best international practice. Part of the problem may be due to staff capacity constraints. The launch of JobPath in 2015, which outsources employment services for the long-term unemployed to private sector firms and bodies, can be seen as a response to these capacity constraints.

There are also concerns about the effectiveness of many ALMPS—education, training, and employment schemes—in getting their participants back to work. Our review suggests that only about one-third of activity and expenditure on ALMPs relates to the kinds of programmes that are likely to be effective.

The Intreo service model is based on a social contract of rights and responsibilities (the 'Record of Mutual Responsibilities'), which stipulates that DSP is committed to providing comprehensive income support and employment services to its clients, who in turn must commit to a range of obligations to actively seek work and to take up any work placement, work experience, and/or training place notified by the Department. Clients sign the contract, accepting that failure to adhere to its terms may result in the reduction or withdrawal of income support payments. Arguably, it is incumbent on the state, as a party to that contract, to ensure that any education, training, or work experience programmes that it recommends or requires its clients to undertake should be of a type and quality that have a reasonable prospect of enhancing their likelihood of achieving suitable employment. The evidence reviewed here suggests that the state does not yet appear to be in a position to uphold its side of the contact.

Unemployment fell from 15 per cent in 2012 to 8.7 per cent at the end of 2015. This is a significant and very welcome fall. It is difficult to assess how much ALMPs contributed to that fall, although it is likely that the main driver has been on the demand side of the economy. ALMPs have more influence on the composition than the scale of unemployment, particularly the share of LTU in the total. LTU increased steadily as the crisis deepened, but the fact that it has fallen more rapidly than short-term unemployment in the more recent years of recovery would suggest that the activation strategy is having an impact. As unemployment falls, achieving further reductions in unemployment, and particularly LTU, are likely to pose greater challenges and require greater efforts due to the composition of those remaining in unemployment.

REFERENCES

CSO (Central Statistics Office). 2015. 'Quarterly National Household Survey, Quarter 4, 2014'.

Department of Finance. 2010. *EU/IMF 2010 Programme of Financial Support for Ireland: Programme Documents*. Dublin: Department of Finance.

Department of Social Protection. 2013. 'Pathways to Work 2013'. Dublin: Department of Social Protection.

Grubb, D., Singh, S., and Tergeist, P. 2009. 'Activation Policies in Ireland', OECD Social, Employment and Migration Working Papers No. 75. Paris: OECD.

Indecon. 2013. *Indecon's Evaluation of JobBridge: Final Evaluation Report*. Dublin: Indecon International Economic Consultants.

Kelly, E., McGuinness, S., and O'Connell, P. 2013. 'Do Active Labour Market Policies Activate?' In *Using Evidence to Inform Policy*, ed. P. Lunn and F. Ruane. Dublin: Gill & Macmillan.

Kelly, E., McGuinness, S., and Walsh, J. 2015. 'An Evaluation of the Back to Education Allowance'. ESRI Presearch Series No. 47. Dublin: ESRI.

McGuinness, S., O'Connell, P., and Kelly, E. 2014. 'The Impact of Training Programme Type and Duration on the Employment Chances of the Unemployed in Ireland'. *Economic and Social Review*, 45(3): 425–50.

McGuinness, S., O'Connell, P., Kelly, E., and Walsh, J. 2011. 'Activation in Ireland: An Evaluation of the National Employment Action Plan', ESRI Research Series 20. Dublin: ESRI.

Martin, J. 2014. 'Activation and Active Labour Market Policies in OECD Countries: Stylized Facts and Evidence on their Effectiveness', UCD Geary Working Paper 2014/09. Dublin: University College Dublin.

Martin, J. and Grubb, D. 2001. 'What Works and for Whom: A Review of OECD Countries' Experiences with Active Labour Market Policies'. *Swedish Economic Policy Review*, 8(2): 9–56.

Murphy, M. 2015. *JobBridge: Time to Start Again?* Dublin: Impact.

NESC. 2011. 'Supports and Services for Unemployed Jobseekers: Challenges and Opportunities in a Time of Recession'. Report No. 123. Dublin: Government Publications.

O'Connell, P. 2002. 'Are They Working? Market Orientation and the Effectiveness of Active Labour Market Programmes in Ireland'. *European Sociological Review*, 18(1): 65–83.

O'Connell, P. and Joyce, C. 2014. 'International Migration in Ireland'. UCD Geary Institute for Public Policy Working Paper Series WP 2015/07.

O'Connell, P., McGuinness, S., and Kelly, E. 2012. 'The Transition from Short- to Long-Term Unemployment: A Statistical Profiling Model for Ireland'. *Economic and Social Review*, 43(1): 135–64.

OECD (Organisation for Economic Co-operation and Development). 2013. *OECD Economic Surveys: Ireland*. Paris: OECD.

Savage, M., Callan, T., Keane, C., Kelly, E., and Walsh, K. 2014. 'Welfare Targeting and Work Incentives', In *Budget Perspectives 2015*, Paper 3. Dublin: ESRI.

14

Inequality

Kathleen Lynch, Sara Cantillon, and Margaret Crean

INTRODUCTION

The aim of this chapter is to analyse the impact of austerity policies on levels of economic inequality in the Republic of Ireland. Although the focus of the chapter is on economic, social-class-related inequality, the effects of austerity were not only economic; they were embodied, lived out in physical and mental distress: the 'ordinary suffering, la petite misère' (Bourdieu 1999: 4) of those who were impoverished and dispossessed (Bissett 2015). Inequalities found expression in anxieties and fears about unemployment, emigration, poverty, and debt, all of which adversely impacted emotional and mental health (Mental Health Commission 2011; Corcoran et al. 2015).[1] The harms of austerity have been visible on the streets through increased homelessness and begging, in the distressed calls to national radio stations and helplines, in letters, comments, and articles in newspapers and social media, and in Dáil questions and expositions.

This chapter outlines the inequality impact of the socializing of private debt arising from both the collapse of the Irish banking sector and the concurrent fiscal crisis emanating from the narrowing of the tax base and an over-reliance on transient taxes from the construction sector (Keane 2015).

The chapter begins with a brief overview of the concept of equality, introduces an intersectional approach to inequality (Yuval-Davis 2006),[2] and

---

[1] Male suicide rates were 57 per cent higher by the end of 2012 than if the pre-recession trend had continued. While female suicide rates were almost unchanged, there was a 22 per cent increase in female self-harm and a 31 per cent increase in male self-harm between 2008 and 2012. Data is based on those presenting in hospitals (Corcoran et al. 2015).

[2] Intersectionality is a sociological term denoting the fact that, while each social division has a different ontological basis irreducible to other social divisions, because human beings are indivisible, all social divisions are interconnected (Anthias 2013). Experiencing inequality in one social position, for example, as a working-class person, is interwoven with other social divisions, including gender, ethnicity, age, immigrant, care, or disability status. Moreover, as institutions and social systems are also intersecting socio-political realities, the injustice experienced in one social system, for example in the field of economic relations, impacts on all other system relations simultaneously, including the political, the cultural, and the affective.

highlights how the political, cultural, and the affective (care) domains of Irish social life interact with economic injustices, to exacerbate or mitigate their impact (Baker, Lynch, Cantillon, and Walsh 2004). It gives an overview of the key economic inequality trends over the period 2008 to 2015, analysing changes in income inequality, consistent poverty, and deprivation. It examines the distributional impact of budgetary policies in a range of areas and highlights the regressive impact of increases in indirect taxation. It investigates the impact of austerity policies, not only at an aggregate level but also in terms of household characteristics, and in terms of the experience of particular vulnerable groups over the period of austerity. The final part of the chapter examines some of the ideological roots of Ireland's adherence to austerity policies: it explores the impact of anti-intellectualism, consensualism, neoliberalism, and the ideology of charity in framing and legitimating Ireland's response to the crisis.

INEQUALITY AND AUSTERITY

Inequality is not singular in its form or origin; it is a set of relationships, and there are at least four major social systems that can generate injustices relationally: the economic, the political, the cultural, and the affective.[3] All of these operate intersectionally to exacerbate or mitigate the impact of injustice (Baker et al. 2004; Lynch, Baker, and Lyons 2009). Within the economic system, addressing inequality is concerned with re/distributing wealth/income/resources justly between social groups, especially between classes. The resolution of injustice is through equalizing the distribution and redistribution of income, wealth, and resources. Within the cultural systems, addressing inequality is about ensuring there is respect and recognition of differences, including differences in belief, gender, language, ability, sexuality, colour, age, marital/family status, and ethnicity (including Travellers' ethnicity). The resolution of injustice is through ensuring respect in cultural relations in media, legislation, education, the arts, symbols, and emblems. Within political systems, addressing inequality is concerned with parity of representation in the exercise of power in formal politics, work organizations, schools, households, crèches, families, and all types of non-governmental and voluntary organizations. The resolution of power-related injustices is through ensuring parity of representation in power relations, having a 'politics of presence' (Phillips 1995: 5) so that those who are affected by key decisions are at the decision-making table. Within the affective system, addressing

---

[3] In/equality is about relationships, between two or more people or groups of people, regarding some important aspect of their lives. For a full discussion on the meaning of equality and how systems-based inequalities intersect see Baker et al. (2004: 21–46 and 57–72).

inequality is about ensuring that people have equal access to love, care, and solidarity, and that there is an equal sharing of the burdens and benefits of love, care, and solidarity work between genders and other social groups. The resolution of affective injustices is through relational justice.

What is significant about the interface between systems of inequality is that while inequality may be primarily generated in one system for a particular group, the impact of this inequality is not confined to that system; it has secondary effects across other systems. Economic inequalities do not just have an economic impact; they impact on power relations, and cultural and care relations: those who are working class are less respected and frequently powerless to influence decisions that affect them adversely (Kirby and Murphy 2011). They suffer disrespect for their lifestyle, housing, and tastes, and are often seriously under-resourced and disrespected in their care and love work (Dodson 2013).

Having a more nuanced, intersectional understanding of how inequality operates relationally, within and between social systems, is critical to developing a holistic understanding of the impact of austerity policies. It captures how austerity adversely impacted on the most vulnerable, generating and reinforcing multidimensional experiences of injustice for those most powerless in Irish society.

THE ECONOMIC IMPACT OF AUSTERITY

The extraordinary boom period of the Irish economy from the late 1990s to 2008 was followed by a period of intense recession. Mean annual equivalized disposable income per individual fell to €20,681 in 2013, and deprivation rates across all households more than doubled from 13.7 per cent in 2008 to over 30 per cent in 2013. These economic and labour market changes have had a stark impact on the standard of living across the Irish population (Keane et al. 2015).

While the focus of this chapter is on the impact of austerity over a short time frame, the level of economic inequality in Ireland must be understood in historical context. Since the 1970s, the top 10 per cent (those with incomes over €200,000 involving 18,741 tax cases) have had a rising share of gross income, while the share of the remaining 90 per cent has fallen (O'Connor and Staunton 2015: 30–1). Measures of market incomes—that is, incomes accrued before the impact of taxation or social transfers are calculated—show that Ireland is one of the most class-divided, unequal countries in gross income terms across the Organisation for Economic Co-operation and Development (OECD). Ireland relies heavily on social transfers to reduce inequality. Consequently, cuts to welfare provisions, increases in indirect taxes that are universal in character, and reduced spending on public services have a greater impact on inequality in Ireland than in comparator countries where market income inequalities are not so substantial in the first instance.

INCOME INEQUALITY

Measured in terms of the Gini coefficient, the aggregate level of income inequality did not alter significantly over the period of boom, bust, and austerity.[4] In Ireland it was estimated at 0.317 in 2007, widely regarded as the height of the boom, and at 0.312 in 2012. There has been an increase, or a return, in the Gini coefficient to its 'usual' 0.31 to 0.32 range since then (Callan et al. 2013). What Gini figures conceal, however, is the distributive impact of austerity across social groups.[5]

As Table 14.1 shows, there were some significant shifts in the share of income going to different classes/groups over the period of austerity. In 2008, the poorest 10 per cent (decile) had 3.5 per cent of equivalized income and this was reduced to 3.2 per cent in 2013; in contrast, the share of the top 10 per cent had increased from 24.4 to 24.5 per cent. The fall in average income of the bottom decile at 18.4 per cent was the largest fall across the income

Table 14.1. Changes in share of equivalized income by decile, Ireland 2008–13

Deciles*	2008 %	2009 %	2010 %	2011 %	2012 %	2013 %
1	3.5	3.6	3.2	3.0	3.0	3.2
2	5.1	5.2	5.0	5.0	4.9	5.0
3	5.9	6.1	5.9	6.0	6.0	6.0
4	6.8	7.0	6.8	6.9	6.9	6.8
5	7.9	8.1	7.8	7.9	7.9	7.7
6	9.1	9.3	9.1	9.2	9.1	9.0
7	10.4	10.6	10.3	10.5	10.5	10.4
8	12.2	12.3	12.0	12.4	12.4	12.3
9	14.7	14.8	15.2	15.2	15.2	15.2
10	24.4	23.2	24.7	24.0	24.0	24.5

* Decile 1 represents the poorest 10 per cent and decile 10 represents the wealthiest 10 per cent.
Source: Central Statistics Office (CSO), SILC 2013: Statistical Release 2015 Table B: <http://www.cso.ie/en/releasesandpublications/er/silc/surveyonincomeandlivingconditions2013/>.

[4] The Gini coefficient is a summary measure of income distribution and the most commonly used measure of inequality. The Gini coefficient is a number between 0 and 1, where 0 equals perfect equality in income and 1 equals perfect inequality.
[5] The Gini coefficient does not show the relationships between those on high, low, and middle incomes. The same 'level of inequality', as measured by the Gini coefficient, can be found in countries with quite different relationships between high, low, and middle income earners (O'Connor and Staunton 2015: 34).

distribution and implies a much sharper fall in the income of the bottom decile than the fall in average income. Thus, while aggregate income inequality has not altered significantly, there has been a transfer of income to the better off from those who are poorest.

BUDGETS 2009–15

An analysis of the cumulative distributional impact of tax, welfare, and public service pay policies through budgets 2009–15 shows substantial income losses at all levels (Keane et al. 2015).[6] As Figure 14.1 shows, over much of the income range there were percentage losses in a fairly narrow range of between 10 and 11 per cent. The greatest income losses were for the highest

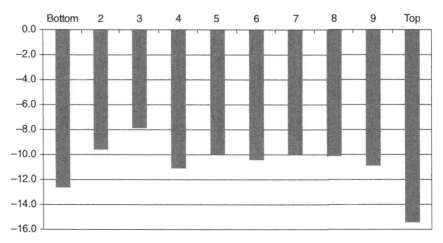

Figure 14.1. The impact of Ireland's budgetary policy 2009–15 on equivalized income deciles

Source: Keane, C., Callan, T., Savage, M., Walsh, J. R., and Colgan, B. 2015. 'Distributional Impact of Tax, Welfare and Public Service Pay Policies: Budget 2015 and Budgets 2009–2015', *Quarterly Economic Commentary*, Winter 2014: 45–56. Dublin: Economic and Social Research Institute.

---

[6] This analysis includes a wide range of measures taken over the seven years, including the main changes to income tax: cuts to income tax credits and the width of the standard rate band; the introduction of Universal Social Charge and subsequent revisions; the elimination of the pay-related social insurance (PRSI) ceiling; the net changes in welfare payment rates over the period, with pension payment rates retaining the increase awarded in October 2008, and working-age payments ultimately reduced below their 2008 levels; net reductions in Child Benefit payment rates, with cuts in earlier years only partly offset by an increase in 2015; reductions in Jobseeker's Allowance (JA) for the young unemployed; the impact of the public sector pension levy pension-related deduction (PRD); explicit cuts in public service pay in 2010 and in 2013; reductions in public service pensions; the introduction of the local property tax (LPT); abolition of the Christmas bonus in 2009, and its partial restoration in 2015; and cutbacks in certain elements of the Household Benefits Package.

income group (about 15.5 per cent) and the lowest income group (close to 13 per cent).

Comprehensive as this cumulative distributional analysis is, it is confined to measuring the impact of specific policy changes, that is, tax, welfare, and public service pay; it does not include the direct effect of the recession in terms of levels of unemployment, the distribution of forms of employment, falling self-employment, and lower wages, all of which resulted in higher-than-average losses for the bottom decile (Callan et al. 2013). Also, what must be added to the mix, albeit more difficult to estimate (Keane et al. 2015), are the distributional consequences of cuts in services, rising rents, the property collapse, and exposure to debt.

Consistent Poverty and Deprivation

To assess the impact of austerity on the most vulnerable, we focus on consistent poverty and deprivations indicators, as these are the most sensitive measures. As Table 14.2 shows, the proportion of the population experiencing basic deprivation more than doubled during austerity: it increased from 13.7 in 2008 to 30.5 per cent in 2013. And there was an increase in the level of consistent poverty from 4.2 per cent to 8.2 per cent. The most severe deprivation was experienced by lone parents: their 63 per cent deprivation rate is nearly double that of 2008. Deprivation also increased among the unemployed (55 per cent, up from 37 per cent) and people not at work through illness or disability (53 per cent, up from 36 per cent).

Table 14.2. Real incomes, poverty, and deprivation rates, Ireland 2008–13

	2008	2009	2010	2011	2012	2013
Real Income—Equivalized Disposable Income per Individual Deflator Base Year 2012						
	€	€	€	€	€	€
Mean	24,290	23,326	22,950	21,920	20,856	20,893
At Risk of Poverty Threshold 60% of Median Income	12,409	12,064	11,564	11,133	10,621	10,425
Poverty and Deprivation Rates	%	%	%	%	%	%
At Risk of Poverty Rate	14.4	14.1	14.7	16.0	16.5	15.2
Deprivation Rate: Two or More Types	13.7	17.1	22.6	24.5	26.9	30.5
Consistent Poverty Rate	4.2	5.5	6.3	6.9	7.7	8.2

Source: CSO SILC 2013: Statistical Bulletin 2015 Table A: <http://www.cso.ie/en/releasesandpublications/er/silc/surveyonincomeandlivingconditions2013/>.

Households and One-Parent Families

Consistent poverty rates also rose for all households across different age groups over the period of austerity (Figure 14.2). There was a very notable (4.8 times) increase in consistent poverty among adults over 65 years living alone, from 0.6 to 2.9 per cent between 2009 and 2013. Although the relative impact of austerity on households with children under the age of 18 years is not as great as that on older people (over 65 years) living alone, the absolute rate of consistent poverty for 'other households with children under 18 years'[7] and 'one parent and children under 18 years' was high pre-austerity and very high post-austerity: it rose to 15 per cent for the former and 23 per cent for the latter. One-parent families with dependent children have had, and continue to have, post-austerity, the highest consistent poverty rate of all households. Given that 87 per cent of lone-parent households are led by women (CSO

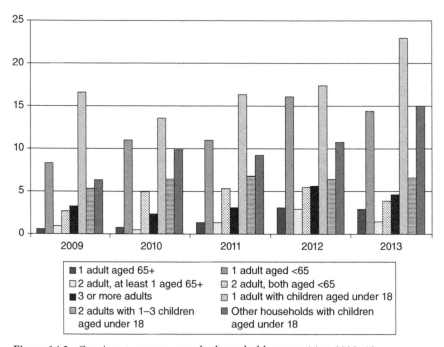

Figure 14.2. Consistent poverty rates by household composition 2009–13

Source: CSO Statbank, SILC data, <http://www.cso.ie/px/pxeirestat/Statire/SelectVarVal/Define.asp?main table=SIA16&PLanguage=0>.

---

[7] This includes households with two adults and four or more children, or those with three or more adults and four or more children.

2011), consistently high rates of poverty in this group is both a strongly gendered and classed issue.

Taxation and Inequality

While taxes on wages and salaries in Ireland are generally progressive, indirect taxation is highly regressive in class terms (Barrett and Wall 2006; Leahy, Lyons, and Tol 2011). As is shown in Figure 14.3 the poorest 10 per cent in Irish society were heavily penalized through indirect taxes throughout austerity, and this continued post-austerity (Collins 2014). While the poorest 10 per cent pay a very low amount of direct taxation due to very low absolute incomes, they pay almost 30 per cent of their income in indirect taxation compared with 5.7 per cent paid by the wealthiest households. Moreover, they pay 30.64 per cent of their overall income on taxation compared with the 29.69 per cent paid by the wealthiest 10 per cent (Collins 2014: 19). The average for the remaining deciles is 20 per cent. The introduction of a higher rate of value added tax (VAT) (increased from 21 to 23 per cent) in the budget of 2012 was particularly regressive, especially when combined with the

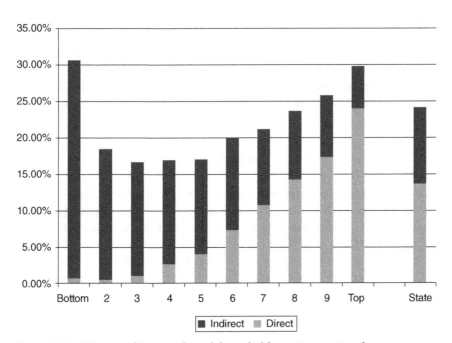

Figure 14.3. Direct, indirect, and total household taxation as % of gross income equivalized data

Source: Collins, 2014: 19 (based on Table 8).

introduction of other direct charges, such as prescription and water charges, and property taxes.

AUSTERITY IN A CARE-LESS STATE

The governments in power during the austerity era in Ireland allowed and enabled social-class-related economic inequalities to persist in some cases, and to rise in others, through the imposition of indirect taxes and charges that did not discriminate between rich and poor. While there were economic costs for all classes and groups, those who were already impoverished prior to the crisis became more impoverished during it. Ireland was and remained a care-less state in the sense that the government disregarded the needs of some of its most vulnerable and powerless citizens during the austerity period, especially if they were unable to be or not sufficiently resourced, and/or not politically powerful enough to exercise political influence.

Austerity heralded an increase in marginalization for many, including people relying on disability support services,[8] children, carers, and the physically and mentally ill, especially if they were reliant on public services (Burke 2014; European Foundation Centre 2012; Mental Health Commission 2011; NESC 2013; Oxfam 2013). Because it is not feasible to analyse the impact of all those adversely affected, the forthcoming discussion will highlight the injustices experienced by children, certain immigrant groups, Travellers, and youth. Being among the most vulnerable, their experiences during austerity exemplify the care-less attitude of the government to powerless citizens during the crisis.

Children

While consistent poverty among adults (18–64 years) almost doubled, rising to 8.2 per cent in 2013, as shown in Figure 14.4, consistent poverty among children (0–17 years) also almost doubled, but from a higher base, from 6.2 per cent in 2008 to 11.7 per cent in 2013. Thus, the proportion of children in consistent poverty remained 50 per cent higher than that of adults after six years of austerity. Not surprisingly, the rise in poverty was exemplified in enforced deprivation more than doubling: 37.3 per cent of children experienced enforced deprivation of basic items such as good clothing, heat, and nourishing food in 2013, compared with 17.9 per cent in 2008.

---

[8] Between 2008 and 2010, the proportion of people with disabilities at risk of poverty rose by 26.16 per cent in Ireland (European Foundation Centre 2012: 5).

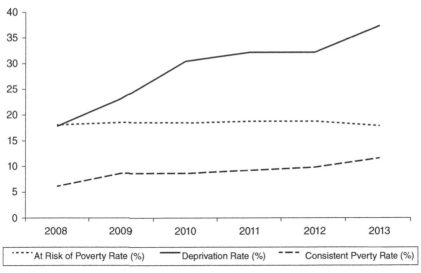

Figure 14.4. Children and poverty, 2008 to 2013
Source: CSO 2015.

Immigrants and Travellers

Much of the infrastructure for monitoring and addressing racism in Ireland has been removed since the crisis (Baker et al. 2015). The absence of this was noted by the European Commission against Racism and Intolerance (ECRI) (2013). It has listed a number of serious failings on the part of Ireland in relation to addressing issues of racism, including Traveller and Roma-related racism.

Because of the absence of appropriate monitoring mechanisms, measuring racial and ethnic-related inequalities both pre- and post-austerity, is difficult. What we do know, however, is that Black Africans and European Union (EU) nationals of minority ethnicity were particularly likely to experience discrimination prior to the crisis, and that this pattern continued post-crisis (Kingston, McGinnity, and O'Connell 2013; McGinnity et al. 2013, 2014). Racial stratification is a persistent feature of the Irish labour market (Joseph 2015).

Although Travellers are recognized as an extremely marginalized ethnic minority in Ireland, cuts in funding for services and supports for Travellers exceeded that enforced on most other groups by several multiples during austerity (Harvey 2013). While the overall reduction in government current spending between 2008 and 2013 was 4.3 per cent, the same period saw an incomparably large disinvestment in the education, welfare, and health of Travellers. Traveller education experienced an 86.6 per cent reduction in expenditure from 2008 to 2013; spending on Traveller accommodation was reduced by 85 per cent, and there was a 29.8 per cent cut in funding for

Traveller youth projects. Given that Travellers are heavily reliant on state supports in health, education, housing, and welfare, the cuts to their services were especially pernicious.

Youth

The Eurostat Dashboard of EU Youth Indicators shows that Ireland had a persistently high percentage of 15 to 24-year-olds (19 per cent from 2009–12), not in education, employment, or training. Yet funding for youth work services was cut by almost 30 per cent over the austerity period, from €73.1 million to €51.4 million.[9] Cuts to unemployment assistance payments were also disproportionately targeted at people under 25 years of age. And there has been a substantial rise in student poverty: 22.7 per cent of students were at risk of poverty in 2010 compared with 33.7% in 2014.[10]

Emigration has also affected young people disproportionately: 49.3 per cent of those who emigrated in 2011 were 24 years of age or younger, while 46.7 per cent were in this age group in 2012 (CSO 2012). And Ireland had higher levels of emigration per capita than other Western European countries affected by the Eurozone crisis. In rural areas alone, 25 per cent of families have experienced the emigration of at least one member since 2008 (Glynn, Kelly, and MacÉinrí 2013). The social and emotional costs of involuntary emigration for individuals, families, communities, and the wider society are not fully captured by economic analysis of loss or gain.

IDEOLOGICAL ROOTS OF INEQUALITY

Austerity, as both ideology and practice, was promulgated throughout Europe in response to the financial crisis, and was not unique to Ireland (Coulter and Nagle 2015). It was a way of rationalizing the impoverishment and suffering of large groups of people on the grounds that prosperity would come at some unspecified time in the future to unspecified persons. In many ways, austerity was a ruse, a charade that secured the privileges of the wealthy and powerful while purporting to offer economic security to the poorest at some indefinable future time in return for suffering in the present (Clarke and Newman 2012).

---

[9] Public Expenditure Report 2013, Department of Public Expenditure and Reform, December 2012.

[10] European Anti-Poverty Network Ireland, <http://www.eapn.ie/eapn/training/poverty-in-ireland>.

However, there are uniquely Irish factors that contributed to the deeply inegalitarian austerity policies implemented in Ireland, arising in particular from both historical and contemporary framing of equality issues. Thus, this final section of the chapter examines some of the ideological roots of inequality in distal and proximate terms. It explores the ways in which anti-intellectualism, consensualism, charitable ideology, and the rise of neo-liberalism contributed to legitimating inequality in the public mind.

Anti-Intellectualism and Consensualism

The closing down of dissent is a powerful mode of censorship and anti-intellectualism in public life. As Ireland's fledging state infrastructure for monitoring and highlighting inequalities was removed in considerable part during the crisis (Baker et al. 2015), the impact of austerity on many vulnerable groups is difficult to measure.

What we know, however, is that equality was only ever promoted in its weakest form, in terms of a liberal equality of opportunity framework, and even then only when Ireland was required to uphold it by EU law, and/or when it did not challenge the deep-rooted economic inequalities (Baker et al. 2015). Ireland's resistance to equality and social justice as principles of public policy has long-standing foundations in religious conservatism and anti-intellectualism in the socio-political sphere. The post-colonial elite who laid the foundations of the state were known for their deep-seated conservatism, being defined as 'the most conservative revolutionaries who ever lived' (Fanning 1983: 52). In post-independent Ireland, communist, socialist, and even social democratic politics were demonized as dangerous by leaders of church and state, especially in the 1930s (Allen 1997; Lee 1989: 184). A deep-seated anti-intellectualism, founded in religious conservatism, actively promoted social and political consensualism (Inglis 1998). Feminism was an inadmissible intellectual and political subject, so invisible it did not even merit demonization for most of the twentieth century (Connolly 2002). Its lack of impact was reflected in how women's status was defined by motherhood in the Constitution, confining many women to a life of economic subservience and child-bearing in male-dominated households (O'Connor 2000). Policies for people with disabilities were largely those of tolerance and segregation, laced with charity (McDonnell 2007), while those who were lesbian or gay had to fight for their basic rights via the courts (Gilligan and Zappone 2008; Rose 1994), and children's rights were poorly protected both in law and in practice (Garrett 2012).

The absence of a strong critical left and feminist analysis of public policy over an extended period of history was not unrelated to the fact that the post-colonial elite in economic, political, and cultural life actively subdued dissent politically and intellectually (Garvin 2004: 3). Moreover, a deep-seated consensualism dominated intellectual life (Lynch 1987) that had roots in Catholic corporatist values. Within this frame, it was assumed that society comprised an organic whole, sharing common goals, no matter how divided it was in social class, gender, and racial or ethnic terms. Given the centrality of Catholic social teaching in the organization of Irish social and cultural life (Inglis 1998), it was not surprising that consensus-led corporatist thinking found institutional expression in the social partnership system devised in response to the financial crisis of the 1980s. Whether one agreed or not with social partnership, consensualism had serious consequences for trade unions and community groups (Allen 2010; Meade 2005): it created a social myth that those who benefited from economic and social inequalities would concede their benefits through simple negotiation, something that did not happen (Allen 2007; Doherty 2011; Kirby 2002).

And in the later 1980s, there were also new political voices arguing for the legitimation of economic inequality, particularly the neoliberal Progressive Democrats Party (PDs). Given that neither of the two major parties of the state, Fianna Fáil and Fine Gael, were ideologically very distant from the PDs, and that they had actively implemented policies that promoted economic inequality, on occasion with the compliance of the Labour Party as a minority coalition partner (Allen 1997; Kirby and Murphy 2011), a new neoliberal consensus built on 'consumer capitalism' rather than 'Catholic capitalism' grew (Inglis 2008: 13–22). It gave rise to a form of 'neoliberal corporatism' that was deeply class-based and inegalitarian (Dukelow and Considine 2014a: 418). Although there was a brief interlude in the 1990s when the election of Mary Robinson as President heralded a shift in public policy towards openness and dissent, a new intellectualism, and a move towards equality, such a movement did not survive her departure from office (Kirby, Gibbons, and Cronin 2002).

Neoliberalism

Because consensualism became a virtue and dissent a vice, this created a political and intellectual void that was readily filled by a virulent, globally powered neoliberalism in the 1990s and 2000s (Lynch, Grummell, and Devine 2012; Phelan 2007). Neoliberalism bore fruit for the very wealthy, including corporate wealth: it institutionalized the ideology and practice of low taxation as Ireland's selling point for global capital investment. Relatedly, low wealth and income-related taxation reduced the tax base, providing a strong rationale for downsizing public services and reducing dependency on state welfare services and supports, even when necessary.

The most strategic organizational example of institutionalized neoliberalism was the Public Service Management Act (1997), designed to 'modernize' the entire public service. The new legislation, and its related accountability systems, instituted a market-led technicist approach to operating public services that was strongly driven by business rhetoric and logic. People became customers in a market, rather than citizens with rights (Collins 2007: 31).

Thus, when the financial crisis came, there was no major forum of intellectual dissent to resist the ideology of austerity; indeed, the government itself adopted a deeply neoliberal position (O'Rourke and Hogan 2014). The potential loci of dissent, be these in trade unions, civil society, or the academy, had been either incorporated into the state machinery (Allen 2010; Meade 2005) or were silent in an increasingly market-led academy (Lynch 2006). Moreover, the ideology of the 'customer citizen' provided a strong rationale for individualizing responsibility, exonerating the state from having a duty of care for its citizens. Religious conservatism and consensualism had paved the way for a market-led neoliberalism. A neoliberal vision evolved, 'where ethical actors are confined to contemporary versions of Victorian charitable works' (Merriman 2005: 497).

CHARITY

The legitimation of austerity in Ireland was also enabled by the deep-rooted practice of responding to inequalities through charitable acts rather than institutional reform. While responding to injustice through voluntary charitable acts has deep roots in many religious traditions, it found political expression in Ireland in the prolonged resistance by the Catholic Church to the state control of health, welfare, and education services (Lee 1989). Welfare-as-charity also framed the wider state project, as Ireland implemented welfare regimes in the post-war era that were heavily reliant on means-tested provisions with a focus on poverty alleviation rather than universal provision.[11] This strong allegiance to charity was evident during the crisis as the language of *generosity* framed the terms of the debate about social expenditure. Welfare was characterized as a form of unsustainable benevolence:

> In keeping with the framing of the crisis as a crisis of public expenditure, 'generosity' became a new term in the semantic field of social protection. Political debate about the generosity of the system emerged as a justification for its

[11] In 2008, for example, 25.2 per cent of all social protection payments were means-tested compared to 11.1 per cent for the EU27 (Eurostat 2012).

retrenchment, especially in the early stages of the crisis. (Dukelow and Considine 2014b: 59)

As charity-defined welfare also leads to social judgement, between the deserving and undeserving, it provided a moral rationale for cuts and indirect taxation on particular groups, especially when the so-called 'undeserving' were demonized through media misrepresentations (Devereux, Haynes, and Power 2011). Thus, the prevalence of a strong charitable ideology in Ireland provided political and moral justification for cuts in social expenditure.

What is ironic about the construal of social welfare as charity is that there are multiple social expenditures in Ireland that are not classified as welfare but are effectively the very same as welfare in redistribution terms: the very generous tax relief on pensions that accrue an income of over €60,000 per annum; the wide range of tax reliefs for leasing agricultural land and the extensive EU payments under the Common Agricultural Policy; and the multiple tax reliefs for businesses, including the Employment Investment Incentive scheme of tax reliefs for business expansion, the research and development (R&D) system of tax credits, the three-year corporation tax exemption scheme, and the Seed Capital scheme.[12] And it is equally ironic to attack those on social welfare as non-taxpayers,[13] given the high proportion of their income, 27.4 per cent, paid in indirect taxes alone (Collins 2014: 13), a proportion that is more than twice the corporation tax rate of 12.5 per cent.

CONCLUSION

The huge debt imposed on the Irish people by the global financial and political powers (European Central Bank (ECB), EU, and the International Monetary Fund (IMF)) was morally indefensible. However, the burden of the austerity programme that ensued was based on the political choices and ethical decisions of successive Irish Governments, not the Troika. Mitigating the impact of austerity on the vulnerable, through reducing economic inequality, was not a major objective of government policy, either prior to or during the period of austerity.

Using an intersectional egalitarian approach (Anthias 2013), the chapter shows that those most adversely affected by austerity were people who were relatively powerless politically and/or already impoverished and marginalized: they were more likely to be working class than middle class, children and

---

[12] <http://www.djei.ie/enterprise/businesssupport.htm#_Tax_reliefs>; <http://www.teagasc. ie/advisory/eupayments.asp>; <http://www.knowyourtax.ie/services/farmers/>.

[13] In an interview after the 2014 budget, Finance Minister Michael Noonon, remarked: 'It's impossible to deliver relief with tax cuts to people who don't pay tax' (thejournal.ie 2014).

youths rather than adults, and Travellers rather than settled. Lone parents, disabled people, carers, and certain immigrant ethnic minorities were also strongly affected.

The role of ideologies in legitimating inequality both prior to and during the crisis must not be underestimated. Austerity was not only practised, it was preached as a moral virtue and a cure for impoverishment, 'the population were told that if they took pain for a short number of years, they would reap rewards later. It was almost as if there had to be atonement for the party years of the Celtic Tiger' (Allen 2012: 428). Those exercising power also drew on metaphors of charity and neoliberal concepts of individualized responsibility to denigrate dependency on public goods and services. Basic economic and social rights were increasingly reframed as forms of state benevolence that had to be withdrawn to save the corporate whole. Health, welfare, and educational services were represented as burdens on 'taxpayers', ignoring the simple fact that all people pay tax indirectly if not directly, and that public services are used by the great majority of people in Ireland.

While it commenced prior to austerity, the practice by government departments of defining users of state services in market language, as 'customers and clients', gathered a pace during the crisis. Public services were defined increasingly as being available on a market basis rather than as a human right; they were framed as a form of state benevolence that had to be withdrawn to 'save' the country during the crisis. And dissent was peripheralized through the promotion of an ideology of inevitability (Ryan 2003). Nowhere was this more evident than in the media, where the myth that Ireland's entire taxation system was progressive was sold by journalists and politicians to legitimate tax cuts and privileges for the better off (O'Toole 2015).

REFERENCES

Allen, K. 1997. *Fianna Fáil and Irish Labour: 1926 to the Present*. London: Pluto Press.

Allen, K. 2007. *The Corporate Takeover of Ireland*. Dublin: Irish Academic Press.

Allen, K. 2010. 'The Trade Unions: From Partnership to Crisis'. *Irish Journal of Sociology*, 18(2): 22–37.

Allen, K. 2012. 'The Model Pupil Who Faked the Test: Social Policy in the Irish Crisis'. *Critical Social Policy*, 32(3): 422–39.

Anthias, F. 2013. 'Moving beyond the Janus Face of Integration and Diversity Discourses: Towards an Intersectional Framing'. *Sociological Review*, 61: 323–43.

Baker, J., Lynch, K., and Walsh, J. 2015. 'Cutting Back on Equality'. In *Defining Events: Power, Resistance and Identity in Twenty-First Century Ireland*, ed. R. Meade and F. Dukelow. Manchester: Manchester University Press.

Baker, J., Lynch, K., Cantillon, S., and Walsh, J. 2004. *Equality: From Theory to Action*. Basingstoke: Palgrave Macmillan.

Baker, J., Lynch, K., Cantillon, S., and Walsh, J. 2004. *Equality: From Theory to Action* (2nd edn). Basingstoke: Palgrave Macmillan.

Barrett, A. and Wall, C. 2006. *The Distributive Impact of Ireland's Indirect Tax System*. Dublin: Combat Poverty Agency.

Bissett, J. 2015. 'Defiance and Hope: Austerity and the Community Sector'. In *Ireland under Austerity: Neoliberal Crisis, Neoliberal Solutions*, ed. C. Coulter and A. Nagle. Manchester: Manchester University Press.

Bourdieu, P. 1999. *The Weight of the World*. Cambridge: Polity Press.

Burke, S. 2014. *Measuring, Mapping and Making Sense of Irish Health System Performance in the Recession*. Dublin: UCD School of Medicine.

Callan, T., Nolan, B., Keane, C., Savage, M., and Walsh, J. R. 2013. 'The Great Recession, Austerity and Inequality: Evidence from Ireland'. *Intereconomics*, 6: 335–9.

Clarke, J. and Newman, J. 2012. 'The Alchemy of Austerity'. *Critical Social Policy*, 32(3): 299–319.

Collins, M. 2014. 'Total Direct and Indirect Tax Contributions of Households in Ireland', NERI Working Paper 2014/No. 18. Dublin: Nevin Research Institute.

Collins, N. 2007. 'NPM: A New Orthodoxy'. In *Modernising Irish Government: The Politics of Administrative Reform*, ed. N. Collins, P. Butler, and T. Cradden. Dublin: Gill & Macmillan.

Connolly, L. 2002. *The Irish Women's Movement: From Revolution to Devolution*. London: Palgrave Macmillan.

Corcoran, P., Griffin, E., Arensman, E., Fitzgerald, A. P., and Perry, I. J. 2015. 'Impact of the Economic Recession and Subsequent Austerity on Suicide and Self-Harm in Ireland: An Interrupted Time Series Analysis'. *International Journal of Epidemiology*, 44: 1–9.

Coulter, C. and Nagle, A. (eds.) 2015. *Ireland under Austerity: Neoliberal Crisis, Neoliberal Solutions*. Manchester: Manchester University Press.

CSO (Central Statistics Office). 2011. *Census 2001, Profile 5: Households and Families*. Dublin: Stationery Office.

CSO (Central Statistics Office). 2012. *Population and Migration Estimates April 2012 with Revisions from April 2007 to April 2011*. Dublin: Stationery Office.

CSO (Central Statistics Office). 2013. *Survey of Income and Living Conditions SILC*. Dublin: Stationery Office.

CSO (Central Statistics Office). 2015. Income and Poverty Rates by Age Group, Statistical Indicator and Year: 2008–13. Dublin: Stationery Office.

Devereux, E., Haynes, A., and Power, M. 2011. 'Tarring Everyone with the Same Shorthand? Journalists, Stigmatization and Social Exclusion'. *Journalism*, 13(4): 500–17.

Dodson, L. 2013. 'Stereotyping Low-Wage Mothers Who Have Work and Family Conflicts'. *Journal of Social Issues*, 69(2): 257–78.

Doherty, M. 2011. 'It Must Have Been Love…But It's Over Now: The Crisis and Collapse of Social Partnership in Ireland'. *Transfer: European Review of Labour and Research*, 17(3): 371–85.

Dukelow, F. and Considine, M. 2014a. 'Outlier or Model of Austerity in Europe? The Case of Irish Social Protection Reform'. *Social Policy and Administration*, 48(4): 413–29.

Dukelow, F. and Considine, M. 2014b. 'Between Retrenchment and Recalibration: The Impact of Austerity on the Irish Social Protection System'. *Journal of Sociology and Social Welfare*, 41(2): 55–72.

ECRI (European Commission against Racism and Intolerance). 2013. *Report on Ireland: Fourth Monitoring Cycle*. Available at: <http://www.coe.int/t/dghl/monitor ing/ecri/Country-by-country/Ireland/IRL-CbC-IV-2013-001-ENG.pdf> (accessed 11 March 2015).

European Foundation Centre. 2012. *Assessing the Impact of European Governments' Austerity Plans on the Rights of People with Disabilities*. Brussels: European Foundation.

Eurostat. 2012. 'Social Protection: Social Benefits by Function'. Available at: <http://appsso.eurostat.ec.europa.eu/nui/show.do?dataset=spr_exp_eur&lang=en> (accessed 6 July 2016).

Fanning, R. 1983. *Independent Ireland*. Dublin: Helicon.

Garrett, M. P. 2012. 'Adjusting Our Notions of the Nature of the State: A Political Reading of Ireland's Child Protection Crisis'. *Capital & Class*, 36(2): 263–81.

Garvin, T. 2004. *Preventing the Future: Why was Ireland so Poor for so Long?* Dublin: Gill & Macmillan.

Gilligan, A. L. and Zappone, C. 2008. *Our Lives Out Loud: In Pursuit of Justice and Equality*. Dublin: O'Brien Press.

Glynn, I., Kelly, T., and MacÉinrí, P. 2013. *Irish Emigration in an Age of Austerity*. Cork: University College Cork.

Harvey, B. 2013. *Travelling with Austerity: Impacts of Cuts on Travellers, Traveller Projects and Services*. Dublin: Pavee Point.

Inglis, T. 1998. *Moral Monopoly: The Rise and Fall of the Catholic Church in Modern Ireland*, 2nd edn. Dublin: University College Dublin Press.

Inglis, T. 2008. *Global Ireland: Same Difference*. New York: Routledge.

Joseph, E. 2015. 'Racial Stratification in the Irish Labour Market: A Comparative Study of Differential Labour Market Outcomes through the Counter-Stories of Nigerian, Polish and Spanish Migrants in Ireland'. PhD thesis, School of Social Justice, University College Dublin.

Keane, C. 2015. 'Irish Public Finances through the Financial Crisis'. *Fiscal Studies*, 36(4): 475–97.

Keane, C., Callan, T., Savage, M., Walsh, J. R., and Colgan, B. 2015. 'Distributional Impact of Tax, Welfare and Public Service Pay Policies: Budget 2015 and Budgets 2009–2015'. In *Quarterly Economic Commentary, Winter 2014*. Dublin: Economic and Social Research Institute.

Kingston, G., McGinnity, F., and O'Connell, P. 2013. 'Discrimination in the Irish Labour Market: Nationality, Ethnicity and the Recession', UCD Geary Discussion Papers, WP2013/23. Dublin: University College Dublin.

Kirby, P. 2002. *The Celtic Tiger in Distress: Growth and Inequality in Ireland*. Basingstoke: Palgrave.

Kirby, P. and Murphy, M. P. 2011. *Towards the Second Republic: Irish Capitalism in Crisis*. London: Pluto.

Kirby, P., Gibbons, L., and Cronin, M. 2002. *Reinventing Ireland: Culture, Society and the Global Economy*. London: Pluto.

Leahy, E., Lyons, S., and Tol, R. 2011. 'The Distributional Effects of Value Added Tax in Ireland'. *Economic and Social Review*, 42(2): 213–35.

Lee, J. J. 1989. *Ireland, 1912–1985: Politics and Society*. Cambridge: Cambridge University Press.

Lynch, K. 1987. 'Dominant Ideologies in Irish Educational Thought: Consensualism, Essentialism and Meritocratic Individualism'. *Economic and Social Review*, 18(2): 101–22.

Lynch, K. 2006. 'Neo-Liberalism and Marketisation: The Implications for Higher Education'. *European Educational Research Journal*, 5(1): 1–17.

Lynch, K., Baker, J., and Lyons, M. 2009. *Affective Equality: Who Cares? Love, Care and Injustice*. Basingstoke: Palgrave Macmillan.

Lynch, K., Grummell, B., and Devine, D. 2012. *New Managerialism in Education: Gender, Commercialisation and Carelessness*. Basingstoke: Palgrave.

McDonnell, P. 2007. *Disability and Society: Ideological and Historical Dimensions*. Dublin: Orpen Press.

McGinnity, F., Quinn, E., Kingston, G., and O'Connell, P. 2013. *Annual Monitoring Report on Integration 2012*. Dublin: Economic and Social Research Institute.

McGinnity, F., Russell, H., Watson, D., Kingston, G., and Kelly, E. 2014. *Winners and Losers? The Equality Impact of the Great Recession in Ireland*. Dublin: Equality Authority and Economic and Social Research Institute.

Meade, R. 2005. 'We Hate It Here, Please Let Us Stay! Irish Social Partnership and the Community/Voluntary Sector's Conflicted Experiences of Recognition'. *Critical Social Policy*, 25(3): 349–73.

Mental Health Commission. 2011. *The Human Cost: An Overview of the Evidence on Economic Adversity and Mental Health and Recommendations for Action*. Dublin: Mental Health Commission.

Merriman, V. 2005. 'A Responsibility to Dream: Decolonising Independent Ireland'. *Third Text*, 19(5): 487–97.

NESC (National Economic and Social Council). 2013. *The Social Dimensions of the Crisis: Evidence and Implications*. Dublin: National Economic and Social Council.

O'Connor, N. and Staunton, C. 2015. *Cherishing All Equally: Economic Inequality in Ireland*. Dublin: TASC.

O'Connor, P. 2000. 'Ireland: A Man's World'. *Economic and Social Review*, 31(1): 81–102.

O'Rourke, B. and Hogan, J. 2014. 'Guaranteeing Failure: Neoliberal Discourse in the Irish Economic Crisis'. *Journal of Political Ideologies*, 19(1): 41–59.

O'Toole, F. 2015. 'The Myth of Ireland's Progressive Tax System'. The Irish Times, 29 September. Available at: <http://www.irishtimes.com/opinion/fintan-o-toole-the-myth-of-ireland-s-progressive-tax-system-1.2370113> (accessed 6 July 2016).

Oxfam. 2013. *The True Cost of Austerity and Inequality: Ireland Case Study*. Oxford: Oxfam.

Phelan, S. 2007. 'The Discourses of Neoliberal Hegemony: The Case of the Irish Republic'. *Critical Discourse Studies*, 4(1): 29–48.

Phillips, A. 1995. *The Politics of Presence*. Oxford: Oxford University Press.

Rose, K. 1994. *Diverse Communities: The Evolution of Gay and Lesbian Politics in Ireland*. Cork: Cork University Press.

Ryan, A. B. 2003. 'Contemporary Discourses of Working, Earning and Spending: Acceptance, Critique and the Bigger Picture'. In *The End of Irish History? Critical Reflections on the Celtic Tiger*, ed. C. Coulter and S. Coleman. Manchester: Manchester University Press.

thejournal.ie. 2014. 'Michael Noonan: 'Austerity as We Know it is Over''. Interview, 14 October. Available at: <http://www.thejournal.ie/michael-noonan-austerity-is-over-1723791-Oct2014/> (accessed 11 April 2016).

Yuval-Davis, N. 2006. 'Intersectionality and Feminist Politics'. *European Journal of Women's Studies*, 13(3): 193–209.

15

Housing

Rob Kitchin, Rory Hearne, and Cian O'Callaghan

INTRODUCTION: FROM CRISIS TO CRISIS

Housing can be an incredibly emotive issue. Shelter and a sense of home is essential to our well-being, which is why the right to housing is enshrined in the conventions of the United Nations (UN), and, in turn, ratified by most national governments. Housing provides us with sanctuary and a sense of identity and belonging. Housing is also seen as an asset: the most expensive purchase most families make or an investment for landlords seeking a steady yield. Building and selling houses can be highly profitable, but they can also bankrupt households, builders, developers, and banks if the market plummets. Losing one's home is highly distressing, as is the sense that one cannot afford a home due to changing house or rental prices. Living in substandard housing or being homeless can be detrimental to one's mental and physical health. Providing high-quality, affordable, and securely tenured housing for all citizens is thus a core stated ambition of most governments. However, there is a marked difference between rhetoric and reality, in part due to the ideology of ruling parties and the machinations of vested interests, but also due to housing being a complex and costly endeavour. Furthermore, there is also, increasingly, a tension between housing as a form of shelter (its use value) and housing as an asset class (its exchange value), particularly in light of the financialization of mortgage markets (Aalbers 2008; Downey 2014).

The central thesis we advance in this chapter is that housing in Ireland is perpetually in crisis. What is more, the crisis in housing pre-dates the crash of 2007/8, building up for at least twenty years and evolving through three distinct phases: 1993–2006 (the Celtic Tiger years); 2007–12 (the crash); 2013– (unstable, uneven, and partial rebalancing). The crises of phases two and three were created by the outcomes and policies adopted during phase one, and have been deepened by recent austerity policies that lacked strategic foresight, placing severe stresses on households and the housing sector.

CRISIS PHASE ONE: 1993–2006
(THE CELTIC TIGER YEARS)

The exact start date of the Celtic Tiger era is still debated, but most commentators accept it was between 1991 and 1995. From the early 1990s the Irish economy began to transform, with a notable rise in key economic indicators such as gross domestic product (GDP) and numbers in employment. As the economy grew, the population increased through immigration and natural increase, and average household size shrank through alterations in family structure. Between April 1991 and April 2006, the population of Ireland increased by 704,129 (20 per cent), the number of households by 440,437 (43 per cent) (CSO 2014a). The demand for housing thus expanded rapidly, as did the need to produce a more diversified stock that would cater for different sizes and types of household. While population and households fell in some localized areas, it increased overall in each local authority, and in some it expanded very rapidly. For example, in Kildare and Meath, the number of households grew by 85 per cent and 87 per cent. This demand had a number of effects—a construction boom, surge in house prices, a large increase in household and mortgage debt, bank indebtedness, over-zoning, urban sprawl, and long-distance commuting—each of which could be considered a crisis in its own right given its dramatic transformative effect and demands.

Between January 1991 and December 2006, 762,631 housing units were completed in Ireland, peaking with 93,419 units being built in 2006 alone (see Figure 15.1; DECLG 2016). Even allowing for replacing obsolescent stock, clearly more units were being built than there were households being formed, especially in the period 2002–6. Nonetheless, house prices rose dramatically. The average new house price rose from €78,715 in Dublin and €66,914 for the country as a whole in 1991, to €416,225 in Dublin (a 429 per cent increase) and €322,634 for the country as a whole (a 382 per cent increase) in 2007 (DECLG 2016). Second-hand homes followed the same trend, with rises in Dublin of 551 per cent and of 489 per cent outside the capital. In the same period, house building costs and wages merely doubled (Brawn 2009). In Q3 1995, the average second-hand house price was 4.1 times the average industrial wage of €18,152; by Q2 2007, second-hand house prices had risen to 11.9 times the average industrial wage of €32,616 (Brawn 2009). Not unsurprisingly, the total value of household mortgage debt increased dramatically, from €47.2 billion in 2002 to over €139.8 billion at the end of 2007, with the average size of a new mortgage (€266,000) being nearly double the 2002 figure (CSO 2008). During this period a 'bubble economy', underpinned by the expansion of debt to households based on perceived increases in the value of their homes, drove economic growth (Ó Riain 2014). Moreover, given rapidly rising prices and a strong rental market, the buy-to-let (BTL) market flourished, with a significant number of households becoming 'amateur' landlords. At the same

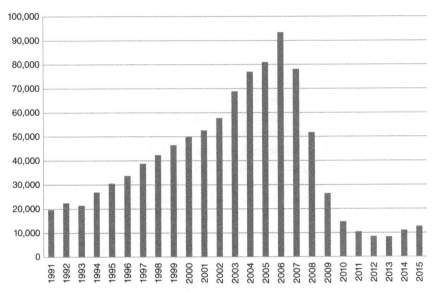

Figure 15.1. Number of completed housing units per annum, 1991–2015
Source: DECLG 2014.

time, state investment in social housing was waning whilst demand was growing, with a turn to the private sector to provide accommodation through a rent supplement scheme. Further, social housing built during the 1950s was coming to the end of its life, needing either substantial refurbishment or replacement.

Given the demand for prime land for development, pressure was placed on local authorities to zone more land; consequently, the cost of land rose dramatically, especially in 2004–6. Land prices jumped in value from just under €10,000 per hectare in 1998 to over €58,400 per hectare in 2006 (Savills HOK 2007). The result was that land became a significant component of housing cost: up to 50 per cent, against a European average of 10–15 per cent (O'Toole 2009). To enable developers to bid for land and to afford the cost of building, bank lending increased substantially. In 2003, the indebtedness of Irish banks to overseas banks was just over 10 per cent of Irish GDP. By 2008 this had risen to 60 per cent of GDP, with over 60 per cent of bank assets tied up in property-related lending (Honohan 2010).

Given the cost of land and housing, households who wished to buy a home but who had limited resources were forced to either buy property that did not suit their future needs, with the aim of trading up later, borrowing beyond their means (e.g. 100 per cent or interest-only mortgages, or taking out multiple loans), or buying in an area further away and commuting. These factors created a context in which a growing number of households had a vested interest in property prices rising further, thus extending a debt-based model of home ownership and perpetuating these trends. Furthermore, the reliance on long-distance commuting led to extensive urban sprawl and the growth of smaller towns around the principal cities and towns.

Somewhat ironically, all of these changes were celebrated by the government, the construction sector, and the media during the Celtic Tiger era. They were taken as a sign that Ireland was catching up with the rest of the developed West in terms of its economy and property sector. It was suggested that a virtuous circle had been created whereby people stepping onto the property ladder were immediately gaining the benefit in their prime asset rising in price, and moreover they had more choice in housing options than ever before; the government was collecting significant tax revenue (value added tax (VAT), capital gains tax, stamp duty, development levies) that could be reinvested into improved services and infrastructure; and the property and banking sector were flourishing whilst helping to bring in overseas investment. Whilst price rises were staggering, potential purchasers and investors were assured that there was still plenty of scope for further expansion. And anyone who suggested that these changes were potentially very harmful to households by saddling them with huge debt and unsustainable commutes, and to the wider Irish economy by reducing competitiveness and producing a bubble that was sure to burst, were roundly attacked by politicians, the media, and the property sector. The worst that could happen, they were told, was a soft landing, wherein prices levelled off to modest growth, and construction slowed in pace. But the bubble did burst, with devastating consequences for citizens, companies, and the state.

CRISIS PHASE TWO: 2007–12 (THE CRASH)

As the global economy slowed and the global subprime banking crisis began, house price rises in Ireland started to slow in September 2006, levelling off in March 2007, and remaining static until November 2007. From December 2007 to February 2012 they fell consistently, before bottoming out and remaining stable until June 2013 (see Figure 15.2). From the peak to the bottom, prices fell by 57.4 per cent in Dublin (houses 55.9 per cent and apartments 63.7 per cent) and 48.7 per cent in the rest of the country (CSO 2015). Ireland experienced one of the deepest house market collapses on record. What was happening with house prices was a barometer for the wider housing sector. As 2008 started it was clear that the promise of a soft landing was empty and all of the issues built up over the course of the Celtic Tiger years exploded into a new set of crises as the property bubble burst and the Irish banking sector collapsed, culminating in the Irish bank guarantee of September 2008, the

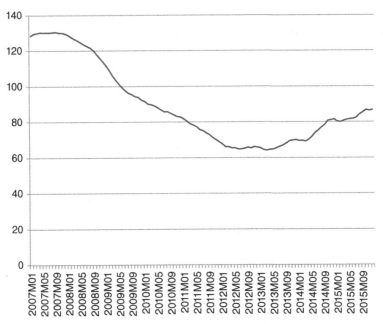

Figure 15.2. Change in property price index: 2007–14
Source: CSO 2015.

creation of the state-owned National Assets Management Agency (NAMA) in September 2009 (which bought €74 billion of distressed property loans from the Irish banks), and the €85 billion International Monetary Fund (IMF)–European Union (EU)–European Central Bank (ECB) bailout in November 2010 (see Kitchin et al. 2012).

Whilst the global financial crisis was the trigger for the Irish crisis, Irish banks were only slightly exposed to US subprime loans; rather, they were massively exposed to property and development loans in a bubble market (O'Toole 2009). Moreover, it soon became clear that not only were prices overinflated, but that there was a massive oversupply of housing stock and over-zoning of land. Between 2005 and 2007, 252,403 housing units were completed in Ireland (connected to the electricity grid), with another 78,144 added in 2008 and 2009 as legacy construction slowed (DECLG 2016). This was despite the fact that the 2002 census had reported 177,254 vacant units (excluding holiday homes) and the 2006 census 216,533 vacant units (excluding holiday homes) (CSO 2014a). Put simply, housing units had been built in excess of demand across the entire country, with several local authorities having vacancy rates, excluding holiday homes, above 15 per cent. The extent of the oversupply was clarified by the 2011 census, which reported that 230,056 units were vacant (excluding holiday homes), 168,427 houses and 61,629 apartments out of a total housing stock of 1,994,845 (CSO 2012). Allowing that one would always expect some units to be vacant in any housing market (*c*.6 per cent) then oversupply was approximately 110,000 units. With supply outstripping demand, there was no demand to support existing prices, moreover, due to the banking crisis, there was no credit to enable purchases.

The most visible manifestation of the oversupply issue were, and continue to be, unfinished estates. After some speculation as to how many such estates existed, the National Survey of Housing Developments reported that there were 2,846 documented unfinished estates in Ireland, present in every local authority (Housing Agency 2010; see Figure 15.3). With respect to the units on these estates, 78,195 were complete and occupied, 23,250 complete and vacant, and 19,830 under construction, with planning permission in place for a further 58,025 units. The 2013 survey recorded 1,811 estates, which all had outstanding issues of planning and development (estates with issues of vacancy only were excluded), on which there were 82,432 dwellings: 57,642 complete and occupied, 8,694 complete and vacant, and 16,135 under construction (19.6 per cent) (Housing Agency 2013). Only 193 recorded development activity. Of these, 82,432 dwellings, 47.9 per cent, had incomplete roads, 18.7 per cent incomplete footpaths, 21.9 per cent incomplete lighting, 19.4 per cent lacked potable water, 18.6 per cent lacked fully operational storm water systems, and 19.4 per cent lacked fully operational waste water systems. Of 4,033 planned open space areas, only 2,205 were complete.

Those households who found themselves residing on these unfinished estates have also had to contend with anti-social behaviour and vandalism, an unsafe environment for children to play in, a diminished sense of place and community, and often poor access to services such as schools, crèches, medical centres, and public transport (Kitchin, O'Callaghan, and Gleeson 2014). In cases where an estate management company was meant to be operating, low levels of occupancy made such companies unviable, meaning that service provision has been patchy or non-existent (Mahon and O'Cinneide 2010). There has also been the stress of an uncertain future with regards to the situation improving and personal finances concerning mortgage payments and negative equity.

Severe cutbacks in government spending and austerity budgets meant that a minimum-policy, minimum-cost approach has been taken with respect to unfinished estates, with the government initially allocating just €5 million for tackling health and safety issues (e.g. knocking down unsafe structures, fencing off and tidying up areas) and seeking to establish Site Resolution Plans (SRPs) for each estate. SRPs are plans collectively put together by all vested interests—local authorities, developers, banks, residents—and provide a roadmap for how to deal with issues on an estate, but crucially are voluntary and have no statutory tools beyond existing legislation (difficult to apply to bankrupted entities), nor finances beyond the government fund. As such, the extent to which outstanding problems are addressed through SRPs varies widely between different local authorities and different estates.

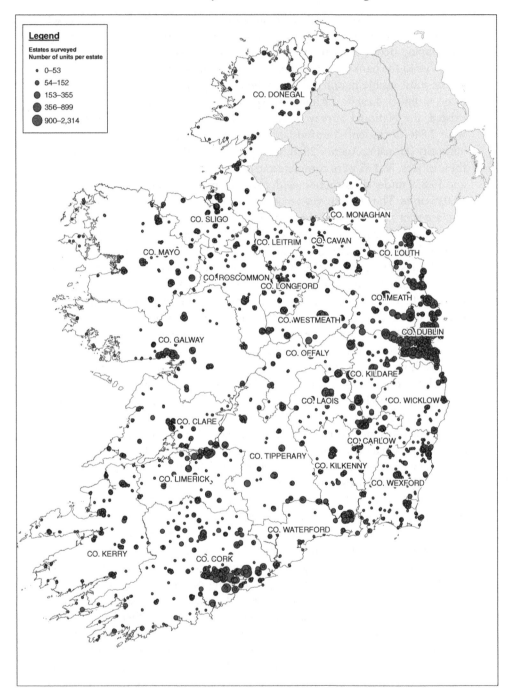

Figure 15.3. Location of unfinished estates and number of units per estates, 2010

Source: Housing Agency <http://www.housing.ie/Housing/media/Media/2010%20National%20Housing%20Survey/2010-National-Map_Location-of-Surveyed-Developments.pdf>.

Beyond vacancy and unfinished estates, there has been a concern related to the quality of dwellings constructed during the Celtic Tiger era. Building control and standards were deregulated in Ireland in 1990, with local authority planning enforcement only undertaking inspections on 10–15 per cent of sites and not at all stages of development. Self-certification, plus high-volume construction, meant that many substandard units were built, along with units that only met minimum standards. Many units or extensions were built without planning permission or building control certification, making them now difficult to sell as banks tighten up the conditions for lending. The highest profile case relates to Priory Hall in Dublin, where 187 apartments were found to breach fire hazard regulations, with residents forced to vacate their homes for two years whilst continuing to pay mortgages, but there have been numerous other similar examples. Further, there are estimated to be in excess of 20,000 homes whose foundation hardcore and building blocks are contaminated with pyrite, though the Department of Environment, Community and Local Government (DECLG) presently only recognizes 74 estates containing 12,250 units, predominately located in Dublin City, Fingal, Meath, Kildare, and Offaly (DECLG 2012).

In addition to oversupply of dwellings, there was also an oversupply of zoned land and commercial premises. In June 2008, there were 14,191 hectares of serviced zoned land in the state, enough for up to 462,000 potential new units (DECLG 2016). In addition, there were another 30,000 hectares of unserviced zoned land. In many parts of the country there was enough zoned land for dozens of years of supply (Kitchin et al. 2010). For example, in Monaghan, a mostly rural local authority with a housing stock of 21,658 units in 2006, there was enough zoned land for an additional 18,147 units. Not unsurprisingly, land prices plummeted by between 75–98 per cent in value post-2007. In Dublin, some 782,500m^2 of office space (23 per cent) was vacant in 2010 (Savills HOK 2010). After a substantial growth in the construction of hotels during the Celtic Tiger era, at the end of 2008, 15,000 guest rooms (26 per cent) were deemed to be in excess of demand (Peter Bacon and Associates 2009).

As the housing market plummeted and the wider economy crashed, with unemployment rising from 4.6 per cent in Q4 2007 to peak at 15.1 per cent in Q3 2011, and households facing tax rises and pay cuts, increasing financial pressure was placed onto households (CSO 2014b). Faced with paying high payment rates on their mortgages, many households struggled to keep up with payments. In Q3 2009, 3.3 per cent of principal residence mortgages were in arrears by over ninety days. By Q3 2013, this had peaked at 12.9 per cent (99,189 mortgages), with 18.4 per cent in some level of arrears (141,520) (Central Bank 2016). With respect to BTL mortgages, 21.2 per cent (31,227) were in arrears of over ninety days, with 27.4 per cent (40,426) in some level of arrears in Q3 2013. And as house prices dropped, the number of households in negative equity grew to include more than 50 per cent of residential properties with a mortgage (RTÉ 2012). Similarly, rent arrears to local authorities, boroughs, and town councils increased from €32.8 million in January 2008 to €58.5 million in December 2011 as tenants struggled to pay their bills (DECLG 2016).

The huge house price rises in the Celtic Tiger years, followed by the financial pressures of the crash, had significant spillover effects with respect to social housing demands and homelessness. In 1999, there were 39,176 households on the social housing waiting list, rising to 48,413 in 2002, 56,249 in 2008, and 98,318 in 2011 (DECLG 2016). The vast majority of people on the list are because they cannot afford private rental accommodation and are unable to purchase a property. Between 1994 and 2007, 47,769 social housing units were built in Ireland, plus, between 1999 and 2007, 9,378 were acquired through purchase and 1,201 long-term leases acquired through the Rental Accommodation Scheme (RAS) (DECLG 2016). At the same time, 22,633 local authority units were sold to tenants (many of these funded by mortgages provided by local authorities, a large proportion of which are now in arrears). However, the austerity programme implemented by two governments from 2008 onwards dramatically reduced state investment in social housing. The capital expenditure for social housing was reduced by 80 per cent (from €1.3bn to €275m) between 2008 and 2013, and funding for the National Regeneration Programme reduced from €121 million in 2008 to €80 million in 2013: a 34 per cent reduction. Between 2008 and 2013, 10,745 social housing units were built (nearly all—8,267—in 2008–9, much of it replacement stock in regeneration schemes), 3,293 were acquired through purchase, and 8,707 long-term leases were acquired through RAS. While some stock was being built or acquired, then, social housing needs were outstripping the state's ability to supply suitable affordable accommodation. Indeed, the proportion of social housing stock in Ireland has fallen from 18 per cent of all residences in 1961 to 8 per cent in 2011 (CSO 2012). The shortfall in social housing is made up through privately rented accommodation subsidized by rent supplement. A total of 97,260 households were receiving rent supplement in late 2010, an increase of 63 per cent on the previous three years, with spending rising from €70 million in the mid-1990s to €516.5 million in 2010. Even with the state providing social housing or rent supplement, the financial and other pressures placed onto individuals and households during the crash saw a rise in homelessness: between 2008 and 2011 the number of homeless households increased by 68 per cent to 2,348, with 3,808 people in accommodation for the homeless (Housing Agency 2011).

Further, much social housing stock is acknowledged to be in poor condition and also in areas with strong social and economic disadvantage, with social problems, high unemployment, drug addiction, gang-related crime, and low education participation rates. After extensive local community campaigning, prior to the crash the decision was taken to implement large-scale regeneration schemes in north Dublin (Ballymun) and other Dublin estates, Limerick (Moyross and St Mary's), and a number of regional towns, including Sligo, Dundalk, and Tralee. The funding mechanism for such regeneration was public–private partnerships (PPPs), involving a transfer of local authority land to a private developer who would then build and sell owner-occupier housing and commercial/retail units in return for providing a reduced amount of new social housing and some community facilities on the remainder of the site (Hearne 2011). The use of PPPs for regeneration would, it was argued, create a better social mix, diminishing concentrations of social and low-income housing (DEHLG 2005). These schemes collapsed with the crash as both private and public finances evaporated. This left thousands of local authority tenants living in substandard conditions whilst awaiting relocation, and many hundreds permanently relocated in preparation for regeneration. Given that old units were slated for demolition (so at least half were empty), and the reduction in local authority maintenance budgets, conditions in these estates deteriorated further, condemning families to live in unhealthy and unsafe environments. At the same, planned investment in Traveller accommodation also stalled during this period, with 361 Traveller families living on unauthorized sites, 2,717 in private rented accommodation, and 663 in shared housing in 2013 (DECLG 2016).

CRISIS PHASE THREE: 2013– (UNSTABLE, UNEVEN, AND PARTIAL REBALANCING)

The levelling off in the fall in house prices, followed by a gradual and then rapid increase of prices in Dublin (rising by 24.1 per cent between October 2012 and 2013, before levelling off again in response to Central Bank interventions), is indicative of the start of a new phase in the ongoing housing crisis. This phase sees the continuation of serious problems of phase two, such as social housing need, private rent rises, mortgage arrears, negative equity, and unfinished estates, but varying levels of change depending on the extent to which solutions are put in place and the wider economy starts to recover. For example, the numbers receiving rent supplement fell by 23 per cent from 2010 to 74,080 in 2014 (*Irish Times* 2014a). Large-scale de-zoning has significantly reduced the amount of serviced zoned land. By Q3 2015, mortgage accounts remaining in arrears had dropped to 92,291 (12.3 per cent), with 65,584 in arrears for over ninety days (8.7 per cent) (Central Bank 2016). With respect to BTL mortgages, 30,288 (22 per cent) were in arrears at the end of June, with 24,890 (18.1 per cent) in arrears of over ninety days. Moreover, by December 2014, 49,000 households had been issued with legal letters seeking repossession, and full court proceedings to repossess homes have been initiated in 23,751 cases (Weston 2014). On the BTL side, 18,000 mortgage holders had been issued with repossession letters and 8,618 with court proceedings.

The new or deepening crises in this period are a lack of supply in some areas and associated rising housing and rental prices, continued problems of social housing provision, and rising homelessness in response to a changing rental market. Whilst there was oversupply in every single local authority for both houses and apartments (with the exception of south Dublin for houses) in 2011 (Kitchin et al. 2012), the extent of this oversupply varied geographically. Much of rural Ireland had extensive levels of vacancy. In Dublin, the overall vacancy rate for the four local authorities was 8.3 per cent (43,707 units) (CSO 2012). While the vacancy rate of houses was low, with only small pockets of oversupply, the vacancy rate for apartments was 16–19 per cent. Since 2011, despite emigration nationally, population and households have been growing in Dublin through natural increase, labour migration, and household fragmentation. Moreover, the levelling off of prices instilled confidence that the bottom of the market had been reached. In combination, the result was an increase in demand by investors trying to maximize return on investment and rental yields and households looking to enter the market. What oversupply there was in the capital has thus been absorbed. With respect to new supply, however, construction has remained moribund. Between January 2012 and December 2015 only 40,471 units were built nationwide, 8,785 of which were in Dublin (see Figure 15.1; DECLG 2016). Assessments by both the Housing Agency and the Economic and Social Research Institute (ESRI) suggest that c.8,000 units are required per annum in Dublin (Housing Agency 2014; Morgenroth 2014). The ESRI estimate that all but 14 per cent of required units needed nationwide will need to be in the greater Dublin region (four local authorities plus Meath, Kildare, Louth, and Wicklow). In contrast, they estimate that many counties will not need new supply because of existing oversupply (Donegal, Kerry, Mayo, Tipperary, Leitrim, Sligo, Cavan, Roscommon, and Longford are projected to still have oversupply in 2021). Overall, it is estimated that between 12,500 and 16,000 new units per annum are required, a rate that is actually quite modest—typically over the past forty-five years new build has been 20–30,000 per annum, rising to 40,000+ post-1998. The effect of very little new supply for either purchase or rent, but rising demand, has led to the inflation in prices. The Daft.ie (2016) Report for Q4 2015 details that rents nationally are up 32 per cent since their lowest point in 2011, and in Dublin rents are less than 1 per cent below their previous peak and in some cases are higher than the peak of the boom.

One effect of rent increases is that families who are income insecure—low wage, uncertain hours, flexible working, dependent on welfare—who reside in private rental accommodation cannot afford rent increases and rent supplement is not sufficient to cover the gap, with more than half of those receiving rent supplement having to top up their rent. Consequently, they are being priced out of their homes in favour of those who can afford the new rental price. These families find it difficult to find alternative private rented accommodation due to rent inflation across the rental sector and landlord preferences for tenants not reliant on rent supplement. With no social housing available, these families find themselves homeless. Nationally, homeless charity the Simon Community reported that in 2012, there was an increase of 24 per cent in those using their services, to over 5,000 individuals (*Irish Times* 2014b). The Dublin Region Homeless Executive (DRHE) detail that, in 2015, a total of 5,480 adult individuals accessed homeless accommodation during 2015 in Dublin (DRHE 2016a). As of January 2016, there were 769 families homeless in Dublin, living in emergency homeless accommodation (DRHE 2016b).

Without a significant increase in the level of supply, competition for property is going to get worse, with rising purchase and rental prices and increasing homelessness. In theory, a lot of the right criteria for creating supply exist. There is an excess of demand; there are 6,400 acres of zoned serviced land available in the four Dublin authorities for 132,000 units (DECLG 2014); there are a lot of outstanding planning permissions still in effect and local authorities want to give permission for developments that meet development plan/zoning criteria; and material and labour costs are significantly lower than the boom time. Yet despite these conditions and the need to create supply it is clear that a hangover from phase two of the crisis is blocking development. The state's finances are limited, there are competing demands for scarce resources, and the government is reluctant to significantly increase capital spending on housing and associated infrastructure. The banks are in a weak state and reluctant to lend for development. Builders and developers have no initial capital to draw down additional finance. With respect to land, it may be the case that owners are reluctant to put it into development because they bought it in the boom and cannot afford to develop at present housing prices. With respect to planning, it may be that developers are seeking permissions that contravene development plans or are trying to alter existing permissions. The property industry also argues that the system needs streamlining and simplifying. Crucially perhaps has been the emergent tension between different types of investment finance in Irish property markets. In the post-crash era the state introduced a series of new financial measures, including the establishment of NAMA and Real Estate Investment Trusts (REITs), which bundled together property portfolios, thus making it easier for international funds to invest in Irish property assets. The rate of return on these investments is often more favourable and seen to be less risky than it would be to invest in new construction projects. NAMA's need for rental growth is likely to be one of the reasons the government is refusing to give private tenants (the majority of those on social housing lists) relief through rent controls. By pushing for maximum commercial returns, NAMA is working against the interests of those looking for an affordable and secure home. The combination of these factors is fuelling a set of related supply-led crises that seems likely to continue for a number of years.

CONCLUSION

The last twenty-five years has seen a tumultuous set of changes with regards to Ireland's housing sector and market. Throughout the entire period it has been transitioning through three phases of crisis. In the first phase, there were crises of creating enough supply, very quickly causing prices to rise to levels that were unaffordable for low- and middle-income households and reducing competitiveness, a significant increase in household debt and bank debt to precarious levels, over-zoning of land and dramatic price increases, and the expansion of urban sprawl and long-distance commuting. The unfolding of this phase was shaped by the adoption of neoliberal ideas and practices with respect to governance and economy. This prioritized market-led development, deregulation, PPPs, and low corporate taxation. Both the construction and banking sectors saw a relaxation of regulatory oversight. The state started to withdraw from social housing provision, instead relying on the private rental sector, and when it did provide social housing it was through PPPs. While demand was high, the property sector was afforded a range of very generous tax breaks and incentives. Moreover, there was a laissez-faire uncoordinated approach to housing and planning policy. Although a national spatial strategy was introduced in 2002 it was never implemented and was ignored by local authorities. Instead, the planning system became developer-led, being pro-growth in ethos with a presumption for development operating, and was consistently undermined by localism, clientelism, and cronyism. In short, Irish policy was uncoordinated, piecemeal, and favoured development interests, with too few checks and balances, thus enabling a property bubble to rapidly inflate, accompanied by an oversupply of stock.

The result was that when the property bubble burst, the fallout was catastrophic for households, the state, and the wider economy. House prices plunged, estates remained unfinished, households were faced with extensive mortgage arrears and negative equity and/or poor build quality, the social housing waiting list extended, and more households became homeless. Rather than a radical change in policy, however, the Irish Government's response to the crash was to persist with the same neoliberal ethos, protecting the interests of the banking and development sector through bank bailouts and the creation of NAMA, enforcing austerity measures that placed significant stresses on households, and making little to no changes to housing and planning policy, other than to significantly cut the resourcing of the responsible departments and local authorities and to massively reduce capital spend on regeneration and new social housing stock. Moreover, it scrapped entirely the National Spatial Strategy and National Development Plan that might have provided a strategic framework, instead replacing them with short-term initiatives split across different government departments (Kitchin 2015). Further, most policy has been minimal effort, minimal cost in nature, with few legislative and policy changes, and a hope that the market returns and economy recovers and serendipitously fixes the problems. In part, this was due to the same government being in place post-crash as pre-, followed by diktats from the IMF–EU–ECB as part of the sovereign debt bailout. But was also the result of an unwillingness to implement reform and put in place a strategic, coordinated approach to development, which Irish politicians have long resisted, given the roll of planning in local politics and the strength of the property lobby (Kitchin et al. 2012). Instead, policy related to housing and planning remained fractured and fragmented in the years immediately after the crash, lacking any systematic or integrated framework.

Instead of the market returning and fixing the problems, a third phase in the crisis has emerged in which, in selected areas, demand has risen, oversupply has been mopped up, but no new supply is being created. This has driven up purchase and rental prices, but also created rising homelessness. A number of inter-related issues have contributed to the poor planning for future demand, including a piecemeal, reactive rather than proactive housing policy, a decimated construction and domestic banking sector, and a lack of long-term housing and planning statistics and active predictive forecasting based on demographics and planning policy. Somewhat belatedly the government response was Construction 2020 (Irish Government 2014). It detailed seventy-five action points, though they are not framed within an overall holistic framework. However, rather than setting out concrete policies, it charted a roadmap for finding solutions rather than providing solutions, proposing a set of new committees, task forces, review groups, and consultations. In effect, it was a strategy for thinking about action (see also the four recent reports by the National and Economic Social Council (NESC) on housing, nos 138, 140, 141, 142[1]). Key elements of the strategy such as a revised national spatial strategy are still not in place in early 2016, let alone implemented. Just as supply and demand became disconnected in the Celtic Tiger years, policy responses and the post-crash crises have become disconnected, hopelessly out of sync with each other in terms of the actions needed and the temporal speed and resourcing required. The consequence is that the stresses and pressures of

---

[1] <http://www.nesc.ie/en/publications/publications/nesc-reports/>.

a failing housing sector and austerity measures continue to bear down on households.

In our view, two things need to happen to help address the crises we have discussed. First, the government needs to fast-track Construction 2020, reframing it into a holistic, sustainable, and non-cyclical approach to housing and planning—that frames them as a sector and public good, not a simply a vehicle for capital accumulation—and start implementing policy and programmes. At the top of the agenda must be prioritizing the creation of supply in selected areas, including an extensive social housing building programme, to tackle the issue of homelessness, and resolving unfinished estates, making them safe and attractive places to live. We appreciate that, to date, policy-making in Ireland has been piecemeal, with different elements introduced at different times by varying governments and ministers with different ideological ambitions and a limited time horizon (the next election as opposed to fifty years' time), and also the multi-scalar and multi-agency nature of delivery and governance of housing, and the diversity vested interests with different modus operandi and ambitions operating in the sector and seeking to influence policy and delivery. However, it is vital that a holistic approach is quickly established and enacted, rather than becoming bogged down in politics and inaction (it is interesting that policy to guarantee banks and bailouts costing billions can be taken overnight, but measures to tackle long-term housing crises can be neglected for years).

Second, the government needs to lessen austerity measures and be a more proactive player in the housing sector, using construction and investment in social housing and selected public infrastructure as a way of tackling housing issues at the same time as growing the economy, as well as taking a more active role in the private rented sector. This includes using NAMA to provide sites, stock, and finance for the provision of social and private housing without seeking to gain maximum commercial return, thus overinflating prices. The private rented sector now accounts for a fifth of all households, and in urban centres it is even more significant with almost 40 per cent of people renting in Galway, 35 per cent in Dublin, and 29 per cent in Cork. Government could pass regulations to restrict the rate of rent inflation in any one tax year to, for example, 5 per cent, and then recoup a higher rate of tax on rental incomes where a landlord has breached this cap. However, there are no moves to do so. The reason is that housing policy remains dominated by the interests of the property industry, including the banks, developers, estate agents, solicitors, landlords, and increasingly, international capital and vulture fund investors who are buying up huge swathes of Irish residential property, and who all seek rapidly rising property prices. Unless there is a more proactive, coordinated response, the crises of phase two will affect households for much longer and the crises of phase three will deepen, worsen, and last for much longer.

REFERENCES

Aalbers, M. B. 2008. 'The Financialization of Home and the Mortgage Market Crisis'. *Competition and Change*, 12(2): 148–66.

Brawn, D. 2009. *Ireland's House Party: What Estates Agents Don't Want You to Know.* Dublin: Gill & Macmillan.

Central Bank. 2016. 'Residential Mortgage Arrears and Repossessions Statistics'. Available at: <http://www.centralbank.ie/polstats/stats/mortgagearrears/Pages/releases.aspx> (accessed 21 March 2016).

CSO (Central Statistics Office). 2008. *Construction and Housing in Ireland.* Available at: <http://www.cso.ie/en/media/csoie/releasespublications/documents/construction/current/constructhousing.pdf> (accessed 21 March 2016).

CSO (Central Statistics Office). 2012. *Profile 4: The Roof over our Heads.* Available at: <http://www.cso.ie/en/media/csoie/census/documents/census2011profile4/Profile_4_The_Roof_over_our_Heads_Full_doc_sig_amended.pdf> (accessed 21 March 2016).

CSO (Central Statistics Office). 2014a. 'Irish Censuses'. Available at: <http://www.cso.ie/en/census/> (accessed 21 March 2016).

CSO (Central Statistics Office). 2014b. 'Quarterly National Household Survey'. Available at: <http://www.cso.ie/px/pxeirestat/Statire/SelectVarVal/Define.asp?maintable=QNQ22> (accessed 21 March 2016).

CSO (Central Statistics Office). 2015. 'Residential Property Price Index'. Available at: <http://www.cso.ie/en/releasesandpublications/er/rppi/residentialpropertypriceindexdecember2015/> (accessed 21 March 2016).

Daft.ie. 2016. *Daft.ie Rental Report.* Available at: <https://www.daft.ie/report/q4-daft-rental-report-2015.pdf> (accessed 10 March 2016).

DECLG (Department of Environment, Community and Local Government). 2005. *Housing Policy Framework: Building Sustainable Communities.* Dublin: Stationery Office.

DECLG (Department of Environment, Community and Local Government). 2012. *Report of Pyrite Panel.* Available at: <http://www.environ.ie/en/PyriteReport/FileDownLoad,30735,en.pdf> (accessed 21 March 2016).

DECLG (Department of Environment, Community and Local Government). 2016. 'Housing Statistics'. Available at: <http://www.environ.ie/housing/statistics/housing-statistics> (accessed 21 March 2016).

Downey, D. D. 2014. 'The Financialisation of Irish Homeownership and the Impact of the Global Financial Crisis'. In *Neoliberal Urban Policy and the Transformation of the City: Reshaping Dublin*, ed. A. Maclaren and S. Kelly. Basingstoke: Palgrave Macmillan.

DRHE (Dublin Region Homeless Executive). 2016a. 'Homeless Accommodation Usage 2015'. Available at: <http://www.homelessdublin.ie/accommodation-usage> (accessed 21 March 2016).

DRHE (Dublin Region Homeless Executive). 2016b. 'Homeless Accommodation Usage Q4 2015'. Available at: <http://www.homelessdublin.ie/publications?tags=38> (accessed 21 March 2016).

Hearne, R. 2011. *Public Private Partnerships in Ireland: Failed Experiment or Way Forward for the State.* Manchester: Manchester University Press.

Honohan, P. 2010. *The Irish Banking Crisis: Regulatory and Financial Stability Policy 2003–2008*. Irish Central Bank. Available at: <http://www.centralbank.ie/press-area/press-releases/Documents/TheIrishBankingCrisisRegulatoryandFinancialStability Policy2003-2008.pdf> (accessed 21 March 2016).

Housing Agency. 2010. '2010 National Housing Survey'. Available at: <http://www.housing.ie/Our-Services/Unfinished-Housing-Developments/2010-National-Housing-Survey> (accessed 21 March 2016).

Housing Agency. 2011. *Housing Needs 2011*. Available at: <http://www.environ.ie/sites/default/files/migrated-files/en/Publications/DevelopmentandHousing/Housing/FileDownLoad%2C27864%2Cen.pdf> (accessed 21 March 2016).

Housing Agency. 2013. '2013 National Housing Survey'. Available at: <http://www.housing.ie/Our-Services/Unfinished-Housing-Developments/2013-National-Housing-Survey> (accessed 21 March 2016).

Housing Agency. 2014. *Housing Supply Requirements in Ireland's Urban Settlements 2014–2018*. Available at: <http://www.housing.ie/Housing/media/Media/Publications/Future-Housing-Supply-Requirements-Report.pdf> (accessed 16 March 2016).

Irish Government. 2014. *Construction 2020: A Strategy for a Renewed Construction Sector*. Available at: <http://www.taoiseach.gov.ie/eng/Publications/Publications_2014/Construction_Strategy_-_14_May_2014.pdf> (accessed 21 March 2016).

Irish Times. 2014a. 'Rent Supplement Recipient Numbers Fall by 23%', 24 September. Available at: <http://www.irishtimes.com/news/social-affairs/rent-supplement-recipient-numbers-fall-by-23-1.1939335> (accessed 21 March 2016).

Irish Times. 2014b. 'More Social Housing and Funding are Urgently Needed', 30 April. Available at: <http://www.irishtimes.com/news/politics/more-social-housing-and-funding-are-urgently-needed-1.1777785> (accessed 21 March 2016).

Kitchin, R. 2015. 'Why the National Spatial Strategy Failed and Prospects for the National Planning Framework', 24 July. *IrelandAfterNAMA*. Available at: <https://irelandafternama.wordpress.com/2015/07/24/why-the-national-spatial-strategy-failed-and-prospects-for-the-national-planning-framework/> (accessed 21 March 2016).

Kitchin, R., Gleeson, J., Keaveney, K., and O'Callaghan, C. 2010. *A Haunted Landscape: Housing and Ghost Estates in Post-Celtic Tiger Ireland*. Working Paper 59, National Institute for Regional and Spatial Analysis. Available at: <https://www.maynoothuniversity.ie/sites/default/files/assets/document/WP59-A-Haunted-Landscape_1_0.pdf> (accessed 21 March 2016).

Kitchin, R., O'Callaghan, C., Boyle, M., Gleeson, J., and Keaveney, K. 2012. 'Placing Neoliberalism: The Rise and Fall of Ireland's Celtic Tiger'. *Environment and Planning A*, 44(6): 1302–26.

Kitchin, R., O'Callaghan, C., and Gleeson, J. 2014. 'The New Ruins of Ireland? Unfinished Estates in the Post-Celtic Tiger Era'. *International Journal of Urban and Regional Research*, 38(3): 1069–80.

Mahon, M. and O'Cinneide, M. 2010. 'Housing Supply and Residential Segregation in Ireland'. *Urban Studies*, 47: 2983–3012.

Morgenroth, E. 2014. *Projected Population Change and Housing Demand: A County Level Analysis*. QEC Research Notes 2014/2/3, ESRI, Dublin. Available at: <https://www.esri.ie/pubs/RN20140203.pdf> (accessed 21 March 2016).

O'Toole, F. 2009. *Ship of Fools: How Stupidity and Corruption Sank the Celtic Tiger.* London: Faber and Faber.

Ó Riain, S. 2014. *The Rise and Fall of Ireland's Celtic Tiger: Liberalism, Boom, and Bust.* Cambridge: Cambridge University Press.

Peter Bacon & Associates. 2009. *Over-Capacity in the Irish Hotel Industry and Required Elements of a Recovery Programme.* Available at: <http://www.ihf.ie/docu ments/HotelStudyFinalReport101109.pdf> (accessed 21 March 2016).

RTÉ (Raidió Teilifís Éireann). 2012. 'Over 50% of Irish Mortgages in Negative Equity–Davy', *RTÉ News*, 17 August. Available at: <http://www.rte.ie/news/2012/0817/ 333979-negative-equity/> (accessed 21 March 2016).

Savills HOK. 2007. 'Values Approach €60,000 Hectare'. *Irish Agricultural Land Research* May. Available at: <http://www.savills.ie/pdfs/articles/166.pdf> (accessed 21 March 2016).

Savills HOK. 2010. *Dublin Office Market in Minutes.* Available at: <http://pdf.euro. savills.co.uk/ireland-research/market-in-minutes/market-in-minutes–dublin-office- q2.pdf> (accessed 14 October 2011).

Weston, C. 2014. 'Banks Issue Legal Proceedings to Repossess 50,000 Homes', *Irish Independent*, 14 December.

16

Migration

Irial Glynn and Philip J. O'Connell

INTRODUCTION

The Great Recession and austerity had a series of profound impacts on Irish migration patterns. Outward migration increased dramatically, and inward migration declined, particularly in the depths of the recession from 2009 to 2012. Initially, emigration was dominated by the departure of relatively newly arrived immigrants. Between 2011 and 2013 emigration of Irish nationals exceeded that of non-Irish nationals, but that pattern was reversed again in 2014 and 2015.

This chapter begins with a review of the main trends in migration, documenting inflows and outflows and showing their impact on the structure of the population. It then examines the impact of the recession on immigrants in the Irish labour market, examining the extent to which immigrants were adversely affected by the contraction in employment and increase in unemployment. The discussion then turns to emigration, exploring trends in outward migration, the reasons for such patterns, the situation of Irish emigrants abroad, and the impact that this latest wave of emigration had on Irish society.

PRINCIPAL TRENDS IN MIGRATION

For most of the last two centuries, migration to and from Ireland has ebbed and flowed with the fortunes of the economy. The last two decades have been no different in this respect. In the mid-1990s, in the context of rapid economic growth and convergence with the Western European core, a long-established pattern of net outmigration, where outflows of emigrants exceeded inflows of immigrants, shifted to net inward migration, as shown in Figure 16.1.

The gross migratory inflow increased from around 20,000–25,000 per annum in the late 1980s to over 50,000 per annum after 2000 and to over 150,000 in the twelve months to April 2007. The impact of the Great Recession, with the dramatic decline in labour market conditions, can be clearly seen after 2008, with a sharp fall in the inflow to 42,000 in the twelve months to April 2010. Immigration then recovered somewhat to over 60,000 in 2013/14. Emigration declined during the period of rapid economic growth, to a low of 25,600 in the twelve months to April 2002. Emigration increased with the onset of the Great Recession, to 72,000 in 2008–9 and to 89,000 in 2012–13, but fell again to just over 80,000 in 2013–14 and 2014–15. As a result, net migration, which had peaked at a net inward flow of almost 105,000 in 2006–7, turned negative in 2009–10 and, having bottomed out at −34,400 in 2011–12, was down to -11,600 in 2014–15. Immigration plunged sharply after 2007, and emigration, which was already on the rise from about 2005, reflecting increased circular movement within Europe after European Union (EU) enlargement, increased steadily throughout the crisis period.

Table 16.1 shows cumulated migration between April 2008 and April 2015 by nationality. Over that period, total emigration amounted to 560,000 while immigration was 407,000: a net outward migration of 153,000 over six years. Irish nationals were the single largest mobile group: 263,000 Irish nationals emigrated during the crisis, and 120,000 returned. The return migrants would have included both those who had emigrated at an earlier time as well as those who emigrated during the crisis and retuned after a brief period abroad. Over the entire period there was net outward migration of 143,000 Irish nationals.

There was also substantial mobility among the nationals of the new post-EU enlargement member states (EU NMS). Over 110,000 of them left Ireland

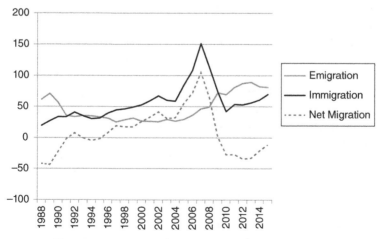

Figure 16.1. Gross and net migration flows, 1987–2015

Source: CSO, *Population and Migration Estimates*, various years.

Table 16.1. Total inward, outward, and net migration, 2008–15

	Inward	Outward 1,000s	Net
Irish	120.5	263.5	−143.0
UK	27.5	25.4	2.1
Rest of EU15	57.0	77.3	−20.3
EU12 NMS	84.6	110.8	−26.2
Rest of world	117.9	83.7	34.2
Total	407.3	560.7	−153.4

Source: CSO 2013, 2015, _Population and Migration Estimates._

between 2008 and 2015. This was a significant outward migration, equivalent to almost 45 per cent of the estimated population of EU NMS nationals resident in Ireland in 2008. However, substantial inward migration continued among this group: almost 84,000 EU NMS nationals migrated into Ireland during the crisis, with the result that net emigration among this group amounted to just over 26,000.

Nationals of the older pre-enlargement states, excluding the UK ('old EU13'), were also highly mobile: over 77,000 emigrated and 57,000 immigrated, yielding a net emigration of 20,000 between 2008 and 2015. While these movements are small in numerical terms, they are significant when compared with the population of old EU nationals in Ireland.

Migration from the rest of the world, a very broad category which accounts for almost 30 per cent of all inflows, increased: inward migration was almost 118,000 during the crisis, offset by outflows of 84,000, yielding a net inflow of 34,000. Most of the inflow from outside the EU related to inward migration of highly skilled workers, with employment permits to meet skill shortages, as well as students.

So while there was a substantial migratory outflow during the Great Recession, this was partially offset by an inflow of immigrants, especially from outside the EU. This can be seen in the data on the number of foreign residents in Ireland, which peaked before the recession at over 575,000, or 12.8 per cent of the total population, in 2008. Their numbers declined during the recession, to 550,400 in 2010, but recovered to 578,000 in 2015, slightly exceeding the pre-recession peak. The single largest group of non-nationals is from the EU NMS. There were 133,000 nationals of the EU NMS in 2006 (accounting for 3 per cent of the total population) and this increased to 248,000 in 2008— (5.5 per cent of the population). That number declined in the recession to 228,600 in 2013, but increased again to over 237,000 in 2015.

The number of immigrants from the old EU 13 (excluding the UK) has fallen from over 52,000 in 2010 to less than 32,000 in 2015, a sharp decline of 40 per cent. Nationals from the rest of the world (outside Europe) have

Table 16.2. Total population 2006 to 2015, classified by nationality

	2006	2008	2010 *1,000s*	2012	2014	2015
Irish	3802.4	3909.5	3994.7	4035.0	4045.3	4057.4
Total Non-Irish	430.6	575.6	560.0	550.4	564.3	578.0
UK	115.5	117.9	115.9	113.0	114.9	115.5
Old EU13	43.8	50.8	52.4	45.5	38.1	31.7
EU NMS	132.5	247.7	233.0	229.4	230.7	237.4
Rest of World	138.8	159.2	158.7	162.5	180.5	193.4
Total Population	4232.9	4485.1	4554.8	4585.4	4609.1	4635.4
	%					
Irish	89.8	87.2	87.7	88.0	87.8	87.5
Total Non-Irish	10.2	12.8	12.3	12.0	12.2	12.5
UK	2.7	2.6	2.5	2.5	2.5	2.5
Old EU13	1.0	1.1	1.2	1.0	0.8	0.7
EU NMS	3.1	5.5	5.1	5.0	5.0	5.1
Rest of World	3.3	3.5	3.5	3.5	3.97	4.2
Total Population	100.0	100.0	100.0	100.0	100.0	100.0

Source: CSO 2013, 2015.

increased in number since 2010—to 193,000 (or over 4 per cent of the total population) in 2015. This is consistent with the data on immigration presented in Table 16.2, and may be partly related to the influx of highly skilled immigrants to meet skill demands in particular sectors, particularly information technology (IT) and health.

THE IMPACT OF THE RECESSION ON IMMIGRANTS IN THE LABOUR MARKET

Employment is a key element of economic integration and social inclusion. It leads to financial independence, and allows people to contribute to society and avoid the risk of poverty and social exclusion in their host country. Through employment, immigrants can build networks, develop their language skills, and increase participation in society. Job loss can be associated with poverty, psychological distress, and broader social exclusion. In general, immigrants are more exposed to the consequences of economic downturns, and in this section we explore the impact of the recession on immigrants in Ireland.

Most research on immigrants in the labour market focuses on patterns of employment and unemployment among labour market participants. However, the first element of immigrant integration concerns continued presence in the country. We have seen that, during the recession, there was substantial outward migration, particularly among the relatively recently arrived nationals of the EU NMS, offset to some extent by inward migration, and that the population of old EU country nationals declined significantly. A second dimension of integration is participation in the labour market. Throughout the boom, asylum seekers awaiting decisions on their refugee claims were denied the right to work in Ireland. Asylum seekers are accommodated collectively in Direct Provision centres and receive small allowances. This exclusion from participation in the Irish economy and society remained unchanged throughout the recession.

A second group with restricted access to the Irish labour market saw that access become further restricted during the recession when, in 2009 under a revised policy, spouses, partners, and dependents of general employment permits holders could not access the Irish labour market without applying for their own employment permit. Such permits allow access to a restricted range of occupations and require a labour market test. This was part of a wider set of revisions to policy at the onset of the recession, which, in other respects, could be regarded as increasing restrictions on 'outsiders', particularly immigrants from outside the EU, while liberalizing certain provisions for those already resident in Ireland, such as extending the time period that holders of employment permits could remain in the country to look for work following redundancy.

In examining observed patterns of labour market activity, it is essential to be aware that our statistics reflect the results of a selection process in which those who had a particularly negative experience of the labour market may have exited the country and are thus not observed. Table 16.3 tracks the trends in employment by nationality since 2004. The role of immigrants in meeting the demand for labour in the booming Irish economy between 2004 and 2007 is clearly evident. The number of non-Irish nationals in employment increased from 164,400 at the end of 2004 to 341,500 at the end of 2007—the peak of employment and immigration. This represented a very rapid increase of immigrants in the labour market, from less than 9 per cent to almost 16 per cent of total employment, between 2004 and 2007. Over that three-year period, the total number of non-Irish nationals in employment more than doubled. The growth in numbers from the EU NMS was particularly strong: over 300 per cent.

After 2007, however, immigrants began to lose ground in the Irish labour market. Total employment fell by over 14 per cent between the end of 2007 and the end of 2012. While employment among Irish nationals fell by 13 per cent, it fell by 21 per cent among non-Irish nationals. Non-Irish nationals accounted for almost 16 per cent of total employment in 2007 but this share had fallen below 15 per cent by the end of 2012. Employment among NMS nationals contracted by over 26 per cent between 2007 and 2012, and among UK nationals by 18 per cent. The biggest employment losses occurred

Table 16.3. Employment by nationality, 2004–15 (Q4)

	2004	2007	2012	2015	2004–7	2007–12	2012–15
			1,000s			*% Change*	
Irish	1735.1	1814.5	1579.9	1682.24	4.6	−12.9	6.5
Non-Irish	164.4	341.5	269.2	300.9	107.7	−21.2	11.8
of which:							
UK	43.6	56.8	46.5	53.5	30.3	−18.1	15.1
EU13	27.3	32.4	29.1	17.5	18.7	−10.2	−39.9
EU NMS	40.9	171.3	125.9	137.9	318.8	−26.5	9.5
Other	52.6	81.0	67.7	92.0	54.0	−16.4	35.9
Total Persons	1899.05	2156.0	1848.9	1983.0	13.5	−14.2	7.3
		%					
Non-Irish	8.7	15.8	14.6	1542			

Source: CSO (2016). *Quarterly National Household Survey.*

in construction, in the wholesale and retail trade, and in accommodation and food services; these sectors had expanded substantially with large increases in migrant labour during the boom years.

In the more recent context of economic recovery, total employment increased by almost 5 per cent between 2012 and 2015. Employment among Irish natives increased by 6.5 per cent and among non-Irish by almost 12 per cent—a significant rebound. The rate of growth was greatest (36 per cent) among those from outside the EU, reflecting demand for skills in short supply among Europeans (10 per cent). Employment of nationals of the older EU countries (other than UK) continued to decline, by a dramatic 40 per cent between 2012 and 2015.

The national unemployment rate increased from 4 per cent of the labour force in 2007 to 15 per cent in 2012 (see Figure 16.2). Unemployment increased by over 220,000 people overall; by 185,000 among Irish nationals and 36,000 among non-Irish nationals. As the recession deepened, the gap in unemployment rates grew wider between Irish and non-Irish nationals. At the end of 2007 the unemployment rate among Irish nationals was 4.4 per cent, compared with 5.8 per cent among non-Irish nationals: a gap of less than 1.5 per cent. Following substantial job losses in late 2008 and early 2009, the unemployment rate among non-Irish nationals was 15 per cent in 2009, 5 per cent higher than among Irish nationals. Unemployment continued to grow until the middle of 2012, although the gap between Irish and non-Irish nationals declined somewhat. Since then unemployment has trended downwards, so that by Q4 2015, the unemployment rates were 8.3 per cent among Irish and 10.3 per cent among non-Irish.

During the period of the Celtic Tiger and in the context of the large influx of new immigrants, a substantial body of research emerged showing that

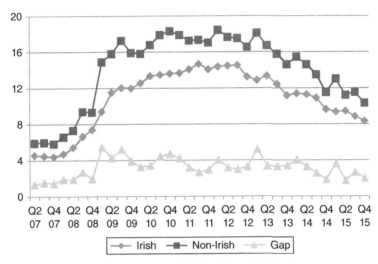

Figure 16.2. Unemployment rates, Irish and non-Irish nationality, 2007–15
Source: CSO, *Quarterly Household Survey*, various years.

immigrants suffered multiple disadvantages in the Irish labour market. Unemployment was shown to be consistently higher among immigrants than natives (McGinnity et al. 2013). Immigrants tended to be overeducated: employed at occupational levels below their skill level (Barrett and Duffy 2008; O'Connell and McGinnity 2008). There was also evidence of substantial wage penalties, whereby immigrants earned less than Irish nationals, and this varied by national group (Barrett and McCarthy 2007). Higher rates of discrimination in the labour market were also reported among immigrants (O'Connell and McGinnity 2008). Given that these studies sought to control for the composition of immigrant groups—in terms of age, education, gender, and so on—these results point to an *immigrant penalty* associated with the status of immigrants per se, rather than to any personal or human capital characteristics that might lead to poorer labour market outcomes. We have already seen that the recession led to a dramatic deterioration in the Irish economy after 2008 and that immigrants were more exposed to its consequences, with greater employment losses and higher unemployment. Given this experience, and against the backdrop of disadvantage experienced by immigrant groups during the boom, it is important to assess whether immigrant *penalties* persisted or increased during the recession.

McGinnity and colleagues (2014) compared labour market outcomes in 2007 and 2012 in their assessment of the impact of the Great Recession. They found that, in 2007, at the end of the boom, all migrant groups, apart from old EU13 and EU NMS, had lower employment rates than Irish nationals, with

Africans showing by far the lowest employment. All nationality groups experienced a fall in employment by 2012. However, controlling for other relevant factors, the employment gap between Irish and all other groups narrowed during the recession. They found a similar pattern in relation to unemployment: most non-national groups experienced higher unemployment risks than Irish nationals in 2007. The unemployment gap was particularly high for Africans. All groups, including Irish nationals, experienced a sharp increase in unemployment. However, the relative gap in unemployment between Irish and other groups did not generally increase—with two exceptions: the rise in unemployment among the EU NMS group was somewhat steeper than that of the Irish, and the size of the African disadvantage increased over time. These results suggest a general pattern of persistence rather than intensification of immigrant penalties over the course of recession. Kelly and colleagues (2015) found that labour market outcomes for newly nationalized immigrants deteriorated in 2012 and 2014, relative to Irish nationals' unemployment, but this appears to have been due less to the impact of the business cycle and more to the personal characteristics of this particular group: there was a marked increase in naturalizations of immigrants from 2011, and many were refugees who had been excluded from the labour market for extended periods of time while awaiting decisions on their asylum claims.

Barrett and colleagues (2014) examined the impact of the recession on the immigrant earnings gap. They found that average hourly earnings increased by 7.5 per cent among Irish nationals between 2006 and 2009 while immigrants' earnings fell by over 8 per cent. Disaggregating among immigrants, they found that all EU groups experienced increases while non-EU nationals' earnings fell. They also found that, when relevant characteristics were controlled for, the large increase in the wage gap between immigrants and Irish nationals between 2006 and 2009 was eliminated, suggesting that the gap was driven by changes in the composition of the immigrant workforce. A key element of this was a decline in the employment share of graduates among immigrants. Indeed, the analysis found that, controlling for these differences, the immigrant wage penalty actually declined, suggesting that immigrants had become better integrated into the labour market over time.

Corroboration for these somewhat surprising findings about immigrant experiences during the recession can be found in the analysis of discrimination in the Irish labour market by Kingston, McGinnity, and O'Connell (2015). They examined the extent to which self-reported discrimination varies across different national ethnic groups, and whether discrimination increased between 2004 and 2010. They found that immigrants experienced higher rates of discrimination both in looking for work, and in the workplace, in both boom and recession. There was substantial variation in discrimination across national ethnic groups. In looking for work, ethnicity was particularly important: Black Africans and EU nationals of minority ethnicity were particularly likely to experience this form of discrimination. In the workplace, most national ethnic groups, apart from White UK and White EU13 groups, were more likely than White Irish to experience discrimination in 2004. In 2010, the Black African, White NMS, and White Non-EU groups experienced more discrimination than White Irish nationals. However, contrary to expectations, they did not find that discrimination increased significantly in the twin contexts of recession and the growth in the immigrant population between 2004 and 2010. In looking for work, the gap in reported discrimination between immigrants and White Irish fell between 2004 and 2010: in the workplace the gap remained relatively stable. In seeking to explain why reports of discrimination did not increase during recession, Kingston and colleagues (2013) suggest many immigrants in 2004 were newcomers and that by 2010 many immigrants might have gained more experience and knowledge of the Irish labour market, and have established networks. Similarly, on the employers' side, as immigrant groups became more established in the Irish labour market over the 2004–10 period, employers may have become better able to identify the work-related characteristics of immigrant job applicants in a process where familiarity breeds tolerance rather than contempt.

Notwithstanding differences in interpretation, these studies share a common pattern of findings that suggest that while immigrants suffer multiple disadvantages and penalties in the Irish labour market, these disadvantages do not appear to have intensified during the Great Recession. Indeed, there is some evidence to suggest that wage penalties and discrimination in looking for work may have declined over the period, perhaps in spite of the recession.

EMIGRATION

The Scale of Emigration Pre- and Post-Recession

Ireland has a long history of emigration. Millions departed throughout the nineteenth century, especially from the Famine (1845–52) onward. Indeed, the Irish moved across the Atlantic at a rate more than twice that of any other European country (per capita) from the 1840s to the turn of the twentieth century (Hatton and Williamson 1998: 75). This was reflected most starkly by the demise of Ireland's population from over 6.5 million in 1851 to less than 4.5 million just fifty years later. Indeed, over 2.5 million Irish-born people resided abroad in 1901 (Delaney 2011). After partition in 1922, emigration continued from the newly independent southern state, especially in the 1950s and 1980s, two decades marked by serious economic difficulties. In contrast with earlier trends, most emigrants went to England rather than America. During the 1950s, Ireland shared the ignominy of being the only country in Europe to see its population decline with East Germany, such was the effect of emigration (Daly 2006: 183). The return of significant economic problems in the 1980s resulted in sizeable out-migration taking place again.

Many of the 1980s generation of emigrants later returned during the 'Celtic Tiger' era. People continued to leave Ireland during this period although the scale and character of emigration changed considerably. From 2002 to 2007, between 11,000 and approximately 13,500 young Irish citizens travelled to Australia each year as part of that country's working holiday scheme (Gilmartin 2013: 11). New Zealand ran a comparable programme that attracted around 2,000 Irish per annum. Approximately 10,000 Irish citizens also registered for national insurance numbers in the UK annually during the same period (Walter 2008). Considering the low levels of unemployment in Ireland at the time, much of this movement was not the result of domestic economic pressure but a desire to leave, sometimes temporarily, for lifestyle-related and professional reasons.

During the Great Recession, emigration from Ireland rose considerably. Whereas 245,900 people left the country in the eight years between 2000 and 2007, nearly 610,000 departed between 2008 and 2015. First, immigrants began to leave in increasing numbers. Thereafter, Irish citizens started to catch up and subsequently overtake their foreign counterparts between 2011 and 2013, before numbers decreased somewhat, as demonstrated in Figure 16.3. It is the departure of Irish citizens, rather than foreign citizens,

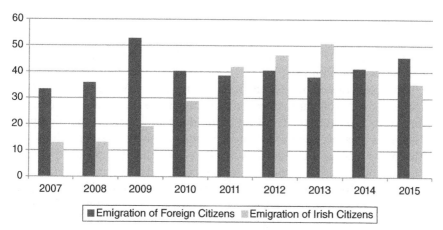

Figure 16.3. Emigration from Ireland by nationality, 2006–15
Source: CSO, *Population and Migration Estimates*, various years.

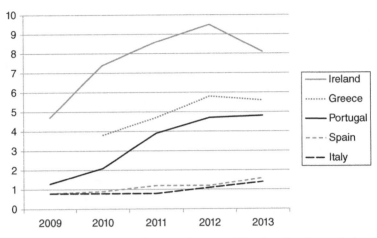

Figure 16.4. Gross emigration of nationals per 1,000 of national population from selected European countries, 2009–13

Source: Eurostat 2015 and Recchi and Salamońska 2015.

which has dominated national debates about emigration because of the notable ties these people have with communities and families in Ireland and because of how much the Irish state has invested in their education. Moreover, the net migration of foreign citizens between 2009 and 2015 was approximately –10,000, compared with a net migration rate of over –140,000 for Irish citizens in the same time period.

Recent Irish emigration patterns contrast starkly with those of other Eurozone countries that also introduced a range of austerity measures in the wake of the economic crisis, and experienced economic contraction and high unemployment, most notably Portugal, Italy, Greece, and Spain (see, for example, Matsaganis and Leventi 2014). As shown in Figure 16.4, the rate of departure among Irish citizens reached much higher levels per capita than in these other crisis countries.

The higher rate of migration from Ireland may have been due to Irish citizens' access to labour markets, particularly the UK, Australia, and Canada, which recovered from the Great Recession more rapidly than other European economies. Such access was facilitated by the existence of working holiday visa agreements between Ireland and Australia, New Zealand, and Canada, which allowed young Irish citizens to stay in these states for up to two years. Furthermore, Irish emigrants possessed valuable transnational human capital desired by liberal labour markets that emerged quite rapidly from the crisis. They also spoke the same language and shared similar cultural traits as their hosts and were able to call upon extensive Irish networks to further facilitate such moves abroad (Glynn 2015).

Reasons for Leaving

Economic crisis and austerity provided a significant impetus for many to leave, as can be seen in Figure 16.5, which shows reasons for emigration over time. A major survey of Irish emigrants conducted by Glynn, Kelly, and Mac Éinrí (2013) found that, in 2008, the most popular reason for emigrating was 'to travel'. But soon after the crisis hit, the vast majority of emigrants were leaving 'to find a job'. While unemployment was a major driving factor, underemployment and lack of job satisfaction also spurred many to emigrate. Although the economic recession was not a major motivating factor for some when leaving, it may have played a significant role in their ability to return.

The Central Statistics Office (CSO) (2014, 2015) estimates that, between 2009 and 2015, almost half of those aged over 15 who moved abroad were employed before they left Ireland. A quarter comprised students and nearly 20 per cent were unemployed (see Figure 16.6). The CSO data equate roughly with that produced by Glynn, Kelly, and Mac Éinrí (2013) for Irish emigrants. Glynn, Kelly, and Mac Éinrí found that a sizeable proportion of those who had been employed in full-time jobs before they emigrated left because they wanted to travel and to experience another culture, as had occurred throughout the early 2000s. These were often people with transferable qualifications in demand in other countries, such as IT professionals. Others, such as medical professionals, left because they were dissatisfied with their career prospects and employment conditions (see Gouda et al. 2015; Humphries et al. 2015). Although austerity measures contributed to a rise in the emigration of health

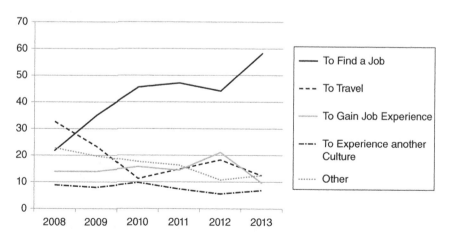

Figure 16.5. Reasons for departure (in per cent) of Irish emigrants, 2008–13
Source: Glynn, Kelly, and Mac Éinrí 2013.

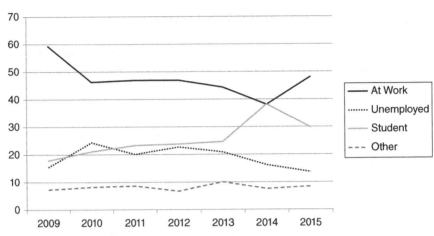

Figure 16.6. Economic status (in per cent) of emigrants aged over 15, 2009–15

Source: CSO, *Population and Migration Estimates,* various years.

professionals, young Irish doctors and nurses had always departed in substantial numbers, so this did not represent an entirely new phenomenon.

Among those Irish emigrants who were either unemployed or underemployed before departing, the rationale for emigration was more straightforward: most emigrated in order to find work. Students who graduated in the years hardest hit by the recession struggled to break into the job market in Ireland. Fewer graduate positions presented themselves and various students who emigrated after completion of their course cited the competition that they often faced from more experienced candidates who had lost their job and who consequently applied for junior positions. Many left for further study, but the majority of new Irish graduates who emigrated did so to find work.

EFFECTS OF EMIGRATION

Impact on Migrants

The emigrant experience generally appears to have been a positive one for those Irish citizens who left in recent years (NYCI 2013: 9; Ryan and Kurdi 2014: 42–3). While less than half had full-time jobs prior to departing, almost 85 per cent found full-time jobs abroad (Glynn, Kelly, and Mac Éinrí 2013: 65). This enabled many to experience a higher standard of living abroad. Whereas Irish emigrants rated their quality of life at home before departure at an average of 5.5 out of 10, the equivalent average rating for their quality of life abroad measured 7.9. Emigrants were also much happier with their jobs, salaries, and employment prospects (Glynn, Kelly, and Mac Éinrí 2013: 66–8). Unfortunately, no equivalent information is available for foreign citizens who left Ireland.

While many Irish emigrants, particularly those living in Australia and New Zealand, emphasized the positive aspects of living abroad, they sometimes experienced homesickness and many spoke about the difficulties that can arise when living in a different country from one's family. Although emigrants benefited financially from their move, they frequently paid an emotional price for leaving. Understandably, emigrants missed their families most of all (Glynn, Kelly, and Mac Éinrí 2013: 69–71).

Impact on Irish Society

While almost half of adult emigrants from 2009 to 2015 were in full-time employment prior to leaving, over half were not, and most would presumably have been in search of employment had they remained. Therefore, emigration helped to substantially reduce national unemployment figures and the burden on the state to provide social protection. This was particularly true for those previously employed in the construction industry, who made up 17 per cent of Irish emigrants who moved between 2008 and 2013 (Glynn, Kelly, and Mac Éinrí 2013: 39). Between 2000 and 2008, construction companies built an average of almost 68,000 residential units every year, whereas between 2008 and 2013, the average number built per annum was less than 14,000. Similarly, the public health sector reduced the number of its employees by 11 per cent between 2007 and 2013 (HSE 2014). The moratorium on recruitment to the public sector resulted in many newly qualified health and education professionals leaving Ireland—almost 10 per cent of emigrants came from the health and social work sectors, and over 5 per cent from the education sector. If Irish citizens had been unable to access labour markets in the UK and outside the EU in the numbers that they have been, it is very likely that Ireland would have experienced even higher rates of unemployment than it did in recent years.

Emigration can have significant disadvantages for those left behind. Mosca and Barrett's (2014: 1) study of Irish people over the age of 50 found that 'depressive symptoms and feelings of loneliness increase among the parents of migrant children'—especially for mothers. The consequences of emigration for local communities are difficult to measure. Glynn, Kelly, and Mac Éinrí (2013) found that a clear majority—65 per cent—of respondents to their representative national household survey viewed emigration as having either a 'negative' or 'very negative' impact on their area. A series of common themes emerged from responses to an open-ended question asking household respondents to elaborate on this issue. The most frequent topics to emerge concerned a perceived loss of general 'vibrancy' and 'energy' associated with younger residents of the locality and the emergence of a 'generation gap'. Respondents also mentioned that there were less people involved in community activities and clubs, as well as an overall reduction in 'community spirit'. Less-accessible rural areas appeared to feel these ramifications most due to their smaller size.

A notable reduction in the number of people aged in their twenties in Ireland has also taken place in recent years due to high emigration rates and low birth rates in the late 1980s and early 1990s. The number of 20 to 24-year-olds and 25 to 29-year-olds in Ireland dropped by over a third and over a quarter respectively between 2008 and 2015 (Kenny 2015). This has caused some researchers to raise the issue of whether this may lead to an increasingly unfavourable age dependency ratio in the future (NYCI 2013: 82).

Graduates are clearly over-represented among Irish citizens leaving. Glynn, Kelly, and Mac Éinrí (2013: 35) found that the number of Irish emigrants with a tertiary education qualification is over 64 per cent. Another 6.5 per cent had completed skilled apprenticeships, which usually involved four years of vocational training. By contrast, those who did not complete their secondary school education or attain an equivalent qualification were significantly under-represented among emigrants when compared with the Irish population more generally, as shown in Figure 16.7. This is because

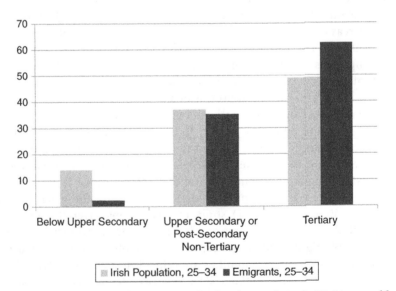

Figure 16.7. Education levels (in per cent) of Irish population's 25–34 year olds in 2012 compared with Irish emigrants, 2008–13

Sources: OECD 2014 and Glynn, Kelly, and Mac Éinrí 2013.

countries such as Australia and Canada operate immigration policies that seek to attract people with higher-level skills in demand in their labour market. No such barriers exist to deter unskilled Irish citizens from moving to Britain or other EU states, yet emigration rates among those with lower education or skills appear to be relatively low. Perhaps the prospect of encountering stiff competition for low-skilled jobs in other EU countries, the convergence of wages between Ireland and the rest of the EU, and the maintenance of the relatively generous Irish welfare system (Cannon and Murphy 2015: 8) means that the costs and risks of migrating are too high for unskilled Irish citizens.

The CSO (2014, 2015) has recently begun to provide education profiles for migrants over 15 years of age. These show a more mixed picture than that set out in Figure 16.7. Unfortunately, the data do not distinguish between nationalities. These aggregate data suggest that less than half of all emigrants from Ireland over the 2009–15 period had third-level education. This is substantially less than Glynn, Kelly, and Mac Éinrí's (2013) estimate that 64 per cent of Irish emigrants who left between 2008 and 2013 had a third-level education, and suggests that Irish nationals were over-represented among the gross outflow of graduates during the recession.

Whether these patterns represent a 'brain drain' is unclear, and it is necessary to consider immigration flows as well as emigration. Indeed, many Irish citizens returning from short-term working holiday visas have been counted among the immigrant inflow in subsequent years. Table 16.4 shows accumulated migration flows over the previous twelve months from April 2009 to April 2015 by level of educational attainment. Almost 240,000 third-level graduates emigrated from Ireland since May 2008, virtually 45 per cent of the outflow. However, the immigrant inflow is dominated by the highly qualified: between 2008 and 2015 almost 190,000 graduates migrated into Ireland, 53 per cent of the total inflow. This resulted in a net outflow of

Table 16.4. Inward, outward, and net migration by educational attainment, May 2008–April 2015

	Immigration		Emigration		Net	
	000s	%	000s	%	000s	%
Higher Secondary and Below	111.6	31.3	211.1	40.0	−99.7	58.3
PLC*	25.4	7.1	44.1	8.4	−18.7	10.9
Third Level**	189.1	53.0	237.2	44.9	−48.2	28.2
Not Stated	31.0	8.7	35.5	6.7	−4.5	2.6
All	356.9	100.0	528.0	100.0	−170.9	100.0

Note: * Technical or Vocational, Advanced Certificate or Diploma
** Third level degree or above
Source: CSO 2014, 2015.

–48,000. Among those with secondary education, there was a substantial exodus (211,000) but the influx was just over half this (112,000). As a result of these divergent patterns, net migration of those with secondary education (58 per cent of the total) far exceeds net emigration of graduates (28 per cent).

With regard to the demand side of the labour market, the moratorium on recruitment to the public sector resulted in many newly qualified health and education professionals leaving Ireland. Since there were so few new jobs available in these areas, it seems difficult to term the outflow of graduate emigrants as a brain drain since these emigrants' skills would most likely not have been fully utilized in Ireland if they had remained—at least in the short term. Nevertheless, if Ireland requires a large number of medical workers and teachers in the future that cannot be met by annual graduate figures, will emigrants return?

Obviously, some degree of return takes place every year. Between 2010 and 2015, for example, almost 100,000 Irish citizens returned to the country, although this paled in comparison to the outflow of over 240,000 Irish citizens (CSO 2015). Whether emigrants return or not, however, depends partly on the immigration regimes of destination states, as well as on conditions in Ireland. The UK has remained the single most popular destination for Irish emigrants, who can remain there indefinitely. Yet the majority of Irish emigrants since 2008 have moved to non-EU destinations, namely Australia, Canada, the USA, New Zealand, and the Gulf States. Most Irish migrants initially move to one of these destinations on temporary permits, such as a one- or two-year working holiday visa or a skilled work permit of a limited duration. It is difficult to foresee how many Irish emigrants will be able to transfer from temporary visas to permanent residency in non-EU destinations, as this often depends on a wide variety of economic and social factors in the host countries. Ireland's economic situation and the availability of jobs were the two most common factors that Irish emigrants indicated would influence their chances of returning (Glynn, Kelly, and Mac Éinrí 2013: 102). Nevertheless, a 2014 survey of medical professionals who emigrated from Ireland concluded that doctors, nurses, and midwives are emigrating from Ireland in search of better working conditions, clear career progression pathways, and a better practice environment (Humphries et al. 2015).

Return migration of Irish citizens remained low in 2014 and 2015 despite the Irish economy's recovery. In addition to labour market demand and working conditions, other factors likely to influence return flows of Irish emigrants include the state of the public finances, the availability of housing, the quality of public services, and the distribution of the tax burden in financing those services.

CONCLUSION

The Great Recession and austerity had a series of profound impacts on Irish migration patterns. First and foremost, outward migration increased dramatically, particularly from 2009 to 2012 in the depths of the recession. Initial emigration was dominated by the departure of relatively newly arrived immigrants.

Immigration fell sharply after 2008 but has been increasing again since 2013 with economic recovery. These trends would suggest the sharp fall in inward migration was a temporary response to the recession and we are likely to see renewed inflows in response to anticipated economic growth.

The substantial migratory outflow during the Great Recession was partially offset by an inflow of immigrants. Within this general trend, it appears that, over the course of the recession, there was high net migration of Irish, as well as other Europeans, with the exception of UK nationals. Part of this appears to be related to skills: this chapter has shown that Irish emigrants were disproportionately drawn from those with higher education, and additional evidence suggested that the share of graduates among the immigrant population declined over the crisis. While this bears the appearance of a brain drain, it should be noted that the outflow of graduates during the recession was at least partially offset by an inflow of highly qualified immigrants, which also included returning highly qualified Irish emigrants. The highly skilled inflow also included a growing number from non-European origins: this is attributable to the employment permits regime, which is designed to address skills shortages from outside the EU.

Immigrants were hit hard by the recession: they experienced a greater fall in employment than did Irish natives, and they suffered higher rates of unemployment. Prior to the recession, immigrants suffered multiple disadvantages in the Irish labour market: they had lower employment and higher unemployment, they tended to be overeducated and underpaid, and experienced higher rates of discrimination than Irish nationals. However, taking into account changes in the composition of the immigrant population, the employment, unemployment, and wage gaps that existed prior to the recession did not widen. Contrary to expectations, the recession did not make things worse. Discrimination is high among visibly different ethnic minorities, but this did not increase, and there is some evidence of a fall in discrimination against ethnic and national minorities. This would be consistent with Fanning's (2015) argument that there was no evidence of a political backlash against immigration during the economic downturn, although he does note evidence of an increase in racist incidents.

The surge in emigration of native Irish in recent years, even continuing after the worst of the recession was over, can be characterized as having some positive effects at an individual level for migrants achieving employment and career progress, as well as helping to ease the pressure on the labour market and on the public finances. However, this has come at a significant social cost and it will be some time before it will be possible to measure the full extent of the losses incurred by families and communities as well as how this will affect the supply of highly skilled workers to the economy.

REFERENCES

Barrett, A., Bergin, A., Kelly, E., and McGuinness, S. 2014. 'Ireland's Recession and the Immigrant/Native Earnings Gap', IZA Discussion Paper No. 8459. Bonn: Forschungsinstitut zur Zukunft der Arbeit.

Barrett, A. and Duffy, D. 2008. 'Are Ireland's Immigrants Integrating into its Labor Market?'. *International Migration Review*, 42(3): 597–619.

Barrett, A. and McCarthy, Y. 2007. 'Immigrants in a Booming Economy: Analysing their Earnings and Welfare Dependence'. *Labour*, 21(4–5): 789–808.

Cannon, B. and Murphy, M. P. 2015. 'Where are the Pots and Pans? Collective Responses in Ireland to Neoliberalization in a Time of Crisis: Learning from Latin America'. *Irish Political Studies*, 30(1): 1–19.

CSO (Central Statistics Office). 2013. *Population and Migration Estimates*. CSO: Dublin.

CSO (Central Statistics Office). 2014. *Population and Migration Estimates*. CSO: Dublin.

CSO (Central Statistics Office). 2015. *Population and Migration Estimates*. CSO: Dublin.

CSO (Central Statistics Office). 2016. *Quarterly National Household Survey: QNHS Release-Time Series Tables*. Available at: <http://www.cso.ie/en/qnhs/releasesandpublications/qnhspostcensusofpopulation2011/> (accessed 28 June 2016).

Daly, M. E. 2006. *The Slow Failure: Population Decline and Independent Ireland, 1920–1973*. Madison, WI: University of Wisconsin Press.

Delaney, E. 2011. 'Directions in Historiography: Our Island Story? Towards a Transnational History of Late Modern Ireland'. *Irish Historical Studies*, 37(148): 599–621.

Eurostat. 2015. *Emigration by Five Year Age Group, Sex and Citizenship*. Available at: <http://ec.europa.eu/eurostat/en/web/products-datasets/-/migr_emi1ctz> (accessed 11 September 2015).

Fanning, B. 2015. 'Immigration, the Celtic Tiger and the Economic Crisis'. *Irish Studies Review*, 24(1): 9–20.

Gilmartin, M. 2013. 'Changing Ireland, 2000–2012: Immigration, Emigration and Inequality'. *Irish Geography*, 46(1–2): 91–111.

Glynn, I. 2015. 'Just One of the "PIIGS" or a European Outlier? Examining Irish Emigration from a Comparative Perspective'. *Irish Journal of Sociology*, 23(2): 93–113.

Glynn, I., Kelly, T., and Mac Éinrí, P. 2013. *Irish Emigration in an Age of Austerity*. Cork: University College Cork.

Gouda, P., Kevin, K., Evans, D., Goggin, D., McGrath, D., Last, J., Hennessy, M., Arnett, R., O'Flynn, S., Dunne, F., and O'Donovan, D. 2015. 'Ireland's Medical Brain Drain: Migration Intentions of Irish Medical Students'. *Human Resources for Health*, 13(11): 1–9.

Hatton, T. J. and Williamson, J. G. 1998. *The Age of Mass Migration: Causes and Economic Impact*. Oxford: Oxford University Press.

HSE (Health Service Executive). 2014. *Annual Report and Financial Statements 2013*. Dublin: HSE.

Humphries, N., McAleese, S., Matthews, A., and Brugha, R. 2015. '"Emigration is a Matter of Self-Preservation. The Working Conditions…are Killing Us Slowly": Qualitative Insights into Health Professional Emigration from Ireland'. *Human Resources for Health*, 13(35): 1–13.

Kelly, E., McGuinness, S., O'Connell, P., González Pandiella, A., and Haugh, D. 2015. 'How Did Immigrants Fare in the Irish Labour Market over the Great Recession?' UCD Geary Institute Working Paper WP2015/13. Dublin: University College Dublin.

Kenny, C. 2015. 'Recovery? Tide of Emigration is Turning, but Slowly'. *Irish Times*, 29 August.

Kingston, G., O'Connell, P., and Kelly, E. 2013. *Ethnicity and Nationality in the Irish Labour Market: Evidence from the QNHS Equality Module*. Dublin: Economic and Social Research Institute, Equality Authority.

Kingston, G., McGinnity, F., and O'Connell, P. 2015. 'Discrimination in the Labour Market: Nationality, Ethnicity and the Recession'. *Work, Employment and Society*, 29(2): 213–32.

McGinnity, F., Quinn, E., Kingston, G., and O'Connell, P. 2013. *Annual Monitoring Report on Integration, 2012*. Dublin: ESRI and the Integration Centre.

McGinnity, F., Quinn, E., Kingston, G., and O'Connell, P. 2014. *Annual Monitoring Report on Integration, 2013*. Dublin: ESRI and the Integration Centre.

Matsaganis, M. and Leventi, C. 2014. 'The Distributional Impact of Austerity and the Recession in Southern Europe'. *South European Society and Politics*, 19(3): 393–412.

Mosca, I. and Barrett, A. 2014. 'The Impact of Adult Child Emigration on the Mental Health of Older Parents', IZA Discussion Paper No. 8037. Bonn: Forschungsinstitut zur Zukunft der Arbeit.

NYCI (National Youth Council of Ireland). 2013. *Time to Go: A Qualitative Research Study Exploring the Experience and Impact of Emigration on Ireland's Youth*. Dublin: National Youth Council of Ireland.

O'Connell, P. and McGinnity, F. 2008. 'Immigrants at Work: Ethnicity and Nationality in the Irish Labour Market', *Economic and Social Research Institute (ESRI) Research Series*.

OECD (Organisation for Economic Co-operation and Development). 2014. *Education at a Glance 2014*. Paris: Organisation for Economic Co-operation and Development.

Recchi, E. and Salamońska, J. 2015. 'Bad Times at Home, Good Times to Move? The (Not So) Changing Landscape of Intra-EU Migration'. In *A Political Sociology of the Euro-Crisis*, ed. V. Guiraudon, C. Ruzza, and H. J. Trenz. Basingstoke: Palgrave Macmillan.

Ryan, L. and E. Kurdi. 2014. *Young, Highly Qualified Migrants: The Experiences and Expectations of Recently Arrived Irish Teachers in Britain*. Middlesex: Middlesex University.

Walter, B. 2008. 'From "Flood" to "Trickle": Irish Migration to Britain 1987–2006'. *Irish Geography*, 41(2): 181–94.

17

Culture

Donald Taylor Black

INTRODUCTION

The author has been a documentary filmmaker for over thirty years, and a substantial number of his films have been about art and artists, whilst others have addressed socio-political themes. After the economic crash, he wanted to make a documentary focusing on the subject, but was only too aware it was being constantly addressed by newspapers, by current affairs journalists on radio and television, and discussed online. As an independent filmmaker, the author was convinced that a creative documentary should be the way to interrogate what was happening, and considered that focusing on artists who were making work about the crisis might be a useful and illuminating method of doing this.

Skin in the Game: Artists and the Crisis

The feature-length film was made with finance from Bord Scannán na hÉireann/The Irish Film Board (IFB) and initially called *Stuffing the Tiger* (Black 2012). It began shooting on 25 February, the day of the 2011 general election, and was intended to follow a number of artists from varied disciplines and genres for twelve months, documenting 'a year in the life of the recession' through their work and their voices. Ultimately, it followed these artists over nineteen months. With a new title, *Skin in the Game* (2012), it received its first public screening at the 57th Cork Film Festival on 16 November 2012. The phrase 'skin in the game' was not well known in Ireland then; it means that executives who own shares in the companies for whom they work are less likely to make unwise decisions because it would put their personal wealth at risk; 'skin' is a synecdoche for self or person involved and the metaphorical meaning of 'game' is the gamble being undertaken or the field of endeavour involved. It has been frequently alleged that it was originated by Warren Buffett, but the late William Safire, best known for his syndicated column in the *New York Times Magazine* ('On Language') has disputed this (Safire 2006). The phrase became more familiar when extracts of transcripts from the so-called 'Anglo Tapes' were published in the *Irish Independent* from June 2013, and broadcast on radio: senior executives of Anglo Irish Bank were regularly heard using it.

The documentary examines the work of ten artists; it is chronological in structure, using captions, with dates, to remind the audience where we are in our timeline, as well as a number of short animations by David Quin, plus brief pieces contributed by writer Roddy Doyle, which act as punctuations throughout the film. It is not merely a collection of artworks with opinions from the makers, but also about the process of making art and the nature of creative inspiration.

Skin in the Game opens with three captions, which very briefly contextualize the background to the crash, the bank bailout, and Ireland's loss of economic sovereignty, with the arrival of the 'Troika'. Then, under a montage of bank exteriors/signs and the main title, we hear Ian Monahan and Dermot O'Brien's austerity song, 'We Built This House...', which uses the metaphor that Celtic Tiger prosperity was a house built without foundations.

It is polling day and we hear from a representative of the arts collective, UpStart, talking about their project of commissioned images which were printed on 500 election-sized posters, and attached to lampposts throughout Dublin (one says: 'Due To Foreseen Circumstances, We Regret To Inform You That Ireland Has Been Cancelled'). Then we see Fergus O'Neill in his studio, discussing how his small graphic design business collapsed in 2009, and showing us posters that he now sells from his website. Based on the celebrated 1939 British propaganda image 'Keep Calm and Carry On', they say 'Fuck It, Sure It's Grand'.

Next we see David Quin producing his thirty-second-long satirical animations, *Cutbacks*, which he began in April 2009 ('frustrated with Mr. Cowan's government, the Lisbon Treaty and the second referendum'); he wanted to make his own 'quick and effective' statements 'without joining a political party'. He uses the characters of the singing Jedward twins to make the political point that the newly elected coalition government is merely more of the same.

The film continues with choreographer/director Muirne Bloomer rehearsing community group, City Fusion, during their section of the 2011 Dublin St Patrick's Day Parade, based on *Brilliant*, a specially commissioned short story for children by Roddy Doyle, about how the 'Black Dog of Depression' has taken away Dublin's funny bone. For the first time, in the history of the parade, according to Bloomer:

there's something so related to the state of the country.

Then, we see a sequence of images, including a familiar one from the project by artist Maser and songwriter Damien Dempsey: 'Greed is the knife and the scar runs deep.'

Painter Brian Maguire opens his section, with the words:

I'm not sure whether anger is the correct term, I just feel gobsmacked about the stupidity of it all.

Discussing his painting of the unfinished Anglo Irish Bank headquarters on the north bank of the Liffey, *Contemporary Ruin* (seen exhibited in the Kerlin Gallery), he says that, as a visual artist, he looks for an image, which is also a metaphor and in this case it is:

a sculptural monument to what they'd done...they'd created a dereliction.

Over shots of 'ghost estates' and abandoned developments, we hear the first of the specially written pieces by Roddy Doyle, this one a monologue about a man who has been made redundant but is too ashamed to tell his family. As we see footage of rural ghost estates, the voice of photographer Anthony Haughey explains his project 'Settlement', which he began in 2010; then, in the Gallery of Photography in Dublin, he discusses some finished images of uncompleted Celtic Tiger houses, simultaneously beautiful and unworldly.

When researching *Skin in the Game*, the author was determined not to produce a film filled with a procession of angry engaged artists, and poet Gerald Dawe (2011) is certainly not known for his political work. He introduces a poem, 'Every Dog Has His Day', by explaining that he wrote it, 'basically out of rage as much as anything else', after reading about a disgraced banker who had escaped to America and was 'conducting himself as if nothing had happened', lounging on his luxury boat berthed in a marina. However, Dawe makes the point that, by the time he began to write the poem using Audenesque irony, his anger had 'distilled to an icy calm'.

Musician Christy Moore, on the other hand, has regularly written or sung about the injustices that he sees around him. However, he explains that, although he has tried to write about the recession, so far the attempts have foundered because they were too full of rage. Instead, he has found songs from other composers and often amends lyrics, or inserts particularly relevant references. Moore then gives an example, by performing 'In Zurich', a political song by American singer-songwriter Jim Page, which discusses a demonstration there, where the Swiss police defend the banks with plastic bullets in their guns.

David Quin's second animation features a speech allegedly made by Taoiseach Enda Kenny at the 2012 World Economic Forum in Davos, where he blames the global financial collapse on the Irish people, stating that it was:

nothing to do with Anglo, nothing to do with nutters in the property sector... nothing to do with the fact that our financial regulator was asleep for twelve years in his office.

Then, the Kenny puppet reassures his Davos audience by emphasizing that:

> we're taking them in hand and we're kicking their asses—they have twenty years
> of austerity ahead of them and they deserve every bit of it!

Not all the artists featured are well known in their particular fields. One is
Frank Buckley, whose installation, *The Billion Euro House*, was built in
the Glasshouse, a new but unlet office building in Smithfield. He obtained
€1.4 billion worth of shredded banknotes in compressed briquette form from
the Central Bank and constructed a house out of them, where he now lives and
works. He is seen in the process of completing it, and we hear him saying that
one of its major benefits is that it 'creates debate'. We cut to a Raidió Teilifís
Éireann (RTÉ) radio studio, where poet Rita Ann Higgins is about to read 'The
Builder's Mess', about ghost estates, from her latest collection, *Ireland Is
Changing Mother* (Higgins 2013).

Next we see activist footage of the clearance of Occupy Dame Street in
March 2012: a young male participant explains how the Gardaí came in the
middle of the night. Then, by Skype from New York, in an editing suite in the
(now closed) Factory in Barrow Street, Dublin, filmmaker Paul Rowley,
describes how his film, *Divestment*, was compiled from business jargon,
having spoken to a friend who had experience of a company in 'lock down
in a war-room situation' when a crisis had engulfed the organization, while his
co-director, Nicky Gogan, adds that a friend of hers, 'a property portfolio
manager from one of the banks', also passed on a glossary of contemporary
financial slang. This is illustrated by a clip:

> We were allowed to sweat the assets—we had skin in the game.

The documentary's second photographer, Seán Hillen, thinks that:

> [T]he idea that we can be apolitical is a political position.

Here he makes work for his 'Ghost Shops' project, which he calls his 'contemporary war photography'. The images play with layers and reflections, as
his camera looks through windows at rubbish inside the door: unopened
letters, cigarette butts, and old retail stock. It then cuts back to artist Robert
Ballagh, who has designed inter alia Irish banknotes, opening Frank Buckley's
completed installation.

The next sequence deals with the (so-called) 'Stability' Treaty, initially
lampooned in a spoof referendum broadcast, by David Quin's puppets of
Enda Kenny and Minister for Finance, Michael Noonan. Then, over a montage of posters, there is another Roddy Doyle-scripted monologue, which
sounds slightly like a poem, or even a rap, as a woman considers which way
she will vote.

David Monahan is a photographer who has been working on a series of
portraits of those about to emigrate, called *Leaving Dublin*, later published as a

book (Monahan 2014); he explains first about how emigration used to make him sad, until recently when a government minister called it 'a lifestyle choice', which made him feel angry. This was Michael Noonan, who, in a speech, claimed young people 'were not emigrating because of unemployment in Ireland'.

The film cuts to choreographer David Bolger, of CoisCéim Dance Theatre, describing the creative origins of his production, *Touch Me*, which began:

> from hearing the background, the soundscape of marches down O'Connell Street, of a discontent of people... it was the sound of the marching that kept seeping into the [rehearsal] studio that made me feel that what I was working on didn't seem to connect at all with what was going on outside and I pretty much decided... I'd have to do this piece.

Touch Me was premiered at the Project Arts Centre in Dublin, and, as Bolger talks, we see extracts from it. Using original music by Kenneth Edge, the images relate to the collapse of the property market, including model 'Monopoly' houses; responses to the question 'What makes you sad?' include 'what we've done to our country, what we've done to our beautiful country'.

In a final Roddy Doyle-scripted dialogue, two young men discuss possible cities to which they might emigrate, as we see a montage of aeroplanes and trains departing and shots of destination boards. The documentary closes with Barry McCormack performing his song, 'Spring', the lyrics of which focus on the aftermath of a political protest against those to blame for the damage caused by austerity; while the demonstrators have a drink before going home, they debate the state of the country.

After its Cork premiere, *Skin in the Game* was screened at the Irish Film Institute in Dublin, around the Access Cinema circuit, which consists primarily of screens within regional arts centres, and at conferences and film clubs. It was nominated for an Irish Film and Television Academy (IFTA) Award and was invited to a number of festivals, primarily in Ireland and the USA, winning Best Documentary at the Irish Film Festival in Boston. Up until the time of writing, *Skin in the Game* has not been transmitted by an Irish broadcaster.

OTHER ARTISTS AND THE CRISIS

Of course, a number of other artists were also involved in making art which engaged with the crisis, including photographer Mark Curran, with his multimedia show at the Limerick City Gallery of Art, *The Economy of Appearances*. It drew together previous related projects such as 'Southern Cross' (1999–2001) and 'The Breathing Factory' (2002–5), which critically surveyed globalization during the Celtic Tiger; Ausschnitte aus EDEN/Extracts from EDEN, which investigated a declining industrial mining region of the former East Germany; as well as 'The Market' (2010–). In addition, there was new work completed in Amsterdam, which included profiles of bankers and traders and documentation from Dublin, London, Frankfurt ,and Addis Ababa, and a 3D representation of an algorithmically generated soundscape, which represented 'contemporary financial capital functioning through the conduit of the financialised nation state'.

In *Power Plays* (2011), broadcast in RTÉ Television's *Arts Lives* series, Fintan O'Toole, *Irish Times* columnist and former drama critic of the *New York Daily News*, lamented the fact that Irish theatre, at least since the mid-1990s, had failed to engage with contemporary national issues, particularly during the boom years. He urged playwrights and theatre companies to rise to the challenge of showing a society in crisis.

In 2012, the commercial theatre produced *Anglo: The Musical*. Written by Paul Howard, with music by Tony O'Sullivan and David McCune, it used puppets and included songs with titles such as 'We All Partied', 'Put Another Nought on the End,… He's a Friend', and 'I Hate to Say I Told You So, But I Did', sung by a puppet of writer and economic commentator David McWilliams. There were also puppets of Brian Cowen, Bertie Ahern, and Enda Kenny, on a leash, held by Angela Merkel. During the previews there were problems, as Howard explained (Freyne 2014):

> The DPP were sending us letters saying they were concerned about it and Sean Fitzpatrick's lawyers were sending us letters saying they wanted to see the script… By then the theatre was booked and there were buses around town with *Anglo: The Musical* on the side and we'd already sold tickets.

Although no Anglo employees were named, changes were made and two scenes were cut completely:

> Then on opening night there were all these people taking notes in yellow legal pads.

Colin Murphy's play, *Guaranteed!*, about the bank guarantee, was produced by Fishamble in May 2013 and toured the country. Characters included: The Regulator, The Governor of the Central Bank, The Taoiseach, and (Anglo Irish Bank CEO), David Drumm. When Murphy, a former deputy editor of *Magill*, was asked why the subject had not been previously tackled by any of Ireland's larger subsidized theatre companies, he replied (Hunt 2013):

> It is surprising that in a nation of writers and theatre that it hasn't been done… But I don't want to take credit for being the first person to come up with the idea.

He is perhaps referring to the fact that it was first staged as part of Fishamble's 'Tiny Plays for Ireland' season, in a 600-word version in 2012. *Guaranteed!*

was later made into a low-budget feature film, as *The Guarantee* (2014), directed by Ian Power, with backing from TV3 and the IFB. Murphy wrote a follow-up, *Bailed Out!* in September 2015.

Radio dramatists have addressed the political and economic situation probably more frequently than theatre writers, many broadcast in RTÉ's *Drama on One* series (Brew 2015). Notable examples included two plays written and directed by filmmaker John Boorman: *The Hit List* (2011), starring Brendan Gleeson and Stephen Rea, where two white knights blackmail their bankrupt betters who had brought Ireland to its knees; and *2020* (2012), a satirical journey into a future Ireland: not only post-Tiger but also post-Euro. Novelist Belinda McKeon contributed *Dropping Slow* (2012), which focused on Maeve, who is now defiantly at peace in her new oasis, a ghost estate under the Arigna Mountains, while Pat McGrath's *Small Plastic Wars* (2015) featured a central character who tries to cope with unemployment. In 2015, Conor Malone's award-winning play, *The Fund*, was a fictional piece, based on the actual story of Grenadian-born economist, Davison Budhoo, and his 150-page letter of resignation from the International Monetary Fund (IMF) in 1988.

In the field of 'classical' or 'art' music, Jenn Kirby reacted to the Irish political situation with her piece, 'Economic Fluctuation' (2010). Kirby (2015), co-director of the Dublin Laptop Orchestra, explains that:

> The pitches for the violins are generated from economic statistics, such as the rate of inflation, migration and the live register.

Tape sources include the anti-austerity protest in November 2010 and Dáil Éireann debates. She has stated that the aim of this composition:

> is to highlight public frustration through the sonification of real data and statistics and also illustrate the divide in the perception of the Government and that of the public.

A later piece, also inspired by the crisis, 'Big Scary Numbers' (2012), begins with two voices reciting, without emotion, a new alphabet: 'A is for Austerity, B is for Bailout' then, after the letter 'Z', the speakers call out the 'big scary numbers', taken by the composer from the Central Statistics Office (CSO) website. The performers end with the final statement, 'Due to cutbacks, we are unable to finish this piece', and then leave the stage (Kirby 2015).

The Spinning Heart (2012) is perhaps the best-known novel about the recession, winning for its author the Irish Book of the Year in 2012 and the 2013 Guardian First Book Award. Set in a fictional village near Limerick, it is told through a chorus of twenty-one victims of the crash, by means of interlocking short stories, each attempting to tell their own kind of truth (Ryan 2012). Julian Gough's satirical novella, *Crash! How I Lost a Hundred Billion and Found True Love* (2013), differs radically in tone and features his regular protagonist, Jude, who is the last person in 'Squanderland' to purchase property:

a vastly expensive wooden henhouse with no roof. With the country facing total ruin, Helen Dunkel, Chancellor of 'Frugalia', and Bertrand Plastique, President of the European Bank of Common Sense and Stability, take charge.

The Mark and the Void, a comic novel by Paul Murray (2015), is narrated by Claude, a French financial analyst who works for a fictional foreign investment bank, based in the International Financial Services Centre (IFSC), and features his thoughts on Ireland, from the position of an outsider in the country, and comments on international finance, as a participant: 'In short, the whole world was massively in debt, but it didn't seem to matter; then suddenly, almost overnight, it did. Someone, somewhere, realised that the global boom was in fact a pyramid scheme, a huge inflammable pyramid waiting to catch light.' There is a bank with strong similarities to Anglo, called the 'Royal Irish Bank', the (anonymous) Minister for Finance is diagnosed with cancer, but the IMF is referred to by its real name.

The importance of culture in Ireland and its history is well documented, and, indeed, is one of the selling points used by state agencies to lure tourists to the country. As Lenny Abrahamson, director of acclaimed feature film *Room* recently commented, 'Ireland's presence globally is through its culture, that's our strongest identifier' (Keegan 2016). Its national, and indeed international, importance is therefore not to be underestimated. What the examples from *Skin in the Game*, and other artists highlighted, illustrate is that a number of practitioners from all genres, including photography, music, dance, literature, film, and theatre, as well as the visual arts, used their creative imaginations to depict the crisis and the impact it had on all walks of Irish life. Naturally, it is usually easier for individuals, such as poets, novelists, or visual artists, who can at least begin work without raising funding, as compared to groups or those working in theatre or film, who need to either access finance directly or persuade commissioners, or cultural producers, to make space in the schedules of their organizations. This was all against a backdrop of severe cuts in funding to the arts and a decline in income for the vast majority of artists, as the recession took hold around the country. Despite these constraints, Irish artists contributed significantly, both addressing the crisis (and its impact on the Irish people) and inspiring subsequent conversations, both in Ireland and further afield, about austerity.

FUNDING THE ARTS

In *Skin in the Game*, the author deliberately focused on artists making work about austerity and the recession and their attitude to what was happening to the community around them, rather than how the economic situation had reduced government spending on arts and culture, and its effect on the income of artists. However, it is important to assert that this happened and discuss the effect that it has had. The 2009 *Annual Report* of the Arts Council/An Chomhairle Ealaíon highlights how challenging the year had been for the arts in Ireland. The report emphasizes that the council's funding had been cut by €8.3 million, more than 10 per cent in one year; this, along with other factors such as decreases in the sales of artists' work, in corporate philanthropy, and in sponsorship, were having a serious impact on artists and arts organizations. The Arts Council had to make significant adjustments to its strategies, as a result of the cuts, and by September 2011, following four consecutive years of reduced funding, amounting to 21.5 per cent, the organization was 'in crisis management' (McBride 2015). The government reduced the budget of the Arts Council to €56,668,000 in 2014, a total loss of 31.7 per cent over the seven years since the highpoint in 2007. Consequently, it decided to commission a strategic review and this gave the organization the opportunity, according to its director, Orlaith McBride, to 'renew its original vows' and 'reaffirm our remit in statute'. This 'complete paradigm shift' and 'deliberate dismantling of policy' meant that the Arts Council had to assess its 'changing relationships' with its clients and: 'Be a development agency for the arts focussed on the public good' (Arts Council 2014). In 2008/9, it funded approximately 340–50 organizations; this was radically reduced to around 235 in 2014. Nevertheless, the fact that there were 1,706 individual applications from artists for 'bursaries, awards and schemes' that year and only 375 were successful, and €2,969,112 was awarded from applications totalling €18.4 million, clearly demonstrates the inadequacy of state funding. The basic grant-in-aid for 2015 remained similar to 2014, but there was an extra €2 million for the 1916 commemorations, which brought the total to €58,593,000; and 2016 saw the first increase for nine years, when the government made available €60,120,000. However, during the recession, the Arts Council lost approximately one-third of its employees, and McBride is of the firm view that the worst thing about austerity has been the cuts coming:

drip, drip in such an insidious way … people have been emasculated in a slower way.

James Hickey, chief executive of the IFB, has commented that screen production fared quite differently during the crisis (Hickey 2015). The IFB, which received its highest ever funding from the government in 2008 (€23.19m) (IFB 2009), suffered cuts in funding of 40 per cent over six years (down to €14m in 2014), and the staff of the IFB decreased from eighteen to twelve. Notwithstanding this, the production of Irish-made cinema, television, and animation increased. Wildgust (2015) highlights substantial growth between 2012 and 2014, with a 37 per cent increase in independent production activity with the highest ever figures in 2014. That year, the IFB invested just under €10 million, generating production expenditure of more than €42 million from IFB-funded projects. Hickey says the reason is that 'film crosses over the zone from arts/

culture to industrial activity' and '. . . has been very successful at creating jobs'. In addition, the screen production sector benefits from foreign direct investment (FDI), principally owing to the benevolent tax regime, which stimulates incoming productions. This incentive, known as Section 481 (S481), has been both extended and developed, with the investor-based system being replaced in 2014 by the new S481 film credit. Ireland did well from the previous version for two main reasons, first, it applied to television and drama, as well as cinema films, which was not the case in the UK at that time, and, second, because the USA was, according to Hickey, 'the first major industrial economy to recover from recession'.

Despite the consequent increase in employment, particularly from high-end television drama, financed by FDI and the S481 tax relief scheme, such as *The Tudors* (2007–10), *Ripper Street* (2012–16), *Vikings* (2013–), and *Penny Dreadful* (2014–16), Irish independent film and television production has not expanded across all budget levels and genres, because of the decrease in the IFB's capital funding. Furthermore, the national public service broadcaster, RTÉ, has suffered severely owing to its system of financing by a combination of the licence fee and advertising revenue, which declined significantly during the recession. In this way, the 'industrial activity' has thrived while the cultural aspect of the sector has suffered, and this has meant there are less Irish-produced (and controlled) films and television being made, except for predominantly low-budget features; according to James Hickey, it is Irish writers who are suffering the most. The internationally financed television drama series are hardly ever written by Irish citizens or Irish-based writers, whereas actors and crew benefit, including 'heads of department' (such as cinematographers, production designers, costume designers, editors, and make-up designers), and even directors. The other problem is that, as Hickey explains, there is a 'complicated eco-system for audio visual production in Ireland'.

Of course, RTÉ as a statutory corporation, a 'semi-state' body, is outside of the IFB's sphere of influence. Nevertheless, because its spending on indigenous production has been reduced substantially from €324 million in 2008 to €211 million in 2014, it does have an effect on the 'complicated eco-system' in which it operates, particularly the cutting of the commissioning budget (i.e. expenditure incurred on commissioning activities) of RTÉ's Independent Production Unit, from €75 million in 2008 to €41 million in both 2013 and 2014 (RTÉ Independent Productions 2013).

RTÉ announced in September 2015 that its continuing 'restructuring' had led to break-even financial results for the second consecutive year (RTÉ 2015). Despite a €5 million reduction in funding in the 2014 national budget, with some growth in commercial revenue, RTÉ returned a small financial surplus, in line with 2013, notwithstanding director-general Noel Curran's statement that 'the overall media market continues to be highly competitive and fragmented'. This result followed a 'major restructuring' of all RTÉ's operations, with its operating cost base reduced by 30 per cent, compared to 2008;. Moya Doherty, chair of RTÉ's board, admitted that 'cutbacks in production . . . have impacted on the creative economy at large'.

TRENDS IN ARTS AUDIENCES

In 2006, the Arts Council commissioned research 'to provide up-to-date information on the behaviour and attitudes of Irish people' in terms of their opinions on, and participation in, the arts, including attendance at cultural events. It reported that Irish people generally had very positive views towards the arts, with 86 per cent of respondents believing that 'the arts play an important and valuable role', while almost 70 per cent agreed that 'spending on the arts should be safeguarded in times of economic recession'. The comparable figure eight years later was 60 per cent, still a clear majority against cuts.

From 2009, the Target Group Index (TGI) surveys, *Arts Attendance in Ireland*, were published by Arts Audiences, an initiative of the Arts Council and the Temple Bar Cultural Trust (Carmody 2015). The evidence from the first edition stated that 1.8 million adults (or 51 per cent of the population) responded that they attended an arts event at least once during the year, and this excludes commercial cinema and rock or popular music concerts. In 2010, this declined to 1.5 million, or 42 per cent of the population. In 2011 and 2012, the overall figures remained almost the same. During the same period, cinema attendance remained stable, at approximately 1.8 million.

However, the most recent report, *The Arts in Irish Life 2014*, gives a figure of 65 per cent for 'last-year' attendance, up from 56 per cent in the previous year (Kantar Media 2015). It also states that levels of attendance have shown particular increases among lower-income groups most particularly, a rise of 11 per cent for those households with incomes of under €30,000. Despite this, in 2014, there was an increase in those who say that cost (or 'can't afford') is a factor in not attending arts events, up to 29 per cent of the population, compared to 17 per cent in 2006.

CREATIVE FORTUNE AND CONCERNS
DURING THE CRISIS

As demonstrated above, despite funding cutbacks, losses in income, sponsorship, and philanthropy, Irish artists created challenging work during the recession and subsequent partial recovery, including art which dealt with the crisis itself and other significant cultural production. Artists in Ireland, and in many other countries, are used to hard times because the higher amounts of state support that existed during the Celtic Tiger years were the exception rather than the rule, thus they have always needed to be flexible to adapt to prevailing conditions. This recent, and particularly harsh, economic period, however, has encouraged, particularly amongst young and emerging artists, a spirit of collectivism and cooperation that should be applauded. Furthermore, some positive initiatives or benefits developed as direct, or indirect, results of austerity.

One such benefit was the Abbey Theatre's purchase of the adjacent property at 15–17 Eden Quay in 2012 (Abbey Theatre 2012). The acquisition of this building had been an aspiration for some time because it overlooks the Liffey and provides an opportunity, not only to expand the existing theatre, but also to realign it towards the river. Nevertheless, during the 'boom', it was always considered too expensive; ironically, however, the drawback now is that the capital cost of developing the site is currently beyond the theatre.

Another noteworthy initiative is the Gate Theatre's introduction of Wednesday matinées for most of its productions from late 2014. This policy began after older audience members lobbied Gate director, Michael Colgan. There have been benefits for both parties, as these midweek performances now attract the second largest houses after Saturday nights, and it has given additional income to the theatre, with minimal additional expenditure (Colgan 2016).

As far as private philanthropy is concerned, the largest publicly known instance has been the €7 million donation, in 2009, from rock band U2 and the Ireland Funds (€5m from U2) to establish Music Generation, the national music education programme for young people, although its origins pre-date the recession and can be dated to a government feasibility study as early as 2001; it also receives state money. Five years later, in 2015, U2 donated a further €2 million, along with €1 million from the Ireland Funds, for the expansion of the project. In 2011, the government had attempted to further encourage philanthropy, by making an additional €1 million available to the Arts Council to provide 50 per cent of the costs of a fundraiser in arts organizations; there has been some limited success, but this is very unlikely to make a substantial difference overall.

In 2011, Business to Arts, a not-for-profit organization, made the timely decision to establish Fund it, an all-island crowdfunding website for the cultural and creative industries. Over its first five years, €3.7 million has been pledged, with €3,416,000 raised from 60,244 pledges for 891 successful projects. The performance category had the highest number of projects, with the music category achieving the highest amount of funding (FitzGerald 2016).

The year 2016 has been a very successful one for Irish film. The Sundance Film Festival, the leading US showcase for independent cinema, selected and screened six feature films and one animated short, all with funding from the

IFB. The previous week, nominations for the 88th Academy Awards included a record number of nine with Irish connections. Lenny Abrahamson's *Room* received four and John Crowley's *Brooklyn* was nominated three times: both were nominated for Best Picture. The IFB gave financial support to both films, which were international co-productions: *Room* was initiated in Ireland and *Brooklyn*, adapted from Colm Tóibín's novel, in the UK. There were further nominations for two other Irishmen: Michael Fassbender (Best Actor for *Steve Jobs*) and Benjamin Cleary (Best Live Action Short for *Stutterer*). Although neither of these films received funding from the IFB, Fassbender and Cleary have been involved in previous productions which received backing from the Broadcasting Authority of Ireland (formerly the BCI), and the IFB. Ultimately, Benjamin Cleary and Brie Larson won Oscars.

The IFB has been at pains to stress that its current grant-in-aid is 40 per cent down since its pre-crash peak in 2008 and it has received the same amount from the government between 2014 and the present, with some extra administrative finance in 2016; consequently, it does not have sufficient resources to regularly produce international success and encourage vital new talent. As the chief executive stated (Clarke 2016b): 'It needs that *consistency* of [adequate] support.' This is not merely self-serving because the major talents behind *Room* and *Brooklyn*, such as Abrahamson, Guiney, and Crowley, have been supported by the IFB for a considerable time, since the IFB was restored in 1993 by the then Minster, Michael D. Higgins. This international success has come as a result of long-term investment. The director of the Irish Film Institute also emphasized that, in order for the arts in Ireland to continue these successes, the restoration of funding was required, otherwise 'this recent awards-season success will be very short lived and unsustainable' (Keane 2016). As film critic Donald Clarke (2016a) wrote:

> In the two decades since the reconstitution of the Irish Film Board . . . film-makers have steadily learned their trade, funders have tentatively dipped in toes and the public have become used to the idea that good films come from places other than southern California. Creating a suitable environment for filmmaking is akin to making a suitable environment for exotic wildlife. You need to plant the vegetation early.

The damage caused by the government's cutting of arts funding has vastly outweighed any gains. The subsequent closure of many cultural organizations has taken away access to the arts from citizens. On the eve of the general election in February 2016, the National Campaign for the Arts (NCFA) stated that 'the next and subsequent governments' must take account of Article 27 (1) of the United Nations (UN)'s Universal Declaration of Human Rights:

> Everyone has the right freely to participate in the cultural life of the community, to enjoy the arts and to share in scientific advancement and its benefits. (NCFA 2016)

Perhaps the worst example of a cultural opportunity going to waste occurred when the Daniel Libeskind-designed Bord Gáis Energy Theatre, said to be 'the best appointed performance space on the island' (O'Toole 2014), was offered to commercial bidders by receivers appointed by the National Asset Management Agency (NAMA). Heather Humphreys, Minister for the Arts, was strongly criticized for not taking the opportunity to purchase it, on behalf of the state, at a bargain price.

In 2012, University College Dublin (UCD) historian, Professor Diarmaid Ferriter, resigned from the board of the National Library of Ireland, in protest at government policy on culture. He stated that the Irish Government paid 'lip service' to the importance of the library and other cultural institutions while 'it seeks to emasculate these institutions' (Carbery 2012). A number of commentators saw this (Duncan and Wall 2014), and a proposal to introduce entry charges to the National Museum of Ireland (since withdrawn) (journal.ie 2014), as further evidence that a substantial majority of politicians—not only within the then Fine Gael–Labour Government, but from all parties—for all their surface enthusiasm, have, at worst, disdain of, or, at best, a negligible commitment to arts and culture in Ireland. Roy Foster, Carroll Professor of Irish History at Oxford University, has been particularly critical:

> the worlds of Irish politics and Irish culture exist in parallel universes. A series of philistine or distracted ministers for the arts . . . have made it embarrassingly clear that their interests lie elsewhere, while influential civil servants have over the last year or so [2013] reduced the powers and scope of organizations such as Culture Ireland, a semi-state body with a brilliant record of promoting creative new initiatives. (Foster 2013: 23–4)

CONCLUSION

Despite cuts in funding, income, and philanthropy, artists from all genres continued to make art during this difficult time period in Irish history, and a significant minority explored the crisis and its impact on the Irish people. The partial recovery has seen a levelling off of cutbacks, and there were some successes for the arts in Ireland along the way. Although there were positives to come out of the recession, many of these benefits were due to factors such as FDI and tax incentives, such as the Section 481 scheme. However, it is clear that the future of the arts and culture in Ireland depends on long-term investment and the further reversal of cuts which occurred during the years of austerity. Without long-term planning and investment, the arts in Ireland will suffer as a consequence.

REFERENCES

Abbey Theatre. 2012. 'Behind The Scenes'. Available at: <http://www.abbeytheatre. ie/abbey-theatre-purchase-of-eden-quay-site/> (accessed 28 March 2016).

Arts Council. 2006. *The Public and the Arts 2006*. Dublin: Arts Council.

Arts Council. 2009. *Annual Report and Accounts 2009*. Dublin: Arts Council.

Arts Council. 2014. *Inspiring Prospects: Arts Council Strategic Review 2014*. Dublin: Arts Council.

Black, D. T. 2012. 'Stuffing the Tiger', *Film Ireland*, 143: 34–5.

Brew, K. 2015. E-mail to author: 7 September.

Carbery, G. 2012. 'Ferriter Resigns in Protest from Board of National Library'. *Irish Times*, 24 May. Available at: <http://www.irishtimes.com/news/ferriter-resigns-in-protest-from-board-of-national-library-1.523450> (accessed 1 March 2015).

Carmody, U. 2015. Telephone interview with author: 15 September.

Clarke, D. 2016a. 'Irish Oscar Nods Were Due to Great Expectations'. *Irish Times*, 16 January. Available at: <http://www.irishtimes.com/opinion/donald-clarke-irish-oscar-nods-were-due-to-great-expectations-1.2498776> (accessed 29 March 2016).

Clarke, D. 2016b. 'Where Did It All Go Right? The Secret of Irish Cinema's Success'. *Irish Times*, 22 February. Available at: <http://www.irishtimes.com/culture/film/where-did-it-all-go-right-the-secret-of-irish-cinema-s-success-1.2541478> (accessed 29 March 2016).

Colgan, M. 2016. Telephone interview with author: 27 March.

Dawe, G. 2011. 'Every Dog Has His Day'. *The Stinging Fly*, 19(2): 114.

Duncan, P. and Wall, M. 2014. 'National Museum Considers Closures and Entrance Fees to Deal with 2015 Funding Crisis'. *Irish Times*, 31 October. Available at: <http://www.irishtimes.com/news/ireland/irish-news/national-museum-considers-closures-and-entrance-fees-to-deal-with-2015-funding-crisis-1.1982600> (accessed 1 March 2015).

FitzGerald, C. 2016. E-mail to author: 31 March.

Foster, R. 2013. 'Macmansions, Cellars and Garrets: Surveying the New Ireland'. *Juncture*, 20(1): 20–5.

Freyne, P. 2014. 'Paul Howard: What I Learned from Making *Anglo: The Musical*'. *Irish Times*, 7 September. Available at: <http://www.irishtimes.com/culture/books/paul-howard-what-i-learned-from-making-anglo-the musical-1.1920670> (accessed 12 April 2016).

Gough, J. 2013. *Crash! How I Lost a Hundred Billion and Found True Love*. ebook: DailyLit.

Hickey, J. 2015. Interview with author: 20 February.

Higgins, R. A. 2011. 'The Builder's Mess'. In *Ireland Is Changing Mother*. Tarset: Bloodaxe Books.

Hunt, C. 2013. 'Drama Aims to Make Sense of Boom and Bust'. *The Independent*, 23 June. Available at: <http://www.independent.ie/lifestyle/drama-aims-to-make-sense-of-boom-and-bust-29365763.html> (accessed 2 September 2015).

IFB (Irish Film Board). 2009. *Annual Report 2009*. Dublin: Irish Film Board.

journal.ie. 2014. 'National Museum Closure Threat Recedes as Minister Humphreys Provides €2m in Extra Funding'. *journal.ie*, 5 December. Available at: <http://www.

thejournal.ie/national-museum-funds-closing-1816691-Dec2014/> (accessed 2 March 2015).

Kantar Media. 2015. *The Arts in Irish Life 2014*. Dublin: Kantar Media TGi for the Arts Council.

Keane, R. 2016. 'Director's Note: February at the IFI'. *IFI Programme*, February, Dublin: Irish Film Institute.

Keegan, R. 2016. 'Irish Film Board Has Growing Ambition for its Industry after 2016 Oscars'. *LA Times*, 26 March. Available at: <http://www.latimes.com/entertain ment/movies/la-ca-mn-irish-film-board-20160327-story.html> (accessed 5 April 2016).

Kirby, J. 2015. E-mail to author: 5 September.

McBride, O. 2015. Interview with author: 16 February.

Monahan, D. 2014. *On Leaving*. Dublin: The Small World Press.

Murray, P. 2015. *The Mark and the Void*. London: Hamish Hamilton.

NCFA (National Campaign for the Arts). 2016. 'NCFA Manifesto: General Election 2016'. Available at: <http://ncfa.ie/news/ncfa-manifesto-general-election-2016> (accessed 28 March 2016).

O'Toole, F. 2014. 'Culture Shock: Wake Up, Minister: You Can Help Save Daniel Libeskind's Bord Gáis Energy Theatre'. *Irish Times*, 23 August. Available at: <http://www.irishtimes.com/culture/culture-shock-wake-up-minister-you-can-help-save-daniel-libeskind-s-bord-gáis-energy-theatre-1.1905041> (accessed 6 September 2015).

RTÉ (Raidió Teilifís Éireann). 2015. 'RTÉ Reports Break-Even despite Ongoing Financial Challenge'. Available at: <http://www.rte.ie/about/en/press-office/press-releases/2015/0909/726776-rte-reports-break-even-despite-ongoing-financial-challenges/> (accessed 13 September 2015).

RTÉ (Raidió Teilifís Éireann) Independent Productions. 2013. *Annual Report*. Dublin: RTÉ.

Ryan, D. 2012. *The Spinning Heart*. London: Doubleday Ireland/Dublin: The Lilliput Press.

Safire, W. 2006. 'On Language'. *New York Times Magazine*, 17 September.

Skin in the Game. 2012. Donald Taylor Black, dir. (Poolbeg Productions) [DVD].

Wildgust, R. 2015. 'The Irish Film Industry: An Overview'. *Sunday Business Post*, 8 February. Available at: <http://www.businesspost.ie/the-irish-film-industry-an-overview-2/> (accessed 23 March 2016).

Index